ST. MARY'S COLLEGE
ST. MARY'S CITY

W9-ADZ-698

A HISTORY OF
SPAIN

31417

A HISTORY OF
SPAIN

BY *Jean Descola*

Translated from the French by

ELAINE P. HALPERIN

NEW YORK *Alfred·A·Knopf* 1967

L. C. catalog card number: 62–17520

THIS IS A BORZOI BOOK,
PUBLISHED BY ALFRED A. KNOPF, INC.

Copyright © 1962 by Alfred A. Knopf, Inc. All rights reserved. No part of this book may be reproduced in any form without permission in writing from the publisher, except by a reviewer, who may quote brief passages in a review to be printed in a magazine or newspaper. Manufactured in the United States of America, and distributed by Random House, Inc. Published simultaneously in Toronto, Canada, by Random House of Canada, Limited.

PUBLISHED, JANUARY 1963
SECOND PRINTING, MAY 1967

Originally published in French as HISTOIRE D'ESPAGNE
© 1959 by Librairie Arthème Fayard

TO

my mother and father

PREFACE

HERE ARE a thousand and one ways of writing the history of Spain. One can be entertaining or earnest, sentimental or pedantic, passionately involved or coolly objective, emphasizing either action or people. Which is more important, military history or the history of ideas? Must we choose between historical logic and cloak-and-dagger intrigue? I do not believe that Spain's destiny throughout the ages evolved in a single direction. Not that Spain sprouted like a mushroom on the tip of Europe; but no other country has been so wanting in obedience to those rules of continuity that make the writing of history simple for certain nations. It is impossible to speak of Hispanic unity without serious reservations. Spain's growth chart is a broken line. The truth is that the Spaniard himself has fashioned, destroyed, and refashioned Spain. In electing to look upon Spain as a living person I have therefore heeded Menéndez y Pelayo's admonition: History is a work of art—*la belleza estatuaria de la historia*. It is also a skeleton to

which the chronicler's imagination as well as his knowledge
lends flesh and blood.

Each "age" of the Spaniard, every moment of his life, is
typified either by a hero or by a painter whose broad canvas
portrays the heroes of an epoch. All the figures of the Golden
Age—that extraordinary phenomenon, that extension of
body and soul, that imperial and mystical extravagance—
are represented in the paintings of El Greco. The same is
true of Goya, who painted the kings, ambassadors, beggars,
and guerrillas of the revolutionary period. And if I devote
almost equal space to John of the Cross and Philip II, and
to the life and work of Lope de Vega, it is because the
personality, the human presence of so many Spanish heroes,
is perhaps more important than their message. This is my
"interpretation" of Spanish history. But can any history be
written without interpretation?

*Genealogical charts of the kings of Castile, of the ancestry
of Charles V, and of the Habsburgs and Bourbons are to be
found on pages 484–90.*

CONTENTS

CONTENTS

A HISTORY OF
SPAIN

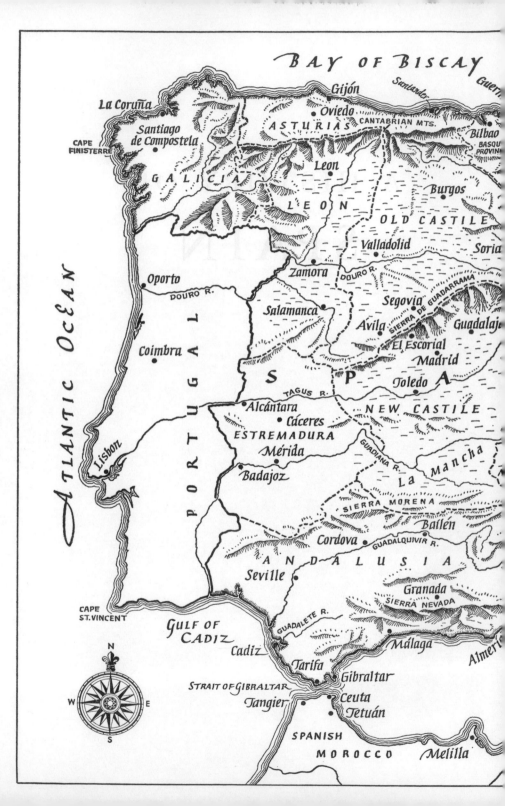

FRANCE

Bayonne
St.-Jean-de-Luz
Toulouse
Narbonne
mplona
VARRE
P Y R E N E E S
ANDORRA
Perpignan
Huesca
EBRO R.
Saragossa
Lérida
CATALONIA
ARAGON
Barcelona
Tarragona
Teruel
N
V A L E N C I A
Valencia
MINORCA
MAJORCA
Palma
IBIZA
BALEARIC ISLANDS
Alicante
A
Murcia
Cartagena
MEDITERRANEAN SEA
Algiers
A L G E R I A
Scale of miles
0   100   map by palacios

❧ PART · I ☙

THE AGE OF
Viriathus

SCIPIO: Subdue your ardor, young man. . . .
I swear to you that you shall know no other master but yourself, and that all the riches that are
mine to bestow shall be yours, if only you will
consent to lay down your arms.

VIRIATHUS: I possess by birth the fearless
spirit of Numantia. To think of vanquishing me
is utter madness. . . . Your forces, were they
yet more formidable than they are, would, I assure you, never compel me to succumb.
                    —CERVANTES, *Numance*

I

Initial Charm

$\mathcal{S}$PAIN, MY FRIEND . . . For one speaks convincingly only of what one loves. And, perhaps more than any other country, Spain demands of whoever comes to it, not so much love as a kind of lucid conspiracy between mind and heart. To sense its deepest significance without sacrificing critical judgment, to drink long of this noble wine and yet not become intoxicated by it—this is a primary condition for a study of Spain, subordinate to only one other—affection. And I love Spain.

Spain is a living being. As soon as one crosses the Bidassoa, or some other Pyrenean *puerto*, one is struck by the similarity between the people and the country. One need go no farther to discover that the Spaniard himself is Spain incarnate. The sharply etched skyline, which literally seems to stand out when first seen, is no more than the Spaniard's backdrop, as if he himself chose or fashioned it according to the dimensions of his artless conceit. Here, the scenery resembles man, not man the scenery, so akin to human attributes is the flavor of its tartness, languor, and aridity. The land more than suggests man; it is impregnated by him, it retains his odor. It smells of man. Even in his absence, man is here. In the *cueva* of the Altamira one is less inclined to admire the stag's canter or the buffalo's death agony than the primate who 15,000 years ago boldly etched the contours of these animals on the glacial rock. One hears the hoarse cries of the Magdalenian tribe; one glimpses the helmeted sorcerer, and the rhymed echo of his incantations still haunts the vaults of the magic cave. Man is present. One can ride for hours over the roads of Old Castile without encountering a soul; two parallel lines—ocher earth and blue-black sky—stretch out endlessly without so much as a human shadow to mar the resounding monotony. But one senses that man is not far away. He is sleeping in the fields, overcome by the noonday heat; or he appears suddenly, coming round a hill, his mantle over his shoulder, his staff in hand. For those who know Spain, who have come to it from all sides, this sense of a human presence becomes a habit. To one who wanders aimlessly in the Despeñaperros pass, flies over the golden serpentine of the Guadalquivir River at sunset, or, dreaming on the terrace of some Moorish palace at Tangier, gazes at the Andalusian coast; or to one who merely inhales the vanilla-flavored odor of the gorse soaked by Navarrian rains, the illusion is the same: this deserted country has the countenance of man and his expression. It frowns, smiles, becomes agitated, and the wind, sweeping in from Guadarrama, breaks over the ramparts of Ávila, intoning Theresian prayers. Spain is a living being.

And so it is with the history of Spain. One must not seek a logical chain of events or a continuity of political design. To some extent, certainly, the impact of nature on the fate of Spaniards has at times probably modified the character of these events. The extraordinary diversity of the Iberian Peninsula and its unusual position in relation to Europe have determined the site of human groupings and, at times, governed their migrations. The departure of so many conquistadors from the *meseta* was not fortuitous. Hunger rather than appetite for adventure drove them to other shores. But the geographical peculiarity of Spain and the extraordinary richness of its landscape were merely pretexts for the Spaniards. Their genius has interpreted these. If we are to understand something of the mystery of Spain we must turn away for a moment from its natural beauties and look at the man seen earlier in the middle of the Castilian plain, set there squarely like a stake in the ground. It is the Spaniard that makes Spain comprehensible. "When I say Spain I herald the man," asserts Antonio Machado, the melancholy poet of Segovian twilights. This statement might serve as the motto for all of Spanish history that emphasizes the human element. Silhouetted against the half-light of the crests that dominate the *campos*, the Spaniard confronts his History. He relates and comments on this tragi-comedy which he has composed and in which he is the protagonist. He performs, not before a blackboard or a theatrical curtain, but against a backdrop animated by a thousand forms. Like the Announcer in Paul Claudel's *Le Soulier de Satin,* the Spaniard stands on the threshold of the First Day, and after the first trumpet blast, gives the three traditional raps that proclaim the beginning of the play: "The setting for this drama is the world and especially Spain."

Where Europe Ends and Africa Begins

The Spaniard has inscribed his history on the strangest of all parchments—the Iberian Peninsula. If we look at a map of the world we will see that the geography of Spain is most unusual. Situated at the western extremity of an ancient continent, it represents a springboard for the discoverers of the New World. But this is not all. What an odd shape! Is it a quadrangle or a pentagon? Strabo compared it to the shape of an ox, the neck formed by the mountainous mass connecting Spain with France; the tail is Cape St. Vincent and the fore legs lean against the Bermeo headland near Bilbao and against Cape Gata, while the hind legs extend to La Coruña and Gibraltar. Seen in profile it looks like one of those iron helmets worn by sixteenth-century men in armor. The visor falls over Vigo and the gorget encloses the Atlantic coast of Andalusia, from Huelva to Algeciras. The clear-cut helmeted profile, elongated by a goatee, resolutely confronts America. This is Portugal. The first glimpse of Spain is quite disconcerting, so amazing is its shape. We see a country that is part of Europe politically, but separated from it by an almost continuous mountain wall. The Atlantic façade, so vital for its expansion toward America, is made up, in part, of Portugal. Does this mean that because of Spain's wide-open Mediterranean seaboard the coast to the south is clear? The very opposite is true. At the beginning of the Middle Ages, Arab conquerors crossed the eight-mile-wide Strait of Gibraltar and occupied Spain for nearly eight centuries. They left an indelible imprint. The Mediterranean was neither a natural frontier nor a means of expansion, but rather a one-way invasion route. The Highway of St. James and the Strait of Gibraltar have determined the fate of Spain and shaped its history. Spain's tragedy is to have been neither part of Europe nor part of Africa.

What do we see when we fly over Spain? To the north, the chain of the Pyrenees extends from Biscay to Catalonia —a great, crenelated wall, 280 miles long, dotted with glittering peaks and softly curving valleys winding toward the ports. Leaping the Balkans, the Pyrenees join the Caucasus, the two coming together over the Carpathians like segments of an arc in an ideal circle which, from Maladetta to Mount Elbrus, enclose Europe and block it off from the Orient.

In the center is rugged Castile, with its wind-swept *meseta*, veined and traversed by the romantic Sierras. It is both extremely hot and extremely cold—"nine months of winter, three months of inferno." There is neither green vegetation nor torrential rain on this yellow-ocher plateau, hardened by the frost and baked by the sun, pungent to the taste like unripe fruit.

In the south, Andalusia, that oriental garden with its burnished cities named after wines and fruit—Málaga, Granada, Jerez—slopes gently toward the sea. Water is plentiful. It gushes here and there in the Campiña of Cordova, or trickles down from the Sierra Nevada in glacial rivulets, slowly warmed by the pebbles of Genil. The gold-speckled Guadalquivir flows in a hundred different places among the *marismas*. Large-horned oxen trample the soft ground. The delicate silhouette of a pink flamingo standing on one leg is profiled against the horizon. Then Africa . . .

Separated from Europe by the Pyrenees, and tending to feel excluded from it, Spain has, for more than seven centuries, constantly kept her gaze turned longingly toward the West. All the while it was obsessed by this longing, a different destiny was in store, pushing it toward Africa, delivering it over to the now cajoling, now brutal embrace of its Moorish conqueror. It is indeed surprising that Spain remained faithful to Europe—torn as it was between Europe and Africa, occasionally seduced by the appeal of its Arab masters, but more often resisting their demands. By keeping hatred for the conqueror alive in the hearts of the Christians, the Moslem persecutions surely abetted Spanish nationalism. The torture inflicted on the pure young Flora along the banks of the Guadalquivir impressed the throngs more than did the Catholic Kings when they affixed the gold cross and banner of Castile to the tower of the Alhambra. Similarly, the muffled persistence of theological thought, the solitary inner conflict of saintly adventurers, Charles V's forsaking an empire for the cloister—all this did more to maintain religious orthodoxy than the execution of heretics at Seville. And while it is obvious that, in the long run, these shameful deeds harmed rather than benefited the Church, we know that St. John of the Cross's cry—"One single idea of man is worth more than the whole world!"—has echoed in our hearts for the last four centuries, as has, in the black Toledo sky, the dazzling gesture of El Greco.

Such is the value of certain attitudes, certain messages, which, over and above the confusion of combat and the crash of arms, crystallize the genius of a people. Thus Spain's loyalty to Europe—often praiseworthy and at times heroic—has been kept alive by the Catholic tradition. Imagine what would have become of Spain under Arab domination if, gradually forgetting the teachings of Christ, it had been converted to Islam! A Mohammedan Spain, set down between the Pyrenees and Gibraltar as early as the seventh century —what a thorn in the side of Europe! It did not happen, but it could have.

What a curious fate! More than any other country perhaps, Spain was plagued with the problem of alien masters. With singular adroitness, due more to instinct than to political acumen, it was able to free itself from foreign domination and occasionally even to draw inspiration from it. Emerging from the shadows of prehistory, Spain felt too early the impact of Phoenician intrepidity, Greek beauty, Punic courage, and Roman wisdom. It borrowed its institutions from the Goths, and the sensuous splendor that adorned its piety from the Moors; from the Jew it inherited its disquiet and the brooding gaze of the persecuted with which, at times, it viewed the world. Nonetheless, and despite its servitude, by remaining faithful to Christian customs, Spain was able to recover its independence and forge its own unity.

Often defeated by historical events, but more often triumphant, an immutable principle seems to have influenced Spain's outlook; at times it hastened and at times it obstructed the march of events. Throughout chaotic periods of anarchy or apparent submission, a compelling, persistent continuity prevailed. Unflagging spirituality and adherence to medieval disciplines prevented Spain from capitulating to the Arabs. Had it yielded, its history and probably the face of the world would have been different.

More Than a Peninsula

Altamira speaks of Spain as a "perfect peninsula." Only the Pyrenean isthmus connects it with Europe. Maurice Legendre has coined the term *plusqu'île* ("more than a peninsula"), for, although as isolated as an island, Spain has "The power, complexity, and unity of a continent." What terrible cataclysms long ago split this bit of Iberia from the Pyrenees at one fell blow, breaking the thick mass of a future Europe into enormous fragments? Streaked by the mighty outlines of the *meseta* and joined to tertiary mountain chains, Spain just missed becoming an island, yet remained a continent.

Indeed, Spain's *meseta* alone warrants calling the country a continent. This vast plateau, composed of very ancient terrain, represents half of the Iberian mountain chain. In the north it is bounded by the Cantabrian Mountains, in the northeast and east by the Iberian range, in the south by the Sierra Morena, in the west by the Portuguese and Galician ledges. Near by are the basins of the Ebro, the Guadalquivir, and the lower Tagus. In the extreme north and south, the imposing Pyrenees and the Cordillera Bética—an extension of the Riff mountain range—hem Spain in. It is a closed continent, which perhaps explains the origin of its name, *Spania*, "hiding place." And the Sierras encircle it like a belt.

Why the word *sierras?* Because the Spanish mountains stand out against the skyline as plainly as the teeth of a saw. As for the Pyrenees, they owe their name to the fact that they were once volcanic. One night shepherds lit a fire to seek protection from the cold and to cook their food. The flames, fanned by a strong wind, caught bushes and trees and spread to the adjacent forests. Thus, legend ascribes the etymological origin of "Pyrenees" to the Greek word *pyr*, which means "fire."

East and south, from the foothills of the Pyrenees to the Strait of Gibraltar, Spain is bathed by the Mediterranean; west and north, by the Atlantic. Its coastline looks as if it had been drawn by the hand of an artist. From Cape Creus to the Bay of Algeciras, the Mediterranean seaboard describes four large arcs of a circle, overhanging Africa like a garland. The Atlantic coast, from Fontarabia to El Ferrol, stretches taut, like a wire. From La Coruña to the Portuguese frontier it is notched and uneven, curving softly between the Guadiana River and Tarifa. Bristling with rocks or coming to rest in lagoons, edged with clay or dropping sharply into the sea, the Spanish coast is so varied that at times it resembles a Norwegian fiord, at times a Breton cliff.

The Ebro—the Iberus of the ancients—begins in the foothills of the mountains of Old Castile. In the course of its majestic descent to the Mediterranean it is joined by all the rivers of Navarre, Aragon, and Catalonia, and refreshes large cities such as Saragossa and Logroño. The Guadalquivir, "the great river" of the Arabs and of ancient Boetis, fed by the torrents of the Sierra Nevada, irrigates the farms of Cordova and the countryside of Seville. Commending the Guadalquivir for its hair-tinting waters, the poet Martial writes: "Boetis, with hair decked by a crown of olive leaves, 'tis in thy limpid waters that golden tresses are made to shine." These are the colors one often sees in the Guadalquivir when morning comes to the Arenas Gordas of the legendary Tartessus. The Guadiana—called Anas ("wet nurse") by the Celts and Ouadi Anas by the Arabs—starts in a basin bounded by the Sierra Morena in the south and the hills of Toledo in the north. In the prairies of La Mancha it meanders and becomes lost, then turns into a spring, "the Eyes of the Guadiana." Finally, reaching the frontier of Portugal, it curves southward and flows into the ocean. The Celtic name Tag, which means "strangulated," suits the Tagus. A stream rather than a river, and beginning close to Molina de Aragon, it cuts a path through narrow valleys and gorges. Pursuing its capricious course, it empties its goldflecked waters into the Atlantic at Lisbon. Also flowing in the direction of Portugal is the Douro, a river that witnessed the fall of Numantia. Its waters nourish the blossoming jasmine. Finally, there is the Minho; springing up in Galicia, it expires in Portugal.

Legend has it that when the Phoenicians came to Spain, they found so much precious metal that, not knowing how to carry it off, they plated their anchors and the iron fittings of their vessels with gold and silver. Later, Fulvius Flaccus, after conquering the Spaniards, demanded and obtained from them 124 gold crowns, 31,000 pounds of gold ingots, and 170,000 pounds in coin. Justinian claims that there was so much gold in Galicia that workers in the fields sliced clumps of gold-filled earth with their plowshares. The same was true of silver. Guadalcanal was the most famous silver

mine. It supplied enough wealth to construct the Escorial.
Mines abounded—cinnabar mines so dear to Emperor Augustus, copper mines at Almadén whose poisonous fumes
mingled with the aroma of rosemary and myrrh, iron mines
at Mondragón, to say nothing of Catalonian lead, Galician
tin, and the antimony of Santa Cruz de Mudela. Successive
Spanish invaders tore up the earth with their pickaxes before bothering to develop the land. Vestiges of the Romans'
round wells and the Moors' square towers testify to the invaders' cupidity. Stone also appealed to these roadbuilders
and artists. Alabaster, bloodstone, granite, and marble of all
colors were extracted with great difficulty from the Sierras.
The 500 pillars of the Cordova mosque and the Roman aqueduct at Segovia attest to the excellence of Spanish stone.

Mountains, two oceans, rivers, metals, stone, to say nothing of timber, flowers, and fruits! Spain's abundant vegetation is certainly due in large part to its diversified climate.
Asturias, covered with holly oak and beech trees, forms
quite a contrast to the triple-tiered hills of Albaida in the
east. Here wheat, flanked by vineyards, is grown on the
lower tier; at the top, surrounded by locust and almond
trees, the dark green plumes of cork oak and evergreen
sway. Save for an occasional hickory planted close to a
church, the Castilian plains are treeless. Shade is rare, and
the horizon is so clear that the outline of church steeples can
be seen from a great distance. Plants and fruits are scarce,
but in summer the golden stacked harvest is ruffled by the
biting wind that blows from the plains. In the Basque country, where rains bring out the brilliant colors, oak trees, arbutus, and heather drip with pearly moisture. The sweat of
labor smells of crushed mint. With strong, regular strokes
of their *lavas*—double-pronged forks—peasants, wearing
felt berets, split the yellow earth. In autumn the vintagers
stomp the glossy Biscay grapes to make their tart *chacolí*.
In Aragon, all along the Ebro, the land is fertile when irrigated. The capital of Aragon, *Zaragoza la harta*—"satiated
Saragossa," as it used to be called—is brimful of oil, although parched for water. What a contrast between Aragon

and its neighbor, the rich, powerful, and hardy Catalonia!
Not that nature is much more clement here than elsewhere,
but the people, so amazingly energetic and industrious,
learned to domesticate the earth and to extract from it all
they needed, and more. Whether we visit the green valleys
of Andorra or Cerdaña, the Costa Brava with its Barbary
fig trees or the interior of villages with names as dazzling as
the Tarragonian sky—Castelfullit de la Roca, Arénys de
Mar, San Felíu de Guixols, Seo de Urgel—we see that the
Catalonian, willful, combative, and tenacious, has made his
influence felt. Catalonia would not be the same without him.
Then we come upon Valencia. . . . "Clusters of palm trees
lifting up their branches like choirs imploring the heavens,
then bowing, sad and disheartened.". . . The Albufera, the
Arabs' "small sea," has not changed since Blasco-Ibáñez.
Boats glide through its rushes in an aquamarine light. The
huerta of Valencia performs its four annual miracles: four
harvests of hemp, wheat, beans, and corn. And the fruits
and flowers! Oranges—20,000,000 orange trees!—white
mulberry bushes, carnations, dates, aloes, almonds, even
palm cabbages and date palms—*dátiles de raposa*, the
Valencians call them. Farther south are Alicante with its
heavy wines and Murcia—"a race of vintagers"—with its
cupolas of blue tile. Approaching Albacete the land begins
to look somber. The fir trees that border the horizon seem
gloomy. Gloomier still are the immense stretches of alfa, the
campus espartarius of the Romans.

Which of us has not thrilled to the mere mention of Andalusia? Certainly its delights must be exceptional to have survived the purveyors of folklore and shoddy literature! At the
bottom of the ox's outline, extending from the Pyrenees to
the *Peñón*, are the eight Andalusian provinces—Jaén, Málaga, Granada, Almería, Cordova, Seville, Huelva, and Cadiz. Actually, Andalusia comprises three different regions:
the Sierra Morena, the valley of the Guadalquivir, and the
Sierra Nevada. The Sierra Morena consists of ledges that
descend from La Mancha to Portugal and bears little resemblance to the classical image of Andalusia. The domi-

nant color is gray—gray-green of olive trees and myrrh, dark gray of pines. At a distance the flocks that graze on the meager hills are barely distinguishable from the silvery gray of the shrubs and the cork oaks. Linares, La Carolina, Peñarroya—what a leaden landscape! South of the Sierra Morena are the plains of the Guadalquivir. This is the Bética of the Romans, its *vegas* gilded by vineyards. The Cordova countryside looks like a fleshy fruit, and Seville is there with all the familiar cities—Sanlúcar de Barrameda, Jerez de la Frontera, Cadiz, the *tacita de plata*, the little silver bowl that reflects the metallic brilliance of salt marshes. At the foot of the Sierra Nevada, Granada aligns its three crimson columns. And Spain ends at Tarifa. A single stride and one is in Africa. . . .

Such is this country, at once splendid and miserable, alternating between extreme abundance and poverty, combining Anatolian steppes, Swiss mountains, Tuscan plains, Judaean desert, and Moroccan beach. In some places it resembles Wales, in others the Languedoc slopes. Such is the physical environment that witnesses the birth, growth, work, and death of the Spaniard.

But who was the first Spaniard?

The First Sanctuaries

To make his acquaintance, where should we seek him but at Santillana? Exactly 110 years ago, a hunter who had lost his way discovered one of the shrines of prehistory. Let us enter the cavern of Altamira. We see, as if etched in a single stroke, the timid herd of stags, the madly galloping, polychromatic buffalo, the wild horse with slender ankles, and the massive wild boar. . . .

The ground is still strewn with ophites, carved shells, bones sharpened into tools by the Paleolithic tribes. Here, in the flickering torchlight, the Troglodytes whetted their flints and, with long, uncertain strokes, copied on stone the winged flight of their steeds. But what is the meaning of those vaguely human bodies in the half-light, crowned with birds' skulls, those profiles of old bearded men with aquiline noses, those hands with palms upturned as if in offering or prayer? It must be that the grotto, hung with votive pictures and cluttered with totems, was not so much the abode of the primate as the sanctuary of malevolent or friendly genii. Evidently, man, even at this early stage, sensed in pictures a magic power to tame animals and ward off bad luck or the fury of the elements. To whom did these oddities, crowned with bird beaks or clothed in bearskins, address their grotesque gestures, and what kind of cult did they practice around the ruddy night-light of those early fires? It is not too farfetched to suppose that the Quaternary savage who succeeded the beast came quite early to fear a divinity, and perhaps even offered it his growling prayers. Yes, already there was fear, but not yet love, although the vague apprehension that froze the bowels of the cave men long before the advent of *Homo sapiens* had something of the artless presentiment of faith. So much so in fact that on the Altamira stone, among the claw marks made by wild beasts, one can perceive in the primitive design some features of the Iberian cast of mind. Similarly, the swaying of shapeless forms seems to represent a savage prelude to the Golden Century's Dance before the Ark.

There are vestiges of the Bronze Age in Galicia, the Balearic Islands, and Catalonia. Who inhabited the peninsula at that time? And whose hands fashioned the curious tombs of Olerda, the cyclopean ledges along the great wall of Tarragona? Medieval legends mention the migrations of the children of Japheth, father of the white race. Modern ethnologists suggest the dolichocephalic Basques. Whether they came from Asia Minor, Africa, or the mysterious Atlantis, nothing remains of Spain's first settlers save a few stones.

Centuries went by. Egypt, which had already been ruled by twelve dynasties, observed the rotation of the planets and elaborated its code of law. Hiram, king of Tyre, formed an alliance with Solomon, and ships loaded with cedar and

Tyrian purple made their way to the Orient. But the Spaniards of the future, concentrated in the *meseta*, were hunting buffalo, shepherding their flocks, harvesting wheat, and fashioning weapons. They had no thought of using arms against men, for they were ignorant of war. Their weapons were designed to capture animals or to give protection from wild beasts. They were divided into clans, several clans constituting one tribe, ruled by a single chief. Pastoral preoccupations, the worship of tribal gods, the beginnings of handicrafts, and perhaps the domestication of horses and oxen—such, apparently, was the simple rustic life of these unknown peoples at the dawn of Spanish history.

The Iron Age, heralding as it did an era of invasions, modified the physiognomy of the population. The peninsula, until then walled in, suddenly seemed to burst asunder as if under the impact of a cosmic cataclysm. The door was opened wide to migration. From then on, Spain became a spiritual crossroads and a racial melting pot.

At about this time the country acquired a name. The Hebrews called it Sepharad "border," or "edge." The Greeks christened it Hesperia, "the Occident," or He Spania, "the sparse." The name Hispania endured. More significant, however, was the term "Iberia," which derived from the Celtic word *aber*, "harbor" or "river." And indeed, the first known inhabitants of the peninsula were precisely the Iberians who came from the valley of the Ebro. They were to occupy a large part of western Europe.

These "river men," or Iberians, probably moved up from the Atlas Mountains by way of the Strait of Gibraltar. They were short, dark, spare, fleet, and hot-tempered. They liked war, were hospitable, and built altars. A traveler today, chancing upon some farm in the Spanish countryside at nightfall, might be reminded, by the man who opens the door, of the high-strung, Iron Age Iberian, patriarchal and courteous.

The Celts arrived from the north by way of the Pyrenees and joined the Iberians. These warriors were tall, blond, and hardy. Adept at using weapons, they were respected for their discipline and military knowledge. Important regions in northern Spain still bear old Celtic names—the Cantabrian coast, from *kent aber*, "river site" or "water site," and Asturias, from *as thor*, "high mountain."

Apparently the fusion went off smoothly. Tough and aggressive, the Celts taught the Iberian shepherds new ways of handling metals as well as the elements of a still rudimentary architecture. At the same time, they provided new blood. From this ethnic and social alliance the Celtiberian came into being—a curious mixture of Berber and Indo-European, believed to be the first Spaniard.

The religious mentality of the Celtiberians tended toward totemism or fetichism. They scarcely advanced beyond the level of superstition, although they did show great concern for the dead. This is borne out by the numerous tombs discovered in Aragon. Next to the cadaver, the Celtiberians placed familiar objects, such as spears, shields, jewels, and sometimes even a horse's bridle. Their notion of the hereafter seemed to be dominated by storms, tempests, illnesses—all the pitfalls that might beset them in the dark forest. And when, with hands pressed against the granite dolmens, they invoked the gods, it was less to implore their protection than to appease their anger. Love had not yet penetrated these savage breasts. God was the rumbling voice of thunder, the large blood-colored *S* that lightning inscribed in the asphalt sky of those early days.

The Phoenicians and the Blood Cult

The industrious and warlike Celts left such a great imprint on the rest of the population that, for a long time, they were thought to be the sole inhabitants of Spain. Four centuries before the birth of Christ, a Carthaginian admiral made the following entry in his log: "Where the ocean waves come together and clash as they move through the basin of our sea, the Atlantic begins. The Pillars of Hercules are there. . . . The nearby lands to the left belong to Libya. The other region is exposed to a brisk north wind. It is occupied by the

Celts." But they were not the only inhabitants. Long before
Spain attracted the interest of Carthage, several small
groups—the Bastuli, Turdetans, Ausetani, and Ilergetes—
had begun to reside in the country. The original Spanish
population, which became mixed very early, soon acquired
the basic characteristics of the two mother races. There is no
doubt that the Spaniard's unusual originality, which helps to
explain his often inexplicable nature, springs from the fusion
of these two very different races: the imaginative, tempera-
mental Iberian, the powerful, disciplined, slow but efficient
Celt. The Spaniard of today cannot disavow either.

Other influences were at work. Since early antiquity, the
route to tin led through Spain. In fact, Oriental expeditions
moved across the Pillars of Hercules and followed the Spanish coastline to avoid danger in reaching the Scilly Islands,
off the southwestern coast of England, which were then
known as the Cassiterides. Here the Phoenicians amassed
tin. In their voyages to Spain they were not content merely to
drop anchor. They also established counting houses, the
largest of which was in Cadiz. As skilled in trade as in navigation, these hardy adventurers taught the natives the science of writing and the use of money. Scarcely a trace of
their spiritual and social influence persists; yet it must have
been considerable, for this was probably young Iberia's first
contact with the Orient. So varied are the findings in ancient
cemeteries that the inferences to be drawn from them are
necessarily contradictory. It is well-nigh impossible to assess
the influence of the Phoenicians by examining the amazing
collection of drawings—sea horses, rhinoceroses, men
draped in the manner of the ancients, grave-looking women,
sphinxes, and griffins. In the province of Albacete there are
remains of a temple, the *cerro de los santos*. Amid blocks of
age-old stone a curious statue has survived—the figure of a
woman holding a drinking vessel in both hands. A large
shawl with pleated panels is draped around her ample, be-
jeweled breast. What is she staring at with her large, vacant
eyes? Is the offering of this voluptuous priestess intended for
the cruel Tanith? Here, in these magnificent ruins, where the
Egyptian lotus lies beside the caduceus, where crumbling,

colorless fragments and shapeless, foliated moldings are
faintly illuminated by the tarnished gilt of Mycenaean
masks, is it possible to discern the role or nature of the
Phoenicians' religion? Yet it seems likely that they did attempt to modify the primitive Celtiberian cult by introducing
their own ritual, their Oriental imagery, and, above all, their
pantheon. For in antiquity invaders were usually preceded
by their gods. This is altogether logical, for obedience to
law stemmed mainly from the injunction: "God wills it."

Thus, the Celtiberians, instead of worshipping sun and
moon, began to invoke the Phoenician idols, Melkarth and
Astarte. In adopting new gods they also learned about the
propitiatory power of blood, which they expressed through
human sacrifices.

The symbol of blood, so common to all religions, was first
introduced by the Phoenicians. If we examine legend more
closely, we find, in the very heart of Lebanon, the myth of
Aphrodite, Astarte's twin sister. Enraptured women dipped
their hair into the purple waters of the river of Adonis.
Served by temple slaves, the first soothsayers consecrated on
altars decked with anemones the bleeding body of the god
who died for love. Gathered around these bonfires was a
great throng, the same that later was to crowd around the
holocausts of the Inquisition. From the shores of Byblos to
Jebel Musa, the grotesque notions of the flagellants swept
over the roads where asphodel and white mulberry met.
Four thousand years later, other flagellants were to become
the screaming escorts of members of the Holy Office, during
the Inquisition, when heretics were burned at the stake—a
reminder of the days when Tyrian priests spilled the blood
of innocent young victims at the feet of Baal.

The Greeks and the Cult of Beauty

Around the seventh century B.C. the Greeks came to Spain.
Ampurias, on the Cantabrian coast, was the site of their first
settlement. In the beginning it was merely a commercial center (*emporios* in Greek means "market"). But soon it grew
more important. Taking advantage of a temporary decline

in Phoenician power, the Greeks gradually extended their influence into the interior. When they landed on the rugged Spanish shores they had already known many centuries of civilization and were a well-governed, clever, artistic race. Their influence in Spain was considerable, and had beneficial effects. It was both commercial and aesthetic. Indeed, Spanish art dates from the time that settlers from Phocis came to the Costa Brava. They gave the natives a knowledge of beauty and taught them the use of wine. From the painted urns and delicate statuettes that have been dug out of Ibero-Greek ruins, the impact of Hellenic ceramicists and sculptors is plain to see.

The blood-cult of Astarte was succeeded by that of Artemis, the huntress, daughter of Zeus, whose temple was discovered in the region of Valencia. But in Alicante another goddess, Elche, appeared and heralded the Spanish Virgin. "Here the town of Herna stands. Between two deserted shores, there flows the sonorous Alebus!" So commented Rufus Festus Avienus a little later. Shimmering, like a mirage, the Vinapalo winds through the forbidding countryside. Elche and its date palms—this is the region of flowers and water, babbling canals and purple-mottled pomegranates, lusterless sun.

At the end of the nineteenth century, the amazing bust of the Lady of Elche was exhumed here. In her we see, under a hieratic miter framed with large gold conches, the very countenance of Beauty. She has large, sad eyes, a long, narrow profile, and lips more disdainful than sensuous. A certain solemn movement of the shoulders is enhanced by the heavy priestess's coif. A luxurious three-strand necklace adorns the proud breast, from which a saintly sigh seems to escape. Erect and grave, she has the melancholy grandeur of Velázquez's haughty princesses. What noblewoman of Tartessus sat for this work of art? Although it dates from the Greek occupation, it already seems Spanish in style, and recalls not Salammbô, the statuesque Carthaginian princess, but Carmen, the gypsy girl of Seville, seething with quiet voluptuousness. Incredible though it seems, over the years the Lady of Elche has been confused with the Virgin.

An extraordinary legend seized upon this pagan divinity, stripped it of its sacerdotal character, and metamorphosed it into the Virgin Saint, carried to the banks of Santa Pola by ocean waves. Each year on the Feast of the Assumption, the people of Alicante piously celebrate the feast of Mary, Mother of God, patroness of Elche, which, for the occasion, takes on the features of glowing Iberia. There is nothing disrespectful to the Virgin in this. The Spanish imagination tends to mix, in all good faith, the sacred and the profane; to transpose the gestures and the forms of art into mystic feeling; to extract beauty from the physical world, to plunge it into the purifying fire of love and to fashion from it the countenance of God. Perhaps this is what the Spaniards learned from the Greeks. "Let us see ourselves reflected in Thy Beauty!" exclaimed St. John of the Cross.

Carthage and the Advent of the First Guerrilla

Whereas the Greeks were generally tolerated by the native population, the same cannot be said of the Phoenicians, who were constantly under attack. As a consequence, they sought the protection of their brother-race, the Carthaginians, who rushed to the rescue. But, as always happens in such circumstances, the rescuers soon became conquerors and then masters instead of allies. In the Balearic Islands and along the Andalusian coast, Carthage replaced Tyre.

The Carthaginian settlements in Iberia, at first commercial and pacific, were quickly converted into military bases. Punic rule, which extended the entire length of the African coast from Cyrenaica to the Pillars of Hercules, clashed with Roman imperialism. And Spain constituted a reservoir of men and natural resources. How could Rome allow Carthage this advantage? Before long Iberia loomed as one of the main prizes in the tremendous struggle that pitted Carthage against Rome, and Hannibal against Scipio Africanus.

The Spaniards played an important role. During the First Punic War and Hannibal's campaign in Italy, they were allied with the Carthaginians, only to turn against them

shortly and to become their mortal enemies. At the siege of
Saguntum they displayed extraordinary heroism.

Livy relates that before the victorious Carthaginians entered the beleaguered fortress, the people of Saguntum lit an
immense bonfire, burned all their belongings, and threw
themselves into the flames. Women strangled their children,
then plunged to their death from the top of the citadel. The
battle proved decisive. After the fall of Saguntum, the Roman ambassador appeared before the Carthaginian senate
and demanded reparations. He raised the bottom of his toga
and said: "I have here either peace or war. Which will you
choose?" "Choose for yourself," the senators replied. "Then
I choose war," replied the Roman. But Hannibal had not
held up his offensive to await the outcome of these formalities. At Cartagena (Carthago Nova) he had amassed a formidable army of 100,000 infantry, 12,000 cavalry, and 100
elephants—the "bulldozers" of Hamilcar Barca—and was
preparing to march on Rome. Many Spaniards (they can
truly be called Spaniards now) were in his army.

Thus, at the beginning of the Second Punic War, two hundred years before the birth of Christ and two thousand years
before Napoleon, Spaniards experienced foreign intervention, civil war, and the bitter taste of fruitless victories. Their
policies were most disconcerting. They fought recklessly,
changing sides and tactics unscrupulously, making alliances
one day and breaking them the next. They seemed incapable
of gratitude, at times even of remembering where their best
interests lay, more intent on the present than on any long-
range plan. They can scarcely be blamed for this. Their
sights were fixed on the shores that carried thousands of Roman or Carthaginian triremes to and fro. They simply
fought the enemy. For them the enemy was Phoenician,
Greek, Carthaginian, or Roman—whoever dragged javelins or rolled carts over soil for which they felt a vague responsibility. Their progress since Altamira can be measured
by this growing awareness, not of national identity—it was
still too early for that—but of property. They reacted instinctively like peasants who brandish their scythes when
their fields are threatened. But they were also soldiers. A

new figure, the guerrilla, emerged from their midst and advanced resolutely, shoving others aside. He influenced the entire course of Spanish history and occasionally marked it with his blood.

What did the ancestor of the remarkable Spanish infantryman look like? He was armed with two short javelins—*chuzos*, they were called—a double-edged sword, occasionally a slingshot, and almost always a pitchfork. He used the pitchfork to pierce the horses' shins, thus halting the enemy cavalry. The same weapon was employed later in the New World to capture wild bulls. Toreadors had a similar weapon, the *media luna*, for bull-fighting. The guerrilla carried a small round shield called a *cetra*, made of wood or wicker and encased in leather. On his head he wore a kind of miter, and his goatskin shirt resembled the battle dress of the English during World War II. He was shod in heavy leather boots called *abarcas*. The Spanish mercenary, accustomed to hand-to-hand combat from his experience with bull-fighting, was as resourceful as he was brave. He went into battle preceded by a chariot drawn by bulls on whose foreheads he had attached bundles of straw smeared with pitch. He would set the straw on fire, and the terrified beasts would rush at the enemy, dispersing them. But more than courage or guile, the guerrilla had the kind of imagination that deeply impressed his foreign masters. For example, to ford rivers he built rafts and used inflated goatskins to float them, thus inventing the first pneumatic boat.

Barca's Spaniards often crossed swords with Scipio's Spaniards as the fortunes of war changed. Finally Rome conquered Carthage and turned to Spain. It took two centuries for the Roman legions to complete their victory. In Lusitania (Portugal and Estremadura) they were fiercely contested. This "resistance," now synonymous with patriotism, was personified by a young shepherd, Viriathus.

Viriathus!

One would never think from his harangues to the Lusitanians that he had begun life as a herdsman. As he stood on a

hillock, the light of the brushwood fire stressed the stubborn
angle of his chin and jaw. His eyes were very dark and his
face swarthy. It was difficult to recognize the former cowherd in this aquiline-nosed Alcibiades. He rebuked his men
severely. But his voice was persuasive, his gestures noble, as
he denounced Galba's deceit. Had Galba not promised the
Lusitanians fertile lands if they ceased fighting the Romans? On the appointed day, Lusitanian patriots gathered in
small groups at the meeting place, bringing with them all
their belongings. It turned out badly, however. They were
surrounded by Galba's troops, then plundered and massacred. Nine thousand were slain and 20,000 prisoners, including Viriathus, were sold as slaves in Gaul! This was the famous *Pax Romana!*

Viriathus escaped. He traveled from village to village,
tireless and bitter, repeating his warning, his battle cry: "Remember Galba!" Meanwhile the praetor had been removed
from the Roman senate for breach of trust. He was replaced
by Caius Vetilius as consul of Ulterior Spain. The new consul was even more tyrannical than his predecessors, and Lusitanian resistance grew. Viriathus bred hatred for the Roman she-wolf in the hearts of his companions. They were a
rugged lot, clothed in animal pelts and armed with spears.
Viriathus marched on Cadiz at the head of 10,000 men but
was forced to beat a hasty retreat. The centurions, standing
shoulder to shoulder, and using their shields for protection,
bore down on the Lusitanians with a mass of iron armor
plate that was studded with swords. Trapped on all sides
and driven to the mountain, the Lusitanians lost their pluck.
Some considered negotiating with the Romans. "Never,"
Viriathus declared, proudly tossing his head. Then he revealed his plan. He would lure the Roman army into open
terrain, pretend to flee, and lead them to the floor of a valley
near the city of Tribola. Stationed on top of the mountain,
the patriots would have an easy time crushing the Roman
legionaries with their javelins. The operation went according
to plan. Vetilius' soldiers were enticed into the Sierras and
trapped by a shower of javelins and rocks. Four thousand
Romans died, and the praetor himself fell into the hands of

a Lusitanian, who laughed at the sight of the plump official. He slit open his belly to punish him for having such a fat one, or so he boasted.

Rome began to chafe at being defied by a cowherd. A third consul, Caius Plautius, was dispatched, only to be routed at Évora. A fourth, Claudius Unimanus, suffered a similar fate. He surrendered his eagles and praetor's insignia to Viriathus. The Lusitanians were not ungenerous, if we are to believe an epitaph written by a Roman soldier and discovered later not far from the battlefield. It read: "Caius Minutius, centurion of the tenth legion, I fainted from wounds received in battle against Viriathus. I was left for dead by General Claudius Unimanus, then revived and tended by Eubutius, a Lusitanian soldier. I survived for a few days and I am sad to die without rewarding my benefactor in the usual manner of the Romans." Actually, mercy was rare in this relentless conflict between Roman imperialism and Spanish patriotism. The Lusitanian who tended the enemy and dressed his wounds was the same who, fighting beside Viriathus, rolled heavy rocks down on the helmeted Romans. Yet sometimes a breath of fresh air cooled the hot eve of battles.

In the senate, uneasiness succeeded anger. Instead of pursuing a struggle whose outcome was both dubious and costly, would it not be better to acknowledge the sovereignty of Viriathus? Opinions were divided. Should they offer Viriathus full Roman citizenship? No, that would be going too far. What about a cleverly worded treaty of alliance? While jurists sought the proper wording, Viriathus consolidated his political and military position. He probably had more trouble keeping his tribes united than holding the Romans at bay. He realized that an Iberian empire could not be established at this time, that Rome would ultimately triumph. But he wanted the struggle to be as long and cruel as possible! Whenever there was a lull in the fighting, he would mount his horse and gallop from village to village, exhorting his fellow patriots to renewed faith and courage. His influence spread and he soon became the leader of Castile. The fierce Celtiberians accepted his rule. He assembled tribes, amassed auxiliary troops, and concluded agreements with neighboring groups. So persuasive was he that nothing was refused him. Moreover, his conduct was irreproachable. He slept on the ground with his soldiers and distributed booty impartially, keeping nothing for himself. All of Lusitania united under his dynamic leadership.

The succession of consuls continued. Fabius Aemilianus, brother of Scipio Aemilianus Minor, conqueror of Carthage, hurled an army of 15,000 infantry and 2,000 cavalry against Viriathus. Fortune smiled upon the new consul, but not for long. He was replaced by Fabius Servilianus. Would the latest arrival succeed where all the others had failed? Servilianus decided on extreme measures. No quarter was to be given these barbarians! Prisoners were either executed or mutilated, in the hope that news of this would spread terror. But Viriathus was not intimidated. One night, he crept into Azuaga—a small town situated between Peñarroya and Fuente del Arco—which was under Roman attack. There he raised the flagging spirits of his warriors. He drafted a plan of battle and at dawn launched a violent offensive against Servilianus. Once the Romans were in close pursuit, Viriathus cleverly inveigled them into a narrow defile and barricaded all avenues of escape with heavy rocks. Servilianus and his army were trapped. Would Viriathus starve or stone them to death? Staging the kind of about-face characteristic of his political adroitness, Viriathus offered the Romans peace. They accepted. The proposal went to the senate, where plans were made to implement it. Great was the joy on both sides. Yesterday's enemies were to become friends. But no! A haughty voice was raised. "Not a shameful peace, unworthy of Rome, but total victory!" Scipio Aemilianus had spoken. One could but listen in silence to the man who had just destroyed Carthage.

For ten years Viriathus had humiliated one Roman consul after another. How would he treat Aemilianus? Like all the others. Resorting to tactics which had succeeded so often, Viriathus pretended to accept battle at the appointed place. He slipped away at the last minute, luring the Romans into regions with which he alone was familiar. There he tried to surround them. But Scipio was not tricked. Instead of seeking direct contact with the Lusitanian leader, he unleashed all his forces against Viriathus' allies. He ravaged their country and pillaged their towns. Was Viriathus weary of war? All we know is that he sent three of his lieutenants to Scipio to negotiate for peace—the peace that Rome had already promised.

Thoroughly skilled in the art of war, Scipio Aemilianus was even more adept in diplomacy. He received the three rugged mountaineers with all the pomp generally reserved for ambassadors. First they were put in steam baths and anointed with perfumes. Then they were ushered into the banquet hall under an arch of glittering swords held aloft by the centurions. The place of honor next to Scipio was set aside for them. What homage to these sons of the Sierras! They were ill at ease, paralyzed by shyness. Clothed in muslin *syntheses*, they were made to recline on a couch of honor and served course after course by Roman slaves. Most of the dishes were totally unfamiliar, for in their mountain retreat their food had been coarse and hastily consumed. Now they ate loirs seasoned with poppy, peacock eggs, cow udders, young wild boar stuffed with birds, and crawfish warmed on a silver grill. Amphorae, filled with the heavy wine of Marseille and Setia, were passed back and forth. The wine scorched their throats, for they were accustomed only to fresh mountain water. Were they the guests of Petronius, they wondered, or was Trimalchio himself their host? Soon the three Lusitanians were befuddled with drink. But headier than the coarse wine of Corsica was the flattery. Scipio leaned toward them and murmured in their ears. Surely such brave generals could find a better way to live than to hide like trapped animals. They were wasting themselves on a hopeless undertaking. Sooner or later. . . . Carthage, too, had grown stubborn. They belonged in Rome, where their talents would be appreciated. But on one condition, a trivial one, a mere formality . . . and Scipio lowered his voice to a whisper.

Early the next morning, Viriathus' emissaries returned to

the mountains. Their heads felt heavy. Heavy, too, were
their horses, weighted down with gifts—silver vases, golden
goblets, engraved weapons; and for the women, jars of oint-
ment and make-up—white lead for their foreheads, ocher for
their lips, antimony powder for their eyelashes. How beautiful the women of Tartessus would look! At night they
reached the Lusitanian encampment. Everyone was asleep.
By now their heads had cooled and their resolve hardened.
They already saw themselves clothed in Roman togas. Poor
fools! Before Viriathus' tent they hesitated a moment. Then
they raised the flap and listened. Their leader was asleep.
They stared at one another, then slid into the tent without
a word.

Viriathus' officers and tribal chieftains were in the habit of
meeting with him every morning. When they gathered at the
usual hour, they let out a cry of horror. Their general was
dead—assassinated! The culprits were soon apprehended.
Soldiers drew their swords in rage. But the three Lusitanians smiled knowingly. They had merely carried out
Scipio's orders. Ask Rome if no one believed them. And what
about the money they had been promised? When the senate
learned of the crime, it was indignant. It demanded that the
murderers be put in irons and Scipio severely censured. But,
on reflection, it decided that the death of Viriathus had
ended an insoluble problem. Without their leader, the rebels
could be brought to heel. The criminals would not be paid
the promised sum. Scipio would be disavowed officially. But
privately he would be congratulated for having succeeded
where so many Roman generals had shamefully failed.

Viriathus was given a hero's funeral in the presence of the
entire army. He was eulogized for his admirable character as
well as for his victories. He had been such a great man, yet
so modest! Sober, abstemious, simple in his tastes, he had
shunned pomp and display. Anecdotes were related, one in
particular. Viriathus had eaten very little at his wedding
banquet. When dessert came, he mounted his horse, lifted
his bride up behind him, and galloped off to the mountains
without a word to his companions. Often he would abruptly

put a stop to conversation and leave. Too great to be familiar, he was too hard on himself to be indulgent toward others.

Their leader dead, the Lusitanians dispersed. Some sought refuge in the mountains. Others continued to battle the Romans for honor's sake. In the end they capitulated. Two years after the glorious obsequies for Viriathus, his warriors settled in Roman colonies and accepted their new masters. Traveling from Cáceres to Lisbon, passing through the Los Barreros defile, one comes upon a village—Valencia de Alcántara—that symbolizes Spain's triple personality. It boasts a Moorish tower, a medieval church, Nuestra Señora de Roque Amador, and the walls of the Roman city of Julia Contrasta.

Here, a century before the birth of Christ, elderly shepherds with a military bearing gathered in the evening around a marble fountain. They spoke of the weather-beaten herdsman, slender as a vine shoot, who preferred the fresh waters of freedom to the Falernian wine of the invader. Frequently they looked toward the east, as if they heard the gallop of a horse, or as if the smell of blood and curdled milk from the Lusitanian caves still mingled with the fragrance of fig trees in the Plasencia valley.

Even had Viriathus lived, he would not have been able to conquer all-powerful Rome. But he would have delayed victory as long as possible. To be sure, the struggle did continue even after his death. But how could increasingly isolated and uncoordinated attacks be effective against Roman discipline and organization? One by one the Iberian garrisons fell. Surrounded on all sides, only the *meseta* resisted. In this last stronghold of Spanish independence the ancient Celtiberians seemed indomitable. Scipio resorted to extreme measures in an effort to conquer the tough heroes whom great patricians—Metellus, Marcellus, Lepidus, Pompeius, and Mancinus—despised as barbarians!

What noble barbarians they were! Eight thousand Celtiberians were entrenched in the grottoes of Numantia, and only half of these were armed. Against Roman armor they brandished the spears and pointed staffs of their cave-dwell-

ing ancestors. Yet, poorly equipped though they were, they
kept Rome at bay for a long time. The entire Roman army
under the leadership of Mancinus was forced to capitulate.
Before the portals of the city, Mancinus himself, nude, his
hands tied behind his back, was exposed to the ridicule of
the Spaniards.

Romans seemed to react to Spaniards in much the same
way as the stag reacts to a pack of hounds: they fled as soon
as the Spaniards appeared. But when Scipio arrived before
the walls of Numantia, the situation changed. First he established discipline, ridding the camp of courtesans, traders,
and canteens. Women and wine made soldiers soft, he said.
He surrounded the beleagured city with a continuous line
of circumvallation consisting of a deep trench and a rampart
twelve feet high and five feet thick. This was flanked by
seven crenelated towers in which crossbows and catapults
could be placed. To prevent the Numantians from escaping
down the Douro River, Scipio had spiked iron chains
stretched from one bank to the other. Determined to take
every necessary precaution regardless of expense, he ordered that seven encampments be built, not of canvas, but of
stone, in case the siege was long. It lasted only eight months.

An army of 60,000, one of Rome's greatest generals, a gigantic enterprise—all this was too much for the defenders of
Numantia. Exhausted, with no food save the flesh of corpses,
they were forced to dispatch plenipotentiaries to Scipio. He
sent them back with word that he demanded unconditional
surrender. Enraged by this message, they massacred their
emissaries on the spot. Then they became drunk on *celia*—
their national brandy—and prepared to die. Some ran spears
through their bodies; others took poison; still others seized
torches, set their houses on fire, and flung themselves and
their children into the flames. A few, pointing their spears
downward, jumped from the tops of the towers, hoping to
take some of the enemy with them.

A morning came when no more noise was heard. All the
Numantians had perished. Aemilianus' centurions entered
the ruins of the dead city. They found only corpses and
charred remains. "Five feet of embers and burned land!"

So the historian Polybius, who was present, reported. Even the horses were unable to flee, for the women of Numantia had cut their shins, thus forcing them to die with their masters. Nothing was left among the ashes but goblets of fine clay, decorated with fanciful birds, which these unhappy heroes had clinked together before their final ordeal.

Five miles from Garray, on the road from Soria to Burgos, all that remains of Numantia can be seen from the hilltop overlooking the junction of the Tera and Douro rivers. The faint outline of streets paved by Celtiberian soldiers and later by the Roman cohorts, is just barely visible. Here Spanish resistance ended. However, a few strongholds in the Cantabrian and Asturian mountains held on. It took a whole century to crush them once and for all. In 38 B.C., Emperor Augustus declared Spain a province of Rome. Pacification was an accomplished fact.

Rome and the Latin Legacy

More knowledgeable as a result of Phoenician and Greek penetration, and hardened by the Punic Wars, the Spaniards now received from Rome the wonderful legacy of the Latin language. The Romans not only built highways, theaters, circuses, bridges, aqueducts, and temples; they also brought their political and juridical institutions and their concepts of social and family life. But the Latin language was perhaps Rome's greatest contribution. The Iberians spoke a quite rudimentary tongue. Some philologists believe that the Basque dialect derives in part from it. Be that as it may, Latin, with its extraordinary resonance and its practically unlimited means of expression, took the Spanish elite by surprise. Virgil's death coincided with the final stage of pacification; this was the golden age of Latin literature. It was then that the poet Martial sang the praises of his native Aragon city—Bilbilis, near Calatayud—in beautiful Latin verse. Latin was the language of law and logic; it was used by the Church Fathers to teach the Christian doctrine. The introduction of the Latin language completed Spain's initiation into the Roman way of life.

Schools and libraries were founded and a new world of knowledge and culture was opened up. Although Spain borrowed much from the intellectual treasures of Rome and rapidly assimilated its customs and institutions, it was much less receptive to its religious influence. The many gods, most of them originating in Greek, Egyptian, or Asiatic mythology, the complicated liturgy and prayers, the hierarchy of prelates and priests—all this was alien to the Spaniards, whose cults had been far simpler.

But Rome's contribution to Spain was not solely intellectual; it was abundantly material as well. Historical evidence attests to the astonishing effort made by this sovereign Roman people to achieve eternal supremacy over the world. The results were amazing, judged even by our own present-day standards. The Romans built aqueducts, notably one in Tarragona, more than 650 feet long and 85 feet high, and another, 90 feet high, in Los Milagros. Picture for a moment the intricacies of their highways, the Segovian aqueduct with arches of pure granite, Caracalla's thirty-four roadways, to say nothing of the powerful stone projection over the roaring Tagus, where Trajan's triumphal arch surmounted the Alcántara bridge! Roman engineers burst mountains asunder, subdued rivers and controlled their stormy waters, and erected amphitheaters black with people, dams capable of holding back 350,000,000 cubic feet of water, and a bridge more than a half mile long! In the turquoise sky of Segovia, the remains of arches, punctuated here and there by the white wings of storks, still attest to the grandeur of Rome.

Such was the resplendent décor of Roman Spain at the beginning of the Christian era: a suitable setting for the stone effigies of the Spanish *imperators*, whose proud profiles were to be seen everywhere. Then, during the reign of Augustus, an event occurred, commonplace in itself, but incalculable in its consequences: the birth of Christ. Did these conquerors, drunk with pride and convinced that they were building for eternity, realize that one day this newborn child of Bethlehem would shatter their empire?

2

Caesar and Jesus Christ

ONE OF THE first acts of the Roman administration was to partition Spain into provinces. In the beginning there were two Spains, Citerior and Ulterior, one on each side of the Ebro. Then, under Augustus and Tiberius, Ulterior Spain was divided into Lusitania (Portugal and Estremadura) and Baetica (Andalusia), while Citerior Spain became Tarraconensis (northern Spain). The provinces of Galicia and Asturias date from Caracalla. Later, Diocletian created three new provinces: Carthagenensis (near Cartagena), Baleares (the Balearic Islands), and Tarraconensis Mauretania (Tangier). Spain's tendency to spill over toward the sea was apparent even at this early date.

The Roman Peace

Spain had now become a Roman colony, educated as well as protected by the empire, which taught its language and way of life. It introduced some new ideas that were quite stimulating. The brave but primitive Spaniards experienced an unaccustomed pleasure in learning to use subtle shadings of expression, and their untutored tongues began to experiment with the art of rhetoric, which knowledge of Latin made possible. Law, art, architecture, became intelligible when explained in Latin. The Romans epitomized intellectual clarity, juridical order, and method; their example helped the

Iberians to realize their own potentialities. To be sure, Rome, the heir of Greece and at times its imitator, transmitted a civilization and a set of doctrines that were inspired by the Athenians. Latin thought had not blossomed spontaneously in the forum; it sprang from Hellenism. Although Greco-Latin in character, Rome's influence helped to make Spain what it is today.

The Augustan epoch was marked by large-scale construction. Towns sprang up—the military city Legio Septima Gemina (Leon); another that housed retired veterans, Emerita Augusta (Mérida); also Pax Augusta (Badajoz), Caesarea Augusta (Saragossa), Toletum (Toledo), and Complutum (Alacalá de Henares). Emperor Augustus governed Spain wisely and skillfully. He made every effort to win the affection of his subjects, and he was most successful. Commerce, the arts, and agriculture were his special concern. During his reign a Spaniard for the first time was appointed consul. Augustus' acts of mercy were legion. Instead of forcing the Spaniards to bargain for the rights of citizenship, he granted it generously to all who seemed worthy. As a consequence, the Spaniards adored him, literally and figuratively. They built altars in his honor and worshipped him. The gracious emperor-god was gratified. He took special pride in the title "Father of Our Country," bestowed upon him by the grandsons of the defeated Numantians.

Did Roman domination forge Iberian unity? Actually this was a matter of indifference to the Romans. In teaching the crude Spaniards fine manners and modes of thought, a more flexible and exact language, their main purpose was to win allies for the defense of the empire. The emperors aimed at fashioning peoples as diverse as the Cantabrians, Lusitanians, and Asturians in the image of Rome, poured from a Latin mold. They only half succeeded. On the whole, the Spaniards proved to be precious allies, and Julius Caesar was proud to count among his personal guard the cream of the Iberian cavalry; yet the unruly nature of the Spaniards was such that they never became the model colony the imperial government had hoped to establish. On the other hand, Rome gave Spain an administrative framework that served as a basis for the first Christian organizations. By providing Spain with effective institutions, a politcal and juridical system, and, above all, an intellectual climate, the Romans unwittingly prepared the way for the Christian ferment. Christianization was the natural corollary of Romanization and its new patterns of thought. The convergence of Roman history and Christianity, the fact that the Gospel spread partly as a consequence of the unification of the Mediterranean world, the adoption by early Christian societies of the Roman administrative structure—all this may seem surprising at first, particularly when one remembers the martyrs. Yet it is altogether evident that, disappointed in Pallas Athene, Rome was unalterably attracted to Jesus. The *Pax Christi* quite logically succeeded the *Pax Romana*. In a few admirable phrases, Bossuet has summed up one of the great moments of history: "Caesar won the Battle of Actium. . . . The armies of Egypt and the Orient, led by Antony, were dispersed. . . . Herod of Edom, who owed everything to him, was forced to yield to the victor. . . . Egypt became a province of Rome. . . . He drove the rebellious Cantabrians and Asturians to the Pyrenees. . . . Triumphant on land and sea, he closed the temple of Janus. . . . The entire universe lived in peace under his rule and Jesus Christ was born into the world."

The Death of Seneca

A brilliant galaxy of Latin writers of Spanish origin appeared during the very first years of the Christian era. The most celebrated were Columella, Pomponius Mela, Lucan, Martial, and Quintilian. Three others exerted a considerable influence on the men of their day although they left no great works behind them: the rhetorician Antonius Julianus, the geographer Turianus Gracilis, and the jurist Porcius Latro, who taught Ovid law. And lastly there was one, Seneca, the philosopher, whose message, though occasionally at variance with his life, has been handed down to us with all its pure resonance unimpaired.

In the heart of Baetica, at Cordova—the center of Hispano-Roman intellectualism—Lucius Annaeus Seneca was born, four years before the advent of Christ. His mother, Helvia, had taught him early the practice of virtue. He came to Rome as a young man to study rhetoric. There he took lessons from the Stoic philosopher Attalus and from Fabianus and Sotion, the Pythagoreans. He registered for the bar and pleaded his cases so successfully that he reportedly aroused the jealousy of Caligula. He was named quaestor and shortly afterward senator.

At the height of his glory, Seneca was exiled to Corsica by Messalina, wife of Claudius. He was pardoned by Agrippina, who, acting in concert with Burrus, entrusted him with the education of Nero. Then tragedy struck. For five years the philosopher had struggled against the influence of the newly freed slaves. He had been untiring in his efforts to stir the conscience of the prince, to awaken some spark in this unfortunate man, torn by passions, to make him cry out for something other than sensual pleasure. But his persistence had been in vain. Disheartened, Seneca left the court. His retirement was all too short-lived. Rightly or wrongly, he was implicated in the conspiracy of Piso, and Nero decreed his death. Very calm, this disciple of Attalus ordered that a warm bath be drawn. In honor of the libations of Jupiter, he sprinkled the floor and the friends who had forgathered with his bath water. Then he opened his veins.

Seneca's writings and doctrines are even more noteworthy than his career. His monotheism, his irreverence for traditional cults, his religious nonconformism, his eloquence (at times bordering on bombast, which Christian rhetoricians were to imitate), and, above all, his natural stoicism—all this links him plainly to the first Church savants. Tertullian, the gifted and somber master of Christian apologetics, called him "our" Seneca, and was influenced by his literary style. Later, Erasmus, Montaigne, Descartes, and even Pascal spoke of Seneca as one of the greatest philosophers of antiquity. One has but to reread *Epistolae Morales ad Lucilium* to discover once again the fortifying richness, stoical inflexi-

bility, and masculine vigor that made this Cordovan philosopher a forerunner of Christianity.

"Do not permit yourself to be defeated by anything alien
to your mind. Amid the changing fortunes of life, remember
that you bear within you an overriding strength, something
indestructible, similar to the shaft of a diamond, around
which shimmer the trivial happenings of daily life. And
whatever befalls you, whether it be happy or unfortunate, or
even if it seems to degrade you by its contact, meet it with
firmness and honesty, in such a way that one can truly say
you are a man."

We readily recognize in this proud language the very ring
of Christianity! Similarities between Seneca's ethics and
Christian precepts are so striking that in all sincerity some
of our contemporaries have come to believe that the philosopher secretly adhered to Christianity and even had dealings
with St. Paul. There is no documentary evidence to confirm
or verify this hypothesis, too seductive to be true, and his-
torically improbable. Considered highly suspect by the
Church and rejected by the humanists, it has nonetheless
been piously perpetuated up to the twentieth century. Some
fervent defenders of this exciting notion are still to be
found. And why should we disabuse them? At the beginning of the nineteenth century, a small book entitled *Christian Seneca* was distributed in all the confessional schools.
Generations of students were taught that the philosopher of
Cordova was one of Christianity's most brilliant recruits.
Every missionary movement inevitably tends to claim great
men as its own, if thereby its cause can be strengthened.
Without going so far as to say that Seneca was really a Christian at heart, one is forced to acknowledge the tremendous
part he played in the moral education of Spain. Witnessing
the last days of paganism, heralding in his own outlook the
dawn of Christianity, Seneca, more than any other, symbolized the transition between two worlds—the ancient and the
modern.

What an extraordinary destiny was this man's, born of a
great Spanish family, who studied law and, because he had
gained the favor of princes, exerted great influence over the

emperor! He was both a man of the world and a stoic, displaying an independence of mind that was inconsistent with certain of his attitudes. For the truth is that he was wealthy, corruptible, often corrupted, and greedy; yet he professed contempt for material values. What a contrast between his principles and his public life! It persisted up to the very moment of his death, the significance of which is still a mystery. Was it the act of a man filled with bitterness, or a confession that he could not survive the disgrace of a ruler whom he identified with a divinity? For, indeed, nothing obliged him to obey Nero. Involved in one of the darkest episodes in Western history, perhaps Seneca saw the Eternal City in flames and the first martyrs burned along the Sacred Way. Never again would he be able to rid himself of Nero's embarrassing shadow. It would cling to his legend, and history would combine their two names: "Seneca, Nero's preceptor." But we should separate them and preserve only the pure classical image of Seneca. Having failed to humanize his monstrous pupil, the philosopher opened his veins. At the same time, the hapless tutor became the teacher of all mankind.

Legends

Jesus designated Peter as head of the Church. Peter settled in Rome, the capital of the empire. This was a surprisingly courageous thing to do, and it probably furthered the progress of Christianity in Spain, which was a Roman province. "Go ye therefore, and teach all nations!" And what nation was more receptive to the evangelical ferment than Spain, Rome's turbulent ally? The exploits of Viriathus, the epic of Saguntum, the hecatomb of Numantia—these still echoed in the memory of the temporarily defeated Spaniards. Seneca's difficult message taught them an ardent resignation that heralded the Christian watchwords. Stoicism was not new to the first Spanish neophytes. It paved the way for martyrdom.

Christian Spain claimed the protection of St. Paul. What

THE AGE OF VIRIATHUS

are we to believe about this glorious investiture? Did the
Apostle of the Gentiles go to Spain? In his Epistle to the
Romans (15:23–8), St. Paul has this to say:

"But now having no more place in these parts, and having a great desire these many years to come unto you;

"Whensoever I take my journey into Spain, I will come to
you: for I trust to see you in my journey, and to be brought
on my way thitherward by you, if first I be somewhat filled
with your company.

"But now I go unto Jerusalem to minister unto the
saints. . . .

"When, therefore, I have performed this, and have sealed
to them this fruit, I will come by you into Spain."

Thus St. Paul's intention is clearly stated. Moreover, he
was not a man to break his word. Yet nothing is known of his
apostleship in Spain. A text composed in A.D. 96 by St.
Clement I, bishop of Rome, although rather vague, nonetheless seems to shed some light on this question, in which
legend figures more than history. "Paul, having become the
herald of truth in the Orient and in the Occident, reaped a
reward for his faith and taught justice to the entire universe. Having reached the end of the Occident and suffered martyrdom under the princes, he finally left the world
and went to the Holy place." Could "the end of the Occident" be Spain? Lucan wrote "*extremique orbis Iberi.*"

Much later, St. Jerome wrote that St. Paul came to Spain
by way of the sea: "*ad Hispaniam alienigenarum portatus
est navibus.*" Actually this was the quickest route to Spain.
Pliny reported that one could go from Ostia to Tarragona in
four days, and all the way to Cadiz in less than a week. According to the traditional belief, St. Paul made this voyage
in A.D. 63, after his appearance before Caesar and his acquit-
tal. Supposedly he remained in Andalusia for a while, and
then departed for Rome, where he suffered his martyrdom
in the year 67.

What are we to infer from this meager evidence? That St.
Paul planned to visit Spain but had to give up the idea at the
last moment? Or did he go there clandestinely to avoid suspicion? But this is hardly credible, for prudence was not

characteristic of the apostle. And it is difficult to believe that such a man could remain incognito for long. Still more incredible is the failure of this ancient Baetica soil, consumed by sun and marked by the passage of so many peoples, to disclose a single trace of his visit.

But what matter historical evidence! One has but to imagine the handful of silent Andalusians crowded around the visionary from Damascus. He speaks and they drink in his words. The dancing flame of a small brushwood fire now lights up and now obscures their wooden faces. But what an all-consuming fire in their hearts!

St. James's visit to Spain seems even more legendary than St. Paul's. Called by the Master "the Son of Thunder," he supposedly sojourned on the banks of the Ebro a few years before his martyrdom in Jerusalem. But this is a relatively recent notion. No historian mentions it, neither Prudentius, Orosius, Martinus of Braga, nor Gregory of Tours.

"The voice of the apostles spread throughout the land, and their words spread to the end of the world. Jesus, seeing his apostles mending their nets on the banks of the Lake of Gennesaret, called them and sent them out over the high seas, wishing to transform these fishermen into men who fished for human souls." In this text, St. Jerome infers that Christ sent James the Elder to Spain, "over the high seas." Why him, and not Peter, Andrew, or John? The *Apostolic Canons* fix Spain as St. James's field of action. This is explicitly refuted by St. Julian, archbishop of Toledo, and by the learned St. Isidore, bishop of Seville. The Mozarabic liturgy makes no reference to a special ceremony in honor of St. James's mission. On the other hand, rumors multiplied and led to bitter arguments. For a long time there was bickering among parishes, and the controversy reached Rome. At the end of the sixteenth century, when the breviary was revised, Pope Clement VIII removed the sentence introduced by Pius V: "James traveled through Spain and there preached the gospel."

How trivial are the clouds of sterile arguments that hover over the glowing tomb of Zebedee's son! All these futile polemics neither deepen nor detract from the mystery. Nor do they affect in any way the refreshing simplicity of the story told in 1139 in the *Historia Compostellana*.

A certain Luis Lopez reports: "On the twelfth of October, in the year 39, St. James, son of Zebedee, was praying with his disciples near the banks of the Ebro. The night was dark. James had gone but a stone's throw away when suddenly there was a blinding flash of light. Escorted by thousands of angels, the Mother of God appeared. She was seated on a pillar of jasper. St. James the Evangelist was beside her. Accompanied by the chords of a harp, celestial voices intoned the Angelic Salutation. Then the Virgin turned to James and said: 'It is here that I wish to be honored. Build me a temple and let this pillar remain in this place until the end of the world. Here I will perform miracles.' James obeyed Mary's command and soon built a chapel that was called our Lady of the Pillar."

Eight hundred years later, in the vicinity of Amala, in the Episcopal diocese of Iria Flavia, a tomb was discovered which the pious believed to be that of St. James.

If St. Paul's voyage to Spain is doubtful, and if the visit of St. James is to be regarded as poetic fiction, this will trouble none but the pedants. On the austere velvet of history, tradition embroiders scenes and shapes that are woven into the fabric. The authenticity of the event is far less important than its symbolic significance and its influence on Spanish spirituality. Later we shall see that the first martyrs were steeped in Pauline lore. Extending the entire length of the *camino franco*, from the port of Cize to the Puerta de Francos, we will observe an endless column of pilgrims from Santiago de Compostela. Paul of Tarsus and the knight of Santiago were present in spirit on Spanish soil.

Those Rebels—The First Christians

While Martial was extolling his native city, Bilbilis, and rejoicing in having been born a Spaniard—"I am proud of being a Celtiberian, born on the banks of the Tagus; I have the coarse hair of a Spaniard and my legs and cheeks bristle with hair"—and while Lucan, still an adolescent, committed suicide as he recited from his epic poem, *Pharsalia*, the Romans were completing the administrative structure of Spain. Before they came, Spain was a more or less loosely knit group of small independent sovereignties whose origins, customs, and language frequently were different. Under the Romans, Spain became entirely homogeneous. Provinces were divided into districts the majority of whose cities preserved their own tribunals and laws. Some were organized into municipalities, and their inhabitants shared responsibility in the duties of the republic. After a period of probation, the republic granted them the privilege of citizenship. But Rome authorized the imposition of taxes upon those cities that were not in good standing. A good illustration of this is the following rescript issued by Vespasian: "I, Caesar Vespasian, Augustus, supreme pontiff, invested for the eighth time with jurisdictional authority, and for the eighteenth time with imperial authority, consul for the eighth time, greet the quatuorvirates and the decurions of Sabora. In view of the account you have given of your weaknesses and difficulties, I give you permission to build your city in the plain, under my name, as you have requested. I will hold the tribute money you say you have received from Emperor Augustus. Any proposal for additional taxes must be presented to the proconsul. I cannot grant anything of this nature unless those involved are in complete agreement. I received your request on the eighth day before Augustus' calends and I dismissed your envoys three days before these same calends. Stay well.

"Engraved on bronze at the public's expense by the duumvirs, Cornelius Severus and Septimius Severus."

In contrast to the municipalities, which consisted of groups of Spaniards united with Rome, the colonies were composed of Roman citizens living in Spain who enjoyed all the rights and privileges of the republic.

The beginning of the second century was marked by the triumph of the Roman peace. Imperial highways, works of art, amphitheaters, had been completed. Trade flourished and literature abounded. Tarragona was the center of the

Roman administration. Emperor Hadrian was fond of visiting it, perhaps because in this Mediterranean city, its gardens swollen with golden fruits, he was reminded of the colors of Rome; perhaps, too, because of the memory of his adopted father, Trajan, a Spaniard like himself. His visits, announced long before his arrival, were triumphal. Several weeks in advance, Iberians set forth from their villages in Estremadura, in Galicia, or along the banks of the Douro or Tagus. Clothed in brown tunics and smelling strongly of their flocks, they were not embarrassed to rub shoulders with the Roman patricians who had just descended the steps of rose-covered villas to go to the baths. They would stand on tiptoe in their rope sandals to glimpse the centurions' helmets among the thick cluster of swords borne by the legionary guards. Preceded by generals with flamboyant coiffures, the emperor appeared. He was on foot, bareheaded, the bottom of his white toga thrown over his forearm. He wore no adornments except an enormous escarbuncle of Hannibal on his index finger. He smiled at the crowds, and they were delighted by his simplicity. Was he not a child of their own country? Meanwhile, Hadrian, walking slowly toward the amphitheater, was turning over in his mind the speech he would deliver before the wild beasts were unleashed in the arena. Tarragonian honey, Ibiza figs, wheat from the Ebro countryside, no longer sufficed. Rome needed soldiers, more and more of them. Should he wait for the first lion to come bounding out, and the first stream of blood to splatter him, before uttering the warning he was so reluctant to proclaim: "Beware of the barbarians!"

Ah! If it were only the barbarians that worried him! Indeed, the empire's frontiers were not the sole source of danger. A new, increasingly restless sect was threatening Rome's internal equilibrium. It was teaching a curious religion, both loving and austere, invented by the "crucified sophist." Its spokesman, a man called Peter, had had the impudence to install himself in Rome. The celebrated Greek satirist Lucian spoke contemptuously of the "folly of the Cross," yet it was affecting even the most balanced minds; converts multiplied daily. To be sure, Rome was tolerant.

More than tolerant, it readily welcomed foreign gods to its pantheon. It had adapted itself to the Greek divinities and the guardian spirits of Gaul. Why should it refuse the Jew of Nazareth the tribute it had bestowed upon Isis? Hadrian had certainly built temples to Antinoüs, and Nero had paid homage to Atargatis, the Syrian goddess. What troubled the imperial government was not so much the person of Jesus as his revolutionary doctrine. To proclaim that all men were brothers, to vilify the rich and glorify the poor, to preach a strict morality—such notions could scarcely be tolerated by the voluptuous and plutocratic Rome of the Antonines.

During the first two centuries, Christianity evolved quietly on the Iberian Peninsula. Preoccupied with material progress and development, the Romans did not seem troubled by the beginnings of evangelization.

Long after St. Paul's reputed voyage, an episcopal mission, reportedly sent by St. Peter, landed in Andalusia. It included seven bishops, each of whom founded a diocese: Torquatus at Cadiz, Secundus at Abla, Indalecius at Urci, Ctesiphon at Berja, Caecilius at Granada, Hesichius at Cazorla, and Euphrasius at Andújar. These were the first *varones apostólicos.*

Toward the end of the second century, St. Irenaeus, bishop of Lyon, spoke of the churches of Spain. They must have been of rather ancient origin, for the prelate referred to the authority of their "tradition" in regard to heretics. In any case, if Tertullian can be trusted, by the end of the third century not a single inch of Spanish soil was unaffected by Christian doctrines. The era of martyrs dates from this period.

Tarragona manifested a special fervor because of its emperor and its official cult. Christianity, at any rate, was tolerated. But the edicts of Valerian put an end to this. Fructuosus, the elderly bishop of Tarragona, was the first victim of persecution.

With his deacons, Augurius and Eulogius, he was arrested by Roman soldiers and brought before Aemilianus, the governor of the province.

"Art thou acquainted with the decrees of the emperor?"

"No, but I am a Christian."

"His orders are to worship the gods."

"I worship one almighty God who has created the heavens and the earth, the sea and all things."

"Art thou then ignorant that there are many gods?"

"I am."

"Who, then, will be either feared or honored hereafter if thou dost not adore the gods and revere the emperors?"

"I worship the all-powerful Lord."

"Art thou a bishop?"

"I am."

"Thou hast been a bishop."

And the governor decreed that Fructuosus and his deacons be burned alive. On the road to his final agony the bishop refused the traditional glass of wine—"The hour for breaking fast has not yet struck." Dragged to the funeral pile, Fructuosus kneeled. He comforted his martyred companions and his faithful. "What you are about to witness is but the torment of an hour." Then he prayed as the fire consumed him.

Even more moving is the story of little Eulalia of Mérida. Overwrought by tales of the persecution of Christians, she longed to share their fate. At the age of twelve she became obsessed with the idea of martyrdom. In the evening she heard her parents discuss in low voices the news from Saragossa, Rome, and Lyon. One name kept recurring, that of Diocletian. We always think that children are asleep, or that the affairs of grownups bore them. Actually, nothing interests them more. Seemingly absorbed in her needlework, Eulalia eavesdropped. She devoured stories of blood and torture. Oh, to be like St. Blandina and to feel the jaws of the wild beast! One day Eulalia announced her intention of offering herself up to persecution. The note of determination, the thin lips and fixed stare, alarmed her parents. They sent her to the country "to clear her mind." But they had waited too long. No sooner had she reached her destination than she escaped, at nightfall, and returned to the city. The following morning she appeared at the tribunal and declared herself a Christian. The magistrate, taken by surprise, was annoyed. Then he began to joke with her. It is not difficult to visualize the Roman bureaucrat, a good fellow at heart, interested in getting a promotion, but disinclined to display unnecessary zeal. He liked children—perhaps he had children of his own. He smiled at her. But his gentle manner only exasperated Eulalia. Seething with anger, she insulted him. What did the little fool want? The magistrate almost lost his temper. But never mind! With the tips of her fingers she could toss a few grains of salt on the altar, and no more would be said. The little girl made a face at him. What did he take her for? She was a Christian. Rude laughter greeted this profession of faith. A Christian? Really? She certainly was; she would prove it. Standing on her toes to make herself taller, she spit in the priest's face. Then she overturned an idol, scattered incense, stamped on it, crossed her arms, and waited. This time she had publicly committed a flagrant sacrilege. The magistrate was livid. To the torture chamber with her! She was seized by the executioners, who plunged iron nails into her tender flesh. The child sang at the top of her voice and counted the blows. Her torturers became exasperated. Let her wander forever in Erebus, pursued by all the Furies, the bitch! With clenched fists, they battered her, and, sneering, put flaming torches to her body. Eulalia's song grew fainter. Chastely, she covered her satin-smooth, undeveloped breasts with her long hair. Her tresses caught on fire. At that moment snow began to fall on the forum of Mérida. Daylight faded swiftly. As the snowfall grew heavier a sharp wind arose. Such sudden changes of temperature occur frequently in Estremadura. Shivering with cold and weary of their task, the torturers fled in haste, abandoning the little naked girl on the road. Eulalia died, smothered by flames. Night fell. Slowly the snow covered the forsaken virgin with a transparent icy shroud.

Certainly the unconscious played a considerable part in Eulalia's determination to become a martyr. The little girl who went before the magistrate was a fanatic, intoxicated by her visions. Yes . . . maybe. But surely this kind of sublime absurdity is characteristic of martyrs. They obey inhuman laws that defy reason and frighten us. To suffer death in order to affirm Life Eternal—what folly!

But can we forget the wounded dove of Mérida, the silence and the shadow that descended on the public square, or the mercenaries who fled along the banks of the Guadiana, and the blood that trickled, drop by drop, making horrible black puddles in the snow?

Christian Spain Becomes Organized

Not all Spanish Christians were saints. A few came to terms with the empire. Basilides and Martial, bishops of Leon and Mérida, respectively, were among those who solicited *libelli*. This was around the year 250, during the reign of Decius. The emperor was opposed to violent methods of persecution, not for reasons of compassion, but because it did not seem sensible to impoverish the empire by massacring Christians. Martyrdom was unprofitable. Decius thought it simpler to rely upon apostasy. To be left in peace, Christians had but to ask the Roman administration for pagan sacrificial certificates called *libelli*. However, only a handful were willing to accept this hypocritical compromise. Bishops who were so weak as to countenance the certificate of paganism were expelled from the Christian community. Thus the faithful among the Spaniards, supported by St. Cyprian, bishop of Carthage, obtained from Pope Adrian the removal of Basilides and Martial from their sees.

The abdication of Diocletian and Maximian marked the end of persecution. The title of Augustus was conferred on Galerius and Constantine, that of Caesar on Maximinus Daza and Severus. Spain was ruled by the gentle Constantine. Now the Church knew peace. No longer menaced from the outside, it was free to conduct its affairs as it saw fit. The veil of secrecy was lifted. But another, more subtle danger began its work of destruction. The Christians had been completely united against the enemy, free of even the slightest dissent so long as they struggled clandestinely. But no sooner had they got rid of persecution than the black eagle of heresy swooped down upon them—an eagle that was soon splattered with blood. Enemies of the Church could be counted among its own faithful. Yet only yesterday, their arms crossed on the sands of the arenas, martyrs had courted the attack of wild beasts. What can we say of this brotherhood forged in torture by the hand of the tormentor, then torn asunder by peace—of the ardor of proselytes, their tenderness toward one another, their somber enthusiasm, fed by the worst kind of bodily pain? On the rack, it was love rather than doctrine that prevailed. Only God mattered. The admirable vitality and strength of the first communities sprang from the fact that they were tracked and hunted by outside powers. Nothing seemed impossible to groups of neophytes tormented by Rome—so young was their faith, so natural their sacrifice. But religions have this in common with human lives: a time of constructive maturity succeeds a period of unpremeditated heroics. Grave problems arose that had nothing to do with the heart's impulses.

An era of councils marked the beginning of an exhausting and protracted dispute that brought on punishment by fire and tormented Christians until the reign of Philip II. But Truth had to be made more exact, and the Church needed to be organized and strengthened because it was still weak.

The Council of Elvira was the first on Spanish soil. Each province was well represented. Galicia and Tarraconensis named the bishops of Leon and Saragossa, respectively. Lusitania sent three prelates and Carthagenesis eight. The delegation from Baetica was headed by the bishop of Cordova.

The main objective of the Council of Elvira was to abolish idolatry. Apparently the participants had but one concern—to put an end to pagan practices. It is not difficult to picture Christian society at the time of its liberation from paganism. It could scarcely believe what was happening. What, no more martyrs? Eulalia's martyrdom happened only yesterday. Was it possible that after so much bloodshed Christianity would become the religion of the empire? The Church, on the verge of victory after its long ordeal, quite understandably wished to eradicate from the new Christian ritual every trace of idolatry, to destroy every remnant of paganism. And so it was forbidden to hang paintings on church walls, and witchcraft was to be punished by excommunication, and even by death. On the other hand, the Church opened its arms to pagans who expressed a sincere desire to be converted, and everything possible was done to simplify the process. Nor did the council neglect the practical and social aspects of Christianity, but the ethics it expounded was still rudimentary. Bold and sure of itself in the domain of theology, it took slow, measured steps along the path of direct action. Young and tremulous with joy, the Church was intent on testing its methods. It was too early to reverse the old order or to break old habits all at once, no matter how pernicious or evil they might be. This caution is not surprising when one remembers the extent to which Roman customs had permeated Iberia. A complacent and cruel immorality, which the sensuous tide of decadence only served to further, governed human relationships. The imperial civilization, admirable as it was in respect to material, political, and intellectual values, had done nothing for man. To Christianity, man and man's destiny alone mattered; confronting Rome, it adopted a revolutionary attitude. What a thunderbolt in the Roman sky!

The Council of Elvira boldly denounced adultery and stigmatized housewives who whipped their slaves to death. It took a solemn stand against customs that were accepted as a matter of course. In decreeing the celibacy of priests, it stressed the sacred nature of the ecclesiastical function. By creating a hierarchy within the clergy as well as episcopal sees, it laid the foundations of the Spanish Church and established it in the community. But how rash it was to implement such reforms when tyranny, although nearing its end, was still rampant in certain provinces of the Eastern Roman Empire!

The Council of Elvira definitely marked the line between paganism and Christianity; or, rather, it represented the threshold of Christianity, for it met in 306, the year in which Constantine, the future Christian emperor, mounted the throne in the West.

Immediately after consolidating its authority, the Church had occasion to test its strength. Around 320 an Alexandrian priest named Arius sought to reform Christianity. He claimed that Christ was not divine, but human and subordinate to God. This satisfied the barbarians' penchant for simple concepts. The idea that a human could also be a god was beyond their comprehension. Although quite interested in law and science, they were utterly indifferent to metaphysics. The new converts, who had readily accepted countless pagan divinities, proved unreceptive to the mystery of the Trinity.

However praiseworthy Arius' intentions might have been, the threat his heresy posed at a time when Christianity was mustering its strength had to be stamped out quickly. For if Christ were in truth not divine, what would become of Christianity? Constantine was worried and asked Hosius, bishop of Cordova, to go to Alexandria, conduct an investigation, and arbitrate the controversy.

Hosius had participated in the Council of Elvira fifteen years earlier. Then, scarcely forty, he had been at the height of his intellectual and physical powers. He was born in the East, probably in Egypt, and his body bore the scars of persecution. His influence over Constantine had inspired the Edict of Milan, which granted religious freedom.

Hosius was now almost sixty. Neither the abuse of his torturers nor the rigors of a frequently arduous apostleship had diminished the amazing vitality of this man of iron. He was not a casuist. His clear and honest mind was not cluttered with subtleties. One Truth existed, not two. Thus, he was entirely lacking in Oriental ambiguity.

The presence of Hosius on the boulevards of voluptuous Alexandria, coming as he did from the heart of the West, aroused great curiosity. The crusty old man found himself in the world's most polished and elegant city. What a change of atmosphere! "Full of snobs," we would say today in describing Alexandria. Conversation was sophisticated and learned. Attempts were under way to revive the intellectual sparring of the Platonic era. Everyone in this fine society spoke Greek, and Hosius understood only Latin. But the old warrior knew how to make his meaning plain to these frivolous people. He cautioned against idle reverie and preached, albeit in crude terms, a return to the pure and simple primitive faith. A few weeks sufficed for Hosius to form an opinion: in condemning Arianism, the Church dogma must recapture its inflexibility and its original values. This was the burden of his report to Constantine, who was urged to convoke another council.

The first ecumenical Council of Nicaea met in 325, at the emperor's call. As the representative of the emperor, Hosius presided. The Spanish prelate made a deep impression on the Oriental bishops. Indeed, this crude Cordovan with a passion for truth first astounded, then convinced the assembly. The partisans of Arianism decreased in number from twenty to two, and the heresy itself was condemned. But Hosius did not let the matter rest there. In an effort to destroy the heresy altogether and prevent its recurrence, he conceived the idea of reducing the essence of the Christian faith to a clear, concise formula. From the lips of this Spanish bishop came the Nicaean Creed: *"Credo in unum Deum, Patrem omnipotentem . . ."* The boundless clamor of the faithful was to answer the murmur of the old man from Cordova.

At the Council of Nicaea, Hosius met the patriarch of Alexandria, Athanasius. A Father of the Church, already famous for his struggle against Arianism, Athanasius found not only a brother-in-arms in Hosius but a good friend as well. He wrote: "Hosius was well named [Hosius in Greek means "saint"]. His life was irreproachable, unless one can call his ardent hatred of heresy a crime." And it is true that this hero, whose scars were a reminder of Maximian, was indulgent toward other people's faults although uncompromising in defense of orthodoxy.

Another council may have met after the one at Nicaea. Documents on the period are scarce. Inspired by Hosius, the Spanish Church continued to evolve. New episcopal sees were created, and the hierarchy was further elaborated. Arianism did not stir, felled by the blows it had suffered. This was indeed a period of peace for the Church. Relics of this era are scarce—remnants of walls, cemeteries, half-effaced paintings, chapels built and rebuilt several times, churches that were secularized or replaced by the Visigoths. Christian Spain was still feeble. Its framework was frail and unimpressive, its ritual rudimentary. But what the Church lacked most was strong leadership. It boasted only one great man: Hosius of Cordova. His steadfastness stood out among those who surrounded him, men of good will but with little will power. Apparently, as the Church moved further and further away from martyrdom, it became more bureaucratic.

For the first time it was beset with the kind of lethargy that was to threaten it during every peaceful phase of its existence. In periods of freedom, far from thriving, it seemed somnolent. However, it awakened with a start at the first sign of heresy.

The Spanish Church was well aware of the paucity of its human values. It acknowledged its weaknesses and clung to the sturdy oak of a man who was nearing his hundredth year. With unshakable optimism Hosius persisted. Embellish the ritual? We will consider that later. Vocations? We will create them. Leaders? We will train them. What mattered was neither liturgy nor clergy, but doctrine.

At the age of ninety, Hosius presided over the Council of Sardis. Almost all the canons bear his name. "Hosius, bishop of the city of Cordova, says . . ." Once again he was the defender of truth. The council, primarily concerned with episcopal discipline, sheds some light on the rather excessive independence of certain bishops. "Ill-advised and unwise practices must be eliminated. For example, a bishop will no longer be permitted to move from one see to another. His reasons for so doing are very plain. No bishop ever goes from a large city to a smaller one. Consequently, his actions are determined by greed, ambition, and pride." One perceives everywhere the firm, shrewd hand of Hosius. The council met for the purpose of restraining these fourth-century prelates from leaving their residences to attend to private matters. Reading between the lines of the academic style, one can guess at the outcry their activities aroused.

Hosius returned to Cordova. Constantine II succeeded his father. Arianism, which was still rampant, found a powerful ally in the new emperor. Two parties opposed each other: the champions of orthodoxy led by Athanasius, Hosius, and Pope Liberius, and the Arian bishops supported by Constantine II. Emboldened by their protector, and seething with malignant glee, the Arian bishops looked forward to the moment of vengeance. They had deeply resented the humiliation suffered at the Council of Nicaea. And now theological chicanery, complicated by court intrigues and the clash of selfish interests, appeared once again. "Will we ever be rid of that subversive, Athanasius, and of Hosius, whose sermons smell of senility?"

Athanasius soared above this reptilian humanity. And nothing could affect Hosius, who remained at his post. His trembling hand was still at the helm. "He will never die!" his enemies complained. Their numbers increased as he grew older. Constantine banished the Pope because he refused to condemn Athanasius. He called Hosius to Milan, hoping to obtain from him what Liberius had refused to grant. The bishop went to the emperor, refused to yield, and returned to Cordova without signing the deposition against Athanasius. To Constantine's rancorous letters (from a distance, the monarch, closeted with the Arians, dared to threaten Hosius), the bishop answered:

"Hosius to Constantine, the Emperor, I greet you in the name of our Lord. The first time I made my confession to Jesus Christ I was persecuted by your ancestor Maximian. If you, too, wish to persecute me, I am ready to suffer anything rather than to cause the shedding of innocent blood or to betray the truth. If you continue to send me letters and threats, I will refuse you communion. . . . Believe me, Constantine, I am old, I could be your grandfather. . . . Change your ways and think of death. . . . God gave you the Empire and us the Church. . . . I am saying this to save you. As for what you tell me, this is what I think: I cannot get along with the Arians, who are anathema to me, nor can I oppose Athanasius, who represents the Church of

Rome, the council, and myself. . . . I am writing you in a way that seems proper to me. Do not spurn my words."

Unresponsive to this noble outcry, Constantine ordered Hosius to Sirmium, in lower Pannonia. It was a long journey from the Guadalquivir to the Danube. And Hosius was a hundred years old. He marshaled all his strength and went off to fight his last battle. For a whole year every effort was made—even to the extent of inflicting blows—to persuade Hosius to subscribe to Arianism. There was speculation about his failing memory; his family was persecuted. How long would the crowd of torturers, some of whom wore the miter, persist in harassing the old man? Even if, by circumventing his good faith, they got him to accept the arguments of the Arian bishops, Ursatius and Valens, never would he, the creator of the Credo, condemn Athanasius or repudiate Catholicism. The old archangel died on his feet.

For the Church of Spain, which is a part of the recorded history of the fourth century thanks to Hosius, this period was a productive if not a brilliant era. For more than sixty years, the awe-inspiring zealot was tireless in arousing the timid, in lashing out at the want of discipline, and in carrying high and firm the standard of his faith. His death—many were those who sighed with relief!—marked the end of a tumultuous but fruitful phase. For a while the world turned its attention away from Christian Spain. Nothing of great importance was to occur until the end of the fourth century— only a few minor incidents.

Gregory of Elvira created the Luciferian sect. Second-rate personalities were involved. Religious tracts were slipped under coats and passed back and forth surreptitiously. The various chapels quarreled. Theological disputes were begun only to subside in indifference. The events were trivial and the men insignificant.

One woman stands out because of her originality: the nun Egeria, whose *Diary of a Journey to the Holy Places* was a strange tale of remarkable physical endurance. For four years Egeria, who was amazingly cultivated for her times, traveled through Palestine and Mesopotamia, going as far as

Persia. Her primary purpose in writing the diary apparently
was to give an accurate description of the regions she visited.
What she had to say about the religion and history of the
Church of Jerusalem is interesting and demonstrates an objectivity that would be less astonishing in a journalist than in
a nun. Excellent at describing places and a keen observer,
Egeria seemed rather indifferent to mysticism. Although she
claimed that she compiled her notes for the sole purpose of
diverting her companions in the convent, strangely enough
she was at liberty to travel throughout the Orient, and she
visited the mother convent only rarely. The rules evidently
were very lax and the cloister quite free. This roaming ab-
bess, who broke away from her convent and preferred sight-
seeing to prayers, was the first Spanish woman of letters—
twelve centuries before Theresa of Ávila!

The virgin Eulalia's blood, splattered on the forum of
Mérida, bespoke the virtues of the martyred Church. Hosius'
resistance to Arianism aided it in its fight. It now knew and
had proved that it could suffer and give battle—the wheel
and the sword.

But Spanish Christianity, bitter and militant, was wanting
in ideas. The literary style of Prudentius and Priscillian's
knowledge illuminated its heroic action with the light of intelligence.

Nobody knows whether Prudentius was born in Saragossa, Calahorra or Tarragona, but we do know that he was
a Spaniard. As he neared the end of a full life, he resolved to
devote himself to God.

"Oh Rome, I wish to rail against thy idols, to dedicate a
poem to thy martyrs, and to praise the glory of the apostles."

Prudentius was the first Christian writer. His contribution
was not original, but he had a feeling for poetic imagery and
rhythm.

"The shaft of a ray of sun breaks through the shadow that
envelops the earth, and the reflection of a shining planet
gathers up the color of all things." Historian and poet, with
fervent enthusiasm he sang the praises of the first Church
martyrs. A consummate realist, he described in detail and
almost complacently their agonies, the red-hot irons sear-

ing human flesh, the slit bellies spilling their viscera. But Prudentius also knew how to express in tones of caressing tenderness the unhappiness of childhood. His hymn on the massacre of the innocents is a masterpiece of musical freshness . . . *Salvete flores martyrum!*

> *How I envy the innocent company*
> *Of those who, massacred by a violent hand,*
> *Early in the morning, saw their finest day cut short.*

The Priscillian Affair

The end of the fourth century was saved from apathy by a major event—the Priscillian affair—which wrought havoc in the Spanish Church. Because of its repercussions throughout the empire and the conflicting emotions it unleashed, the Priscillian heresy can be likened to one of those great historical trials that divide opinion and persist indefinitely despite the court's verdict. There was, then, a Priscillian trial as well as a Priscillian affair.

Until now Christian Spain had been generous with its blood. It boasted a leader of men, Hosius, who knew how to arouse and control a soft and irresolute episcopate. It had a Pope, Damasus, who restored the catacombs and protected St. Jerome. And later we shall see how much it owed its emperor, Theodosius. But where were its ideas? The heresiarch Priscillian more than filled this gap. Yet Spain beheaded him.

Who was Priscillian? Sulpicius Severus, his old enemy, has pictured him with a vividness that is still fresh:

"Born to noble parents, extremely rich, restless, elegant, eloquent, and learned because he read voluminously, Priscillian was ever ready to hold forth and to argue. . . . To be sure, the man revealed an abundant talent both of mind and body. He was proof against long, sleepless nights, hunger and thirst. Disinclined to accumulate wealth, he scarcely made use of what he possessed. On the other hand, he was extremely vain and took an excessive pride in his knowledge of matters profane. It is even said that when he was very young he was mixed up with witchcraft. No sooner had he begun to transmit his pernicious doctrines than, thanks to his powers of persuasion and his seductive charm, he attracted both nobles and simple folk in great numbers. And crowds of women, avid for novelty, wavering in their faith, and curious about many things, flocked to him. . . ." Thus, Priscillian gives the impression of having been above all a seducer. The people who accompanied the new Messiah and constituted his following included women of the world, who drank in his words, great and noble lords who were dissatisfied with the simple morality of the Church, and scholars (today we would call them researchers).

What did he preach? What was his doctrine? We had to wait until the nineteenth century, when his works were rediscovered, to become acquainted with his ideas. No information can be gleaned from the campaign that Sulpicius Severus waged against him. Priscillian was accused of Gnosticism, Manichaeanism, and Sabellianism in turn. These terms, which sound as though they were borrowed from the medical vocabulary, do express the maladies of that era. The Gnostics acknowledged the conflict between spirit and matter, denounced all attachment to material values, but maintained that the impulse to satisfy the flesh was not reprehensible so long as the heart condemned it. What a curious accommodation with heaven! Mani taught that man was the work of an evil god and that only fasting, Christ's legacy, together with prayer and communal singing, could improve him. As for Sabellius, he denied the three persons of the Trinity. The accusation seems all the more gratuitous seeing that Priscillian never ceased to anathematize the false prophets and to assert his own orthodoxy. He exclaimed: "Anyone who claims that Jesus Christ appeared in the flesh is a man of God, and anyone who denies Jesus Christ, is not a man of God." Is this not an explicit acknowledgment of Christ's divinity?

Priscillian's profound originality lay in his effort to interpret the Scriptures on the basis of divine inspiration. In this he was not unlike St. Paul, who said: "Stifle not the mind nor reject prophecies." Priscillian's position was a bold one, particularly in view of the well-nigh general ignorance of the clergy and its blind, mechanical submission to the canons decreed by the councils. It was also a dangerous position insofar as it postulated the exercise of one's critical faculties and injected scientific ideas into the domain of faith. "Let us invoke not prudence but confidence. God is my witness, the apostles and the prophets are my witnesses." Like St. John and St. Paul, Priscillian never tired of repeating: "Study the Scriptures. . . . Every prophecy requires interpretation."

His voice, at once obdurate and bewitching, foreshadowing the harsh resonance of Jansenism, was truly that of the master. Within the wavering Christian community it evoked a long quiver of hope and fear. Was it necessary, or even possible, to perfect one's faith, probe the Truth, and question things anew? Was it not enough to believe? Was proof necessary? Yes, of course, because the clever savant said so. Around him crowded the curious, the blasé, the "intellectuals," the despairing, all tempted by the dark fruit on the Tree of Knowledge.

At first the Church was nettled, then worried by Priscillian's extraordinary following. It was afraid of losing precisely those learned and clever members it had tried so hard to acquire. Priscillian must be made to see that his ideas were not the orthodox ones. But how? What line should be taken? From the point of view of dogma his doctrines were beyond reproach. His enemies would suffer quick defeat, for they were ignorant and he was very learned. That he was erudite could hardly be held against him. But this deft juggler was also slippery. He foresaw the traps his enemies set for him and foiled their crude tricks. There was such a ring of sincerity in his professions of orthodoxy that even the most suspicious were deceived. Yet there was something mystifying in his conduct and in that of his sect—for it *was* a sect, and it was growing. Reportedly its motto was: "Swear, commit perjury, but do not divulge the secret." What secret? A quintessential doctrine, a rigorous moral discipline that was not suitable for ordinary folk. Far more than Priscillianism, Priscillian himself and his haughty attitude irritated the Church. Not everyone was allowed to enter the charmed circle of poets, philosophers, converted aesthetes, and gentlemen. Women of noble birth, the most cultivated in all of wealthy Aquitania, withdrew from the world to follow Priscillian. What contempt this intelligentsia showed for the zealots of obscurantism! Thirteen centuries later the recluses of Port-Royal were to nurture the same bitter pride.

In 380 the Council of Saragossa considered the Priscillian affair. Although Priscillian himself was not nominally the target, it was he and his disciples who received most of the council's attention. The council forbade the faithful to take home the sacred bread and wine for the Eucharist. It prohibited any bishop from giving communion to anyone who had been excommunicated by any other bishop. A priest who should decide to become a monk because of a desire for stricter rules would be excommunicated. No one could claim the title or functions of Doctor of the Church. In every canon there was inserted a sentence denouncing the practices of the Priscillianists. The works of Priscillian were condemned. But this was not all. His enemies, led by the Bishops of Mérida and Ossobona, requested the intervention of the secular authorities, and from the emperor they obtained a rescript ousting all Priscillianists from their churches and properties.

Priscillian refused to accept defeat. Escorted by his disciples, he departed for Rome. His triumphal procession stretched the length of Aquitania. He preached, and his sermons evoked such acclaim that everywhere he was showered with flowers. Men followed him, and strange women, spellbound by the charmer, joined the procession. For Priscillian was a feminist. He believed that women should occupy a more important place in Christian society than the insignificant one assigned them by the Bible. But at the gates of Rome a disappointment awaited him. Pope Damasus refused to receive him. Priscillian turned back. In Milan he tried to persuade Ambrose, but the Church Father proved unyielding. Repudiated by the religious authorities, Priscillian appealed to Caesar. Exerting all his political influence, he wrested from Gratian a repeal of the decree. Thus, on the temporal level he emerged triumphant. Two of the prelates he had won over made him, a mere layman, Bishop of Ávila. He was now a leader of the Church.

Exasperated by Priscillian's insolent victory, his enemies redoubled their attack. They spread scandalous rumors about him. Calumny eats into a man's reputation like a worm into fruit. "Look at this teacher of virtue, who has taken to witchcraft and debauchery!" Idatius of Ossobona proved the most ferocious in his attempts to discredit the great man. What could be expected of this self-important prelate, as garrulous and greedy as an empty goatskin? Annoyed by the endless denunciations addressed to him, Maximus decided to have Priscillian brought before a tribunal. This was the trial of Trier.

Priscillian's record was scrutinized. What did it reveal? Nothing contrary to established doctrine. However, it was necessary to justify the arrest of an innocent man, to find reasons for indicting him. Was he not involved in witchcraft? And what about his nocturnal meetings with women? And his habit of praying in the nude? These questionable activities warranted the death sentence, at least in the opinion of Idatius, whose ignorance and gluttony had led him to despise Priscillian's erudition and asceticism. Come, to the executioner with him!

Rumors of the trial reached Gaul. When Martin of Tours heard about it he was indignant, and he hastened to Trier. He came before the emperor. "What! You intend to shed a man's blood for religious reasons alone? Is the secular authority empowered to settle dogmatic controversies by the sword? Expel these heretics from the Church if you cannot convert them. But do not harm a hair of their head!" Apparently convinced, Maximus promised to save Priscillian's life.

No sooner had Martin left Trier than intrigues began again with fresh vigor. The trial entered a new phase. The death penalty was demanded. Priscillian and a few of his disciples were condemned to death, and the rest were deported. The rebel was executed on alien soil. Spain would no longer hear his irresistible voice boldly proclaiming: "God permits all His faithful to speak freely with Him."

Martin of Tours returned to Trier shortly after Priscillian's death. When the bishops heard he was coming, they tried desperately to prevent him from seeing the emperor. But the great man was resolute. He insisted that he had to see Maximus and that see him he would. The emperor, concealing with rage the shame he felt for having deceived Martin, flared up. After all, he was the master. And anyway, Priscillian was an impostor! Did Martin dare to defend Priscillian? Did he agree with the heretic's ideas? Maximus repeated what he had been told by the bishops. Martin had better join the ranks of Idatius if he wanted to prove his orthodoxy. Otherwise the emperor would march his legions into Spain and Priscillianism would be drowned in blood. To save Spain from such an ordeal, Martin of Tours joined the persecuting bishops. Heavyhearted, he was present at the ordination of Felix, then returned to Tours. Never again did he attend a meeting of the episcopate.

Priscillian's execution aroused vehement protests. For the first time the secular authorities had intervened in a religious matter and an emperor had abetted and appeased a bishop's spite. It was also the first time that a bishop had assumed the role of executioner. Sulpicius Severus, although intolerant of Priscillianism, called his condemnation "a crime." St. Ambrose likewise disapproved: "The sinner must be allowed to live in order to mend his ways." Not for long did Idatius enjoy his foul victory. He was deposed together with his accomplice, and Maximus, the usurper, soon perished at the hand of Theodosius.

There was more to the affair. Under the cover of heresy another tragedy, at once more sordid and more real, was being enacted. Idatius, an ambitious, unlettered libertine, represented the episcopate. Priscillian, although wealthy, not only led a life of poverty but extolled it. He could praise the evangelical ideal without being suspected of Pharisaism because he and his disciples lived in strict accordance with it. The slightest provocation could reawaken the old anticlerical sentiment of the common people, who dislike seeing their Church dignitaries don the mantle of the rich. Quite understandably, therefore, they sympathized with Priscillian, whose austere and ascetic habits were a tacit censure of the clergy. What about the clergy? This is what Sulpicius Severus thought of the epsicopate: "Today all is in a state of disorder and confusion, mainly because of the bishops. Their hatred, caprice, fear, lack of character, jealousy, factionalism, profligacy, greed, arrogance, apathy, and laziness have finally perverted everything." Although the opinion of this Church historian cannot be taken too literally, it does seem that at the end of the fourth century, bishops were hardly qualified to attack the character or morality of a man like Priscillian. They feared that the apostle of poverty would jeopardize their privileges and reduce their prebends. Some, perhaps, also hoped that Maximus, who loved to plunder, would confiscate the property of the Priscillianists and assign it to them. How alien all this is from the teachings of Christ!

Priscillian's death strengthened his cause; the invasions gave it new impetus. During the first half of the fifth century, the followers of Priscillian settled in Galicia. At once St. Augustine undertook to combat them. Dietinius had succeeded Priscillian, but in this sect all were alike—secretive and evasive. Esotericism was their rule. They claimed to be innovators, and this irritated St. Augustine, who accused them of practicing false doctrines and harboring moral reservations. Their penchant for mystery was such, and they disguised their doctrine so thoroughly, that diabolical powers were attributed to them. But nothing seemed to shake them. They alone possessed the truth.

The first Council of Toledo met in 400 for the purpose of extirpating Priscillianism. It forced the principal leaders of the sect to embrace orthodoxy. But could they be trusted? Evidently Priscillianism was well entrenched. Pope Leo the Great instructed Bishop Turribius of Astorga to invoke the

help of the secular authorities if he should need it to rid
Spain of this sect: "The Church must employ ecclesiastical
tribunals . . . but the severe edict of the Christian prince
will be of valuable assistance, because heretics, fearful of
bodily pain, sometimes have recourse to it as a spiritual
remedy."

Harassed on all sides, constantly threatened with excommunication, Priscillian's last disciples retreated to the diocese of Iria Flavia, their stronghold in northeastern Galicia.
Here Priscillian had been buried. Did he lie next to someone
purporting to be St. James of Compostella? For a long time
fervent worshippers confused the son of Zebedee with the
heresiarch of Ávila. Although Priscillianism was officially
stamped out during the second half of the sixth century, it
continued clandestinely to recruit new disciples. How
many irreproachable Catholics remained at heart faithful to
the teachings of Priscillian!

Were they in the right? The answer is to be found not in
the eleven treatises Priscillian wrote, but in the author himself and in his exemplary life. For indeed he was the first in
the West to speak of asceticism and learning. He affirmed
that man was not a creature of the Devil, but rather that God
had created him in His own image. He urged "all men of
good will" to study, pray, and go into seclusion. By their
condemnation his accusers and judges only exalted him and
debased themselves. Their behavior showed how unbearable
was the thought that this heretic was so true to the Gospel.
And the people whom Priscillian carried along with him
were the lowly and the wretched. Spain never forgot this
young man of great charm, wealth, and noble birth who
chose to live like a pauper among the poor. The shadow of
the heretical bishop still hovers over the roads of Galicia
where he scattered his alms and captured the souls of men.

While Priscillian fought orthodoxy, another Spaniard,
seated on the throne of St. Peter, sought to preserve it. St.
Damasus waged war against the Arians and called upon St.
Jerome to prepare the Vulgate, a Latin version of the Bible.
He beautified Rome, ordered the construction of two basil-
icas, and restored the Catacombs. At the Council of Con-

stantinople he crushed the dangerous pretensions of the local patriarch, who claimed to be first in importance after the Pope.

Another Spaniard, Emperor Theodosius, destroyed paganism once and for all by prohibiting the worship of many gods. A formidable foe of the barbarians, his victories sounded the death knell of the tottering Roman Empire. He was also a man of feeling as well as a great warrior. It seems that after a revolt in Thessalonica, he ordered terrible reprisals, making no distinction between the innocent and the guilty. St. Ambrose, bishop of Milan, demanded public penance of the emperor and refused him the sacraments. The proud Segovian proved recalcitrant and would not comply, but Ambrose stood firm. On Christmas Day, Theodosius finally acknowledged defeat and threw himself at the bishop's feet. In the presence of a large gathering he begged Ambrose's pardon, like a child.

Priscillian aroused the people and was beheaded. Damasus built cathedrals. Theodosius, his head in the dust, humiliated himself before God's representative and smashed the remaining idols. These grandiose gestures heralded the end of the fourth century in Spain as well as the collapse of Roman eminence.

Actually, Rome did not fall; it expired, and with it died the ancient world. Or, to put it a better way, Rome committed suicide. For years, the empire, weakening under its crushing burdens, had been forced to rely on foreigners. For several generations, colonists had been settling in all the frontier provinces—on the hither side of the Danube, in Macedonia, Thrace, Gaul, and Illyria. Doggedly they took up their pickaxes and plowshares. Formerly annexed to Rome, now its allies, Vandals, Suevi, Alans, and Franks gradually worked their way toward the capital. The invasion had begun before the birth of Jesus. Ostrogoth leaders governed the Hispanic provinces in the name of the emperor. Thus, the barbarian was not merely at the gates of the city; he was already inside. A few more months and he was master.

Fortunately, and by a curious reversal, Christianity be-

came the custodian of "Romanism," at least in Spain. Despite
Priscillianism and Arianism—their convulsions lasted until
Reccared—Theodosius' enlightened Catholicism made possible the Christian conquest of Spain. By conferring upon
Christians the extensive rights of citizenship, Rome gave
them political unity and an administrative machinery that
enabled the Church to organize its religious revolution. The
evangelical doctrine required a language to express it, jurists
to codify it, administrators to implement it. Rome provided
these. Caesar's royal gift to this nascent Christianity made
amends for the blood of the martyrs. Theodosius redeemed
Diocletian. And thanks to the Cross, the Roman eagle survived.

Meanwhile, Spain looked toward the north with some
anxiety. From the Manchurian plains and the high plateaus
of Tibet, a silent flood of yellow men began to inundate the
world. Starting from Mongolia, they invaded China, which
was then occupied by the Huns. Hemmed in, almost trapped,
the Huns escaped and spread over the Russian steppes.
There they clashed with the Alans, whom they absorbed.
They moved on until they encountered the Teutons. The
Teutons, in turn, drove the Visigoths, who had settled on
the left bank of the Danube, to the gates of Constantinople.
There they were halted by the legions of Theodosius. But
for how long? Could any army halt this irresistible push toward the West, the sea, the radiant Occident? The panicky
flight suggested an army on the run.

Pressed against the African, Asian, and European frontiers of the orbis Romanus, and contained by the imperial
infantry, the hordes shoved and trampled one another, their
weapons raised, ready for the Roman debacle. The Spaniards, whose fate was now linked to Rome's, prepared themselves for the impact of this fearsome human earthquake.
They expected to see any day a black forest of lancers profiled against the crest of the Pyrenees.

In the twilight of a great century, the triumphant sun of
Numantia slowly descended upon the empire.

3

The Visigoths at Toledo

THEODOSIUS died in 395. The Roman Empire split into two worlds, each going its own way. One remained centered in Rome, where the Pope held spiritual sway; the other, the Eastern Empire, had its capital in Constantinople.

Exploiting the troubles of Honorius, emperor of the West, the barbarians continued their push with renewed vigor. In 406, bands of Alans, Suevi, and Vandals crossed the Rhine and infiltrated Gaul, advanced to the Pyrenees, and ravaged Spain. The Romans were forced to accept them as allies. After pillaging Rome, the Visigoths offered to reconquer Spain for Honorius, who was living in Ravenna. In less than two years the Iberian Peninsula, purged by Wallia of Alans, Vandals, and Suevi, again became a Roman province. As their reward, the Visigoths received the right to occupy Aquitania.

Spain remained a battlefield for several centuries. Vandals and Suevi in turn staged bloody incursions. They clashed with the Hispano-Romans, occasionally aided by the Visigoths. The Visigoths, tempted by Spain as well as Gaul, whose southern portions they occupied, desired the destruction of the empire but maintained allies in both camps.

The invasion of the Huns produced a sacred union of the West against the Asiatics. In 451, on the Catalaunian Plains, a coalition of Romans, Franks, and Visigoths defeated Attila. But the alliance—the barbarians' final convulsive effort against people even more barbaric than themselves—proved short-lived. Internecine quarrels and revolts broke out; treaties were made one day and repudiated the next. Armies on the march tore up the Spanish soil.

The powerful army of the Visigoths impressed their Roman masters. Had the Romans realized, when they invited German mercenaries to defend their imperial frontiers, how great a price they would have to pay for this service? No emperor of the decaying West could prevent the Visigoths from carving out their share of Augustus' legacy. True emperors were no more. They were but pale puppets manipulated by the patricians. The Visigoths did not hesitate to expand their territorial possessions. All of Gaul that lay between the Loire and the Pyrenees was theirs by the law of the survival of the fittest. To this they added Roussillon and lower Languedoc. Their capital was Toulouse.

On the heels of a terrible attack by Remismond, king of the Suevi, the Hispano-Romans were forced to implore the help of Theodoric, the Visigothic king. Theodoric calculated that by hastening to the rescue he would achieve mastery of Spain. He was mistaken; not he, but his brother Euric, became its ruler.

Diplomat and warrior, Euric pushed the Suevi back to Galicia, conquered Tarraconensis, the province of Cartagena, most of Baetica, and almost all of Portugal, Aragon, Leon, and the two Castiles, while the Vandals and Alans moved on to Africa. Simultaneously, in 476, Odoacer, leader of the Heruli, dethroned the last Western emperor, Romulus Augustulus. This occurred at Ravenna; it marked the death of the Roman Empire. Now Gothic monarchs would taste power. Euric, the Visigothic Clovis, ruled a state extending from the Loire to the Pillars of Hercules. But this barbarian was ambitious. He dreamed of a Gallic monarchy with Toulouse as its capital. To him, Spain was but a small part of his future kingdom. Fate decreed otherwise. Although he was lucky in war, his son Alaric II disgraced him. This mediocre, malignant, petty king was defeated at

Vouillé in 507 by Clovis. The result of this important battle was Frankish control of Aquitania and the withdrawal of the Visigoths from Spain. No Gallic king ruled France, nor would one ever do so.

Nor would there have been a Gothic king of Spain if, after the catastrophe at Vouillé, Theodoric the Great, the powerful leader of the Ostrogoths in Italy, had not taken Amalaric, the infant son of Alaric II, under his protection. His armies, which included the Franks, guaranteed the Visigoths Septimania (the eastern Pyrenees, Aude, Hérault, and Gard) as well as their Spanish possessions.

Euric killed his brother, Theodoric II, and took his place. Amalaric was assassinated by Theudis, who proved an energetic and judicious prince. He, in turn, perished at the hands of Theudigisel, his faithful lieutenant. But this reign was brief. Theudigisel, too, suffered a violent death, leaving the Visigothic crown to Agila, who was luckier than his predecessors. A noble Goth, Athanagild, ally of Emperor Justinian, was his adversary. While the Byzantine army conquered the Mediterranean coast without striking a blow, Athanagild routed the troops of Agila, who was slain by his own men. Only Athanagild died a natural death, and this is worthy of note. Until then crimes had determined the royal succession; only painfully, by blood and the sword, had the Visigothic monarchy come into being.

An Episode of the Gothic Era: Galeswintha, the Princess Who Was Strangled

Let us break the chronological thread for a moment and select one of the better ghosts that roam the Neustrian glades. This might distract us temporarily from the quarrels of the Visigoths! But can we call the sorry Galeswintha a ghost?

Upon becoming king of Spain after his victory over Agila, Athanagild transferred the capital from Barcelona to Toledo and was considering a rapprochement with the

Merovingians. With the death of Clotaire, son of Clovis, an opportunity presented itself. The Frankish king had four sons—Chilperic, Sigebert, Haribert, and Guntram. Chilperic inherited his father's share, the kingdom of Soissons, or Neustria, bounded on the north by the Scheldt and on the south by the Loire. The eastern kingdom, or Austrasia, which included the Auvergne, northeastern Gaul, and Germania as far as the Saxon and Slavic frontiers, fell into Sigebert's hands, while Haribert and Guntram divided the kingdoms of Paris and Orléans. Athanagild had two daughters, Brunehilde and Galeswintha. Sigebert asked for the hand of Brunehilde, and their wedding was celebrated with great pomp. Athanagild eyed his close neighbor, Chilperic, now master of the Pyrenees. He wanted him as an ally as well as a son-in-law. The matter was quickly settled. Chilperic's dowry—his "gift of the morning"—was made up of villages along the frontier; Athanagild would give his daughter and wagons filled with gold and silver objects. But Galeswintha had not been consulted.

When the Frankish envoys were presented to Chilperic's fiancée, they found the girl clinging tearfully to her mother. Why should she leave Toledo, her family, and the palace for Rouen, where it rained and the sky was gray? In vain was her sister's contentment with Sigebert extolled. Galeswintha's happiness was here, within the ramparts of Toledo. Besides—she hesitated to say this aloud—the fiancé for whom she was destined did not appeal to her. She was not so unaware as to be ignorant of what the servants were saying. Chilperic was a libertine. He drank until he was senseless and he was extremely fickle. What made them think he would be faithful to Galeswintha? However, the king insisted. A long procession of cavalry started northward, crossed the Tagus, and headed for the kingdom of the Franks. Athanagild accompanied the procession for a while, then turned back. The queen did not have the courage to leave her daughter so quickly. She continued with the others, but when the moment of parting came, her final embrace was accompanied by the admonition: "Be careful, my child!"

Before mounting the carriage that was to take her back, the queen watched the chariot that was carrying her daughter so far away. It grew smaller and smaller as it approached the horizon, until suddenly it turned and disappeared in a cloud of dust.

The long file of Visigothic lords and Frankish ambassadors reached the mountains, where, for many days and nights, they traversed deserted trails and dark chasms. Finally they reached the plain, cooled by sea breezes. Narbonne, Carcassonne, Poitiers, Tours. . . . At the gates of the cities Galeswintha would leave the rough-hewn cart and take her seat in the silver-plated chariot of state, built high, like a tower. Commoners and gentlemen alike acclaimed the princess. Her sorrow was somewhat mitigated by the court that was paid her, for what young girl could remain insensitive to such homage?

Now that Chilperic was free (he had broken off with his favorites), he was burning to meet his fiancée. It had been hard to give up Fredegund, who had accepted summary dismissal without a murmur. She had merely asked permission to remain his wife in the Germanic manner, to live at the palace but as his servant. How could he refuse? At Rouen, which hummed with preparations for the wedding, Galeswintha finally alighted. Chilperic was waiting for her. The sturdy, handsome, though somewhat heavy man was not displeasing to the girl. A few days later the marriage was celebrated. Neustria's lords and warriors, forming a half circle around the royal couple, brandished their swords and swore allegiance. Chilperic, his hand on a reliquary, promised to keep Galeswintha as his wife forever. The following morning, before the notary, the King of Neustria bestowed upon his wife, "in the name of his tender love," a dowry called *morganeghiba*—"a gift of the morning"—the five promised cities: Bordeaux, Cahors, Limoges, Bigorre, and Béarn. Then the grandson of Clovis, complying with a Germanic custom, scattered bits of straw on the braided headdress of the timid Galeswintha.

For several months the young sovereigns of Neustria

knew happiness. Their joy had the color and savor of a honeymoon. She was sweet and good. He was strong, and his wild outbursts, though somewhat terrifying, were not of a nature to displease his frail bride. But after a while he grew weary of this excessively docile woman. She bored him. His appetite demanded spicier fare. He remembered the clever Fredegund. Every day he passed her in the halls of the palace. Her eyes were lowered. Indeed, she had no need to seek the king's gaze, for she knew that her hour was near, that her patience and duplicity would be rewarded. One evening Chilperic could stand it no longer. He seized Fredegund by the arm, took her to his chamber, and threw her on the bed. . . . The next day she was again his concubine. Galeswintha did not reproach her fickle husband. Nor did she insult her smug rival, who regarded the young queen disdainfully. Very simply and with great dignity, Galeswintha asked Chilperic to let her go. He could take back his cities and keep the precious silver and gold she had brought from Toledo. All she asked was permission to return to her parents. The young sovereign vehemently refused Galeswintha's request. He was either remorseful or fearful of scandal. On his knees he implored her to forgive him. Forgive him she did, and took heart. But one morning the palace was in an uproar. Queen Galeswintha had been strangled to death.

Chilperic pretended to be heartbroken. He wept and lamented. But shortly afterward he installed Fredegund in the palace and gave her all the prerogatives of wife and queen. Meanwhile, his crime had filled the court and the army with horror. Certain omens seemed to portend divine wrath. The day of Galeswintha's funeral, a crystal lamp suspended over her tomb fell suddenly upon the marble flagstones but did not go out. The sinister sound, echoing under the vaults, reverberated like a foreboding. Yet Fredegund pursued her brilliant and ferocious career, apparently without incurring any vengeance from heaven. She committed innumerable cruelties, while showing rare political acumen. Galeswintha's assassination was only one of the many deeds with which Fredegund stained the somber fabric of Merovingian history.

The Arian Monarchy

Religion is an intimate part of Spain's history. Throughout the centuries it was a continuous source of inspiration, and explains the behavior of people passionately obsessed with God.

By the end of the fifth century, the man of piety ranked highest, and it was he who instigated political action. Although Arianism had been condemned by the Council of Nicaea and proscribed by Pope Damasus, it appealed to the barbarians. It was easier for them to think of Jesus as a human being. And the ponderous, vengeful God portrayed by Arius had some of the features of their old Teutonic idols. The Spaniards, on the other hand, remained faithful to Catholicism. As a consequence, the hostility that inevitably arises between natives and occupiers was intensified by spiritual conflict. Moreover, it was a Catholic—he had been baptized only recently by St. Remi—who had triumphed at Vouillé over an Arian king. Catholicism or Arianism? The question was posed on both sides of the Pyrenees, for Gauls as well as Spaniards. In short, territorial conquest came to matter less than differences of dogma. Every Spanish war was essentially religious in nature.

Although Euric was an ardent champion of Arianism, he evidently refrained from systematic persecution of the Catholics. But his son, Alaric II, pursued the clergy and the faithful with stubborn hatred. His intolerance cost him Gaul. Similarly, Amalaric, totally unsuccessful in his efforts to make an Arian of his wife, Clothilde, daughter of Clovis, mistreated her so badly that he was thrashed by his brother-in-law, Childebert. Quiescent under Theudis and Theudigisel, Arian intransigence increased with the advent of Agila, when religious disputes became more violent than ever. Cloaked by dogmatic controversy, the clash of interests and personal ambitions grew sharper. Like a noxious fog, the venom of fanaticism poisoned society, turned men against one another, and even made its way into family relationships.

It was not unusual for an Arian father to banish a Catholic son from his home. The quarrel affected the court. Noblemen, lords, and adventurers used Arius and Jesus as pretexts for their intrigues. Such an atmosphere was hardly propitious for the consolidation of royal authority, already undermined by its own excesses. What a contrast to the solid Frankish monarchy which the baptism of Clovis had stabilized! Two very different worlds, separated by the Pyrenees, began to take shape.

Even without the support of Byzantium, Athanagild would probably have worsted Agila, a courageous soldier but despised by his subjects. Anti-Catholicism had definitely brought misfortune to the Visigothic kings! Athanagild doubtless realized this. Instead of hunting down Catholics, he concentrated on dislodging his former allies from the coast of Andalusia. Moreover, he was indebted to the Catholics. As neutrals or as allies, they had helped him toward Agila's tottering throne.

Anxious to put as much distance as possible between himself and the Byzantines, Athanagild transferred the Spanish capital from Tarragona to Toledo. He could not have chosen a better place for defense. Like a flag stuck in the very heart of the *meseta*, on top of a high rock, and encircled by the Tagus, Toledo became the lookout tower of the Visigothic monarchy. Enemy columns, their swords flashing, could be seen far off as they traversed the black Sierras and the blinding desert of Estremadura. But the military importance of Toledo was speedily overshadowed by the part it played in forging Spain's nationality. Only a few stones, the ruins of a church, remain of Visigothic Toledo. Dust has buried the heavy arches of San Ginés. But the evanescence of material things matters little. Until the reign of Philip II, Toledo was the capital of Spain, and even today it remains the center of the Catholic see. Later, in its immemorial sky, which El Greco's eyes were to scan, the prayers of the mystics would rise up like a flame.

Leovigild succeeded his brother Athanagild. This energetic and stubborn prince had a taste for grandeur. Imitating the Byzantine emperors, he ordered his profile engraved on a gold medal. But such grandiose gestures were trivial in view of the power he wielded. After putting down an uprising of the Suevi, and waging several other successful campaigns, he managed to extend his sway as far as Cordova. Elated by his success, the soldier-king now resorted to diplomacy. Reverting to the traditional alliance between Franks and Goths, he demanded the hand of Ingunthis, daughter of Brunehilde and Sigebert, for his son, Ermenegild. Leovigild did not realize that by welcoming Catholic Ingunthis to his court he would hasten the fall of Arianism.

Toledo was still but a bare plateau, swept alternately by glacial and torrid winds, when the wedding of Ermenegild and the great-granddaughter of Clovis was celebrated. The new Spanish capital gave the impression of being an army camp rather than a royal city, full of the sounds of horses neighing, pickaxes at work, and javelins whistling through the air. From the windows of the wooden palace, the blond princess, dressed in a white tunic, her hair braided, could see Gothic soldiers trying out their bows or digging ditches. The only music she heard was the hoarse song of the barbarians, punctuated by the clatter of shields. What an austere setting for a honeymoon!

When Ingunthis accepted Ermenegild in marriage and promised him fidelity, she also vowed to convert her husband to Catholicism, for she had the soul of a true apostle. From the moment of her arrival in Toledo, she considered how best to carry out her plan. It was indeed a bold one. Arianism was the official religion of the Visigothic court. Although there were, of course, a few Catholic priests, the Arian deacons were extremely vigilant. Basically easygoing, Leovigild showed himself to be a halfhearted defender of Arianism. Personally, he thought religious disputes foolish, but the same was not true of his entourage, particularly his wife Goiswintha, Athanagild's widow. She was a fanatical Arian and hated her daughter-in-law. Both women were young and beautiful, and both intended to rule the household. With savage intensity, and in the name of religion, Goiswintha persecuted Ingunthis. How many times the two princesses, fighting like drunken sailors, had to be pried apart! When they ran short of theological arguments they flung themselves at each other like madwomen and tore at each other's hair. Their clothes in shreds, their faces scratched, their earrings splattered with blood—in such a state would these noblewomen end their religious disputes.

Weary of the screaming and the scandalous quarrels, Leovigild sought peace in his own home. He sent Ermenegild to Seville as governor of Andalusia, and the fiery Ingunthis followed him there. Rid of her mother-in-law, and aided by St. Leander, the persuasive bishop of Seville, she redoubled her efforts to convert her husband. Finally, after hesitating for a long time, Ermenegild consented to be baptized a Catholic.

The news exasperated Leovigild. His son's conversion destroyed his dream of unification and jeopardized his authority. Furthermore, he was afraid that, in case of conflict, most Catholics would rally to the side of the prince who shared their faith. In order to reassure the Catholics, and also to seduce them, Leovigild convoked an episcopal council in Toledo. At his instigation the bishops promulgated a decree which stated: "Any member of the Roman Church who embraces Arianism will not have to be rebaptized; he will merely have to be *reconciled* by communion and imposition." Driven by ambition, some bishops did espouse Arianism, but they were only a handful. The great majority of Catholics sensed the trap that lay concealed in the policy of the outstretched hand.

Ermenegild's conversion soon bore fruit. Several Spanish cities submitted to his rule. Realizing that he must act quickly, Leovigild ordered his son to return to Toledo. He knew of Ermenegild's weak and indecisive nature, and he was sure that once he had him home there would be no difficulty. Ermenegild was as pliable as a glove! But Leovigild had underestimated the influence of Ingunthis. The indomitable little woman, flushed with success, constantly encouraged her husband to resist. Whenever she thought he was about to yield, she would scold and inspirit the timid novice. "All Catholic Spain looks to you. You are the sole hope of those who have had to put up with the rule of a heretical king." "But he is my father." "Of course, and you owe him respect. But think of the throngs of believers who send their delegates to you each morning." Leander, standing beside Ingunthis, brandished the crucifix. Thus, without intending to, without even realizing it, Ermenegild was made to play the role of rebel.

Leovigild, who had shown great patience, finally decided to strike. He gathered a large army and marched against his rebellious son. Ermenegild formed alliances with the Catholic Suevi, Galicians, and Byzantines. They occupied the southern sector of Cartagena, and a civil war, aggravated by religious conflict, ensued.

After two years of battle, Ermenegild learned that the king of the Suevi, whose help he had counted on, was dead. Another of his allies, the commander of the Byzantine troops, allowed himself to be bought by the enemy and surrendered Seville. Fearing his father's wrath, the rebel prince fled to a monastery at Cordova in the hope that it would serve as a holy refuge.

At this point, Leovigild's second son, Reccared, intervened. Up to now he had remained in the background. Henceforth he would play an important role. He sought out his brother and urged him on their father's behalf to return to the court, giving assurance that Leovigild would forgive him. The promise proved false. When Ermenegild appeared before the king, he was stripped of all his insignia and rights. Made to don shabby clothes, he was banished by his father to a prison in Valencia. From there he was transferred to a dark dungeon in Tarragona.

The aging Gothic king, believing that reasons of state must come before his feelings as a father, sought in every conceivable way to make Ermenegild renounce the Catholic faith. But nothing, neither threats nor promises, could touch the prince, who no longer needed anyone to strengthen his resolve. Leovigild was completely puzzled. Something had changed his son!

One night, his last on earth, Ermenegild heard in the darkness of his cell the honeyed tones of an Arian bishop.

"Do not rebel, my child. Accept from my hands the com-

munion of Arius. The reward is your father's pardon. What
risk do you run? Nobody will ever know anything about it.
Only you and I are in this prison, and the night alone can
hear our words."

"And Jesus Christ," the prince replied firmly. "Jesus
Christ, the true God and the true man."

The following morning, at the king's command, Sisbert,
Ermenegild's jailer, beheaded the prince. It was April 13,
the holy day of Easter.

Reccared, the First Catholic King

Weakened by grief, and perhaps by remorse as well, Leovigild died the following year, leaving the throne to Reccared.
The new king of Spain had recently learned that unity—already an obsession of the Spanish sovereigns and destined to
remain such until the reign of Philip II—would never be
achieved by Arianism. He recalled those whom his father
had banished, restored confiscated property to their former
owners, and, one year after assuming the throne, embraced
the Catholic religion. Probably the influence of Leander,
leader of the Spanish episcopate, was partly responsible for
his bold decision, and perhaps, too, the somewhat mysterious parting advice of his father. At all events, it took great
courage to brave the anger of the powerful Arian clergy
who had dominated Gothic kings ever since the days of
Euric. Allow Catholic bishops to take their places and their
prebends? Never! A raging wind of revolt swept through
the Arian episcopate. Old Queen Goiswintha headed the conspirators. The time had come for this Jezebel to exercise her
hatred of Catholics! Two heretical bishops, Sunna of Mérida and Atholocon of Narbonne, promised Septimania to
the Franks in exchange for their help. But Reccared was not
intimidated. He arrested the conspirators, then had them
tried and executed. Goiswintha, the deadly mother-in-law,
succumbed in prison, a victim of her own rage.

Reccared consolidated peace at home by crushing the heretics. Next he defeated the Franks, who had attacked him

at the instigation of the Arians. The time was now ripe for the convocation of a council.

The tremendous conclave opened in Toledo on May 8, 589. The king, queen, and the entire court were present. Five metropolitans and sixty-four bishops flanked the most important figure of all, Leander of Seville. Reccared was the first to speak. After congratulating himself on having gathered such a brilliant assembly, he professed his faith in firm, unequivocal terms. He stressed the Son's divinity, of the same essence as that of the Father and the Holy Ghost, and proceeding from it. After anathematizing Arius, who still had a few adherents among those present, he gravely recited the Nicaean Creed: *Credo in unum Deum, Patrem omnipotentem, factorem coeli et terrae, visibilium omnium et invisibilium.* . . . Finally, pounding the golden hilt of his sword with a fist encased in an iron gauntlet, the first Catholic king of Spain made the following declaration: "I, King Reccared, cherishing in my heart this sacred faith and professing it with my lips, this true confession which alone is professed by a Church that has spread over the entire world, with God's help have subscribed to it in my own hand." When the king finished there was complete silence. Then the entire assembly broke into applause and wept. This was an overwhelming and unique event. A prince had allied himself with the apostolic Roman Church, and the union was to have a profound influence on the fate of Spain. From now on her history was linked to that of the Church, for better or for worse. The effects of this union can be seen throughout Spanish history, from Reccared to Franco.

Taking advantage of the assembly's emotion, one of the Fathers, speaking in the name of his colleagues, easily persuaded everyone to profess the Catholic faith and repudiate Arian doctrines. A declaration was drafted and signed. Then Reccared spoke again, this time to request that the Credo be recited in every church of Spain and throughout the Gaul of Narbonne.

Finally, several decrees were promulgated to encourage moral reforms and re-establish ecclesiastical discipline. A homily by Leander ended the meeting.

Arianism was dead. It succumbed under the blows delivered by Leander and Reccared. The Bishop of Seville must be credited with the conversion of Leovigild's two sons. He used his knowledge, eloquence, and friendship with Pope Gregory to serve the Catholic cause. Reccared "the Good," although innately peaceful, was able to foil the efforts of his enemies to exploit the religious crisis. Rarely had royal power and religious authority collaborated so felicitously.

Isidore of Seville, Precursor of Newton

Isidore of Seville was Spain's most eminent prelate during the Visigothic era. A brother of Leander, he succeeded him as Bishop of Baetica. His voluminous works deal with every phase of science, liturgy, and political economy. The *Etymologies*, which comprise at least twenty volumes, are considered a summary of all the knowledge of that era. Actually, they represent an attempt to popularize the teachings of the Alexandrian school, to which the Greeks contributed so much. Isidore also introduced totally new ideas. He acquainted Spaniards with the exact sciences and taught them mathematical logic. A thousand years before Newton, Isidore demonstrated that the earth revolved around the sun. And in seeking to give a lucid exposition of numbers, he established the principles of the decimal system.

It has been said that when he was born a cluster of bees— an omen of eloquence—swarmed over his crib. He showed little aptitude for literature in his early years. One day, downcast because his teacher had scolded him severely, he ran away from home. Wandering aimlessly about the countryside, he came upon a well whose rim, although made of marble, was so worn from the rope rubbing against it that a groove had formed. Impressed, the young runaway decided then and there that perseverance could overcome any obstacle. He returned to his father's house and became one of the greatest scholars of his day. For many years, visitors to the Church of St. Isidore in Seville were shown the marble rim of the well that determined the young student's vocation.

The insipid descriptions in textbooks—"gifted writer,"
"well of science"—scarcely do justice to the man. Isidore
was not a compiler of facts but a scholar and man of action.
During the forty years that he ruled the episcopate of Seville, he was a tireless fighter. He presided over the Fourth
Council of Toledo and directed the discussions with a hand
of iron. It was to him that King Sisinand owed his accession.
Isidore's prestige and enormous erudition greatly impressed
the Visigothic kings, who were quite ignorant. A leader as
well as a humanist, he lent strength and reality to the idea
of Spanish nationalism. In a foreword to his *History of the
Goths*, we find this excellent passage:

"Oh, Spain, thou art the fairest of all the lands that lie between the West and India. Blessed country, and fortunate
in thy provinces, mother of many peoples! Thou art the
queen of all of them. From thee both the Orient and the Occident receive enlightenment."

The initiator of Spanish nationalism, Isidore wanted it to
be Christian. For this he can hardly be blamed, although one
may well regret it. In any case, it was to Christianity, which
he symbolized, that the Spain of that epoch owed its cultural framework. A country cannot exist without an elite.
Spain's elite was stimulated and educated by the Bishop of
Seville. The result was a rich cultural renaissance, inspired
not only by Greco-Latin but also by Oriental antecedents
thoroughly adapted to the needs of the West. Isidore wrote:
"Nothing is more disgraceful than ignorance. It engenders
error and nourishes vice." Although this extraordinary encyclopedist studied geometry, astronomy, and even architecture and navigation, it is obvious that what he meant by
science was grammar and theology. Above all else he required of his clergy a thorough knowledge of the Scriptures.

The diocese of Toledo, with its bishops, Eugenius, Ildefonso, and Julian, stimulated a taste for literature and encouraged the study of theology. These young prelates were
curious about many things—poetry, history, and liturgy.
Julian wrote an excellent account of Wamba's expedition to
Septimania; Ildefonso's naïve, fresh defense of Mary's virginity foreshadowed the *Fioretti*.

Schools, libraries, writers—an intellectual aristocracy gradually emerged and made itself felt at the court. The process soon left the Visigothic kings far behind. However, they were able to keep their crowns so long as Isidore of Seville lived, so long as his thundering voice resounded at epsicopal councils.

Church and State

Never were church and state so closely united as during the reign of the Visigoths. The Councils of Toledo, which ensured the continuity of this union, considered both political and religious problems. Moreover, they met at the king's behest. Surrounded by a few court dignitaries of his own choice, the king was always present and expected to take an active part in the discussion. It is therefore hardly surprising that the secular authorities should have tended to encroach upon the ecclesiastical domain. The monarchy was so fragile! Without the Church it would have collapsed. Naturally enough, these precarious monarchs, many of whom owed their thrones to violence or rebellion, sought protection from the Catholic Church, which had stability. The bishops, Grand Electors with the same privileges as the nobility, reminded the kings of their duties and delimited their authority.

After Reccared's conversion, the codes that governed the Goths and those that prevailed among the Hispano-Romans had to be revised. From then on a single law and a single judge served everyone. This important reform is recorded in the *Liber Judicorum*, which was compiled by the bishops. Later, the juridical texts were assembled in a single enormous volume, the *Fuero Juzgo*, also the work of the clergy. For the first time in the modern period, legislation determined by Christian doctrine and morality triumphed over the brutal law of the survival of the fittest. "We are dedicated to the protection of the prince's authority. But if, out of pity and indulgence, the prince decides that a guilty man may overcome the error of his ways, then let him be merciful!" Pity? Forgiveness? This was a new language, quite unfamiliar to the crude Visigothic society. Isidore of Seville, the great figure of his era, did not hesitate to remind the princes that "a bond of faith unites them and obliges them to proclaim Christian truth and to reinforce their professions of faith by exemplary conduct."

The civil code required not only that the judge be "enlightened and well versed in the study of law," but also that he be moderate in meting out punishment. Thus the Christian ideal was carried over into the institutions of the state.

The Spanish Church, though strongly centralized and tinged with nationalism, did not lose contact with Rome. It often invoked papal authority to justify this or that measure. In actuality, however, relations between the Spanish clergy and the Holy See tended to be limited. Travel between Spain and Italy was somewhat dangerous, for the Vandals controlled the sea. Besides, the Church had proved itself, having fought hard for its pre-eminence. Its large gatherings at Toledo, which made and destroyed kings, had no counterpart elsewhere in the West. Its decrees amazed the entire world, and its theologians had nothing to learn from the Romans. The Bishop of Toledo was the peer of the Bishop of Rome.

For it was in Toledo that the Church of Spain was centered. The Bishop of Toledo, at first the metropolitan of Carpetania, a region of Cartagena, then the metropolitan of Cartagena itself, finally became, at the end of the seventh century, the Archbishop of Spain.

Bishops and Clergy

Ecclesiastical organization remained in harmony with tradition. The kingdom was divided into six provinces: Cartagena, Tarraconensis, Narbonensis, Baetica, Lusitania, and Galicia. These comprised eighty bishoprics. Six were headed by metropolitans: Toledo, Tarragona, Narbonne, Seville, Mérida, and Braga.

Until the reign of Reccared, bishops were elected by the

people and the clergy; the latter, in turn, were elected with
the concurrence of the metropolitans. But little by little the
civil authorities began to meddle in episcopal elections. This
practice was confirmed by the Twelfth Council of Toledo
(681), which acknowledged the king's absolute right to appoint bishops.

The sovereign's excessive interference in ecclesiastical affairs had deplorable consequences. Poorly trained priests
moved immediately to the highest Church positions, and
even laymen went straight "from the army to the sacerdotal
office." How many worldly or unworthy individuals became
bishops merely because they enjoyed the favor of the prince!
How many abuses, even crimes, were committed within the
shadow of the sanctuary! The decrees of the councils disclose the existence of these excesses, which were suppressed
with great severity. Yet there were many illustrious and
saintly priests for every evil bishop.

The councils attempted to make worship uniform in all
the churches. Every parish priest received from his bishop
a practical manual enumerating and describing in great detail the various ceremonies for administering the sacraments.
The Sixth Council decreed: "There must be but one hymn
and one rite in all of Spain." However, it was not enough
to fix the form of worship; a system had to be established for
training the clergy. Candidates for the priesthood were to
undergo a lengthy apprenticeship and were not eligible for
promotion to the deaconry until the age of twenty-five. To
become a full-fledged priest one had to be thirty. Very
early the Church made celibacy obligatory for all priests.
They were forbidden to attend lay festivals, engage in trade,
or travel for pleasure. Their dress was somber—a long robe
and sandals. In every way and under all circumstances they
were expected to set an example. Failure to obey these injunctions would be severely punished. We can readily understand the need for strict regulations: the Spanish Church
was still quite young and a newcomer to a land that had just
rid itself of heresy. It had to be vigilant in order to survive
and endure; for Arianism, like a decapitated snake, still
quivered. Visigothic Spain and its powerful clergy were be-

ing watched by the rest of the world, including Rome. Never before had a barbaric government granted a position of such importance to the Church, and never before had the Church had such an opportunity to test its own methods. Aware that it was under constant observation, the Church demanded of its priests a conduct that was, at all times, in keeping with their station. Nevertheless, some were liars, murderers, and adulterers, for this was the seventh century, an era of reconstruction. The Church did not lack men of quality—there were Leander and Isidore of Seville, Masona of Mérida, and Braulion of Saragossa. But as parishes multiplied it became urgent to train priests for real leadership. It is, however, not surprising that a few black sheep should have strayed from the fold. Murder, robbery, and plunder, which accompanied the Visigothic invasion, had contaminated the Hispano-Romans, and many succumbed. Upon those ecclesiastics who transgressed, swift and terrible punishment was visited.

But unworthy priests were the exception. On the whole, the Spanish Church achieved a moral standard which far surpassed that of the Franks. To be sure, occasionally it was guilty of encroaching upon the civil power, of leaning too heavily on the secular authorities, and using the councils to exercise domination. One should not forget, however, the barbarism that persisted in certain regions of Spain. Pagan superstitions were not dead. People still turned to the village sorcerer, or worshipped idols, springs, or sacred trees. Sodomy, concubinage, incest, and abortion were widespread. The Church's task was essentially to reform. To create order out of chaos, to purge prospective converts of vice and brutality—these were the primary concerns of the Spanish church. Would it have accomplished its purpose had the sovereign refused it the use of his tribunals and executioners? Sermons mattered less than firmness, catechism less than soldiers. Under the brutal and crude regime of the Visigoths, the Church consolidated the organization which St. Peter had received from Rome and which was half a millennium old. Little wonder then that the Church ruled the barbaric Visigoths of Spain. Since the most intelligent, the best men of the day, belonged to the Church, power naturally fell into its hands. But—and this occurred whenever Spain made inordinate use of Catholicism—the Church exploited this power. Perhaps somewhat unwittingly it committed, or allowed, the kind of excesses that it was obligated to suppress.

The Jewish Problem

In tracking down crime and vice, the Church performed a wholesome task and played the role for which it was best fitted. Less fortunate was its tendency to confuse breaches of common law with sins against religion, and to censure both alike. The Sixth Council of Toledo proclaimed: "No one in the royal kingdom will be tolerated who is not a Catholic."

Since the Arians were no longer a threat, this was aimed principally at the Jews. Already, three hundred years earlier, the Council of Elvira had warned Christians not to consort with Jews. But neither civil nor canon law had prescribed any penalties. "On the contrary," as St. Gregory explained, "we must convince the Jews by gentleness and kindly exhortations to rally to our faith; we must not lose them by threats of terror." It was King Sisebut who initiated the policy of anti-Semitism which, for so many centuries, was pursued by the Catholic kings. Brief indeed were the periods of relaxation or reconciliation!

Although Isidore had already warned the Seventh Council that conversion was a matter of free will, and had censured the Gothic monarch for "using violence instead of persuasion to bring people to the Church," he could not prevent Sisebut from persecuting the Jews.

Jewish children were taken away "to keep them from being led astray like their parents." Tribunals ceased to accept testimony given by apostate Jews. Jews were denied the right to own Christian slaves and were barred from the royal service. They were baptized by force. When a king was crowned, he was made to promise that he would not tolerate Judaism.

The situation grew worse when King Chintila issued an edict expelling from the country all Jews who had remained faithful to their own religion. Many, faced with such a choice, declared themselves Christians rather than go into exile. But their protestations of sincerity were in vain; conversions obtained by force were deemed worthless. Hardships increased. The Seventeenth Council of Toledo (702) ordered the confiscation of all Jewish property and decreed that the proceeds should go to the national exchequer. It also enslaved the Jews and forbade them to marry.

Were the councils complying with royal demands in such matters or were they taking the initiative? It is quite clear that as the clergy grew in number and importance, it tightened its grip on the civil power. National synods usurped the functions of a parliament or council of state. Provincial synods claimed jurisdiction over every problem submitted to them. Bishops controlled the public administration. Judges and tax collectors were supervised by the heads of dioceses. Moreover, it was the councils that trained the members of the revenue and law-enforcement agencies and instructed them in their duties.

Thus, the Church moved imperceptibly first from the legislative to the judiciary, then to the executive. Its tendency toward despotism led it to foster, deliberately or unwittingly, a hunger for wealth and a spirit of revenge. This is the grave danger of too close an alliance between church and state.

Most Jews had achieved an enviable position under the shadow of Arianism. Almost all of them had grown rich. Their exclusion from the community and the confiscation of their property conveniently filled the coffers of the treasury in the name of national necessity. Undeniably, the bishops profited from the suppression of an embarrassing adversary. And what a windfall for the Church's finances!

The ferocious tide of racism swept over Spain. The Jew lowered his head before the storm. If he could not flee, he repeated his professions of Christianity. He allowed himself to be stripped, humiliated, and imprisoned. He, a descendant of the first patriarchs, was torn from his family! His children, and even his means of subsistence, were taken from him. No matter! He would remain on Spanish soil. He cringed, he smiled at his persecutors, and he showered them with flattery. He even mumbled thanks. Nothing could break down his atavistic patience. He knew all too well that time was of no moment, that he would have to wait. Upon the brow of the unfortunate Hebrew, though his head was bowed, shone the star of the chosen race.

But his humiliated heart burned with hatred for the Visigothic masters. A few more years—the seventh century was nearing its end—and he would wreak vengeance. For though the Jew accepted insults, he did not forgive them: "An eye for an eye and a tooth for a tooth." The thundering victory of Gibraltar was a triumph for him.

The Last Visigothic Kings and Decadence

In 601, an adolescent, Liuva II, succeeded his father, the good King Reccared. He reigned for only two years. A Gothic nobleman, Count Witteric, had him put to death and took his place, but not for long. He, too, was assassinated and replaced by Gunthemar, who, after a brief period on the throne, was succeeded by Sisebut, the persecutor of the Jews.

Upon the death of Sisebut a fresh period of disorder and intrigue began. The kingly office was becoming a precarious one. With the aid of palace revolutions, and sometimes resorting to criminal acts, both usurpers and legitimate princes strove for power. Such methods were employed by Sisinand, who nevertheless was recognized by the Fourth Council. With the advent of Prince Chindaswinth, a humanist and warrior, and his son Recceswinth, a jurist, restoration of royal authority seemed possible. But their successor, Wamba, was plagued by the worst kind of disorders. First he had to repress a Basque revolt. While he was putting it down, Hilderic, the Count of Nîmes and governor of Septimania, decided to rebel. Wamba dispatched Duke Paul, one of his best lieutenants, to deal with Hilderic. Exploiting his victory, Paul went to Narbonne and had himself proclaimed King of Septimania. After a brilliant sweep through Calahorra, Lérida, Barcelona, Gerona, the Perthus Pass, Roussillon, Agde, Béziers, and Maguelone, Wamba laid siege to Nîmes. A bitter battle ensued. The attackers scaled the ramparts and spread throughout the city. Hunted and attacked on all sides, the usurper sought refuge in the arena. He could hear the screams of the wounded and the shouts of the victors. Hiding in one of the enclosures which in Roman times had housed wild beasts, he watched the triumphant entry of Wamba's foot soldiers. Realizing the game was up, he discarded his royal cloak and shoulder belt, the insignia of command. This supreme act of cowardice saved his life, and he died in prison. Wamba returned to the capital, preceded by a sorry procession of defeated foes, barefoot men with ropes tied around their necks. Behind were the horsemen in shining armor who received the acclaim of the people of Toledo. This was the last triumph of Catholic royalty in the Gothic era.

For the past fifty years, a simple keeper of camels named Mohammed had been preaching a holy war at Medina. He turned his disciples into soldiers and led them to victories over the Persians and the Romans. For a few decades the caliphate of the Ommiads occupied Mesopotamia and most of Asia Minor. Traversing the length of North Africa, the Saracens raced for the sea. Mauretania, with the exception of Ceuta, fell into their hands. An Arab fleet of one hundred and sixty vessels cruised the waters of Algeciras. Sensing danger, Wamba armed his ships and engaged the Arabs, and handed them a crushing defeat. For a few more years the Iberian Peninsula was safe from the Moslem threat. But the Visigothic kings realized that their days were numbered.

When the rebels were put down and the Basques and Arabs defeated, Wamba could devote himself to peaceful pursuits. His first concern was to transform and beautify Toledo. He was well on the way to becoming a great king when he clashed with the usurper Euric, who shattered his career. Inviting Wamba to drink with him at a feast, he offered him a goblet of wine to which a drug had been added.

The aging monarch drank it and fell into a stupor. With Wamba apparently on the verge of death, Euric got him to sign a decree naming him as king-designate. Then this living cadaver was tonsured and clothed in a monk's habit. The following day, when Wamba recovered his senses, he had no choice but to confirm the decree which had been extorted from him. He withdrew to a monastery and Euric mounted the throne. The Twelfth Council of Toledo ratified the act, the nobles gave their approval, and the people remained silent.

The advent of Euric heralded the death of the Visigothic monarchy. Real power was increasingly usurped by the clergy and the palatines. Sisebert, the archbishop of Toledo, headed a conspiracy against Egica, Euric's successor, but it failed. Egica's son, Witiza, gained a reputation for cruelty. He beat to death one of the sons of Chindaswinth, whose wife he coveted, and put out the eyes of the other. He banished the Archbishop of Toledo and gave the see to his son. A great lover of women and wine, he extolled debauchery and publicly encouraged it. The accounts of this troubled reign that have come down to us are contradictory in certain respects, but they all agree on one thing: the Gothic kingdom was slowly rotting.

Before he died, Witiza named his son Achila to succeed him, but a group of noblemen and bishops decreed otherwise. Witiza's enemy, Roderic, duke of Baetica, mounted the throne. Achila made an attempt to regain power, but was defeated and forced to flee to Morocco.

Ominous portents marked the beginning of Roderic's rule. In Toledo there was an ancient edifice known as the House of Hercules. Its doors were always locked, for the people believed that Spain would be destroyed if anyone opened them. During the festivities that accompanied Roderic's coronation, the Toledans requested a new lock for the House of Hercules. This was a time-honored custom which every king had granted at the time of his accession to power. But Roderic refused. Hoping to find hidden treasures, he broke open the locks and chains that had kept the mysterious building sealed. But he was doomed to disappointment.

Instead of the hoped-for riches, he discovered only a canvas depicting men dressed as Arab warriors. Their faces were strange and seemed to breathe hatred. The painting bore the inscription: "These men will soon come and destroy Spain." Hardly had the dismayed king fled the House of Hercules when he was consumed by "fire from heaven." Of course, this is a fable, but events were to bear out the prediction. Roderic was the last Visigothic king, *el último rey godo.* With him, an entire world collapsed.

Reccared's monarchy had failed to fulfill its promise. Who was to blame? Probably his successors, who allowed the vigor of the laws to slacken and gave themselves up to debauchery. Yet it was the Church that wielded authority and bore responsibility for the institutions and customs of the land. One is especially drawn to this fact, for the Church alone gave stability to the Visigothic era. Eager for royal protection, it began by complying with the king's wishes, because it was he who enabled the Church to play a leading role in the state. Then, yielding to the temptation of power, it took the scepter from the weak hands of the Gothic sovereigns. Blinded by power, the episcopate ended up by ruling the kingdom and occasionally siding with the nobility against the monarch. The councils, whose primary object was to limit the royal prerogative, soon became an *instrumentum regni* in the hands of the bishops. They controlled elections and legitimized usurpers. The death of the judicious Isidore speeded the trend toward ecclesiastical omnipotence. The measures against the Jews precipitated the crisis. Such a regime, undermined from within, proved incapable of resisting Islam. As has so often happened, decadence inevitably invited invasion.

Despite its defects and weaknesses, Visigothic Spain represented a considerable improvement over conditions that had prevailed during the fifth century. Without the Church this would have been impossible. The Church gave the nomadic Germans a sense of nationality. It also inculcated in them a love of justice. For their ancestral notion of a leader, it boldly substituted the idea of an assembly, and confronted the king with a representative body strong enough to curb his wishes. The limitation of personal authority by a national assembly was a new concept. It evolved and gave rise to modern democracies.

When the Roman Empire fell, the Church showed great skill in preserving everything that was good in Caesar's legacy—respect for law, humanism, a flair for political organition. It imparted all this to the Visigoths. Roman order adapted to Christian needs—what a grandiose design! However, it was achieved only in part. The Church failed to maintain the uncompromising attitude and inflexible principles that had enabled it to triumph so easily over Arianism. It would have had to purge its all-too-human clergy. Nevertheless, it is remarkable that the Christian doctrine of brotherly love had so quickly and completely affected the turbulent mass of barbarians whose ancestors, not so long ago, had roamed like wolves along the Vistula.

Finally, the disintegration of the state did not undermine the elite. It did not die with the Visigothic kingdom. The torch of faith was handed down from father to son. It was this elite, composed of laymen and clergy, that inspired the Reconquest, that stirred those Christian soldiers who made the Reconquest possible. Spain has never lacked great and powerful personalities. They typify its history: they fashioned, destroyed, and re-created it.

Of the Visigothic interlude there remain only a few simple crosses that point to such treasures as the ruins of church naves, crude jewelry buried in tombs, and, surrounding Toledo, the masses of scattered stones that once served as Wamba's ramparts.

The Arabs drove from the peninsula these big children of the North, at once artless and cruel, who had merely the semblance of kings. For eight centuries Spain was engaged with Islam, fighting or coming to terms with it. Eight centuries were to elapse before the cathedral of spiritual knowledge triumphed over the shadowy mosque, before all the parts of Spain, like pieces in a puzzle, were put together under the silver cross and the banner of Castile.

❧ PART · II ☙

THE AGE OF

The Cid

"My beloved swords, where are you now?
Where are you now my precious swords? Precious, not for having been purchased with gold
and silver, but for having been won by the
sweat of my brow. I took you from the Moorish
king of Morocco, oh my Tizona. You I tore
from the grasp of the Count of Barcelona, my
dear Colada."

—*Romancero*

I

The Caliphate of Cordova

ELEN, it is said, was the cause of the Trojan War. Legend likewise attributes the beginning of the Arab invasion to the beautiful Florinda, known as *La Cava*, "the Bad One." The daughter of Count Julian, governor of Ceuta, she was allegedly seduced by King Roderic. The monarch saw her for the first time while she was bathing in the Tagus at Toledo and promptly fell madly in love with her. Julian reacted to his outrageous behavior the more sharply because, at that time, the guests of his palace were none other than Oppas, Witiza's brother, and Achila, Witiza's son and Roderic's unlucky rival. Everyone in the kingdom who opposed the regime, all the bitter and discontented, sought refuge at Ceuta, where they rallied round the deposed prince. Only a spark was needed to ignite the rebellious assembly; Florinda's honor supplied it.

For a long time Musa ben Nosair, the caliph's delegate at Tangier, had gazed longingly at the Spanish coast. On a clear day it seemed within arm's reach. He could count the houses, follow the movements of ships, and, when the wind blew hard, he could sniff the odor of Spanish oranges. This annoyed the viceroy, ruler of North Africa, who only recently had been defeated by the Arabs of the East—the *Chargins*, or Saracens, as the Visigoths called them.

Musa's warriors liked to go off on raiding parties. The coastline held no secrets for them. When they returned from

a foray they would hasten to the viceroy and recount what
they had seen. Sometimes Jews who had been exiled by the
Gothic kings would provide information about the political
situation in Spain. They described the clergy's tight grip on
the state and the growing weakness of the princes. Achila's
envoys openly invited Arab intervention. They could not resign themselves to defeat and passionately hoped for the
overthrow of Roderic. "Cross the sea," they urged. "You will
be acclaimed as saviors." To forestall resistance, Musa sent
his disenfranchised slave, Tarif, on a reconnoitering expedition. It proved highly successful. Tarif anchored in a small
Andalusian port—later named Tarifa—seized valuable
booty, and returned to Tangier without any trouble.

The viceroy consulted Damascus. Then, choosing his moment carefully, he dispatched an expeditionary force of
7,000 Berbers commanded by Tarik, a Berber general. In
July 711, Tarik and his soldiers crossed the strait called the
Pillars of Hercules by the Greeks, and landed on the Rock
of Gibraltar (Djebel Tarik: "Tarik's mountain"). Here they
established a bridgehead, then converged on Algeciras.
Meanwhile, Musa ordered another 5,000 men into battle.

Roderic hastily assembled an army and met the invaders
between Algeciras and Cadiz. On July 19 a terrible battle
was fought near the banks of the Guadalete. Following an
old Gothic tradition, Roderic arrived in an ivory chariot,
wearing a purple mantle, a gold crown, and silver boots. At
the height of the fray, he abandoned the chariot and
mounted a white horse. The Visigoths, despite enormous
courage, could not hold out against the Arab onslaught.
Screaming Berber horsemen, mounted on small, long-tailed
steeds, swooped down from every direction, their broad
burnooses flowing and scimitars whirling above their turbaned heads. Amidst guttural cries, the whir of arrows, the
neighing of horses, and the clash of armor, the Goths took
flight. When night fell on Jerez the Berbers raised the green
standard of the Prophet. In vain did they look for Roderic.
The only trace of him was his white bemired horse and,
close to it, a silver boot.

One hundred and fifty years after the Battle of Guadalete, a tombstone was discovered at Viseu, in Portugal. It bore the following inscription: HIC REQUIESCIT RODERICUS REX ULTIMUS GOTHORUM. It is hard to imagine the defeated king, fleeing in despair into exile. Even if he had been spared the enemies' blows, how could he have survived the shock of seeing Bishop Oppas and Count Julian, men of his own race, nationality, and religion, riding at the head of the Moslem army and leading the attack?

Roderic's defeat exposed Seville to the invaders. They dashed through it, hastened past Carmona, subdued the last Visigothic forces at Écija, seized Cordova, and finally reached Toledo. Meanwhile, Musa, who wanted to share the victory, effected a landing, crossed the Sierra Morena, and conquered Mérida. At Salamanca he liquidated the small detachment of troops that had remained loyal to Roderic. Then he joined Tarik before the walls of Toledo. Once there, and flushed with pride, the viceroy proclaimed the annexation of Spain in the name of his master, the Caliph of Baghdad. Spain now belonged to the Islamic Empire.

Thus, after fighting off the Roman legions for over three hundred years, Spain became a Moslem colony within the space of a few days. How startled the people of Andalusia must have been to see the armies of the Prophet pouring over the ancient road of Caracalla! Could it be that those dusky little horsemen who swept by in a cloud of dust, those mamelukes brandishing curved swords, were now their masters? Was the King of Spain no more? The reports that had been circulating—the rumors from Toledo about the scandalous life of the princes, the cupidity of the civil servants, and the corruption of the clergy—were they then true after all?

Yes, undoubtedly. But it would be wrong and unfair to place the entire blame for the collapse on the Church alone. To be sure, it had been far more interested in secular than in spiritual concerns. Its learned and elegant clergy, consorting with dukes and counts and electing kings, had done very little to improve the lot of the people. Admittedly, it was impossible to abolish slavery. Such a reform—in the middle of the seventh century—would have been foredoomed. The councils had urged progress in the field of social welfare.

If only progressive measures had accompanied the preaching of the Gospel, even at the risk of incurring the nobility's anger! But this, of course, was asking a good deal of the powerful ecclesiastical oligarchy, which valued its property and prerogatives far too much to jeopardize them by displeasing the princes. In the end, the Church miscalculated. The people know who among their fellow beings look down upon them. When their help is needed by those who only yesterday disdained them, they remember. Passivity is their answer to the contempt of their masters. And so it was that the serfs, mistreated by the sovereigns, wary of the clergy, and feeling neither love nor gratitude—not even hatred—for either, made no attempt whatsoever to stay the tide of the infidels. What, after all, did they have to lose?

For a long time Spain had been plagued by Jewish propaganda. Sisebert's ill-advised persecution of the Jews had led them to seek an alliance with the Byzantines and the Berbers of Africa. A few years before the Moslem invasion, the Spanish Jews reached an understanding with their African brothers. Together they planned an uprising against the Visigothic monarchy; the Berbers were to disembark and move in from the coast. When the plot was discovered, even sterner measures were brought to bear against the Jews. But the evil day had only been postponed. Angered at being treated so badly, the Jews continued to preach revolt. "Death to the Visigoths! May the liberators from the South come quickly!"

Achila and his partisans spoke the same language. Hatred of Roderic plus hunger for power outweighed their patriotism. They were prepared to welcome help from anyone, from the Jews or from Africa, if it would lead to the deposition of the king and enable them to gain the throne. Were these Gothic lords really naïve enough to believe that Tarik's stay would be brief, that when he was sated with plunder he would withdraw and leave the new dynasty to them?

The prince and his companions soon realized their error. Their troops fled with those of Roderic in the face of the Moslem onslaught. Slaves and Jews were more fortunate.

Cleverly setting out to please those who were to toil for them, the invaders treated slaves gently and invested Jews with the responsibility of policing the conquered cities. Naturally, the Jews welcomed such reward for their services; they were happy to perform a task that enabled them to give full vent to their bitterness. The Spanish Christians never forgot this humiliation. They remembered it seven hundred years later when the Catholic Kings signed an order expelling the Jews. It was recalled that the Jews, not content with helping the Berbers invade the country, had provided garrisons in order to humble their fellow Spaniards. Alas, vengeance begets vengeance!

Finally, it was not solely the military daring of a few thousand Arabs and Berbers that accounted for the overthrow of the Hispano-Visigothic regime. The language and religion of Islam were known to Spaniards long before Tarik. Many educated people enjoyed Mohammedan philosophy. Andalusia, with a population of several million, had often looked toward the Strait with nostalgic curiosity. The viceroy of Tangier was well informed; he knew that Cordova would be receptive to his mosques. An army is but the instrument of an idea, and the philosophy of the Arabs had long preceded their mercenaries.

The Religion of the Sword

The first invaders of Spain were the Berbers, who comprised all the peoples variously called Numidians, Libyans, Africans, and Getae by the Romans. The Berbers had been ruled successively by Romans, Vandals, and Visigoths. Around the middle of the seventh century they were conquered by Arabs, nomadic warriors of Semitic origin. These newcomers founded Kairwan, overran Carthage, and governed Africa with the aid of emirs appointed by the caliphs. It took several centuries for the Berbers, who had immigrated gradually, to unite with the Arabs. When they landed on the Spanish coast they had already been converted to Islam, either of their own accord or by force. This

THE AGE OF THE CID

is important. Whether the invaders were Arabs or Berbers, Moors or Saracens, the tie of religion bound them together despite their dissensions. What was the nature of this religion and who was its prophet?

Mohammed, the founder of Islam, belonged to the most illustrious of all Arab races, the Adnan, and to the most influential of all tribes, the Koreish. Raised by his grandfather, Abd-al-Mottalib, then by his uncle, Abu Talib, he became a caravan merchant at a very early age. He married the widow Khadija, who made up in wealth what she lacked in beauty.

Mohammed was born in Mecca in 570, and not much is known about his early life up to the age of forty, when he had a vision. He announced his intention of combating polytheism, which was centered in the temple of the Kaaba, the sacred refuge of Arab divinities. At first Mohammed was ridiculed, but as his message spread among the people, it infuriated and worried the Koreish, the guardians of the Kaaba. Secretly, they resolved to rid themselves of this troublesome prophet. But Mohammed learned of their plan in time and fled to Medina, where he made a triumphal entry. The era of the Hegira had begun.

While elaborating the Koran and organizing a new form of worship, Mohammed created an army. At the head of his troops, he captured Mecca and led expeditions against his neighbors, not all of which were successful. But they served to enhance the prestige of both the new religion and its leader. When Mohammed died almost all of Arabia, as far as Oman, had been converted to Islam.

What did the man from Medina teach? Actually, it was less a doctrine than a collection of precepts and moral rules codified in one hundred and fourteen suras of the Koran. The concept of the universe that Mohammed propounded was not very different from that of the Biblical prophets, from Abraham to Jesus, whose revelations he accepted in their entirety. Nor did he hesitate to borrow largely from the Judaeo-Christian tradition. Is not Mohammed's God—"the only God in heaven and on earth . . . indulgent toward mankind in spite of its iniquity, but terrible in His punishments"—the God of the Hebrews? The creation of the world in six days, Adam, the paradise on earth, the fall of man, the Last Judgment announced by "thundering trumpet blasts," Hell and "seething waters," the celestial paradise "of fruits, palms, and pomegranates" all this is in the Old Testament. Allah addressed Mohammed as follows: "For you God has established a religion which He recommended to Noah. Oh, Mohammed, this is the religion which you are revealing. It is also the religion which we urged on Abraham, Moses, and Jesus, saying unto them: Observe this religion, do not sunder it into sects."

Although similar to Christianity in its concept of God, it is different in several respects. Mohammedanism attributes an inflexible nature to the divinity. This monolithic God, utterly unrelated to man, resembles a machine that creates the world and dispenses justice, oscillating like a sinister metronome between the chosen and the damned. More akin to Baal than to the Christian God, somber and vengeful, He inspires tremendous awe and terror—"thunder sings His praises." Allah, from up high, inexorable and solitary, punishes and rewards. The promised paradise is none other than the Garden of the Alhambra. "The just will live among springs. They will recline on rugs lined with brocade. There will be young virgins like hyacinths and coral . . . and good and beautiful women." In this wonderful place everyone would find his dearest wish gratified. Devotees of the siesta would sleep on "elevated beds" during all eternity.

A shrewd politician, Mohammed invented a paradise that was suitable for his crude disciples, just as Moses, another clever leader, likewise created mirages and depicted the Promised Land. Yet, although this rudimentary notion of an earthly paradise appealed to the nomads of the Hejaz and to the tribes of Africa, it could not satisfy Spaniards who had experienced seven centuries of Christianity. They had been taught—and the humblest of serfs knew this—that God, by virtue of his Incarnation, had identified Himself with man, that the Father, the Son, and the Holy Ghost were one, and that Jesus Christ joined the creator and the creature in a single dazzling unity. The Christian conception of man, partaking of divinity and becoming one with it through the miracle of Love, led Spaniards to spurn Allah, the mighty cadi, demagogue, and provider of houris and thornless lotuses. Besides, Mohammed's sensuous paradise, which stressed only the pleasures of the flesh, had nothing in common with the luminous world of knowledge foretold by the Gospel.

True enough, there were many similarities between the Koran and Christian morality—fasting and prayer, exaltation of virtue and condemnation of sin, exhortations to practice charity. Many a good Moslem put an impious Christian to shame, for there were, of course, just and gallant Arabs. The contrast was less ethical than theological. The clash between these two different worlds led to the Reconquest, which over a span of eight centuries made its way from Covadonga to Granada, gradually encircling Spain in a cordon of fire. The drama thus enacted between Moors and Spaniards was a purely religious one.

It is not easy to describe the relations between Christians and Moslems. They varied from province to province and from century to century, according to the personalities involved and the ever changing political situation. Acute crises were followed by periods of calm. The Koran itself is not consistent. Sometimes it urges tolerance: "Coercions should not be used in matters pertaining to religion. Those who believe in the Gospel will swear by the Gospel. . . . Our God is the same as your God and we are entirely submissive to His will." But the Koran also calls for violence: "When you encounter Infidels, slay them. . . . Wage war against those who believe neither in God nor in the Last Judgment." Omar, the caliph, was more specific: "Our task is to destroy Christians and the task of our sons is to destroy all their surviving descendants." Arab persecution was not comparable to Roman persecution; more underhanded and intermittent, it was much less persistent. Long periods of inactivity alternated with sudden eruptions of violence. But no true and lasting peace prevailed. The Prophet's followers were not all fanatics, and often it was the Christians who spurned the olive branch.

Meanwhile, many Spaniards—pagans, Arians, and slaves of the Jews—embraced Islam. Some of these new converts, whom the Arabs called Muladíes, were sincere, but the majority sought to recover their freedom by currying favor with the victors. Actually, because of the important services they rendered, the Muladíes were given prominent positions by the emirs. By and large, the influence of these superficially Islamized Spaniards (they were Islamized just enough to win the confidence of their masters) proved beneficial to Spain. Quite frequently they were called upon to perform administrative duties, and most of the time they showed themselves to be extremely humane.

The same was true of converted Berbers, who only recently had worshipped the gods of Carthage. Indifferent to religion, they were greatly concerned about their share of Spanish territory. The Arabs had taken the fertile valleys of Andalusia and Aragon, leaving to the Berbers the dry Castilian plains and the deserts of Estremadura. Naturally, the Berbers resented this inequitable division of the spoils. After all, they had been the first to land on the Spanish coast, thus paving the way for the viceroy's troops. The disdainful attitude of the Arabs drove the Berbers to make common cause with the Spaniards. A shared interest—the land to be farmed —together with intermarriage, hastened this fusion.

The Arabs were the sworn enemies of Christianity. They were justly proud of the long way they had come since Mohammed's death. Starting from the Arabian plains, they had conquered Persia, Syria, Egypt, and North Africa. Their empire stretched from India to the Atlantic and from the Caucasus to the Persian Gulf. They were Believers; they wanted the whole world to follow the law of the Prophet. Arab imperialism was essentially mystical in character. Had it not clashed with an analogous movement—Catholic imperialism—it doubtless would have survived indefinitely in Spain.

From Solomon's Table to the Diadems of the Gothic Kings

When Musa learned of Tarik's victory on the Guadalete, he was filled with rage. He hated the Berbers even more than he did the Visigoths and did not intend to forfeit his share of the victory. He ordered his lieutenant to suspend operations until he arrived in Spain. Inasmuch as his plans had proved so successful, he himself would assume command. But Tarik had ideas of his own. He decided to ignore Musa's orders and continued his triumphant campaign, dividing his army into three sections. The first, commanded by a renegade named Mughez el-Rumi, headed for Cordova; the second, under the leadership of Zayd ben Kesadi, was dispatched to guard the coast; the third, under his own direction, moved toward Toledo, the Visigothic capital.

Within a few weeks the large southern cities fell to the Berbers. Mughez captured Cordova with relative ease (his soldiers, disguised as Goths, unwound their turbans and used them to scale the ramparts). Zayd raced to Málaga, Granada, and Seville, and at the last of these was welcomed by Bishop Oppas before the gates of the city. Then Zayd joined Tarik in the outskirts of Toledo; the Visigothic capital offered almost no resistance, thanks to Jewish treachery.

On the whole, the invader was fairly well received. Why should anyone die for the Goths or the monks? This was the feeling of many. Furthermore, the terms laid down by the victors were not too harsh. They levied a moderate income tax of one fifth, and in some cases, one tenth, on the rich. Christians were allowed freedom of worship so long as they remained inside their churches. Seven churches in all were kept open, quite enough to serve the needs of pious Christians. The municipalities enjoyed administrative autonomy. Thus, there was ample reason to submit willingly to the conquerors. In any event, the sight of a few severed heads on the ramparts, or a glimpse of crucified bodies rotting at the top of a hill, soon convinced even the most hesitant.

But it was impossible to prevent victorious soldiers, however merciful, from plundering. Tarik himself set the example. At Toledo he seized the twenty-five gold crowns adorned with precious stones that had belonged to the twenty-five kings who had ruled Gothic Spain from Leovigild to Roderic. On the banks of the Jalón at Medinaceli, Tarik discovered a table made of gold and silver, studded with coral and pearls and encrusted with the twelve signs of the zodiac. Three hundred and sixty emeralds, each representing a degree of the circle, adorned the marble top. "This is Solomon's Table," educated Arabs declared. The Goths probably took it from Rome, where it had lain since Titus had taken it from Jerusalem. Dazzled by this wonder, yet determined to be diplomatic, Tarik added it to his booty. He would offer it to his supreme commander, the Caliph of Baghdad.

Musa landed at Algeciras at the head of 5,000 foot soldiers and 10,000 horsemen. His son, Abdul-Aziz, rode beside him. That devil Tarik had not yet captured everything. Medina-Sidonia, Carmona, Mérida, yielded to the viceroy. It was but a short distance from Mérida to Toledo. Musa was in a hurry to catch up with Tarik—but not in order to praise him, as we may have guessed. Finally the two men confronted each other. Musa was pale with rage and Tarik was wary, fearing his master's temper. To appease him, Tarik offered his own share of the booty, including Solomon's Table, from which he had surreptitiously removed one leg. But the viceroy refused to be disarmed by Tarik's generosity. He charged his lieutenant with disobedience, accused him of assuming too much initiative, removed him from his command, and ordered him whipped and thrown into prison.

Meanwhile, Abdul-Aziz was fighting along the coast. His Gothic enemy, Theodomir, gave him a difficult time. In the Murcian mountains, whither he had retreated, Theodomir resisted every assault. Abdul-Aziz laid siege to Orihuela, but did not dare to attack because of the large number of well-armed troops that manned the ramparts. For the same reason he agreed to negotiate. Moslems and Goths signed a treaty which stipulated, among other things, that Theodomir "would not be deposed or banished from his kingdom, that the faithful would neither kill, capture, nor separate Christians, and that churches would not be burned. In return, Theodomir and his people would pay an annual tribute of one gold dinar per capita, together with four measures each of wheat, barley, fermented wine, vinegar, honey, and oil." Assured of an honorable peace, Theodomir opened the gates of the city. Imagine Abdul-Aziz's surprise when he saw the garrison at close range! The ferocious sentries hiding behind the battlements turned out to be women who had draped their long hair over their chins in order to look like bearded Visigoths. Abdul-Aziz was a good sport. Instead of denouncing a treaty obtained by means of such trickery, he burst into laughter and embraced the shrewd Gothic king.

Musa's treatment of Tarik displeased the caliph, Abd-al-Malik. He ordered the viceroy to free his lieutenant and to use his services in the conduct of operations. Musa obeyed the first part of the command but refused to collaborate with Tarik. Each went his own way. Tarik proceeded down the Ebro, conquered Tortosa, and continued along the Mediterranean to Murcia. Musa fought in the mountains of Galicia. He was consumed with ambition, hoping to conquer all Europe—Gaul, Germany, Italy, and Greece—while another Moslem army advanced into Asia Minor. His relations with Tarik grew more and more bitter, a fact which did not escape the notice of the caliph, who was very annoyed that the campaign was jeopardized by quarreling among his generals. He ordered them both to Damascus. Just as Musa and Tarik reached Syria, each arriving by a separate route, Abd-al-Malik died and was succeeded by his brother, Suleiman. The new caliph received the rivals and gave them an icy stare. The two brilliant strategists looked sheepish. To appease Suleiman, Musa had Solomon's Table brought in and laid it at his feet. The caliph's face brightened. What a marvelous thing! But one leg was missing. Where could it be? Tarik smiled. How would Musa know, since it was he, Tarik, who had found the legendary table. Musa denied this loudly. The caliph lowered his eyes and fingered his beads as if he had suddenly lost interest in the quarrel. Tarik drew aside his white burnoose and produced the missing table leg. Here was proof of his contention. A tremor of rage ran through the caliph's personal guard. The Supreme Commander of the Faithful had been tricked! Scimitars were swiftly unsheathed. Musa began to quake. But Suleiman, continuing to tell his beads, softly pronounced the sentence: Musa must pay a large fine and for an entire day would be exposed to the public, after which he could resume his command. Islam had need of him.

Musa preferred imprisonment or even decapitation to this frightful punishment, which Suleiman had long contemplated. To make matters worse, Abdul-Aziz had fallen in love with Egilona, the widow of the last Gothic king. He married her without insisting that she change her religion; at his request she did, however, take a new name: Zahrabent-Isa, the flower, daughter of Jesus. Accused of partiality to Christianity, Abdul-Aziz was decapitated. His head was placed in a camphor box and sent to Suleiman, who hastened to show it to Musa, saying: "Do you recognize your son?"

Princes of the North

Dumfounded by the lightning Arab-Berber campaign, the Christians sought refuge in the mountains. There they assessed their forces and caught their breath. For a few years they tried to marshal their strength. The boldest among them recruited mountaineers, taught them the art of war, and organized them into armed bands. To obtain the means of subsistence, they raided the Moslem-controlled plains. In 718, during a foray, one of their leaders, Pelayo, was captured and imprisoned at Cordova. He managed to escape and rejoined the Christians in the Asturias. The Moslems sent an army to eliminate this nest of insurgents. Pelayo moved the women, children, and old men to a sheltered spot at the top of the mountain. Then, leading his soldiers, he withdrew east of Mount Auseva to a cave in Covadonga which overlooked a defile. In the valley below flowed the Deva. As soon as the Arabs reached the gorge, the Christians rolled enormous rocks from the heights of the sierra and at the same time riddled the enemy with arrows. Overwhelmed, the Arabs fell back in great disorder. Just then a storm arose, the Deva became a torrent, and its turbulent waves swept away the remnants of the army. Long after the battle, when the Deva, swollen by rains, overflowed, its banks were littered with bones and bits of armor. A chapel, Our Lady of the Battles, was built at Santa María of Covadonga, on the site of this dramatic encounter. This first episode of the Reconquest occurred shortly after the defeat on the Guadalete.

One by one, centers of resistance sprang up in northern Spain, Biscay, Navarre, and the mountains of Aragon. In 724, García Jiménez founded the tiny state of Sobrarbe, a future province of Aragon. Pelayo's son-in-law, Alfonso I, called Alfonso the Catholic, established the capital of Asturias in Oviedo. Gradually the Christians erected strongholds all along the Douro—at Astorga, Leon, Zamora, Salamanca, Segovia, Ávila, Miranda. From these they set forth to reconquer Spain. The Moslem frontier formed the large arc of a circle: Coimbra, Coria, Talavera, Toledo, Guadalajara, and Tudela. A neutral zone, periodically ravaged by both Christians and Arabs, separated the two boundaries. From either side of this no man's land the feeble princes of the north and the emirs eyed one another.

Thus a quarter of a century had scarcely gone by when the ramparts of Catholic principalities arose. To be sure, they were weak, but they betokened the symbolic presence of the Christian monarchy in Spain.

Why did the Arabs permit such nuclei of resistance? Probably because they not only had to defend themselves against their former allies, the Berbers, but also had to cope with a difficult dynastic crisis. Abd-er-Rahman, a member of the Ommiad family, headed the Arab empire at Damascus. Deposed by Yusuf, a prince of the Abbasside family, Abd-er-

Rahman sought refuge in Spain, seized Cordova, and claimed the caliphate. This split the Arab world in two; in the West the would-be caliph of the Ommiads denied the authority of the Abbasside caliph in Damascus.

Twenty years before the advent of Abd-er-Rahman, on October 11, 732, Frenchmen and Moors fought a major battle in the vicinity of Poitiers. The Moors had just devastated the territory between the Pyrenees and the Garonne and were advancing over unprotected fields in the direction of the Loire when they encountered the hastily assembled army of the Frankish prince Charles Martel, son of Pepin of Herstal, major-domo at the court of King Thierry. The Franks were outnumbered, but they carried shields, wore coats of mail, and were armed with heavy axes and long, sharp swords. The Moors went down as if they had been struck with a hammer—which explains why Charles was called the Hammer. Then Pepin the Short pushed the Saracen armies back to the Albères. Later, Charlemagne, exploiting dissension among the Moslems, crossed the Pyrenees. Cities fell like overripe fruit: Pamplona, Huesca, Gerona. . . . But the swift pace of the Frankish troops was halted at Saragossa. They had to turn back. Moving through the Roncesvalles Pass, Charlemagne's rearguard was ambushed. Basque partisans massacred Roland and his companions. "In this battle, Roland, prefect of the March of Brittany, was killed."

Once again the Arabs raided the south of France, striking furiously near Narbonne and Carcassonne. To halt these attacks, Charlemagne created the kingdom of Aquitania. The establishment of glacis in Navarre and Catalonia completed the Carolingian system of defense.

During the eighth century, which was about to end, Spain knew both the bitterness of invasion and the first anticipation of Reconquest. The Franks were at Barcelona. The Caliph of Cordova acknowledged the Hispanic movement. As an ally of Harun al-Rashid, Charlemagne became the protector of the Holy Places and received the imperial crown of the West from the hands of Leo III. Spain turned its gaze to the north—the Christian world's new center of gravity.

Cordova, the Spanish Byzantium

Spain was ruled by new masters. Who were they? Although Abd-er-Rahman I had not ventured to assume the title of caliph, his seventh successor, Abd-er-Rahman III, not only did so but also acquired the necessary prerogatives. Actually, as early as the middle of the eighth century, an Ommiad caliphate at Cordova confronted the Abbasside caliphate in Baghdad.

From his nomadic origins, the founder of the Hispano-Arabic dynasty had preserved a penchant for simplicity. He was tall and blond, perhaps because his mother's people were Berbers, or because of his remote Germanic antecedents. His thin face, framed by long hair, was appealing even though he was one-eyed. He could be both fierce and sentimental. He sent the Caliph of Baghdad the dried heads of Abbasside leaders, wrapped in the black flag that symbolized their dynasty, with the name of each victim on a label suspended from one of the ears. But he also had palm trees planted in his garden in memory of his home in Damascus and wrote the following verses to them: "May the morning clouds drench you with as much water as Spica and Arcturus discharge."

In 756 Abd-er-Rahman took up his abode at Cordova. The Ommiads liked the city, which resembled Byzantium more than either Seville or Málaga, although they described the latter as being as "fragrant as a decanter of unbottled musk."

Of the old Roman and Gothic city there remained only the ramparts, a bridge over the Guadalquivir, the monumental gate called "the Statue," and the residence of the governors—a castle called the Alcazar: *el Ksar*, "palace of the Arabs." A Roman tower stood on the left bank of the river. Facing it on the opposite shore was a mosque. Vast gardens and sumptuous villas stretched to the west of the Alcazar. In a nearby aqueduct, water bubbled from the mouth of a gold-plated lion whose eyes were precious stones. The city

of Cordova sprawled endlessly, being three times longer
from south to north than from east to west and possessing
no fewer than twenty-eight suburbs. It comprised "an area
illuminated by the light of lamps at night," a description
more poetic than precise. At its height Cordova boasted
1,000,000 inhabitants, 260,000 buildings, 80,000 shops,
4,300 markets, 500 mosques, 700 bathing establishments,
and also countless public and private libraries, for it was the
greatest center of the Arabic book trade in the West. In the
only large suburb east of the city, 170 women were employed
to transcribe the Koran in the Kufic alphabet. But Cordova
was not merely a place for pilgrims or writers, nor was it
only a center for the study of mathematics, theology, and
horticulture, which were then very popular. It was also a
thriving metropolis where many business deals were trans-
acted. Its forged iron, silks, and damascened leathers were
renowned throughout the Orient and the Occident. Furthermore, the extraordinary fertility of Andalusia stimulated
considerable economic activity. The Mediterranean coast
swarmed with fishermen and sailors; merchants and middle-
men of all kinds provided the artisans of Cordova with the
raw materials they needed. Glassware, rugs, bound books,
enamel, sculptured ivory—all these were exported to the
West and sold at high prices. In addition, Cordova's exchequer, swelled by export duties and booty, was one of the
richest in all Islam.

When Abd-er-Rahman settled at Cordova the first thing
he did was to build a mosque worthy of the caliphate. Arab
conquerors had already constructed a mosque inside St.
Vincent's, a church which had been erected on the ruins of a
Roman temple. It was customary to divide a place of worship into two parts, one reserved for Christians and the other
for Moslems. But Abd-er-Rahman wanted a temple that
would do honor to Allah. He paid the "barbarians"—a term
used by Arabs to denote Christians—a good price for their
section of the church, tore it down, and built in its place the
primitive edifice of the great Mosque of Cordova. This explains the appearance of arches with red and white voussoirs
in the "horseshoe" style that for a long time were believed to

have been imported from the Orient. Actually they were
Visigothic in origin, as were the decorative themes portray-
ing fruits and plants. For caliphal art was an extension of
Gothic art, which it enriched by its very flamboyance.

Every prince of the dynasty founded by Abd-er-Rahman
was eager to enhance the splendor of the mosque. Hisham I
built galleries where the women could pray and added a
basin for ablutions. Abd-er-Rahman II constructed a southern wing and enlarged the mihrab. Abd-er-Rahman III
erected a square minaret, topped by three gold and silver
apples and a large, vaulted arcade. Here, every Friday, the
muezzins summoned the people to prayer. Hakam III sent
to Byzantium for 320 quintals of mosaics with which to cover
the mosque and hired an expert to supervise the work. He
ordered a pulpit with nine steps, composed of 36,000 pieces
of precious wood held together by gold and silver nails. Finally, al-Mansur further expanded the mosque, and until the
sixteenth century, it remained as he had left it.

Entering the mosque for the first time, one had the impression of being inside a labyrinth of multicolored pilasters:
white-veined blue columns, yellow, red, red streaked with
white, gray and green. The edifice was divided into four
sections. One was reserved for the nobility and clergy, the
other three for the people. In a green and red marble-
columned chapel was placed a Koran inlaid with rubies and
pearls and stained with the blood of Osman, who had copied
it in his own hand. This was the *Zancarron*. Seen from the
side, the vaulted arcades and pillars gave the feeling of a
limitless jungle. Daylight entered the mosque through the
doors and cupolas, and this lent an air of mystery to the
whole. The faithful, walking silently in the dusk, seemed
like wonder-struck knights in a forest of marble, so immobile
were their faces and so measured their tread. Lamps were lit
at prayer time. There were 280 chandeliers and 8,000 oil
lamps! The largest chandelier held 1,500 lamps. Al-Mansur
introduced the use of wax. During the month of Ramadan
three quintals of wax and three quarters of a quintal of rav-
eled cotton were required for the manufacture of candles.
The largest of these, which was placed next to the imam,

weighed sixty-five pounds. The smell of wax mingled with
the odor of the cedar ceilings and the incense of amber and
aloe. On the night of the Ramadan alone, four ounces of am-
bergris and eight ounces of bitter aloes were consumed! But
one is struck less with the fabulous richness of the Mosque
of Cordova than with its mystical atmosphere. This was
doubtless due to the aspect of the interior. Man seemed alone
in a metaphysical forest, thrown back upon himself, separated from the imam by columns of jasper marble. Could
this be ascribed to the distant influence of Arius? A cold yet
salubrious wind blew through the sculptured vaults of the
mosque, more reminiscent of the Jews' rational philosophy
than of the mechanical prayers of Islam.

Such was the extraordinary temple whose minaret rose
above the banks of the Guadalquivir. What a strange destiny it had! Begun as a church, it ended as one. Under the
Romans and Visigoths, it was the cathedral of Cordova;
later it was placed under the protection of the martyr of
Saragossa, St. Vincent. Subsequently half of it was taken
over by Moslems for their rites, then all of it was made into
a mosque by Abd-er-Rahman. Completely torn down and rebuilt, this ancient Christian basilica became one of the most
beautiful temples of the Mohammedan world. Its proportions and architecture retained the general lines of the
Church of St. Vincent. The naves were extended and enlarged, the apse was replaced by a mihrab, and a minaret
supplanted the belfry. The pillars came from Christian Africa, the flagstones were cut by Byzantine workmen; the masons—former prisoners who had been captured in the north
—were Christians. The cost of this prodigious construction
was paid for in part by money given at ransom for Christian
princes. From Constantinople, Narbonne, Tarragona, and
Carthage, workers, artists, and raw materials poured into
Cordova. Later the Christians of the Reconquest also made
alterations on the mosque. Innovations—usually unfortunate
—only served to emphasize the hybrid nature of this sanctuary which was used successively by Christians and Is-
lams. There were too many arches and columns, too many
colors, too much open space. A place of worship should be

enclosed and bare. Thirty years after the Moors left Spain forever, the Catholic Church obtained permission from Charles V to erect a cathedral on the site of the mosque. The architect in charge was too clever to destroy it completely. He built the Christian church over one part of the Mohammedan temple. But this did not prevent Charles V from sighing at the sight of the mutilated remains: "What you have constructed could have been built anywhere; what you have destroyed was unique."

The fact remains that Christian hands dripped blood on the stones of the mosque, just as Moslems labored to install flagstones in the Catholic cathedral. Before the advent of Abd-er-Rahman I, Moslems and Christians worshipped side by side within these walls and their prayers were identical. Their combined orisons burst forth from vaults and portals and hung suspended like stationary dust over the battlements of the Alcazar and the ribbed cupolas. They blended at high noon with the sapphire-colored Cordovan sky.

"Louis XIV" at Cordova

While Abd-er-Rahman, a puritan and scrupulous follower of the Koran, disdained luxury, the same cannot be said of his successors. Abd-er-Rahman II, the grand monarch, aimed at creating in the Spanish capital a brilliant and stately court which would eclipse that of Baghdad.

In selecting Cordova as the city of the caliphs, the Moslems had chosen well. Seneca's birthplace and the ancient capital of Baetica, the Romans' Colonia Patricia, it had retained all its prestige in the eyes of the people. The emirs added to this prestige by extending the outskirts of the city to the sierras and by multiplying villas and mosques. These men of the desert had a passion for water: it flowed profusely through marble canals, among gardens of jasmine and carnations, and burst into pearly sprays in the cool shadows of courtyards.

Abd-er-Rahman's thrift, together with the savings accumulated by Hakam I, made Abd-er-Rahman II's fortune.

His annual income amounted to a million dinars, which made him one of the richest rulers of the Orient. Among the gifts bestowed upon this fortunate prince was the famous "dragon's necklace" that had belonged to Subaida, wife of Harun al-Rashid. From Baghdad and more remote places, he brought the scholars and poets he wanted in his entourage, to say nothing of lovely girls, on whom he doted, provided they came from good families and were virgins. His many wives gave him twenty-four children, an almost equal number of boys and girls. A great builder, the founder of the city of Murcia, an excellent financier and promoter of the arts and sciences, Abd-er-Rahman II lent considerable impetus to commerce and industry. His reign gave Andalusia a brilliance comparable to that of Renaissance Italy, so exceptional was the quality of its science, entertainment, and art.

The tenth century witnessed the apogee of the Cordovan caliphate. It was Arab Spain's "century of Louis XIV." Abd-er-Rahman III was the Louis XIV of his epoch. Twenty-two years old when he mounted the throne, he was blond and blue-eyed, as were most of the Ommiads. From the very beginning of his reign, although he had no desire to do so, he was obliged to wage war against both dissident Moslems and Christian princes. So adroit was he that the agreements he made with both groups benefited him in the end. When co-operation became impossible, he resorted to force.

Among the Spanish population, composed in large part of descendants of Romans and Visigoths, many had readily become converted to Islam, although they did not necessarily accept Ommiad rule. They organized independent centers, which Abd-er-Rahman set out to weaken. The most obdurate of the feudal lords was Omar ibn-Hafsun, whose Visigothic great-grandfather had embraced the Moslem religion. Himself a Moslem, ibn-Hafsun exerted power over a large section of Andalusia. Deliberately, and by successive steps, Abd-er-Rahman succeeded in winning over the refractory cities. Meanwhile, ibn-Hafsun, for no apparent reason, returned to the religion of his father and became a Christian. Thereupon he died, and the Moslems could wreak vengeance only upon his remains. His "impure bones" were exhumed and nailed to stakes facing the Alcazar of Cordova. None of this was to the taste of Abd-er-Rahman, whose lukewarm attitude toward religion was taken for commendable tolerance. But by allowing apostasy to be punished so fiercely he demonstrated his power. There are times when it is necessary to overcome one's aversions.

Strife among the Christians played into the hands of the emir of Cordova. King Sancho of Castile, having failed to get the better of his rival, Ordoño, asked his old grandmother to request Abd-er-Rahman's help. In exchange for the return of ten fortresses, the emir hastened to the rescue and restored Sancho to his throne.

Friend and protector of both Moslems and Christians, and now without enemies in either camp, Abd-er-Rahman turned his gaze toward the Maghreb. He seized Melilla and Ceuta in order to provide himself with excellent strategic bases, as well as to protect his kingdom from the contamination of a religious movement organized by the Fatima sect. Fatima was the daughter of Mohammed. She represented for traditional Mohammedanism what the Reformation later represented for Roman Catholicism. This revolutionary movement endangered the unity of Ommiad rule; at the frontiers of Morocco the garrisons of Abd-er-Rahman held it in check.

The Setting for a Thousand and One Nights

His work done, Abd-er-Rahman III, seventh of the Ommiad line, was free to dream. In other words, he reviewed his life. Before he had assumed power, Andalusia resembled a coat that was torn. With his own hands he had mended the rich mantle which presently adorned Islam. How cruel were the points of the thousand swords that speared Badajoz and Seville! Not content with bending all of southern Spain to the will of the Prophet, he waged war as far as Toledo and even beyond it, now that his flotilla cruised the waters of Moroccan ports. All Moslem Spain was his, and the rest of it as well—the Spain of the Christians. For he made peace with the kings of Galicia, Leon, and Aragon. He crowned his military accomplishments with a diplomatic masterpiece, an alliance with Byzantium. For a long time, and over the head of the Baghdad caliphate, Abd-er-Rahman dealt with the powerful Macedonian dynasty as an equal.

But the Ommiad was not merely dreaming about himself. At the twilight of a full life it was his accomplishments rather than his battles that he liked to remember. A few miles from Cordova he had built a palace which soon became a veritable metropolis: Medinat-ez-Zahra, "city of the flower." Ten thousand laborers worked there for twenty-five years. Six thousand blocks of stone were cut and polished each day. There were 4,000 columns of marble and onyx which had been brought from Rome, Carthage, and Byzantium, and even from the kingdom of the Franks, as well as 1,500 doors coated with polished brass. The Hall of the Caliphs contained sixteen doors, eight on each side. They were set in ebony and ivory arches resting on pillars of transparent crystal. In the center of the room a basin of mercury splattered a porphyry conch with quicksilver. Baths for the court and the people, a zoological park, and vast outbuildings made Medinat-ez-Zahra the most luxurious residence in the world. Approximately 25,000 people lived there— 13,000 male servants, 6,000 female, and 3,000 pages and eunuchs. Seven tons of meat per day were required to feed them. During this same era, the palace of Lothaire, the next-to-last Carolingian king of France, was a wooden "villa" and Beauvais boasted but fifty-three fireplaces.

Abd-er-Rahman preferred Medinat-ez-Zahra to the Alcazar at Cordova, for the capital, with its million inhabitants, was noisy. And so he decided to move his court to Medinat-ez-Zahra. On cool evenings, the caliph would converse with friends in Latin or enjoy the sallies of his blind jester as he sipped a cup of mint-flavored tea. Sometimes very young dancing girls, their legs swathed in transparent chiffon pantaloons, would whirl about, waving scarves to the rhythm of tambourines and flutes.

It was also here that Abd-er-Rahman granted audiences to ambassadors. One day when he particularly wanted to impress some Christian plenipotentiaries, he had matting

spread from the gates of Cordova to the portals of
Medinat-ez-Zahra. A double row of soldiers lined each side
of the way, the tips of their unsheathed swords forming a
canopy of steel over the heads of the intimidated ambassadors, who walked beneath this shining arch. When they
came to the entrance hall they saw a long brocaded rug and,
seated on both sides, richly gowned lords. The Christians
bowed low to each of the noblemen, thinking he was the
emir. They were soon apprised of their error. Finally they
arrived at a courtyard where the ground was strewn with
sand; in the center, his head bowed, sat Abd-er-Rahman. A
Koran, a sword, and a burning fire were in front of him. As
the ambassadors knelt, the monarch raised his head and
said: "Allah has commanded us to request that you yield to
Him," and he pointed to the Koran. "Should you refuse, we
will use force," and he indicated the sword. "If we should
kill you, you will go there," and he held his hand to the fire.
Overcome with terror, the envoys agreed to the conditions
imposed by the caliph and went away without a word.

Thus, depending upon whether he wanted to dazzle or
terrify, the caliph could be either magnificent or unpretenti-
ous. Similarly, if he wanted to cajole or convince, he resorted
either to compliments or to parables. Sometimes, too, he obtained a good deal by offering gifts. Presents cost him little
because he received so many himself. Noble though he was
in many ways, Abd-er-Rahman was not above stooping to
bribery. For a long time his friend Ahmed ibn-Suhaid
longed for the position of vizier. But he was not the sole
candidate. To further his cause he sent the caliph gifts.
Merely to enumerate them is enough to cause one to dream:
500,000 miskals of gold coins, plus 400 pounds of crude
gold, or a total of about 5,000 pounds of gold; 200 bags of
silver ingots, precious woods for incense burners, musk
and camphor; thirty lengths of brocaded silks, five ceremonial tunics, ten fur-lined wraps, seven of which were made
of white fox, six silk robes from Iraq; forty-eight items of
apparel and a hundred pieces of night clothing; a hundred
skins of marten and mink, six ceremonial tents, forty-eight

silk and gold trappings, 4,000 pounds of spun silk; thirty
wool rugs, a hundred prayer rugs, fifteen silk rugs; a hundred pieces of armor for battledress, 1,000 shields, and 100,-
000 arrows; a hundred horses, fifteen of which were Arabian
steeds and five harnessed with brocaded saddles; five mules,
sixty slaves, a large quantity of stone blocks and wood for
construction. It is hardly surprising that this generous donor
was appointed vizier, with an annual income of 80,000
dinars!

Thus, Abd-er-Rahman was fabulously rich. And he knew
how to spend his wealth. This lover of science and beauty
wanted to expose his people to culture and art. From India,
Persia, and Asia Minor, at great expense, he imported not
only books but scholars, poets, and artists. And Andalusians learned to set a table, to enjoy delicate foods, beginning
with hors-d'oeuvres and ending with dessert, to brush their
teeth—in short, they were taught the comforts and refine-
ments of living. Because of his amicable relations with Byzantium, the emir was able to acquaint Spaniards with the
writings of Dioscorides, Plato, and Aristotle. Simultaneously, Jewish thought crept in, contributing precious knowledge about the exact sciences. Astronomy, mathematics,
botany, and medicine opened new horizons to Spanish minds
which until then had been confined by the imperatives of
theology. On the whole, Abd-er-Rahman's greatest service to
Spain was to encourage and promote the introduction of the
teachings of Greece and Alexandria. Like those before and
after him, the emir of Cordova adapted ideas. He was no innovator. Yet something, he felt, was still lacking to complete his fame. During a hot evening at Medinat-ez-Zahra, an
ambition arose and revolved like smoke beneath the ceilings
of cedar, enveloping the marble columns, dimming the alabaster panels and onyx interlacings. In the morning it was
dissipated while, on the highest branch of a tamarind tree, a
nightingale sang. But in the evening it came once again to
visit the pensive emir. For a long time he spurned the temptation. But, after all, why not? Was he not the supreme
head of the Moslem Occident? And so he assumed the title

of Commander of the Faithful—Emir al-Moumenin—which
no other prince of the dynasty had dared to do. Thus he officially confirmed the rupture with the Abbassides of Baghdad. And to lend further significance to his gesture, he
adopted a religious surname: al-Nasser in dine Allah, "he
who fights for Allah." In this way he avenged a less fortunate ancestor, Abd-er-Rahman, who, two centuries earlier,
had been defeated at Poitiers by a Frankish chief.

In 961, Hakam II succeeded his father, Abd-er-Rahman III. The moment the caliph breathed his last,
Hakam mounted the throne at Medinat-ez-Zahra. Palace
dignitaries were the first to pay him homage. Then his eight
brothers swore allegiance, and the doors of the Hall of the
Caliphs were thrown open. On each side of the gallery where
Hakam was seated, high court officials waited, swords
girded over the white tunics they wore as sign of mourning.
A short distance away, on the terrace, bodyguards were stationed; slaves clad in coats of mail, they carried swords inlaid with stones. Below the portals of the vestibule stood the
leaders of the Slavonic eunuchs, dressed in white, swords
in hand. Further back were the eunuchs themselves, arrayed
according to rank. The rear was brought up by the Slavonic
archers, quivers strung across their shoulders. Behind the
eunuchs were long motionless lines of slaves in multicolored
clothing. A row of armored foot soldiers wearing white
mantlets and shining helmets stretched from the end of the
vestibule to the terrace where the bodyguards stood. Gate-
keepers and their assistants guarded the entrance to the
palace. Finally, mounted mercenaries and archers, massed as
far as the eye could see, crowded the road between Medinat-
ez-Zahra and Cordova.

Dawn came. Birds began to sing noisily. But a tremendous rustling drowned out their song. All the people of Cordova were paying homage to their new master. For two days
and two nights nothing could be heard save the muffled
glide of hundreds of thousands of bare feet along the Cordovan road.

2

Convulsions of Reconquest

WHAT WAS the composition of the so-called Arab-Spanish population during the tenth century? When they first settled in Spain, the Arabs pushed far beyond Cordova and Toledo, encountering Charles Martel at Poitiers and the Duke of Aquitania at Toulouse, and harassed Lyon and Narbonne for many years. But in fact the zone they occupied ended at the Toledo-Saragossa-Barcelona line. Although their incursions into the mountains of the north and northeast were occasionally successful, they never managed to hold their positions. Nor were they able to prevent the establishment of the states of Asturias, Galicia, Leon, Old Castile, Navarre, Aragon, and Catalonia. The Spanish territory occupied by the Moslems possessed the weakest of garrisons, consisting of a handful of racially pure Arabs— that is to say, descendants of the Prophet's soldiers, who came originally from Mecca, Medina, or southern Arabia. As the years went by, the number of such Arabs dwindled.

Syrians had joined the first Arab contingents. They were not racially pure, for although Damascus, the seat of the caliphate for a very long time, had remained entirely Arabian, the rest of Syria became mixed as a consequence of continuous Egyptian, Persian, and Greek invasions. The Syrian leaders were feudal lords who owed military service to the caliph. As soon as an order was given, they amassed troops, called *gunds*, and led them into battle. These mercenaries, who were excellent soldiers, settled in Spain. The Caliph of Cordova had great respect for their discipline and military prowess.

The Berbers, on the other hand, showed a marked tendency to withdraw from mixed groups and to cling together. They attempted to escape the authority of the caliph. While the Arabs settled in Seville, Cordova, and Toledo, the Berbers preferred to live in the southern mountains, at Ronda and Granada.

Finally, there were the Slavs. These auxiliary troops, whom the Arabs had never counted on, were formerly prisoners the Germanic armies had brought back from campaigns in the Balkans. They included individuals of uncertain nationality who returned with the Arabs from raids along the Italian coast. The Slavs, for the most part, were slaves. Occasionally, however, some broke away and proclaimed their independence. They set up small colonies in eastern Spain, at Valencia, and in the Balearic Islands.

Because of intermingling with the Romans and Visigoths, Arabs, Berbers, Slavs constituted a people incorrectly called Moors, so that when we speak of "Moorish," "Arab," or "Saracen" Spain we are merely making use of a convenient terminology. Actually, Spain was invaded, not brutally, but in successive waves, by Berbers, Syrians, and Balkan mercenaries led by Arabs. The invaders settled in Spain and became its founders. As the centuries went by, the large number of intermarriages and illicit unions made it increasingly difficult to ascertain what proportion of the so-called Arab population was of pure Arab, or Semitic, blood. Confusion was compounded by the fact that many Spaniards, even bishops, had Arab names. Although the distinction between Christians and Moslems is arbitrary, it is nonetheless a better criterion than race in identifying Spaniards and Arabs. Religious problems did not in fact become acute until the twelfth century, when both the Almohad sect and the Cluniac Movement sprang up. Mohammedanism and Christianity alike begot the black fruit of intransigence. But in the days of the caliphate of Cordova, and even later, politics were independent of religion, and Christian troops willingly served Arab princes so long as this brought them glory and profit. Conversely, Arab armies sometimes came to the rescue of Christian lords when they fought among themselves.

Although the religious problem had not as yet been raised, and did not even trouble the Moslem regime, it nonetheless disturbed the consciences of many. Most of the early inhabitants of Arabic Spain had remained Christian. Any Christian who had kept his faith while residing in Islamic territory was called a "Mozarab." Why? *Mezo-Arab:* half-Arab? *Most-Arab:* having become Arab? *Mozo-Arab:* young Arab? Whatever the etymology of the term, Mozarabs showed great courage in practicing the religion of Christ. To be sure, the Arabs treated them with surprising liberality. Evidence of this can be found in the treaties concluded between Christians and Moslems. The Moslems never hindered the practice of the Christian religion so long as it was carried on with discretion. Naturally, the Mozarabs had to be careful not to wound the religious sensibilities of the Arabs. They also had to accept without rancor the contempt that Believers displayed toward Infidels. Moreover, there were certain restrictions on the practice of Catholicism. Christians could live on good terms with Moslems provided they observed these restrictions, paid their taxes, and made no ostentatious display of their religion. Many, too, out of indolence or self-interest, or merely because they were so inclined, became "Arabianized" and gradually lost their taste for and knowledge of Latin—the mainstay and medium of Christianity. There even existed a kind of snobbery among young Christian intellectuals who, while clinging to the faith of their fathers, professed a keen admiration for Arabian literature. A pious and learned ecclesiastic of the ninth century lamented: "Oh, what a pity! Christians fail to observe their religion and forget their Latin language!" It was quite true that Arab expansion in Andalusia and the emergence of a brilliant Hispano-Arab literature did nothing to further Catholic orthodoxy.

But soon enough, the tepid, for whom religion was but a habit, or those intrigued by novelty, were confronted by pious men who were drawn to martyrdom. One such was Eulogius, who met a violent end. The first to wage inexorable war against Mohammedanism, he scored the sensuous tendencies of Islam, the immorality concealed in the ethical teachings of the Koran, the exaltation of pleasure. He also rebelled against the caliphs' abuse of power. An ardent polemicist and a clever scholar, his sermons and writings infuriated the Moslems but stirred the Mozarabian masses, who had been seduced by the easy solutions offered by Mohammedanism. Hunted by the *mustasafs*, he fled from village to village, vigorously pressing his attack by clandestine means. The people of Toledo chose him as their archbishop, but he never took possession of his see. The authorities eventually caught him and dragged him before the cadi. He was brutally whipped, then beheaded.

One day, in a street of Cordova, some Moslems approached Prefectus, the parish priest of St. Acislus. "What do you think of Mohammed?" they asked him. The priest quoted from the Gospel: "False prophets will arise and work wonders." He was seized, charged with blasphemy, and brought before the tribunal. Condemned to death, he was executed on the day of Bairam before a large crowd.

The example set by such religious "hotheads" infected the Christian population of Cordova. Fanatics entered the mosques and committed unforgivable affronts. They left no stone unturned in their efforts to court the bitter pleasures of torture. There is nothing more contagious than suicide, particularly when it is accompanied by religious hysteria. The bishops were well aware of the seriousness of the situation. Acting in concert with the Moslem authorities, they wisely condemned these extreme forms of behavior. Wisely, because these demonstrations only harmed the Christian cause. The long line of priests and laymen who waited at the cadi's door to insult him as he emerged, the hotheads who seemed to invite execution as if it were a boon, did not aid the Mozarabian cause. As for the Moslems, they deeply resented these insults, which, of course, did not win universal approval. But they also recalled the screaming mob that had carried the severed head of Prefectus through the streets of Cordova. The caliph did not want any more disturbances of that kind.

The story of lovely Flora is a moving one. The daughter of a Christian mother and a Moslem father of Spanish origin, she was secretly reared as a Christian. Her brother, a recent convert to Mohammedanism, denounced her to the cadi. But Flora ran away and sought shelter in a Christian home, where she made the acquaintance of a nun named María. The two girls became friends and together decided to seek martyrdom. Barely twenty, they were both consumed with a longing to die. They went to the cadi and confessed. Similarly, five hundred years earlier, the child Eulalia had defied Caesar's representative. Like the Roman magistrate, the judge of Cordova tried to reason with the two foolish girls, gently urging them to repudiate their statements. But they laughed in his face. Did he take them for children? Exasperated by their stubbornness, the cadi resorted to threats. Did they want to end their days in a harem? The expression on their faces changed. They looked at each other. Should they yield? At this moment Eulogius intervened. He knew Flora, having met her several months after her first experience of torture, and he loved her with a pure love. It was he who had healed her aching sores. "Gently I placed my hands on your wounds. I wanted to heal them with my lips, but I did not dare." Repressing his tender feelings, Eulogius now spoke sharply to Flora: "Better to die than to betray one's God!" The poor man had no difficulty persuading her. Yes, she would choose death, and she would take her friend with her. "I adored her," Eulogius admitted later. But was not his love of God greater, since it inspired his heroic resolve? Of course, when he urged martyrdom on Flora, the soldier-priest knew that he too would be condemned to die. She would precede him to that ineffable kingdom where their disembodied souls would know perfect union.

One sad morning in November, at a place known as "Campo de la Verdad," two young girls mounted the scaffold. The ashen shadows of autumn, streaked here and there with lavender, hovered over the riverbank. . . .

Prelude to Reconquest

The population of Arab Spain was based ethnically on Ibero-Roman-Visigothic strains, fused with Arab, Berber, and even Balkan elements. This mixture, to which must be added the Moslem and Mozarabian religions, was found in Andalusia and along the Mediterranean coast. The basin of the Ebro had remained relatively independent. The center and south of the *meseta* inclined toward Mozarabianism. Old Castile, Leon, and Asturias remained Iberian and Christian. Only the Pyrenees represented a neutral zone of sorts, or rather a retreat where future *guerrilleros* would seek refuge—people who refused to yield to the Arabs, who could not bring themselves to accept either their rule or their religion. Immaterial and mobile, yet as real and definite as the ramparts of a fortress, a spiritual wall divided Spain into two zones: Latin-Christian and Arab-Moslem.

The duel between Christian and Moslems, at first limited to a few skirmishes, soon grew more formidable. Resolve stiffened in both camps, and positions were established. In the year 1000 a new Spain emerged.

It is not my intention to follow the entanglements of the various rulers or the involved political alliances and ruptures of this period. Nor shall we go into the religious quarrels of the northern princes and their intrigues. What interests us is the development of the *"reconquista"* in its totality, the gradual progress of this crusade from the Pyrenees to Gibraltar.

The eleventh century had begun. Let us look at a map of Spain. Far better than a list of dates or battles is a geographical view of the peninsula at the dawn of the second millennium. It will help us to see how much Christian warfare had accomplished during the last three hundred years, and how much still remained to be done.

A chain of Catholic states, both independent and federated, stretched from the northwest to the northeast and, little by little, began to move toward the center.

The kingdom of Asturias, created by Pelayo, had grown and expanded. With Leon as its capital, it extended as far as the Douro. Galicia and Asturias, for a while separate, were now united. Castile, originally part of the kingdom of Asturias, withdrew to become a county and subsequently a state. Navarre, which included the Pyrenean counties, spread to the upper Ebro. Aragon, long a province of Navarre, achieved the rank of kingdom through the right of succession, then absorbed the county of Pallás, an important area in the central Pyrenees.

Finally, Catalonia merits special mention because of the prominent role it played very early in the Reconquest. This old Carolingian region was unified during the ninth and tenth centuries. Little by little, the eastern Pyrenees were brought together under the rule of the Count of Barcelona, himself a vassal of the King of France. Political and ideological ties between Catalonia and the Frankish kings persisted until the thirteenth century. Although the Catalonians received no military assistance from the Capetians, they were aware that they constituted the outpost of Christian France. Forceful personalities emerged. Joffre le Poilu extended Christian rule to the Ebro. Many monasteries were constructed. This "epidemic of masonry," so often promoted by the Catholic Church, spread further and further to the south. It was as if the Christians finally realized that they, too, must build.

Thus, Leon, Castile, Navarre, Aragon, and Catalonia mounted a vigilant guard around the basin of the Ebro—a mobile guard that became an encircling flank. But five hundred years were to elapse before the Christian offensive achieved its ultimate objective—half of a millennium to hold the line on the Douro, to advance to the Tagus, and to conquer western Andalusia.

While the princes of the north were consolidating their positions, the caliphate of Cordova gradually grew weaker. One by one the provinces detached themselves from the central authorities. Viziers and walis demanded independence. In 1031 the caliphate was abolished. No longer did an Arab monarchy exist in Spain; all that remained was a federation of small states, the *taifas*. Cordova itself became a republic. Petty Arab and Berber rulers divided Spanish Islam. Twenty-three *taifas* varying in size, the heirs of the Moslem empire, confronted the Christian principalities of the north.

Spain had become a mosaic: in the south, tiny Moslem kingdoms, controlled by Moslem lords; in the north, agglomerations the size of cantons, under the sway of a noble and evolving into a single sovereign entity. As Mohammedan culture faded and Arab strength declined, Christians took heart and pushed forward. In Cordova people played the flute and recited poetry; in the mountains of the north soldiers drilled. The imaginary frontier separating Moslems from Christians slowly shifted southward. Of course the process was gradual, for the Christians were cautious and the Moslems resisted stubbornly. Then, too, there was no hatred between north and south, nor would there ever be, but simply a curious struggle, interrupted by unexpected truces—a savage game of intermittent, anonymous massacres and joyous armistices.

The crumbling of the former caliphate of Cordova naturally furthered the Christian cause. Ferdinand I, "the Great," the first king of a united Castile and Leon, became the leader of the Reconquest. Exploiting Arab disunity, he laid siege to Toledo, Saragossa, and Badajoz, and exacted tribute from their Moorish rulers. The voluptuous Motadid, patron of poets and sovereign of Seville, crossed to Ferdinand's camp and begged his mercy. Motadid was no coward. Cruel and combative, he kept the severed heads of his enemies in a casket and carefully preserved the name of each victim by attaching a label to the ear. Those he adjudged unworthy of identification he interred in his courtyard and marked the place with planted flowers. Before leaving for the seraglio, where eight hundred courtesans awaited him, he would inhale the fragrance of these blooms. Such was Motadid, son of Aboul Kasim, of the Yemenite family, who now knelt at the feet of the Christian king.

Ferdinand conquered northern Portugal and expelled the Moslems. Finally he launched a large-scale operation against Valencia. But en route he fell ill and had to retrace his steps. He celebrated Christmas in the basilica of Leon; the following day he died "in an aura of sanctity," as the chroniclers put it.

Before his death in 1065, he divided his territories among his three sons. Sancho received Castile and the tributary of Saragossa; García, Galicia and the tributary of Seville; Alfonso, Leon and the tributary of Toledo. Alfonso was his father's successor both politically and spiritually, becoming "Emperor of the two religions."

The reign of Alfonso VI began with a fratricidal struggle between him and Sancho. Defeated, he took refuge with the ruler of Toledo, Mamoun. His stay with the Moslems and his experiences at the court of Toledo proved profitable. It gave him insight into the mentality and psychology of his future adversaries. Upon the death of Sancho, he seized Castile. Pressing his luck, he pretended to support Mamoun's successor, al-Cadir, in the latter's quarrel with the ruler of Badajoz. The Moor rewarded him with the cession of Toledo. The Christian frontier was thus advanced from the Douro to the Tagus. But Alfonso was not satisfied with the title of *Toleti Imperii rex et magnificus triumphator*, nor with the occupation of the first Christian metropolis, the ancient capital of the Visigothic sovereigns. He decided to continue his march southward. Feigning a desire to protect al-Cadir, now ruler of Valencia, from his turbulent neighbors, he besieged Saragossa. Finally he crossed the Guadalquivir, entered Seville, and arrived at the beach of Tarifa, where the Arabs had made their first landings. When he came to the Pillars of Hercules, Alfonso uttered a cry of joy: "At last I have reached the farthest point in Spain!" Pressing spurs to his horse, he pushed into the sea and there faced Africa.

The Cid Campeador, the Man with Two Swords

The career of the Cid is both moving and varied. It reflects the many contradictions of this rugged hero, whose image has often been distorted and falsified by legend.

Bivar is a village in Old Castile, near Burgos. It lies in a barren and gloomy plain, alternately torrid and freezing, streaked here and there with a few thin rivulets of water, and overhung by the purple shadows of the distant Sierras. A bitter wind blows, benefiting only the windmills. Here Rodrigo, son of Díaz, was born. The family was of noble blood, and of Gothic origin, as his name, "Roderic," suggests. The word *Cid* means "lord," from the Arab word *sidi*. As for the sobriquet Campeador, it derives from the Teutonic *champh*, which is also the root word for "champion"—that is to say, the knight who has been chosen for special combat in a duel between rival armies. Thus, no sooner did Rodrigo appear than he became involved in the contradictions associated with his Germanic and Arabic names.

Burgos. . . . The palace of the Infante Don Sancho, son of Ferdinand the Great. Orphaned at a very early age, the Cid was raised at court, where he received the kind of elementary education given to royal princes: a little grammar, some mathematics and law, Latin, and, above all, the art of war. There was no need to teach him Arabic because he had learned it as well as Spanish when he was a child. Arabic was the language he spoke during his entire lifetime.

Upon the death of his father, Sancho became King of Castile. Eager to enlarge his legacy, he made war on his cousins of Navarre and Aragon. The battle of Graus was Rodrigo's first chance to try his hand. For several hours the outcome remained uncertain. Suddenly, at one end of the plain a horseman clothed in black flung himself at the enemy. He unseated several men from Navarre with his sword thrusts, slashed at their golden helmets adorned with plumes, and with his dagger forged an opening among the ungirthed and galloping horses. The example set by this bareheaded young man, who did not even carry a shield, excited the soldiers. The battle resumed, more terrible than ever. In vain did the priests brandish their crucifixes, the Castilians invoking St. James and the priests of Navarre imploring St. Luke. No mercy was shown, no quarter given. But the battle ended without victors or vanquished, and neither side profited by it. However, although he did not achieve complete victory for Sancho, Rodrigo won in this battle the title "Campeador." And here we encounter another inconsistency: his first accomplishment served the cause of a fratricidal war.

Zamora. . . . Sancho was assassinated and a successor had to be chosen. Before the gate of St. Martin at Burgos, the Campeador, in mourning for his king, asked Alfonso VI to swear that he was not his brother's murderer. "I swear it by the Holy Virgin," Alfonso said gravely, but there was an angry look in his eye. Alfonso was proclaimed King of Castile.

The new sovereign deeply resented the Cid's suspicion, but refrained from showing his feelings. He merely deprived Rodrigo of his functions as *alférez* and gradually removed him from public affairs. On the other hand, he gave his cousin Ximena to the Cid in marriage. The young couple had known each other for some time. To avenge his father for the insult that Count Gómez de Gormaz, Ximena's father, had inflicted on him, Rodrigo had taken down the ancient sword of Mudarra, the Catalan, and had used it to slay the offender. From then on Ximena had plagued the king with her complaints, not so much because of her father's death, for the duel had been fair, but because of Rodrigo's taunts. "Every day he comes with a bird in his hand and feeds it at the expense of my pigeons, just to annoy me. My pigeons come to me dying, and their blood splatters my apron. I have told Ruy Díaz about this but he answers me with threats." Their story ended in marriage.

Sent to Seville to collect the annual tribute from Motamid, Rodrigo quarreled with Count Ordoñez, a friend of Alfonso's. Subsequently he led a punitive expedition against the Moorish sovereign of Toledo, an ally of the King of Castile. His success impressed the Arabs so deeply that from then on they never called him anything except the Cid. But Alfonso was not at all pleased with the initiative displayed by this turbulent young man. He exiled the Cid to the manor house in Bivar.

What? Retire already, when he had just begun to live his life? We can almost hear the indignant laughter. Rodrigo cleaned his best sword—Tizona—and considered where to offer his services. The Count of Barcelona was recruiting men, but his terms did not suit the Cid. What about the emir of Saragossa, Moktadir?

Saragossa was the ancient Roman city of Caesarea Augusta, founded upon the ruins of the Iberians' Salduba. It had been given the Arab name of Sarakusta. The city, entirely Moslem, flourished. Its avenues were wide and its houses spacious. It was called "the white city," because its walls had been whitewashed. The climate was particularly salubrious; wheat could be stored here for one hundred years, grapes for six years. Scorpions and snakes died as soon as they neared the town. At one end of the ramparts stood Moktadir's two palaces: the palace of joy, Ksar es-Sorur, and the palace of gold, Medjeless ad-Dhabab. Moktadir received the Cid and his army with open arms. These Christian reinforcements would enable him to win the interminable war he had been waging against his brother Modhafar, king of Lérida. To hasten matters, he had his brother assassinated, but the crime availed him little; he himself died shortly thereafter.

What matter his master, so long as the Cid waged war! He fought for Mutamin, and he fought for Mostain. His method of combat was that of an eagle who swoops down on its prey. The soldiers he defeated were sometimes Christians, sometimes Moslems. He even captured Ramón Berenguer, the Count of Barcelona, whose offers he had refused and who, at that time, was allied with the Moslem king of Lérida. The emirs of Saragossa held the Cid's talents in high esteem, but his enemies thought otherwise. "Mostain unleashed a Galician dog called Rodrigo, surnamed the Campeador. He was the scourge of the country. He waged many battles against the petty Arab kings of the peninsula and caused them all kinds of trouble. . . . He became very powerful. There was no country in Spain that he failed to plunder."

One city remained to be conquered: Valencia. Situated on the right bank of the Guadalquivir, two miles from the sea, it was the most prosperous metropolis of Moslem Spain. What a fine prey for the Cid! He was tired of serving the King of Saragossa and wanted to work for himself. Although by now his fame was well established, he was not satisfied. He desired even more glory, of course, but more than anything else he wanted money. His soldiers were fierce but also expensive. And so he attacked those seigniories that he knew to be wealthy. For the sake of a little gold he would raze entire cities. The Christian Count Ramón Berenguer wrote him: "We know that mountains, sparrow hawks, eagles—in short, almost all the birds—are your gods, and that you have more faith in their omens than in the help of the Almighty. God will avenge the churches you have desecrated and destroyed." For Rodrigo showed remarkable impartiality in his forays. Church or mosque, Arab palace or presbytery, all doors were broken down with equal violence and skill.

The only way of avoiding mistreatment by the Cid was to place oneself under his protection, in exchange, of course, for a certain honorarium. Tortosa, Segorbe, Valencia—almost all the cities of Catalonia accepted the Cid's assistance, his law, and his tariffs. Good years or bad, it cost them between 3,000 and 12,000 gold dinars, depending upon the size and importance of the city. Although he possessed no land of his own, Rodrigo's annual income reached princely proportions. Still he was not satisfied. He also wanted to reign; eventually he was offered an opportunity.

Cadir, the king of Valencia, whom the Cid protected, was slain by a palace official, ibn-Djahhaf. Rodrigo felt he had a

right to intervene, and he headed for Valencia. The terrified
Djahhaf was willing to negotiate with the formidable hero.
While discussions dragged on, the outskirts of Valencia
were besieged by Rodrigo's troops. "The Valencians were
certain they would die. They seemed like drunkards, no
longer understanding what was being said to them. Their
faces grew black, as if covered with pitch, and they lost
their memories completely, as if they had fallen into the
waves of the ocean." Djahhaf tried to hold his own against
his fearsome adversary. He was quite prepared to sign a
treaty provided that he kept the crown he had wrested by
violence from Cadir. Finally Rodrigo lost patience. In 1094
he attacked Valencia.

Twenty months elapsed before the city yielded. So much
resistance exasperated the Cid. "Rodrigo desired possession
of Valencia more passionately than ever. He clung to the
city the way a creditor clings to his debtor. He loved it as a
lover cherishes the place where he has tasted the pleasures
of passion." He cut off supplies to the city, killed its defenders, and wrought all kinds of havoc. "How many were the
magnificent places, unequaled in beauty even by the sun and
the moon, that one could no longer hope to visit, which this
tyrant captured and desecrated! How many charming girls
(when they washed their faces with milk the blood sprang
to their cheeks; the sun and the moon envied them their
beauty and coral and pearls were jealous of their teeth and
lips) felt the point of his lances or were crushed beneath the
feet of his insolent mercenaries!" Occasionally, Valencians
attempted a counterattack. Rodrigo had them seized and
burned live at the foot of the ramparts, in the presence of
their families; or they were thrown to the hounds.

Finally, ibn-Djahhaf capitulated, and Rodrigo took possession of the city. In spite of his promise to spare his life, the
Cid ordered ibn-Djahhaf put to death. Nor was the execution a merciful one. A hole was dug and the Moslem was
buried alive up to his armpits. Flaming torches were put
to him. The executioner leaned over the slowly dying man,
in the hope of detecting a nod of the head or a glance of the

eye that might indicate where treasure lay hidden. For it appeared that the usurper had in his possession, among other things, the famous necklace that had belonged to the sultana, Subaida. When the flames had done their work, the skull of the victim was covered with ashes.

Valencia no longer belonged to Islam, but to the Cid. "Swords have been rampant in thy court, Oh palace! Poverty and fire have destroyed thy beauties. For the present we gaze at thee, we meditate at length and we weep. . . ." Meanwhile, Rodrigo's first gesture was to send Alfonso one hundred horses fitted with lavish trappings, one hundred Moorish slaves, and the keys to the castles he had captured. In this way he showed his desire to make peace with a sovereign he still acknowledged. He converted the great mosque into a cathedral and put Bishop Don Hierónymo in charge—"a man of great prudence and knowledge." His own establishment was in the Alcazar, where Ximena and his two daughters soon joined him. Was the Cid settling down and returning to the Christian faith? In any case, his first words upon entering Valencia left no room for doubt about one thing: "There shall be no master here save myself." This summary dismissal of his Arab overlords rang out like a challenge.

For a few years the man from Bivar ruled Valencia. He administered and legislated. And, after burning so many chapels, he now built them! He did his best to win the confidence of his Moslem subjects while seeking peace with Alfonso. This was a period of remission and spiritual reconquest. Occasionally he would take Tizona down from the wall, run his fingers along the edge of his valiant sword, and draw himself up to his full height. At such moments his family and servants trembled, expecting to see the Campeador re-emerge. Of course, the tiger was growing older. But the gray-bearded warrior did not neglect the defenses of his marvelous Valencian principality. As long as he lived the Cid held the Almoravides in awe, for had they not shoved Alfonso aside and stormed the gates of the city? To his dying breath, he remained the Campeador, but his piety surpassed his military ardor. He became the patron and

protector of the Church. Whence came the booty that included the golden chalice and the two brocaded rugs he
donated to the cathedral of Valencia? Rodrigo had forgotten his former forays. He prayed and asked forgiveness for
his sins: warriors often become devout late in life. When
Rodrigo died, Ximena took charge of his principality. But
not for long was the widow to remain in Valencia.

While the Cid lived, the Moslems did not attempt to capture Valencia. But now their chance had come. Their army
surrounded and besieged the city. Rodrigo's family was
forced to flee. But how could they escape capture? The Cid's
body was embalmed, clothed in full battle dress, and placed
securely on his horse, Babieca. His faithful sword, Tizona,
was put in his hand. Planks were used to support his shoulders, chest, chin, and neck. The gates of the ramparts were
flung wide open, and just as the Moslem army prepared to
plunge inside, it stopped, dumfounded. The Cid was not
dead! He rode at the head of his troops, his cheeks rosy, his
eyes wide open, his beard neatly trimmed; on his chest
hung a large red cross. He looked handsome and fierce.
Amid clouds of dust, soldiers, chariots, women, and children
moved northward, led by this cadaver, who, already growing stiff, was gently bowing his plumed head.

Despite the reinforcements Alfonso had dispatched, Ximena had no choice but to abandon Valencia. Thus it was
that she and her party went in the opposite direction, toward Castile. Ximena rode her palfrey, followed by the coffin studded with gold nails which contained the remains of
the hero, an escort of lords wearing black mantles and bearing escutcheons pointed downward, women covered with
bunting, and finally Babieca, stirrups dangling. When the
procession neared Burgos, the Cid was interred, close to the
altar of San Pedro de Cardeña. Surrounded by banners, the
tomb was in the form of a catafalque. The Campeador's
two swords, Tizona and Colada, glimmered in the mild
dusk, symbols of his twofold struggle and of his dual status
as a Mozarab—Christian and Arab. King Alfonso wept.
Two years later Ximena joined her husband under the mar-

ble mausoleum. The mortal remains of Babieca were buried in front of the gate of San Pedro de Cardeña. The Latin inscription on the tombstone, *Rodericus Didaci Campidoctor*, recalled not only his Gothic name but also his incautious statement: "One Rodrigo lost Spain and another will conquer it." Indeed, at that time, the new master of Valencia wrote to a friend: "It is we Moslems who are victorious. We entered Valencia after it was overcome with shame. The enemy set fire to a large part of the city, but its marvelous body remains. And its lofty landscape, which resembles fragrant musk and red gold, is unchanged; its gardens are filled with trees, its rivers with limpid waters. . . . Praise be God, Ruler of the Eternal Kingdom, for having purged it of pantheists." According to the Arabs, Christians who worshipped a trinity were pantheists.

What are we to think of this mercenary who carved out a kingdom for himself with his sword? And how can we explain his many contradictions? He defied his king yet helped him; he either won his enemies over or burned them alive; he was "terrible in war and gentle in peace," greedy and munificent, a Christian who fought in the service of the Moslems, at once loyal and filled with deceit. One can still see, hanging from the wall of one of the chapels in the Burgos cathedral, an iron chest which the Cid had filled with sand and scrap iron and given to a Jewish merchant as collateral for a loan of six hundred silver marks, saying that it contained all his china and silverware. The Jew had taken him at his word. Ibn-Djahhaf had also trusted the Cid, who promised to spare his life. Although the rascal was a liar, he remained faithful to Alfonso. Patient researchers have attempted to extract from Latin or Arab texts a true picture of the Cid, denuded of all fiction. But this proved a rash and frustrating undertaking. The Campeador, a captive of the poem *The Romances of the Cid*, will always remain in the nebulous no man's land between history and legend.

There is no doubt that he raided, pillaged, massacred, and had men hanged, or that he led hordes of Moors in attacks against the Spaniards. But such was the custom of the times. He has been reproached for his courteous and even amicable relations with the Moslems. But this, too, was quite natural, in view of the times. Rodrigo lived in an era when the Christian and Moslem civilizations were converging. Whereas the passage of time served to blur the memory of ancient Visigothic Spain, the Arabs were very real and always present. In any case, although Rodrigo did help the Arabs in war, he never ceased to be a good Christian. At the height of battle, he would appeal to God in his own naïve and primitive manner: "We render grace unto Thee, Lord our Father, who dwells on high. See what my wicked enemies have brought upon me!" Even when he fought against the Christians he never doubted that God was on his side. Nor did he neglect religious holidays. He observed Lent and practiced charity. Moreover, this restless warrior, who had visions of covering his escutcheon with the royal purple, this impecunious lordling fascinated by gold, whose fingers caressed the fabulous necklace of Harun al-Rashid's beloved wife, this "scorpion's tail," this upstart and lover of horses and war, was also the friend of the lowly and humble. Just before he died, he asked that his property be distributed among the poor, "my sponsors and intercessors with God."

As the Almoravides were threatening his very frontiers and as, little by little, the impact of his "resounding victories" was fading, the dying Cid dictated his last will: "I, Rodrigo of Bivar, named the brave Cid Campeador, victor over the Moorish nations, commend my soul to God. May He admit it to His Kingdom. And may my body, made of this earth, return to the earth. I want my body to be embalmed and oiled with the unguents sent to me by the Sultan of Persia. You must show me to King Bucar and all his partisans, seated on Babieca, with my standard and banners behind me. I command that Babieca be buried and interred. Let no dogs devour my horse, who so often ate the flesh of dogs. May my good warriors and lords, those who shared my board and bread, attend my funeral."

Philip II asked Rome to canonize the Cid, but the request was refused. Too much blood had stained the flaming sword. Besides, it would have been difficult to visualize a saintly halo around the head of the stubborn, leather-helmeted Cid. The Campeador was neither mystic nor ascetic, nor even, as one respectable tradition for long insisted, defender of Spanish Christianity against Islam. Yet in the popular imagination he remains the hero of Mozarab Spain, and the symbol of that curious epoch when one could befriend, assist, and admire the Moslems and still be a good Christian. For Spain was mighty in the days of the Moorish kings.

Almost in spite of himself, the Cid figured in the Reconquest. While he was defending Valencia against the Almoravides, Peter the Hermit was dashing across the deserts of Syria to conquer the Holy Places. The First Crusade ended just as the epic of the Cid drew to a close. The Campeador died in the Alcazar at the very moment that Godfrey of Bouillon was being crowned King of Jerusalem. Thus, in the same year, 1099, the Christian cause lost one champion and consecrated another. The death of the Campeador marked the passing of the eleventh century.

Crusade versus Holy War

A Spanish crusade, timid and sporadic at first, then increasingly formidable, was beginning to take shape. The rulers of the *taifas* were exasperated and worried by the exploits of the Cid, to say nothing of Alfonso's insolent ride to the beach of Tarifa. Like the dissident Visigoths, they too turned to Africa for help.

The Almoravides, founders of Marrakech, were of Berber origin. Masters of the powerful Moroccan empire, but still leading a primitive and rugged existence on the borders of the Sahara, these Lamtounas had been converted to Islam by a marabout. Inflamed by the preachings of this fakir, they mustered their strength, increased the size of their army, and chose a commander in chief, Yusuf ibn-Tashfin. Soon they ruled Africa from Senegal to Algiers. Led by their emir, this semi-barbaric martial horde crossed the Strait of Gibraltar and landed at Algeciras. In 1086, Alfonso VI, who was then besieging Saragossa, changed his plans and hurried to head off the Berbers. The two armies clashed along the banks of the Guadiana, on the plains of Zallaka.

A fearsome battle ensued. The Christian horsemen—some had come all the way from France and Italy—saw swarms of gesticulating warriors swoop down upon them, their lances held high, their faces covered with black veils. Drums beat a sinister tom-tom to the rhythm of their attack. Alfonso fled in full gallop toward Toledo, while the victorious Almoravides collected the severed heads of the enemy and piled them up into a pyramid. Facing this hideous altar, they recited the Prayer of the Faithful. Yusuf was proclaimed the Spanish emir of emirs. Actually, however, neither he nor his son concentrated exclusively on religious objectives. Rather, they attempted to destroy the power of the Moorish rulers—the very people who had requested their help. History is replete with such betrayals. From this time on, these Saharan ascetics, supplanting the Oriental princes, were to incorporate Moslem Spain into the Maghreb. For the time being, the Reconquest was stopped in its tracks.

Once again the Holy War became a war of annexation. Inspired by a mysticism that was all the more fervent because it was new to them, the forbidding envoys from the West, rigid observers of the Law, yearned to reform Spanish Islam. As the missionaries of Mohammed, they intended to realize the austere dream that had sustained them in the deserts of Senegal. But when the pious Almoravides came in contact with gentle Andalusia they were not proof against the temptation to conquer it. The claims of *djihad*—Holy War—were outweighed by those of sovereignty. While Motamid, the ruler of Seville, was rotting in chains, and Alfonso VI, reduced to defensive tactics, was slowly dying of sorrow, the Almoravides completed the submersion of Spain.

The center of Christian resistance shifted from Castile to Aragon. Alfonso I, nicknamed the Battler, was the hero of this phase. In 1118 he charged into the Ebro basin, took Huesca and Tudela, and with the help of the French Count Rotrou, captured Saragossa. Our Lady of the Pillar was reconverted into a Christian church under the direction of Bishop Don Pedro de Librano. Encouraged by his success, and feeling that nothing could stop him now, Alfonso continued southward. And indeed, for the first time, the papacy officially conferred upon the Battler's warriors the title of "Crusaders." This was of major significance; henceforth all expeditions against Spanish Moslems, like the crusades to the Holy Land, were hallowed by Rome.

At the head of his *cruzados*, Alfonso I pushed past Saragossa, reached New Castile, where he took important territory away from the Moors, and then trod upon Valencian soil. As he advanced, many Christians joined his army and captive Mozarabs broke their chains to do likewise. Alfonso seized Murcia and threatened Granada while all of Andalusia trembled. In the mosques, imams recited the prayer of fear, *la azalá del temor*. The Battler camped beneath the walls of Granada, but, loath to tarry, crossed the Sierra Nevada and continued his relentless march. Soon he reached Málaga, which smacked of Africa with its bamboo and palm trees, its scent of pepper and cinnamon. Like the other Alfonso of Castile, this errant prince cast a quick glance at the Pillars of Hercules, then, laden with booty, returned, bringing with him the people he had liberated.

At Fraga, Alfonso suffered his only defeat, but it cost him his life. The crown of Aragon passed to his brother, Ramiro the Monk, apparently a rather insignificant individual. Extremely devout, his ostentatious piety may have concealed a lack of talent for affairs of state. He was derisively called the "monkish king"—*el rey cogulla*. His sole political achievement was to marry off his daughter Petronilla to Ramón Berenguer IV, Count of Barcelona (heir of the man who saved the Catalonian capital from invasion by the Almoravides), thus uniting Aragon with Catalonia.

With the advent of Alfonso VII, the grandson of the victim of Zallaka, Castile once again grew more spirited. The new sovereign was energetic and had himself crowned emperor of Spain at Leon. He secured the allegiance of Navarre and Aragon. Thus, while Castile manifested its intention of unifying the peninsula under its own laws, Alfonso marched victoriously through Andalusia, captured Almería, and pushed on to Gibraltar.

One Fanaticism for Another

Now, from the heart of the Atlas Mountains, the voice of the Mahdi, Mohammed ibn-Tumart, was heard. He claimed that the Almoravides were not following the teachings of the Prophet, that they were committing grave errors and must therefore be overthrown. He convinced the caliph, Abdul Mumin, and entrusted him with the mission of reestablishing the true Kingdom of God. Galvanized by this new fanaticism, the Berber armies embarked on their campaign. They put down the Almoravides of Africa, conquered Marrakech, crossed the Mediterranean, and set up their capital in Seville. Once again the Spaniards had new masters, and once again, in the name of religious reform and orthodoxy, Spain experienced both invasion and its inevitable concomitant, persecution.

The idea of a Holy War, which the Almoravides seemed to have forgotten, was now resumed with fresh vigor. Moslem theologians inspired and directed the military operations; in fact, nothing was done without their advice. "Here is my real army," Yakub al-Mansur, the Almohad emir and Abdul Mumin's successor, said to his staff, pointing to the fakirs. As a wave of puritanism and piety swept over the sects of Mohammed, public prayers and processions preceded and followed every battle. Such austere enthusiasm was not lacking in grandeur, and Tumart's gesture of smashing the amphorae as a sign of penitence attested to a certain noble ardor. But doctrine is one thing and human nature another. The Moslem princes, who for a long time had succumbed to mystical exhortations, soon resumed their quarrels and their pursuit of sensuous pleasures.

Alfonso VIII, the "little king," now ruled Castile. He set the country to rights again and recaptured Cuenca and Logroño from the Berbers. In alliance with Alfonso II of Aragon, who was creating a territorial domain north of the Pyrenees, he reconquered Valencia. But in 1195 he was defeated by Yakub at Alarcos, in La Mancha.

The Day of the Three Kings

Alarcos was the last victory of the Almohades. Under the leadership of Rodrigo Jiménez de Rada, archbishop of Toledo and builder of the cathedral there, steps were taken to organize a mighty army that would wipe out the Almohades' rule, once and for all. Castile, Aragon, and Navarre joined forces, while troops from France, Italy, and Germany marched toward Toledo. Pope Innocent III blessed the Spanish crusade, which was spearheaded by an immense expeditionary force under the triple command of Pedro II of Aragon, Sancho V of Navarre, and Alfonso VIII of Castile. The army of this great Christian coalition crossed the Sierra Morena, not far from the Despeñaperros Pass, and attacked Moslem positions with all its might. Yakub, his head swathed in a green turban, the black mantle worn by Abdul Mumin thrown over his shoulders, sat on a shield and watched the battle. The Spanish cavalry, protected by iron armor, drove into the lines of the Almohades, which bristled with pikes. Navarrese and Castilians forged an opening and the rest of the army followed. They poured into the Andalusian plains and routed the enemy. Yakub fled in such haste that he left the caliph's standard behind. Alfonso had the blue banner, studded with gold stars, hung from the top of the cathedral at Toledo. On the site of the battle, Las Navas de Tolosa, the victors intoned a *Te Deum*. Navarrese, Castilians, Aragonese, and knights from Aquitania joined in prayer to give thanks for their triumph and to attest to their unity. Every year the Church commemorated this important date, July 16, 1212, which was named the Victory of the Cross.

Soldiers still eager for slaughter, three kings seated, motionless, on their horses, winds of decay ruffling princes' sashes and priests' golden stoles, corpses rotting in the harsh summer sun, hymns intoned by countless numbers—such was the grandiose and savage picture on the blood-soaked plain where the Cross of the Living God had been implanted.

The Cross and the Sword

Both the Archbishop of Narbonne and the Bishop of Toledo were present at the Las Navas de Tolosa massacre. Was this a suitable place for prelates? Actually it was, for Spanish unity and the conquest of the Moors must be credited to the clergy. How great was the number of those Christian princes who had been more or less "Arabianized," who seemed quite satisfied with their situation and had no inclination to resist! If the clergy had not wielded a continuous and unflagging influence over the masses as well as the sovereigns, if the monastic orders had failed to provoke and sustain a fiery crusading spirit, the struggle against the Moslems would have come to nothing more than a few ineffectual skirmishes. Priests were constantly needed to stoke the ardor of the Spanish kings, to direct and co-ordinate their efforts, and to hold high the crucifix at the head of embattled armies. When the fighting was fiercest, the presence of monks and chaplains, standard-bearers of Christ—or at least believing themselves to be such—served as a reminder that religious as well as military objectives were at stake. In the future, religious orders were to tighten still further the alliance between sword and cross.

Alfonso the Battler was apparently the first Spanish prince to sense the importance of an organized religious militia for the defense of the peninsula. From the band of knights who had accompanied him to Málaga, he selected those whose performance had been most satisfactory. He formed them into companies, dubbed them Knights of the Holy Savior, and gave them a set of rules. They wore white robes upon which a cross was anchored with open knots. But soon the fame of other orders, which had been created in Jerusalem —the Knights of the Holy Sepulcher, the Hospitalers, or Knights, of St. John, and the Knights Templars—reached Spain. On his deathbed, Ramón Berenguer III, king of Barcelona, requested that he be clothed in the raiment of the Knights Templars.

In the middle of the twelfth century, at a site where pear trees had been planted, two lords of Salamanca founded the Order of San Julián del Pereyro. These religious knights belonged to the Benedictine Order. They wore hoods and red belts and carried shields of gold displaying bare pear trees and crosses fleury.

Upon the death of Alfonso VII, which occurred in the same period, the Knights Templars guarding Calatrava ceded the city to Sancho III of Castile because they feared they would be unable to hold out against the Almohades. Sancho, reluctant to assume the responsibility, let it be known that whoever undertook to defend Calatrava would be amply rewarded. But, since nobody volunteered, St. Raymond, abbot of the monastery at Fitero, and Friar Diego Velásquez, both former soldiers, accepted the task. They garrisoned Calatrava, stocked it with supplies, and built new defenses. In 1158, to emphasize the religious character of the enterprise, St. Raymond founded the Order of Calatrava. A papal bull sanctioned it and placed it under the jurisdiction of the Benedictines. The dress of the new order consisted of a white scapulary and hood. The shield was of gold with a cross fluery.

Calatrava was recaptured by the Moslems after the battle of Alarcos. But the Christians took it back just before the victory at Las Navas de Tolosa, and Alfonso VIII promptly returned it to the knights of the city.

The Order of St. James of Compostela (Santiago) was apparently established at the same time, although an organization bearing the name existed as early as the reign of Ramira, the first victor over the Moors. When the supposed tomb of St. James was discovered, a militia was created for the purpose of lodging and protecting the pilgrims who visited the sanctuary. In 1175, Pope Alexander III gave official recognition to the Order of St. James, which took up quarters in the monastery of St. Mark founded by the prebends of St. Eligius.

True to their mission, the Knights of St. James built almshouses along the highway that ran from France to the tomb of St. James, escorted and lodged pilgrims, and protected them against misadventures. They carried shields of gold displaying cross-shaped swords called *lagarto*, or lizards. Said Archbishop Rodrigo de Rada: "These swords are red because they are dyed with the blood of Arabs." The hilts were heart-shaped, and sea shells ornamented the scabbards. The banners of these knights also displayed sea shells—five of them. The story is told that a knight of the Pimentel family, who followed the corpse of St. James in Galicia as it was being transported by his disciples, had to swim across an arm of the sea. He emerged covered with sea shells, which thereafter became the emblem of St. James the Apostle. Pilgrims going to Compostela would gather shells along the shore and tie them to their hats or coats to symbolize the pious character of their journey.

The first French pilgrim to Compostela whose name we know with certainty was Godescalc, bishop of Puy. He made the journey in 950. But thanks to the belief in the miraculous that was so strong at that time, it was the legendary "Story of Charlemagne and Roland," reputedly composed by Bishop Turpin of Reims, one of the twelve peers, that captured the popular imagination. According to the story, the aging Charlemagne, weary after his many victorious campaigns, was relaxing in his palace at Aix-la-Chapelle, when a "headless Galician" appeared in a dream—St. James the Apostle. He pointed to a starry path in the heavens—*campus stellae*, hence "Compostela"—that led to his burial place in Galicia. Surely Charlemagne would not permit the tomb of St. James to remain in the hands of the Saracens! Charlemagne responded by waging three campaigns and freeing Spain from Moslem rule. During his return from the last of these expeditions, the rear guard of his army met with glorious defeat in the Roncesvalles Pass. Charlemagne obtained revenge, then piously collected the victims' corpses and had them buried like true relics in sanctuaries along the "St. James Highway." He placed the sepulcher of Roland at St. Romain de Blaye, and Roland's famous ivory horn, Oliphant, on the altar of St. Seurin at Bordeaux. Ogier and Oliver were buried in the province of Landes. Meanwhile, Charlemagne built the first church of Compostela and appointed his own bishop head of the Spanish Church.

Somewhat later, certain chroniclers claimed that it was a mistake to attribute these conquests to Charlemagne, that it was questionable whether he had ever been in Spain, preoccupied as he was with the problems then presented by the Saxons. But they protested in vain; the story of Roncesvalles, which sprang from French epic poetry, was too deeply rooted throughout the region of the Pyrenees to arouse any doubts. These believers even gave a precise date for his victories, the year 778.

In the annals of medieval civilization, the *camino franco* played a considerable role. It not only promoted the development of religious institutions but also served as a means of intellectual, artistic, and commercial intercourse between France and Spain. To some extent, the Compostela route nurtured both epic poetry and Romanesque art. Thanks to it, the Pyrenees, far from constituting a barrier, became a powerful link between the two countries.

Itinerant workshops, moving ceaselessly from one place to another, followed the route of the pilgrims in France and Spain. This accounts for the simultaneous appearance of Roman sculpture in both countries. Far from Spanish territory, in Auvergne and Burgundy, which comprised the French sections of the road, remains of the diffuse Hispano-Arabic influence were discovered. Some of these are still extant— for example, the multi-lobed arches of the cathedrals of Bourges and Charité-sur-Loire, and the Andalusian polychrome of dark and light keystones at Vézelay-en-Bourgogne and Puy.

In France, the *camino franco* followed four main arteries: the Via Tolosana, which led from Arles through Toulouse to the Somport Pass; the Via Podensis, from Puy to Ostabat, skirting the sanctuaries of Conques and Moissac; the Via Limosina, connecting Périgueux and Limoges; and, finally, the Via Turonensis, which passed through Tours, Poitiers, and Bordeaux. The last of these was taken by pilgrims from northern France and England, who went through Paris by way of the rue St. Jacques and the faubourg St. Jacques. Their starting point was the Church of St. Jacques de la Boucherie, which was built by a butchers' guild and had a tower that represented the flamboyant style of the past.

There were several meeting points along the way. One of the most popular early in the twelfth century was the famous St. Christine shelter for pilgrims, located between the Aspe Valley and the Somport Pass. Later, thanks to clever publicity about "Charlemagne's mementos" and the legend of Roland, the port of Size and the Roncesvalles Valley were preferred. Shrewd merchants attracted visitors by offering to show them the sites where legendary objects had been found. These included Durandal, Roland's sword, Oliphant, his ivory horn, and even the Bishop of Turpin's slippers.

In Spain, the *camino* passed through Puente de la Reina, Santo Domingo de la Calzada, Burgos, Sahagún, and Leon. During the second half of the eleventh century Alfonso VI built roads, bridges, and almshouses in Castile and Leon for the benefit of the pilgrims, while Sancho Ramiro did likewise in Aragon and Navarre. Eventually pilgrims repopulated some of the cities. Foreigners, called "Franks," settled in sections of certain towns and were granted special privileges. Such enclaves were to be found in Jaca, Pamplona, Sangüesa, and Puente de la Reina.

The city of Compostela profited by this extraordinary migration. In the twelfth century it became the wealthiest commercial center in the peninsula, receiving Moslem imports from Valencia and goods brought in by Norman merchants, whose ships anchored off the coast of Galicia, to say nothing of a constant flow of gifts destined for the local cathedral. It subsidized Christian kingdoms and contributed generously to Rome. After the Reconquest, its prosperity gradually declined as it lost ground to various regions of Andalusia. The Reformation curtailed the influx of foreign pilgrims; the French Revolution dealt it a fatal blow. Only a few scattered pilgrims—scholars, historians, and archaeologists—have continued the tradition.

Meanwhile a new order sprang up in Alcántara, on the banks of the Tagus. A year after the victory of Las Navas de Tolosa, Alfonso IX entrusted the city, which he had recaptured from the Moors, to the Knights of Calatrava. After guarding it for five years, they turned it over to the Knights of San Julián del Pereyro, stipulating, however, that supreme jurisdiction was to remain in their own hands. But the new guardians of the city obtained a papal bull freeing them from control by the Knights of Calatrava, and they changed their coat of arms to a gold shield with a blood-red cross fleury. Among the ruins of the monastery of San Benito one can still find some traces of the knights of Alcántara. Even now emblems and mottoes perpetuate the names of their leaders.

In conclusion, we must mention an order founded in the region of Tortosa by Alfonso II of Aragon—the Knights of St. George of Alfama—which tended to be confused with the Valencian order of Montesa after the disappearance of the Templars.

Every order had a leader, called Master—the Master of the Order of St. James is an example. He was the highest dignitary of the state. The Great Commander—*Comendador Mayor*—ranked second to him and replaced him when he was absent. The *clavero*, in charge of finances, came next, followed by the prior of the organization. The various commanders under the latter's jurisdiction completed the administrative framework. Thirteen members formed the Supreme Council of the Knights of St. James. They chose the Master, advised him on all important matters, and named the commanders.

The authority of the orders equaled and at times surpassed that of kings. Many were the muffled conflicts between the commanderies and the court, and great was the
threat they represented. As a consequence, when the Moors
were banished from Spain, one of the first acts of Ferdinand
the Catholic was to disarm all the orders. Claiming that their
principal mission had been accomplished, he obtained from
Pope Innocent VIII a papal bull naming him sole administrator. From then on, the title of Great Master of the Orders belonged to the Spanish crown, a situation bitterly resented by the knights. Was this their reward for having
liberated the land? However, the Spanish kings could not afford to countenance the growth of such powerful brotherhoods. They felt menaced by the successful wars they had
waged, the tremendous prestige they enjoyed in the eyes of
the people, their military organization, and their wealth,
which had often financed expeditions against the Moors. But
what troubled them most was the somber pride and the
constant severity they displayed toward the sovereign.
Knights alone seemed to be the fit judges of good and evil,
they alone had the right to sermonize, to criticize the Spanish crown openly. Weary of being lectured to, and becoming
more confident of its power, the monarchy did not scruple
to abolish the knights' temporal authority or to destroy their
spiritual influence.

Victims of an incurable nostalgia, for many long years the
orders continued to meet among the ruins of their commanderies. Grass grew between the flagstones of the chapels
as the muffled voices of the last knights subsided within
the barren walls. What could they discuss save the twilights
of battles, St. James galloping on his fiery steed beneath the
exultant sky of Granada, or their saints and martyrs? Suspended like a relic near a large crucifix was the white silk
scapular mantle, its left side embroidered with a picture of
the blood-stained sword of St. James. Now and then one of
the knights would press his lips to its hem.

3

Cathedral and Mosque

W HEN FERDINAND III was invited by his cousin St. Louis (whose mother was a sister of Blanche of Castile) to go on a joint expedition to the Holy Land, he replied: "We do not lack Infidels at home." The King of Leon and Castile thus announced his intention of organizing a crusade of his own in Spain. Presumably he believed that no crusade could be victorious unless love, too, conquered. He alone among all the Catholic kings inspired affection in both Moslems and Jews, this despite the terrible blows he had dealt the Moslems. How surprising to encounter the gentle countenance of charity in the midst of the Spanish Middle Ages, a period steeped in fire and blood! But the kiss of peace bestowed by the Christian princes upon the emirs of Andalusia would not have been possible without the military victories that had come before.

Henry I, son of Alfonso VIII, the victor of Las Navas, was a child when he mounted the throne of Castile. His elder sister, the wise Berengaria was regent. Upon the death of the little king, the Infanta convoked the Cortes and announced that she had decided to yield the crown in favor of her son Ferdinand, whose father was Alfonso IX, king of Leon. In 1217, at Valladolid, the young prince was proclaimed sovereign of Castile.

This aroused the ire of Alfonso IX, who coveted the crown for himself. Encouraged by a handful of partisans, he gathered an army and prepared to march against his son. But the nobles and prelates of his entourage made him listen to reason, arguing that a military conflict between Castile and Leon would only benefit the enemies of Spain. Thus the reign of Ferdinand almost began with an infanticidal war.

No true harmony existed between the kings, yet together they formed an alliance against the Moors. While the King of Leon besieged Cáceres and conquered Mérida and Badajoz, Ferdinand invaded Andalusia and captured Baeza and Andújar. Only after the death of Alfonso IX (he succumbed on the Compostela road, while journeying to offer thanks to St. James for his victories) was Ferdinand able to show the full measure of his strength, bringing war to Cordova, the very heart of Andalusia.

After four years of careful preparation, Ferdinand crossed the Muradal Pass, pushed his drive to Guadalquivir, and, after a siege that lasted several months, captured Cordova in 1236. The city was in a sorry state, very different from its past grandeur. Ferdinand had his banner affixed to the Alcazar and a cross placed at the top of Abd-er-Rahman's great mosque. He also discovered the bells of St. James of Compostela, which the fierce al-Mansur had forced Christian prisoners to carry from Galicia to Cordova. In reprisal, Ferdinand ordered the bells returned to the apostle's sanctuary, whither they were carried on the shoulders of Moslems.

After Cordova, Jaén, and Murcia, the Castilian besieged Granada, where the emir Mohammed al-Hamar had to pay him homage. Encouraged by his success, Ferdinand attacked Seville, the capital of the Almohades. This was a daring thing to do, but the King of Castile had amassed a large army: Aragon, Navarre, Catalonia, and the Moslem kingdom of Granada had all sent him reinforcements. In 1248, after fifteen months of fierce combat, his formidable coalition overcame Moorish resistance. Preceded by a great number of clergymen, Ferdinand led his troops into Seville. The first thing he did was to attend Mass at the great mosque, now converted into a Christian church. Passing the royal procession as they moved in the opposite direction, 100,000 Moslems, men, women, and children, fled to Africa. The power of the Almohades had been broken.

Master now of Seville, Ferdinand meant to complete his conquest of Andalusia by occupying Cadiz and Jerez. At last he came to the sea. Having made peace with the King of Granada, his only remaining enemy, he prepared to pursue the Moslems in Africa. A flotilla was equipped off the coast of Biscay and was about to set out when Ferdinand died.

The Emperor of Three Religions

Ferdinand died with humility. Sensing his end was near, he gathered his people around him, gave them last words of advice, and urged them to continue the crusade. Then he removed his royal insignia, asked that the traditional rope be placed around his neck and a candle that had been blessed be put in his hand; then, begging forgiveness for his sins, he met death to the strains of the *Te Deum*, which had been sung after each of his victories.

All Christianity and even his enemies were moved. The emir of Granada, who had been successively enemy, vassal, and ally of the great Catholic king, ordered public mourning. One hundred Moorish horsemen, each bearing a white torch, went on foot from Granada to Seville to pay him a last tribute. This pious pilgrimage was repeated every year until the fall of Granada.

Ferninand was laid to rest in the royal chapel of the cathedral at Seville. Above the bronze and silver shrine over which a royal mantle had been thrown, there was an epitaph written in Latin, Hebrew, Arabic, and Spanish, a reminder that Ferdinand had ruled equitably and mercifully over Jews, Moslems, and Christians alike. Of course, in order to overcome resistance and establish the kind of peace he desired for his kingdom—a Christian peace—he had had to use an iron first. Heretics were burned, cities were sacked, and people were starved—harsh measures, to be sure, but deemed necessary by the late king. What would have become of Spain, still in its infancy politically and under a constant threat from Africa, if the kings had failed to impose their law? To enforce their will, they were obliged to wage wars. It was to Ferdinand's credit, and his principal claim to fame, that, as soon as he had rid the kingdom of both internal and external enemies, he grew fond of his subjects and allowed Moslems and Jews to preserve their customs, laws, and religion. Such generosity and understanding not only did honor to Ferdinand, "Christ's servant and knight, standard-bearer of St. James," but also to his mother, the energetic and "very wise" Doña Berengaria.

The Stone Cathedral

Ferdinand the Saint's century was one of stone, beginning with the cathedral. Inspired by the great monastic brotherhoods, especially the Cluniac monks, Romanesque art spread throughout the Orient as early as the eleventh century, and Spain was the beneficiary.

In France, Romanesque art varied according to region, each province having its own school. The vault, which was widespread in Burgundy, was almost unknown in Normandy. In Auvergne the façades of churches were studded with colored stones while in Poitou they were embellished with works of sculpture. Languedoc architects boldly built towers and belfries. Spain's churches are illustrative of this diversity.

The Church of St. Vincent at Ávila is of the purest Burgundian style, with a lovely double door and columns adorned with statues of the apostles. The basilica of Compostela, built over the ruins of the humble sanctuary of Santiago, is definitely the work of French masters, and resembles the Church of St. Sernin at Toulouse. One is not at all surprised to find the Languedoc influence here: in the twelfth century, a workshop from Toulouse had been established in Compostela. Certain Narvarrese churches bear the imprint of the Poitiers school, recognizable by its arcades and bas-reliefs.

Romanesque architecture, France's gift to Spain, still somewhat cumbersome and severe despite its occasional capitals and pink brick, spread beyond the Pyrenees via the St. James route, the *camino franco*. Its cold austerity blended with the climate and landscape of northern Spain. The massive buttresses of Romanesque churches weighed heavily on the rugged soil of Navarre and Aragon, like the vaults of a cave.

Around the middle of the twelfth century, the influence of the Cluniac monks began to wane while the Cistercian Order became very popular. Its monasteries multiplied throughout the peninsula and, as it won converts, its conception of religious architecture revolutionized Western art.

Birth of the Ogive

The characteristic features of Gothic architecture, imported from France by the Cistercian monks and destined to spread throughout Europe, were the ribbed vault, or ogival transept, and the flying buttress, which supported the external edifice. The discovery of the flying buttress, which provided structural stability, made possible the reduction of pillars and the substitution of stained glass for walls, thus adding space and light to the house of God.

In France, cathedral towers sprang up almost miraculously, and this burst of enthusiasm spread to Spain. Churches and monasteries multiplied in Catalonia, Navarre, Aragon, and Castile. Among the most highly prized was the convent of Las Huelgas, near Burgos, built and controlled by King Alfonso VIII. It housed one hundred nuns of noble birth and was under the jurisdiction of the Cistercian Order. Its church was pure Gothic in style. Flying from the arch of the *capilla mayor* was a replica of the banner that Alfonso VIII had captured from the Moors in the battle of Las

Navas de Tolosa, the original of which was preserved in the convent.

Ogival arches were to be found in Tarragona, Lérida, Sigüenza, and Tudela. Occasionally one encountered contrasting influences as exemplified by the cathedral of Ávila. Enclosed within the walls of the city like a garrison, it was the first Gothic cathedral in either Castile or France, yet parts of it were built in the Romanesque style. The vault, or *cimorro*, with its turrets and battlements, has the shape and weight of a tower. Similarly, the cathedrals of Lugo and Orense combine the Languedoc and Burgundian styles. Such bold compositions result in masterpieces.

We know almost nothing about the artists who conceived and built these religious fortresses. Only one signed his name in stone: the artist Mathieu, architect of the cathedral of Compostela and the famous Portico of Glory. The latter has three magnificent arches. The one in the center represents the Catholic Church; the others symbolize the churches of the Jews and the Gentiles. "A unique achievement, by far the foremost of the period. In any evaluation of medieval architecture, it must be ranked with the Royal Portal and the transept of Chartres."

French masters crossed the Pyrenees, bringing with them the wonderful secrets that were to benefit Spain. Obscure workmen, they seemed more intent on serving their God than in espousing any human cause. Without their piety, they could not have accomplished their gigantic, anonymous task.

French influence was felt even more keenly during the thirteenth century, when foundations were laid for the so-called "French cathedrals of Spain," and artisans from Burgundy and Normandy built churches in Cuenca, Burgos, Leon, and Toledo.

Begun in 1221 by Bishop Mauricio, the construction of the cathedral of Burgos was completed three hundred years later. Gilded and elegant, it dominates the city. One can see, a long way off, rising in the indigo sky, its two belfries and delicate spires "designed like the setting for a ring." The octagonal dome, as intricate as lacework, seems to rest lightly on the top of the edifice. In the center of the *crucero*, where the nave and transept intersect, a tombstone marks the mortal remains of the hero of Burgos, the Cid Campeador, and those of his wife, Ximena. The cloister, also Gothic in style, which forms one wing of the cathedral, is paved with tombs. One walks over sepulchers containing the bones of illustrious men. The rose windows glow, and the spires, carved like the teeth of a saw, pierce the sky and glisten like Tizona, the Cid's sword.

The cathedrals of Leon and Cuenca date from the same era and are of the same style. Guillaume de Rohan was the principal architect of the cathedral of Leon, which resembles that of Reims. Its beautiful façade contains five ogival arches with openwork galleries. Built with greater austerity, the Cuenca cathedral is noted for its marvelous perspectives.

A little above the Place de Zocodover, dominating the landscape of Castile and the churning Tagus, the great cathedral of Toledo proclaims the grandeur and perfection of Gothic architecture. Constructed by the first Bishop of Toledo during Reccared's reign, converted into a mosque by the Arabs, then torn down by Ferdinand, it was rebuilt according to the plans of a certain Petrus Petri, doubtless a Frenchman. It is surrounded by a network of houses, convents, and obscure streets. One wanders at length along the narrow passageways of Toledo—nail-studded doors, grilled windows, enormous walls adorned with shields, enclosed galleries—before finding one of the eight doors that leads to the basilica. There are 5 huge naves, 370 feet long and 98 feet high, 22 chapels, 750 windows, and a tower almost 300 feet high. These figures eloquently attest to the immensity of the edifice. Pilasters composed of sixteen columns rise to the vault and seem to be embodied in it. Elaborate tombs, stalls of carved wood, marble pillars, monstrances and gold crosses, medallions and rose windows, multicolored jasper— all these give the impression of a forest of stone, bedecked with blazing stained-glass windows. French in structure, the cathedral of Toledo is yet quite Spanish in its massive splendor, replete with mementos of a glorious past. The glamour of that militant period is recalled by Cardinal

Jiménez's ring, the pennant that Cardinal Mendoza flew from the top of the Alhambra, the blue flags of Lepanto, studded with gold stars and suspended from the vault of the church. Below, the Mozarabian chapel serves as a reminder that under the Moors, Christians enjoyed freedom of worship in Toledo. The composite spirit of the Spanish Middle Ages hovers in the shadows of the *capilla mayor*. It still burns and flickers like those night lamps that the ancients suspended over their tombs. Within this immense stone edifice, filled with sacred trophies and sarcophagi, dwells the poetry of the past. The mounting swell of old litanies, the glaucous stirring of statutes in the shades of the evening, the sea-green columns rising like giant algae, give one the illusion of being in a nautical graveyard.

Originally Roman—copied from earlier Aquitanian churches—then Gothic, French in plan and construction, but combining the slender shape of the symbolical ogive and the brilliantly imaginative plasticity of the Arabs, the Franco-Spanish cathedral of the thirteenth century became more and more Hispanic in style during the course of the centuries as its white stone gradually turned to gray. The bold chisel of the Castilian *imagineros* molded the details of its façade. Spanish Renaissance masters added new ornamentation to the ogival architecture, but above all, the comings and goings of millions of faithful, flagstones worn thin under the knees of the penitents, the somber ardors of a God-impassioned people, the echoes of prayers in the dim choirs, a hundred generations of monks—all these together have helped to give a national imprint to Spain's cathedrals. Actually, this Gothic stone is the very substance of the country.

The Cathedral of Spiritual Knowledge—
An Extension of the Mosque

Begun by St. Isidore in the seventh century, the cathedral of spiritual knowledge grew and developed under Ferdinand. In the monasteries, the clergy devoted themselves to the study of science. Although theology remained their first concern, they did not neglect the liberal arts, which were divided into *trivium* (grammar, rhetoric and dialectics) and *quadrivium* (mathematics, geometry, astronomy, and music). However, the birth of Spanish culture was not a spontaneous phenomenon, nor were the Church fathers the sole initiators of scholarship. Both the Jews and the Arabs contributed to Spain's fund of knowledge.

The Jews, who had resided in Spain for many centuries, completely assimilated its customs and language. Many of them embraced Catholicism, some even becoming priests and members of the episcopate. Persecution had not yet affected them, and Jewish thought, traditionally oriented toward metaphysics and philosophy, adapted itself easily to the Spanish mentality. The ardent curiosity of the Jews about the nature of God, their intellectual acuity and readiness to engage in scientific controversy, to say nothing of their inborn pessimism, found a congenial environment. The writings of Bakia ben Pakuda, Ibn Ezra, Judah Halevi, and Abraham ben David show not only extraordinary familiarity with the Scriptures but also a knowledge of science that was amazing for the period. Ibn Ezra, a Jew from Toledo, a minstrel, mathematician, and philosopher, wrote a textbook in which, for the first time, the rules of multiplication were set forth. As early as the twelfth century he conceived the idea of using the zero in both the decimal system and arithmetical computations. It was he who proclaimed that "reason is an angel between man and God." The pioneers in algebra and astronomy were also Jews. Very early in the twelfth century Hispano-Jewish scholars were solving second-degree equations and extracting square roots. Geometry and trigonometry likewise progressed in their hands, and Cheber, a Jew from Seville, resolved the problem of spheric lines, thus making it possible to measure with precision the orbits described by the planets.

The greatest Jewish philosopher of Spain was Maimonides, a physician as well as a theologian, for in those days care of the body went hand in glove with care of the soul. Forever on the move (like Ibn Ezra, who wandered over the

earth from Africa to London), Maimonides was banished
from Cordova, his native city, by the Almohades. He traveled to Morocco, Palestine, and Egypt, working at twenty
different trades,(from the most respectable to the humblest,
continuing his researches no matter how disheartening the
conditions of his employment.) Finally he became a jewel
merchant, but a ship on which he was sailing sank with all
his precious cargo aboard. In the course of his adventuresome
life, full as it was of ups and downs, he had the good fortune
to attract the attention of Saladin, the sultan of Egypt and
Syria, the Moslem hero of the Third Crusade. The victor of
Jerusalem made him his private physician. The vicissitudes
of Maimonides' life did not interrupt his scientific and philo-
sophic studies, which were amazingly broad. He has been
known quite justly as the Jewish St. Thomas, and theologians of all faiths borrowed heavily from his writings. (His
fundamental objective was to reconcile faith with reason, to
demonstrate that there was harmony between the teachings
of the Bible and Aristotle's philosophy. This was the basic
thesis of his challenging work *Guide of the Perplexed*, which
the creator of Thomism was to utilize fifty years later.)

Similarly, it was a Spanish Jew, Cheber, who inspired
Einstein, and another, Ibn Ezra, who influenced Spinoza.
But the philosophy of Maimonides was more original than
that of all the others, for he was perhaps the first who, in
vigorous terms, posed the grave problem so important for
modern man: are religion and science compatible?

At this point Arab and Jewish currents of thought converged. Indeed, Averroës, the leader of Islamic culture and
virtually a contemporary of Maimonides, was likewise imbued with Aristotelianism. His brilliant commentaries on
the Greek philosophers made a profound impression on
Western students of the thirteenth century. Scholars at the
Sorbonne were amazed by his writings, which also inspired
the *Summa* of St. Thomas Aquinas. The brilliant philosophical thought of this Cordovan, together with his extraordinary influence on the intellectual elite of his times, forced the
Church to modify its teachings and inclined it toward the

Averroist conception (the eternity of matter and God's communication with things through the medium of an "active intellect"), while remaining true to basic dogma. Later, Averroës was condemned by both the University of Paris and the Holy See as a materialist and pantheist.

Averroës' life was just as adventurous and tormented as that of Maimonides. Private physician to the victor of Alarcos, al-Mansur, he aroused the jealousy and hatred of the Moslem fakirs. This philosopher who denounced false prophets, whether they were called Mohammed, Jesus Christ, or Moses, who drank wine and ate ham, was bound to be suspect in the eyes of the Believers. Egged on by his entourage, the sovereign of the Almoravides eventually summoned Averroës, anathematized his doctrines, ordered his writings burned, and condemned him to exile. Doubtless al-Mansur neither understood this man, who had added luster to the court, nor grasped his ideas. Averroës attempted to prove to the king that harmony existed between faith and science, but it was all in vain. In 1198, he died a lonely death in Marrakech. Actually, the God of Averroës resembled less Allah or Jehovah than the God of St. John of the Cross, awesome and personal, and not unlike the icy divinity conceived by Auguste Comte.

The Arabs were also prolific historians. Although naturally tending to magnify Moslem exploits, they have left us interesting works on Spain. *History of the Learned Men of Spain, History of the Judges of Cordova*, and *Almohtabis* are still vivid documents, if one makes allowance for the lengthy and inevitable passages that typify Oriental exaggeration and lyricism. Some Arabs even became philosophers of history. During the eleventh century an Arab from Cordova wrote *A Critical History of Religions, Heresies, and Schools*, which delved deeply into the subject. Finally ibn-Arabi, in his *Meccan Revelations*, examined asceticism and mystical phenomena.

But the Hispano-Arab genius was perhaps most brilliantly expressed in epic and lyric poetry. "Go far, far from me, pearl of China. I am content with the rubies of Spain!" exclaimed ibn-Hazm. And the king-poet Motamid not only sang his love for the beautiful Romaïquia but celebrated the charms of his native Cordova as well. "All at once I received the hand of lovely Cordova, that proud Amazon who, sword and lance in hand, had repulsed all those who sought her. At this moment, in my palace, we are feting our union while all the other kings, her rejected rivals, weep with rage and tremble with fear." But war and love did not inspire Motamid as much as nature. "Night spread its shadows over the earth like an immense veil, and by the light of torches I was drinking a wine that sparkled in my cup when suddenly the moon arose, accompanied by Orion. It seemed like a superb and magnificent queen, longing to enjoy the beauties of nature and using Orion as a dais. Gradually the glittering stars came out, surrounding it, each to the envy of the other. This splendor increased from moment to moment as the Pleiades joined the retinue, resembling a queenly banner. What she symbolizes above, I represent here below, surrounded by my noble knights and the beautiful girls of my seraglio, with their dark hair like the shades of evening, and the resplendent wine cups which seem like stars to me. Drink, my friends, drink the fruit of the vine, while these lovely maidens sing melodious songs to the thrumming of their guitars."

Of course, one must not overestimate the intellectual influence of Jews and Arabs on medieval Spain. Arab men of letters and rhetoricians introduced Greco-Latin culture, while the Jews, those great wanderers, imported Oriental science. Both peoples merely transmitted and adapted, but with such subtlety that during the Middle Ages Spanish philosophy was tinged with the colorful imagination of the Semites.

This Judeo-Arab influence was plainly evident in the writings of the famous Raymond Lully, "the Enlightened Doctor." Born in Palma de Mallorca, poet, thinker, and man of action, he traveled all over the world, "apostle of a single idea," that of founding colleges of Oriental language to train missionaries to convert Jews and Moslems. He hoped to convince Christian princes and the Pope of the merits of his novel scheme. A tireless pilgrim, he knocked on every door, but he never succeeded in winning enough moral and financial support to realize his plans. This remarkable precursor of the missionary apostles founded only one college on his native island. Four hundred years later, St. Vincent de Paul espoused the same idea and organized the Lazarists.

When did this eternal wanderer find the time to write his three-hundred-volume work? He probably assimilated his prodigious fund of knowledge during his long trips on horseback. His monumental opus commands respect even today. A distinguished champion of Arab culture, Lully was equally at home in Arabic, Latin, and Catalan, his native tongue. His greatest book, *Ars Magna Lulli*, a treatise on scholasticism to which Descartes referred in his *Discours de la Méthode*, has remained a classic. More readily intelligible are his purely mystical writings, such as *The Art of Contemplation* and especially *The Book of the Lover and the Beloved*. Inspired by Moslem mystics, especially ibn-Arabi of Murcia, the two books constitute the foundation of all Spanish mysticism. Three centuries before St. John of the Cross, the bewitching dialogue between Jesus and the conquered soul revives the dramatic epithalamium of the Song of Songs. Never before had a human come so close to reaching the divine.

A philosopher, Lully was also a missionary and a pioneer. He foresaw and somehow sensed the vast field of action the world offered Spanish Catholicism; he heralded and prepared the way for the great spiritual conquistadors. Martyrdom fired and obsessed him. It was not enough to convert the infidel; one must die in order to save him. Although his somewhat utopian plan of organizing an army of apostles to spread the Gospel failed—his sadness over this is expressed in the poem *Desconhort*—he must be given high honors for martyrdom. He was an old man of almost eighty when he was stoned by the Moslems at Bougie. Mustering enough strength to return to his home in Majorca, he died in 1314. An extraordinary visionary, one of the noblest figures of medieval Spain, he also made a practical contribution. Not only Catalonia but the entire world owes him a considerable debt. Although the compass was familiar to the ancients, it was used unsystematically until the appearance of Lully, who demonstrated its practical applications. Without the compass Christopher Columbus could not have discovered the New World two centuries later.

Dominic de Guzmán, Destroyer of Heresies

Thirteenth-century Arab Spain was marked by heresy in both the Moslem and Christian camps. Within the Arab community, various sects opposed one another, claiming to be inspired by this or that philosopher, including Arius. Some Mozarabic Christians were still faithful to the Visigothic ritual, others adhered to the Cluniac Movement, while many, of course, were mere opportunists. As a result, there existed a generally tolerant attitude that bordered on skepticism. Only the Jews remained Jews.

Christian Spain, although more orthodox than Mozarabian Spain, suffered the consequences of this religious upheaval. The proximity of Islam did nothing to fortify its dogma. Because the people were vulnerable to the many existing heresies and tempted by various intellectual deviations, militant, authoritarian men were needed to keep the stray sheep from wandering out of the fold. Dominic de Guzmán was such a man.

Born in 1170 outside Calahorra, in the very heart of Castile (all the reformers came from the glowing, rugged Douro Valley), Dominic belonged to an illustrious family. Like many others—the Cid, Guzmán the Brave, St. John of the Cross, St. Theresa of Ávila, and future New World adventurers—he, too, was a product of the formidable Castilian countryside, where thick shadows barely veil the light's glare, the noon sun blazes, the night is tender, the Tierra de Campos pebbly white, the vast sky blue. The hidden spirit of Spanish mysticism can never be fully grasped by anyone who is unfamiliar with Old Castile.

Trained at the University of Palencia, Dominic became the regular prebend, then the prior of Osma. The Bishop of Osma, Diego de Azevedo, sent Dominic and a few of his companions to France to combat the Albigensian heresy. This important mission revealed Dominic's true vocation and determined his career.

The Albigensian heresey derived its inspiration from the Catharist doctrine, which was of Slavic origin. It had spread into Italy, Germany, and Flanders before reaching the Languedoc country. Like the Manichaeans, by whom they were influenced, the Cathars acknowledged two equally eternal principles: Good and Evil, the latter the creator of matter. Jesus was an angel sent to save mankind in the name of the principle of Good. The Cathars preached a rigid morality, claiming that only a life of austerity could save man from Evil. Their ideal, quite inaccessible to ordinary mortals, was reserved for a small number of the "pure," or "perfected." The rest, called "believers," would continue to lead a life of their own choosing. To be cleansed of all impurity before dying, they had merely to receive the blessing, the *consolamentum*, bestowed by one of the "perfected." The danger inherent in this heresy was twofold: it relieved the ordinary man of the need to aspire to a good life, and created an elite of proud supermen, ascetics, whose sole duty to their flock was to impart the benediction. The mass of simple believers had nothing in common with these solitary yogis. How discouraging for the good, whose every effort to improve themselves was thus condemned in advance, and how reassuring for sinners who, thanks to the *consolamentum*, were guaranteed salvation at no cost to themselves.

The psychological climate of medieval Christianity explains the extraordinary popularity of the Catharist heresy. The West was facing a real moral crisis. Returning from the Holy Land, the nobility brought with them the sophisticated customs of the caliphate of Baghdad, as well as a new philosophy derived from antiquity. Alexandrian pantheism and Platonic idealism met with favor in the universities. Abelard and Almaric de Bona expounded seductive and curious

theories at the Sorbonne. The Church was powerless in its
struggle against this current of thought. Isolated in monasteries, the clergy devoted itself to prayer and science. There
was very little contact between the priests and the people.
And yet Europe, a prey to mystical fever, needed religion.
While a thirst for expiation devoured true Christians, others
shrewdly used the Church as a means of acquiring advan-
tageous positions. The Catharist doctrine satisfied both
groups. The "perfected," those who had received spiritual
baptism, were the ministers of the cult, honored and
catered to, while the believers wallowed in penitence. Over
their heads, like a black hawk, flew Evil. People who were
ill begged for the *consolamentum* and deliberately died of
starvation in order not to forfeit the benefit of absolution. A
frightful pessimism tormented the souls of men. Since only
certain people could rid themselves of Evil, what was the
point of living?

The weakness or ill-will of the clergy, the intrigues of the
nobility, conducted in the name of religion, the infiltration
of Oriental doctrines and modes of thought—all this jeopardized the very existence of Christianity. Pope Innocent III
was well aware of what was happening and decided to
cauterize the wounds. The Church, under penalty of death,
must cease to be an intellectual laboratory; it must become a
stronghold. It needed soldiers as well as scholars and pious
men. Dominic de Guzmán was such a soldier.

Dominic went to Albi, where, for three difficult years, he
tried to destroy heresy. His method was persuasion, his
weapon syllogism and controversy. His handsome physical
bearing and his oratorical skill drew large crowds, but resulted in few conversions. Dominic preached and exhorted
endlessly, but without success. What a magnificent experience for this devoted young man—he was only thirty-three!
In spite of both declared and concealed hostility he perse-
vered, his enthusiasm never faltering. But soon the
Albigensian heresy was to take a political and then a militant turn. The assassination of the papal legate, Pierre de
Castelnau, by a heretic ignited the powder keg. Innocent III

excommunicated the Count of Toulouse, Raymond VI, and in 1208 launched a crusade against the Albigenses. Under the leadership of Simon de Montfort, the French barons pillaged Languedoc, and set fires and shed blood in Béziers and Carcassonne. Soldiers massacred priests, women, and children. Horrified, Raymond VI requested help from Pedro II, king of Aragon, but in 1213 the Spaniard was defeated and slain at Muret. The war ended with a total defeat for the Albigenses. Despair in his heart, Dominic witnessed the unleasing of all this horror, although he realized the Northern Crusade was really his own. But he had dreamed of a different kind of victory.

After Capetian intervention had liquidated the Albigenses once and for all, thus aiding French unity, Dominic founded his order at Prouille. The first Dominican community consisted of one Norman, one Englishman, one Lorrainer, a Frenchman, a man from Provence, six Spaniards, two natives of Languedoc, and one Navarrese. Probably from the very outset its founder sought in this fashion to indicate the universal character of Christian society. Dominic selected the rule of St. Augustine, with a constitution borrowed from the Premonstratensians. On December 2, 1216, Pope Honorius III solemnly confirmed the Dominican Order. The previous year he had sanctioned the establishment of the Franciscan Order. The two are inseparable, for both were mendicant orders dedicated to rigorous poverty. The Friars Minor of St. Francis of Assisi and the Friars Preachers of St. Dominic were thus created at the same time. Although later their relations were occasionally difficult, it is quite plain that they were alike in their close adherence to the Gospel and to the teachings of Christ.

Dominic and Francis of Assisi—a gentleman of Old Castile and the son of an Umbrian draper—what a contrast! Two men from two different countries; one from the Castilian plains bristling with dark rocks and covered with red sand, winds sighing through the pines and barren mountains protruding into the sky; the other from the hills of Umbria, where olive trees and grape vines grow on the Apennine slopes, where the generous Tiber flows and the voluptuous towns of Spoleto, Perugia, Assisi, hang like grapes on the hillsides. Dominic was what we would call athletic. He epitomized strength and good health and was impatient to battle for his beliefs. He feared nothing and no one. Rather, he seemed to seek adventure. Once he had tried to free a prisoner by offering to take his place; another time, waylaid on the road, he sang merrily as he walked beside his would-be assassin. He remembered the Cid and his own family name, for the Guzmáns were a race of great leaders. But this calm hero was also a charmer. He possessed mass appeal —a handsome, masculine face, a voice that was soft but capable of rolling out like thunder (the echo of this first great Dominican voice still resounds), and his own special way of conversing. Indeed, it was Dominic who first used the direct approach in his preachments. The note of familiarity, the narration of a personal anecdote or a provocative story, reinforced by his powers of persuasion, communicated to others the very warmth of life. At the beginning of his treatise *Dons de l'Esprit*, Étienne de Bourbon, a thirteenth-century Dominican, recalls a remark made by Dominic's biographer, Jourdain: "Wherever he happened to be, tramping the roads with his friars, a guest at someone's family table, or host to great princes or prelates, the blessed Dominic always had something benevolent to say. Examples that evoke a love of Christ and contempt for wordly things sprang to his mind, so that he hardly pronounced a syllable that did not carry weight or make an impression." Physical courage, irresistible persuasiveness, a knowledge of human beings, common sense, and a talent for organization made Dominic essentially a man of action.

Quite different though no less inspiring was Francis of Assisi. The son of a wealthy merchant, he spent his youth in revelry. He was the life and soul of a joyous company of friends, the lord of their banquets, and he sang and danced on the streets of Assisi. They called him the "flower of youth." One day he resolved to mend his ways. He joined the Christians at Damietta and set out to preach to the Sultan of Egypt. Falling ill, he discovered the Cross and became the penitent of Assisi. For Francis, who was far less cultivated than Dominic, it was the human that led to the divine. Poetry, animals, flowers, showed him the way to God. Squirrels would leave their trees to sit quietly in his hands. Peasants sought refuge in the folds of his robe. A winged procession of partridges, cicadas, and larks accompanied *il poverello* on the roads to Cremona and Padua. After eighteen years of penitence, it was to the doves that he recited his Hymn to the Sun: "Praised be Thou, my Lord, for our mother, the Earth, that sustains and nourishes us and produces fruits of all kinds, a great variety of flowers and grasses." This minstrel and gentle vagabond did not resemble Dominic at all. Innocence such as his is hardly of this world. Perhaps the Catalan lacked that spark of gaiety, the grain of folly, the naïve enthusiasm that is the hallmark of a saint. And yet how close they were! In the Louvre, in one corner of a Florentine predella, there is a painting of two monks embracing each other. One is dressed in a coarse, brown woolen robe and his hands bear the stigmata; the other wears a white tunic and black scapulary. But the contrast between the Spaniard and the Italian is as moving as the embrace. The rugged features and broad shoulders of St. Dominic stand out against the Castilian sky as in a painting by El Greco, while the frail figure of St. Francis, resembling a primitive painting of paradise, blends with the lambs and the turtle doves in the delicate Umbrian April.

On August 15, 1217, Dominic returned from Rome, bringing with him the Pope's blessings and words of encouragement. He gathered his friars around him—there were fifteen in all—and gave them the instructions he had received in the Eternal City. Repeating Christ's words, he said: "Go into the whole world and preach the gospel to every creature." The moment had come to separate. Deeply moved, Dominic gave his blessing to his companions and assigned a residence to each. His community was to be divided into small groups which would, in turn, form new communities. But before his disciples left, he reminded them of the most important part of their mission: to study, pray, teach, and preach. In addition, they would have to fast, practice abstinence, observe total silence, and make a vow of poverty. In short, they must meditate and be consumed with zeal in order to instruct and inspire others. Action was the sister of ecstasy.

Dominic himself went to Bologna, one of the intellectual capitals of Christianity. Then he became master of the Sacred Palace and founded the monastery of St. Sixtus in Rome. He taught theology, but he did not give up his itinerant life. He was seen everywhere, barefooted, a pilgrim's staff in his hand, trodding the road from Italy to France and back again. A few years before his death he decided to return to Spain. He had been away from his native land for sixteen years! He headed toward Segovia, passing through the plains of Lombardy and the valleys of the Alps. Finally he came to the Sierra of Guadarrama, the mountains of Segovia, and the royal Roman aqueduct leading to the city. Osma was not far away, nor the castle of the Guzmán family, where he had spent his youth. Along the Eresma, at the foot of the ramparts, Dominic found a grotto in which to spend the night. The faithful crowded around him. Nobles and beggars—*ricoshombres* and mendicants—escorted him with great deference. In the outskirts of Segovia he built the first Spanish Dominican establishment, the monastery of Santa Cruz. Then he continued on his way until he reached Madrid, spreading the word of God and founding new communities. He returned to Bologna exhausted but radiant. Although his end was approaching—he had only three years to live—he could take stock of his accomplishments. There were more than sixty Dominican monasteries throughout the world, and Dominican scholars headed the great universities of Bologna, Paris, and Rome! Could the sublime preacher have anticipated the fame his order was to enjoy in the centuries to come? In 1217 his group numbered fifteen. Seven hundred years later there were 150,000. Powerful personalities, as different from one another as Vincent de Beauvais, Albertus Magnus, Thomas Aquinas, and Savonarola, would wear the white robe and the leather belt. Giovanni da Fiesole became famous under the name of Fra Angelico. Dominicans too were Luis de Granada, Francisco de Vitoria, and an intrepid group of spiritual conquistadors. Today a Lacordaire would be happy to adapt the methods of St. Dominic to the modern world.

The very year of his death, 1221, Dominic had the foresight to create an auxiliary militia, which was known as the Third Order. He himself formulated the duties and rules of the organization. Composed of Christians of good will, and designed to protect ecclesiastical property, it soon became a projection of the monastic ideal into society. Members of the Third Order—first as the Militia of Jesus Christ, then as the Brothers of the Penance of St. Dominic—were to perfect themselves in accordance with Christian precepts while living "in their own century," under the direction of the First Order. To accomplish this they were to offer "continuous and, if possible, liturgical prayers and to perform those works of apostleship that further faith, the Church, and the practice of charity." In short, the Third Order of St. Dominic was to be a supplementary militia, a reservoir of qualified men, a secular elite whose influence was to make itself felt through example. For the first time, thanks to the efforts of this Third Order, laymen co-operated with the clergy. Dominic showed great foresight in placing the scapulary under the protection of the military and the king. The power of religious authority and the potential number of converts were thus increased tenfold. Pope Pius XI later proclaimed the founder of the Dominican Order the "precursor of Catholic Action." The influence of the Third Order was enormous. Ferdinand the Saint, St. Louis, Raymond Lully, Dante, Tasso, and Christopher Columbus all wore its robe. Nor can we overlook the considerable contribution that members of the French branch of the Third Order, founded by Lacordaire, made to the Church of the nineteenth century. Doctors, lawyers, intellectuals, and army officers, organized into specialized groups by the ardent Catholic preacher, constituted an active and vigilant troop instead of a lukewarm band of faithful.

Scarcely had he finished setting forth the regulations of the Third Order when, succumbing to the burden of his superhuman efforts, Dominic returned his soul to God. He had lived half a century. Fra Angelico has portrayed him holding a lily, a star on his forehead—symbols of divine inspiration and purity. But to complete the picture a flaming sword should have been placed in the long, beautifully shaped hand, as a symbol of the exhausting battle Dominic waged against the enemies of Christ.

The stone cathedral and the church of spiritual knowledge stand out against the thirteenth-century sky of Spain, but their construction would have been impossible if the foundations for a political cathedral had not been laid at the same time.

Although still divided into various states, Christian Spain was becoming unified. At the top of the hierarchy was the monarch who governed the kingdom. He was assisted by ministers, other officials, and a Council. A powerful and, on occasion, intractable nobility revolved around the palace. Comprising *ricoshombres*, *hidalgos*, and *caballeros*, it constituted a formidable organization, the *Hermandades*. An exclusively feudal army, reinforced by the military orders, served the royal authority.

The clergy, like the nobility, played an important role in the state, just as it had during the Visigothic era. Grown wealthy thanks to foreign contributions, monks of the Cluniac Movement and the Cistercian Order, who had come to Spain to help their brothers against the Moors, remained there permanently.

A species of third estate arose during the twelfth century. The process was aided by the sovereign, who permitted the representatives of cities to voice their claims before the Cortes. Another agency was the *Fuero Juzgo*, through which privileges and franchises were bestowed on peasants who had developed lands wrested from the Moors by Christian kings. Finally, the Catalonian *Usatges* and the *Partidas* begun by Ferdinand III completed and introduced greater unity into the law, which had hitherto been unwritten.

Respect for the law was imposed on rulers and subjects alike. The condition of peasants and colonists was considerably improved by the introduction of *behetrías* (social contracts between free men and lords) and *cartaspueblas* (popular charters). Instead of being under the control of the suzerain, the serf now collaborated with him. Workers were organized into guilds and brotherhoods. Every group, even reconquered Mozarabs, *mudejares*, and Jews, received statutes.

The outstanding feature of the thirteenth century was the growing importance of the middle classes, which consisted of small landowners, industrialists, and merchants. It was during this period that Castile began to develop its rich resources and to export minerals and agricultural products to Flanders and Germany. At the same time, Castilian ships went to sea. In similar fashion, municipal life began to take shape. In a young Christian kingdom such as this, administration tended to become decentralized; every township, every city, longed for autonomy. The inhabitants of Castile were grouped into *concejos* and then into *cantons* which were practically independent of their lord. Sometimes it was to the advantage of a municipality to unite with others, but Spaniards have always vacillated between particularism and federalism. As early as the Middle Ages, juries were chosen by lot and their verdicts could not be appealed. When the king swore allegiance, he promised, like the humblest of his subjects, to obey the law. He could not levy taxes, conduct the affairs of state, or choose his successor without the consent of the Cortes. Would it be correct to speak of a "medieval Spanish democracy"? Probably not, in the strict sense of the word. But it is nonetheless true that medieval Spain, with its *fueros* and its Cortes, was well ahead of the other Western states as regards human liberty. The message of St. Dominic, the unflagging influence of the Church, to say nothing of the intelligent concern of Ferdinand the

Saint for his subjects, were not without bearing upon this great liberating current. An enlightened monarch, a clergy drawn closer to the people because of the arduous battles of the Reconquest, proved invaluable in helping yesterday's slaves become free men.

Of course, the progress thus achieved was still quite precarious, but so, too, was the political situation of these Christian kingdoms. They were divided, the prey of irritating internal quarrels, and forced to be constantly on the lookout for external enemies. The Moors had not yet left, but already dynastic crises and the revolt of the nobles were beginning to delay the completion of Hispanic unity. However, Ferdinand III deserves his fame. He attempted to combine the Roman notion of Empire and Law with the ethical teachings of Jesus Christ. Three centuries before Charles V, this blessed monarch preserved the legacy of the Gothic kings and nurtured in his heart the Caesarean vision of an imperial and Catholic Spain. Thanks to him, the youthful Iberian states, though fragile, disunited, and threatened, began to exhibit the characteristics of a great power.

The century of Ferdinand, that political springtime of Spain, heralded and prefigured the Golden Century. What were its essential characteristics? Wisdom, order, and harmony. Its symbol? The upward thrust of stone cathedrals in the unsullied mirror of the Castilian sky.

4

The Catholic Kings at Granada

E HAVE NOW reached the dawn of fourteenth-century Spain. Ferdinand III, king of Castile and Leon, pushed his frontiers to Cordova and Seville while the Conqueror, James I, captured the Balearic Islands and Murcia. Almost all of Spain was in the hands of the Christian princes. With the Moslems holding only Granada, it seemed as if the Reconquest was about to be concluded. One more mountain remained to be crossed (in 1950 this would take exactly one hour by jeep!) and the last of the Moors would be vanquished. Yet two centuries or more were to elapse before Granada fell. This unbelievable delay was caused by civil wars and dynastic rivalries, especially local ones. Preoccupied with their quarrels or seeking new alliances, the Spanish kings temporarily abandoned the Reconquest and did not complete it until the end of the fifteenth century. Thus, at the foot of the Sierra Nevada, in the south of Spain, which otherwise was entirely free from Moslem rule, the emirs of Granada were able to maintain an Islamic state.

Navarre Slumbers

Navarre, surrounded by Castile, Aragon, and the French counties, inevitably became the object of intense rivalry. A

French province for over a hundred years, it finally regained its independence around the middle of the fourteenth century. Its kings at this time were Charles II, the Bad, and Charles III, the Noble.

Charles II, known for his underhanded and blundering policies, died a horrible death. Feeling a chill, he asked that a charcoal foot-warmer be placed in his bed. The sheets, cover, and curtains caught fire, and the prince, badly burned, suffered agonies until he passed away two weeks later. His son deserved the title which history has bequeathed him. Although he was not particularly brilliant, he was honest and conscientious, maintaining friendly relations with potentially dangerous neighbors. He gave his subjects an era of peace and prosperity. A descendant of the Valois, and like them in many ways, he was a humanist and surrounded himself with Frenchmen. Pierre Gasrel and Richard Alexandre were his chaplains, Jean Molinier his physician; the Bishop of Bayonne, Barthélémy, advised and assisted him. He bestowed upon the city of Pamplona a charter called the *Privilegio de la Unión*, and at Olite, where the court resided, he built the famous palace of the kings of Navarre. His main concern was to shield his tiny Pyrenean kingdom from war, and in this he was successful. Although known as a collector of medals and manuscripts, a builder of castles in the French style, an intrepid hunter, gallant knight, and lover of art, his chief claim to fame was his love of peace.

Soon Navarre would experience frightful internal struggles. But for the moment, under the king's intelligent guidance, it slumbered. What wisdom lay buried in this vigilant half-sleep!

Alfonso the Learned Brings Wisdom to Castile

In 1252 Alfonso X, the Learned, succeeded his father, Ferdinand III. Although he tried very hard to continue Ferdinand's work, he found it difficult to maintain the positions previously won, for the Moslems had rallied some Moroccan tribes to their side. The closing years of his reign were marred by bitter competition for the succession to the throne. An enterprising monarch, but beguiled by illusions, his attempts to seize everything at once resulted in complete failure. More successful, however, was his pursuit of literature, science, and law. His studies of astronomy, which are still remembered, show that at a time when the laws governing the movement of celestial bodies were as yet a mystery to ordinary mortals, he already grasped them. One day, when the universe, as understood in the thirteenth century, was being explained in his presence, Alfonso exclaimed: "Really, if the world is as you describe it, God should have consulted me. I could have given him useful advice." Impious words, but sensible ones.

Like the Moorish kings of the *taifas*, Alfonso, a genuine intellectual, was able to put aside his political disappointments by studying literature and cultivating his mind. This tolerant prince was a patron of scholars and writers, and their religion was a matter of indifference to him. He wrote poems in honor of the Virgin and had the Scriptures, the Koran, and the Talmud translated into Castilian. But he was known primarily as the author of *Siete Partidas*, a legal code begun by Ferdinand. It clarified Castilian law and dealt in exalted language with religion, the Church, and the duties of royalty. Passages of unquestionable wisdom rounded out its enormous erudition. Why was the work divided into seven parts? "Seven is a very noble number, greatly honored by the wise men of Antiquity." The remark bordered on the comical, but the work scarcely lends itself to jest. It claimed to embrace every branch of law and to anticipate every kind of contract men might devise.

However, when Alfonso was not acting the pedant he could speak with amazing humanity. "Great feeling is aroused against a king, as against any man, who uses ill-sounding or offensive words which he ought never to have uttered, for once he has done so, he cannot retract them. . . . The misuse of words degrades the value of what you say and reveals your weakness. If you are not a man of great worth the world will know it from the language you employ. For, just as one hears a sound when a vase cracks, so a man's common sense is judged by his words." In addition to law, Alfonso studied the art of war. Through his efforts, the people were taught how to plunder, prepare an ambush, set out sentries, surprise an enemy. They also learned what to do in emergencies. Remembering the terrible famines in cities under siege, especially at Calahorra, Alfonso gravely decreed: "A father who is besieged in a castle that he holds from his lord may, if pressed by hunger, eat his son rather than yield the castle without orders from his lord." But one of Alfonso's most important innovations was to abolish the custom of writing public and private documents in the poor Latin of the Middle Ages and to have them written in the young Castilian language instead.

Although his father had disinherited him, Sancho IV, the Ferocious, nonetheless assumed the throne. He certainly earned his sobriquet, for though his reign was brief he suppressed palace revolts with the greatest cruelty. "I am dying of my sins," he confessed on his deathbed; but remorse came too late. His widow, María de Molina, fought like a lioness to preserve the crown for her son, Ferdinand IV, whose succession was threatened by youthful pretenders. She had to contend with nobles, Moors, and the King of Aragon. Upon coming of age, Ferdinand did ascend the throne. He captured Gibraltar, only to die suddenly under strange circumstances, which led to his being called *el Emplazado*, "the Summoned." He had ordered two brothers who were accused of a crime to be thrown from a high wall. Because he had turned a deaf ear to their protestations of innocence, they had retaliated by summoning him to appear before the tribunal of God thirty days hence. On the morning of the thirtieth day, Ferdinand's servants found him dead in his bed! He was succeeded by Alfonso XI, the Avenger, who promptly concluded an alliance with his father-in-law, the king of Portugal, and with Pedro the Pompous, king of Aragon. He defeated the Moors at the Salado River and seized Algeciras; but a sudden illness caused his death, on

Good Friday, in the year 1350, just outside Gibraltar, which the Moors had recaptured. The Avenger left several illegitimate children—one of whom was Henry of Trastamara—as well as one legitimate son, Pedro, later known as Pedro the Cruel.

Pedro the Cruel, a Man of His Times

Pedro was fifteen when he became king. His childhood had been somewhat abnormal. His mother, a Portuguese princess, had no authority over him, while his father's mistress, Leonora de Guzmán, had been assassinated. He grew up without friends. Soon a marriage was arranged. The bride was Blanche de Bourbon, sister-in-law of the French dauphin, the future Charles V. The two youngsters, their hands clasped, advanced slowly on their white palfreys, as if in a dream. Dressed in robes of gold brocade lined with ermine, they were a moving couple to behold. The good people who watched the nuptial procession were enraptured by the young lovers, who looked like figures in a medieval stained-glass window.

Blanche was in love, but Pedro had been coerced into the marriage. Dropping the hand of his bride, he thought of his mistress, María de Padilla, and of the daughter she had given him. After two days of matrimony Pedro grew restive and hastened to join his mistress, who, being the more sensible of the two, sent him straight back to his bride. But after another two days with Blanche he again returned to the woman he loved. Poor Blanche could but weep for her elusive husband, whom she was never to see again.

One evening Pedro, wearing a disguise, walked alone down a street in Seville. A guard ordered him to halt. Impatient, Pedro drew his sword and killed the man. An old lady who witnessed the scene was summoned the following day to testify. The murderer's face had been concealed in the folds of his cape and she was therefore unable to describe him. The only information she could give was that the joints of his knees cracked. All Seville knew of this peculiarity of

the king's person. Could he be the assassin? Pedro confessed his crime to the constabulary. Since, in this case, the
usual punishment—decapitation and exposure of the severed
head to the public at the site of the crime—could not be administered, he ordered that his likeness be sculptured in
stone and placed in a niche near the scene of the murder.
This was done, and the statue can be seen today in the Calle
de la Candileja, "the street of the Old Lady's lamp."

Although known for his lecherousness—María de Padilla
was not enough to satisfy his sensual needs—Pedro condemned the loose conduct of the priests. He took strong
measures against their concubines—the *barraganas de
clérigos*—but could accomplish little because the young
ladies involved enjoyed protection in high places. As a result, he came to feel utter contempt for the Church, and it
was to Jews and Arabs that he offered his friendship. "I have
no better subjects than the Hebrews and the Moors," he often said, half in earnest, half in jest.

Pedro's favorite residence was the Alcazar at Seville,
where he had spent his youth. Served by turbaned Moslems,
he lived there in Oriental luxury, like a caliph, whose habits
he adopted. María de Padilla was the queen of the seraglio
and could often be seen, swathed in pearly gauze, on her
way to the Patio de las Muñecas. She bathed in the pool that
had belonged to the Almohad sultanas. When she emerged,
the people of the palace were expected to scoop up some of
the bath water in the palms of their hands and drink it devoutly. Pedro the Cruel had so ordered. One day an officer
refused to follow the ritual. Outraged, Pedro demanded an
explanation. The officer replied: "Having tasted the sauce,
I am afraid I might be tempted by the bird."

Clouds gathered on Pedro's horizon and seemed to
threaten his voluptuous reign. Choosing a specious pretext,
Aragon declared war on Castile. Pedro was no coward, but
he lacked the necessary funds. He levied taxes on the merchants of the city and then replenished his treasury by pillaging the tombs of his predecessors, Ferdinand and Alfonso.
"King Ferdinand lies buried with a golden crown on his
head. Clothed in precious silks, he holds in his right hand

the large sword with which he captured Seville. A ruby the size of an egg is on the hilt of the sword and a green emerald on the scabbard. His left hand clasps the sheath on which there are also many precious stones." If we add that the finger of the Holy Virgin bore a gold ring with a ruby "the size of a hazelnut" and that two thousand stones—sapphires, emeralds, and topazes—decorated the tabernacle of the burial chapel, it becomes plain that the stakes were considerable.

Leonora de Guzmán had five illegitimate sons by the Avenger. Before going off to war, Pedro decided to rid himself of them, beginning with Fabrique. Entering the Alcazar one day, Fabrique was greeted with a sudden rain of blows that knocked him to the ground. A Moorish slave administered the *coup de grâce*. The corpse was carried into the hall of the *asulejos*, where Pedro the Cruel was finishing his evening meal. Three more sons were killed by Pedro's ruffians, who brought back the heads slung over their saddles. But one head he would never receive—that of Henry of Trastamara.

Henry of Trastamara was an ally of the King of Aragon, a relationship which lent the Aragon-Castile conflict the character of a family vendetta. Military operations served as pretexts for terrible reprisals. Henry's soldiers, who were lodged in a castle, refused to continue fighting unless the wife and daughter of the governor were handed over to them for their pleasure. Apprised of the situation, Pedro captured Trastamara's men and had them quartered and burned. At the same time, Pedro's hirelings were instructed to seek out and slay every prominent individual who was known to be opposed to the king. Woe to the Castilians who were friendly to Henry! Terrible punishment awaited them, like that inflicted on the leading citizens of Miranda, who were boiled alive in cauldrons while Pedro looked on. Weary of so much horror, Castile and Aragon made peace.

Two events that were to have a direct effect on Pedro's personal life occurred the very year in which the two kingdoms laid down their arms. Blanche de Bourbon, the sad, forsaken queen, died in the castle of Medina-Sidonia. Pedro the Cruel had exiled her there, telling her, or so it was said, to make a banner for him with "a background the color of her blood and embroidery the color of her tears." The story was also told that, anxious to be rid of his importunate queen, he ordered one of his men to kill her. When the murderer entered the queen's room she was praying. Turning around, she realized what was afoot and began to moan tremulously: "Oh, France, my noble country, oh, my Bourbon blood! I was just seventeen today. The king has never known me. I am leaving this world like the virgins. Castile, tell me, what have I done to thee?" The assassin did not wait for her to finish, but raised his heavy club and brought it down on the child's head. The skull split open, splattering the wall with her brains. A few days after Blanche's murder, María de Padilla died. She was given a lavish funeral and, the following year, her remains were transported with great pomp to Seville, where they were laid to rest in the cathedral, near Ferdinand the Saint's coffin. A year later, the son that Pedro had had by María de Padilla and whom he intended to make his heir, died of the plague. Pedro had lost the only two people he had ever loved; henceforth his cruelty was his sole companion.

Henry of Trastamara was determined to wreak vengeance on Pedro, the murderer of his mother and brothers. He urged the King of Aragon to resume hostilities. To encourage him, he brought mercenaries from France, promising them the moon and the stars once the war was won. The expression, "castles in Spain," derives from this incident. Pedro was weary and sad. Gone was his spirit, yet he was not one to give up. He made an alliance with the Moslems of Granada, but finding it impossible to launch a frontal attack, he had to limit himself to hand-to-hand fighting. The war seemed to last forever, slackening, then resuming with full force when France and England decided to intervene—the former on the side of Aragon and Henry, the latter aligned with Pedro and Castile. Charles V participated by sending his Grand Companies to Spain, thus ridding France of them temporarily. Led by Bertrand Du Guesclin, 12,000 adventurers swept down the Rhône Valley. They stopped at

Avignon long enough to extract a subsidy from the Pope, claiming that they were going to fight infidels; then they crossed the Pyrenees, joined Henry's troops, and in one fell swoop conquered Castile. Pedro fled to Toledo. At Burgos, Henry of Trastamara was consecrated King of Castile. Du Guesclin was made Duke of Molina and a Grandee of Spain. It was England and Islam that delayed the fall of Pedro the Cruel. In response to his request for help, the Moorish king of Granada besieged Cordova. For long the outcome was uncertain, the Spanish banner flying on the ramparts beside the black flag of the Abbassides. Finally the Spaniards won. English intervention ended more happily. Pedro had enticed the Black Prince to his cause by boasting of his wealth; in particular he mentioned a precious red stone so pure "that it shed light at midnight as if it were noon." Thanks to the betrayal of Charles the Bad, king of Navarre, the English troops went through Roncesvalles and met the armies of Henry and Du Guesclin at Navarrete. Trastamara was defeated and Du Guesclin taken prisoner by the English. But, thirsting for revenge, the terrible Breton paid a huge ransom and rejoined Henry at the siege of Toledo. He cornered Pedro in his castle of Montiel. When night fell, Pedro tried to escape, but instead of the horses he had expected, he found Du Guesclin's mercenaries. He was brought to the commander's tent, where he also found Henry of Trastamara. The half brothers eyed each other with hatred. They exchanged insults, then rolled on the floor, locked in a desperate struggle. Finding an opening in Pedro's coat of mail, Henry pulled out a dagger and plunged it in savagely. In this miserable fashion Pedro I, the Cruel, met his death in 1369; his crimes had enveloped the crown in a mist of blood.

Melancholy of the Trastamaras

Thus, Henry of Trastamara, now called Henry II, the Bastard, was securely established on the throne, but not for long did he enjoy the power so dearly acquired. Allied with France, he waged war against Portugal while attempting to achieve tranquillity within his own country. Nicknamed the "King of Concessions," he died of poison, probably administered by the Navarrese. His son, Juan I, was defeated by the Portuguese and died in 1390 after falling from his horse. The crown went to Henry III, the Sickly. Delicate in health yet courageous, he led a victorious expedition against the Barbarians of Tetuán. Juan II, his son, was two years old when he inherited the throne. His coming marked the beginning of government by favorites, in contrast to the earlier reign of bastards and usurpers.

For thirty-five years the real ruler of Castile was a bastard from Aragon, Álvaro de Luna, who governed in place of Juan II. Constable, prime minister, and Master of Santiago, but above all the king's favorite, Álvaro humbled the nobility. Banished from the court and then recalled, he again met with royal disfavor and was finally arrested, deprived of his property, and condemned to death. He confessed his sins, received communion, and, mounted on a mule, rode off to the gallows to the accompaniment of the town crier's announcement: "This is the justice of the king!" A scaffold was erected on the *plaza mayor* of Valladolid. It was covered with a rug; a cross was placed between two candles. Álvaro raised his head and was surprised to see a hook attached to a high beam. He was told that after decapitation, his severed head would be hung from the hook. "You can do what you please with me once I am dead," Álvaro sighed. Thereupon he held out both thumbs so that the executioner could tie them with the proper cords. His corpse was exposed to public view for three days and his severed head for nine. Álvaro's mutilated remains were buried in a cemetery reserved for malefactors.

The ungrateful prince, Juan II, survived his minister by a few months. He died in 1454, consumed with remorse. "If only I had been the son of a simple officer!" he lamented on his deathbed. The crown then went to his son, Henry IV, called the Impotent, although nobody was altogether certain that the epithet accurately described him. Fainthearted and taciturn, but basically a good man, the new sovereign did nothing to check the rebellion that shook Castile. He married Blanche of Navarre, but as she had produced no heirs, he repudiated her and was married a second time, to the flighty Princess Juana of Portugal. She gave him a daughter, Princess Juana, the Beltraneja, but rumor had it that the real father was her favorite, Beltrán de la Cueva. After Henry IV's death in 1474, the Beltraneja was to be the cause of a war of succession. The contestants were Ferdinand the Catholic, who wished to protect the Castilian crown for Isabella, Henry's half sister, and the King of Portugal, Alfonso V, who claimed it for his niece, the Beltraneja.

The sudden death of Henry IV's half brother, Prince Alfonso, forced Henry to designate Isabella as the heir to the throne, but she had to promise not to marry without his consent. Isabella swore a solemn oath to that effect in the Cortes. Two years later she violated her pledge and married Ferdinand of Aragon against her brother's wishes.

A gust of rage and hatred, accompanied by pillage, swept through Castile. The Archbishop of Toledo led the revolt. In the center of the plains of Ávila an effigy of Henry the Impotent was hung up, with the royal insignia torn from him. Anger smoldered among the masses while the nobles took up arms against the crown. Everything was turbulence and disorder, not unlike the last days of the Visigothic monarchy.

The Cruel, the Sickly, the Impotent. . . . But one must look beyond these nightmarish figures. The court was not the nation. While the princes were intriguing in their palace in Toledo, or wearing themselves out in useless military ventures, the imperious voice of the Castilian Cortes, louder than that of the grandees, could be heard. A powerful and popular reaction set in against the feebleness of a monarchy that was neglecting its duties. The middle classes, petty lordlings, and honest country priests all yearned for a firm and humane rule.

Henry the Impotent died in 1474. Thereupon Isabella, recently married to Ferdinand of Aragon, was proclaimed Queen of Castile at Segovia.

Aragon Prepares for Unity

The great figure of thirteenth-century Aragon was James I, the Conqueror. Victorious in the Balearic Islands and Valencia, James of Aragon combined the courage of a soldier with the prudence of a statesman. Christianity was his first concern, and this was reflected in his policies. Successful in maintaining friendly relations with his French and Spanish neighbors, he signed the Treaty of Corbeil with St. Louis, which fixed the border between France and Catalonia. He married his daughter to the eldest son of the great king Philip the Bold. Toward the end of his life he set out for the Holy Land, but a storm tossed his ship back to the French coast and he never reached his destination. He died in Valencia in 1276, clothed in the garb of a Bernardine monk, inconsolable at having failed to make the pilgrimage to Palestine. This generous and loyal monarch, an indomitable warrior and shrewd politician, yearned to expiate his sins. He had known the love of many women. Torn between remorse and sensual desire, he was reputedly incapable of resisting female charms.

James the Conqueror's unfortunate testament, which divided his kingdom between his two sons, marked the beginning of unrest and strife in Aragon. As successive sovereigns mounted the throne, brothers and cousins betrayed and fought one another. Pedro the Pompous humbled the nobility, while Juan I hunted the hare and gave balls. Martin the Humane brightened the moral gloom of this period by his goodness and wisdom, but his reign was too brief. He died in 1410 without heirs, ending the Aragonese dynasty begun by Alfonso the Battler. The crown of Aragon went to a Castilian, Ferdinand the Just. His son, Alfonso the Magnanimous, established a brilliant court in Naples and then turned his gaze toward the East. This Renaissance prince, more concerned with the affairs of Italy than with his Spanish subjects, bequeathed Aragon and Sicily to his brother, Juan II, king of Navarre.

Castilian by his father, King of Aragon through the action of his brother, and King of Navarre thanks to his marriage, Juan II was in a good position to achieve the unification of Spain. During his reign he bent all his efforts to that end. But Catalonia insisted that Charles was the rightful heir to the throne and this precipitated a fierce civil war. Juan formed an alliance with Louis XI and, in order to put down the Castilians, ceded Roussillon to France. As adroit in diplomacy as he was bold in war, he solved many intricate problems. But his greatest political feat was to marry Ferdinand, a son by his second wife, to the Infanta Isabella, the future Queen of Castile.

In October 1469 at Valladolid, throngs gathered to catch a glimpse of the princely couple. They were more curious than enthusiastic, for there was a good deal of unrest; the nobles were worried and the people sulked. What would happen? ¡Ya veremos!

The Pope of Peñiscola

While Spain was becoming united, the unity of the Christian world, which had been seriously threatened by the great Western schism, was being completed.

But we must go back a little. An Italian, Urban VI, was pope in Rome while a Frenchman, Clement VII, was pope in Avignon. Charles V, king of France, supported Clement VII and persuaded Castile and Aragon to join him, while England and Portugal sided with Urban VI. Aragon intervened in the dispute after the death of Clement. The Cardinal of Aragon, Pedro de Luna, became pope in Avignon and called himself Benedict XIII. All of Spain backed him. As he was on the verge of being captured, he was rescued by a band of Castilians. To the cause of this stubborn pontiff, who was so sure of his rights, the Iberian princes lent their arms and their prestige; but his most enthusiastic supporter was Vincent Ferrier.

Ferrier was born in Valencia and died in Brittany. He traveled constantly throughout western Europe—France,

Italy, Switzerland, and Flanders—preaching and converting. He restored to the Catholic fold hundreds of thousands and baptized a countless number of people. Although he could speak only a Valencian dialect, his heart-warming, clever sermons impressed even Jews and Arabs. He was instrumental in placing Ferdinand on the throne of Aragon, but his touching devotion to Pedro de Luna, whose status as pope he helped to legitimize, was perhaps the most outstanding feature of his career.

Despite Aragonese support and the stubborn eloquence of Vincent Ferrier, Benedict XIII was deposed by the Council of Constance, which named Martin V in his place. The schism was ended, but not the resistance of Pedro de Luna. Neither prayers nor threats had any effect on the proud Aragonese. In 1414, accompanied by two cardinals who had remained faithful to him, he sought refuge at Peñíscola, the Cartago Vetus of Hamilcar. His curia was established on these somber rocks washed by the sea, and it was here that he died, alone but defiant and unyielding.

"Yo el Rey"
"Yo la Reina"

There had been a trend toward unification long before the marriage of Ferdinand and Isabella, although actual consolidation was not yet accomplished. Castile and Navarre had begun to realize the futility of bloodshed, and public opinion welcomed the prospect of unity and peace. Ferdinand and Isabella's wedding in 1469 dramatized this feeling.

Thus, Ferdinand, son of Juan II of Aragon, and Isabella, half sister of Henry IV of Castile, shared the throne of Castile. But a civil war had to be fought before their right to rule was established. They were opposed by a coalition organized in the name of legitimacy. The Archbishop of Toledo, backed by a few discontented noblemen, supported the Beltraneja, and not without reason, for although Henry IV had disinherited her, she was nonetheless his daughter. Henry's alleged impotence must have been open to question, in view of the fact that he had had two wives and several mistresses. Moreover, Isabella was not without enemies. Some accused her of defrauding her niece, who was also her godchild, of the crown. It was likewise whispered that Juan II of Aragon had himself forged a papal dispensation permitting the couple to marry. He was charged with duplicity and a tendency to foster intrigues. All this was, in large part, true. But the ultimate truth was that Isabella, a girl of nineteen, knew her own mind and probably desired power even more than love.

The conflict was resolved by war. Partisans of the Beltraneja, supported by the troops of Alfonso V of Portugal, clashed with the regiments of the Catholic rulers. The outcome, at first uncertain, was favorable to the Segovians. The Beltraneja withdrew to a convent at Santa Clara de Coimbra. At the same time, Ferdinand, succeeding Juan II, who had just died, assumed the crown of Aragon. The result was not a true fusion of the two kingdoms, for each preserved its own administration as well as its own Cortes, but rather a conjugal partnership of a kind that had no precedent in the history of nations.

Los Reyes Católicos! Had there ever been, throughout the ages, such a perfect example of royal collaboration? Handsome and powerful, their combined ages did not come to more than fifty years. What a marvelous fairy tale was this young love crowned with youthful glory!

Let us enter the cathedral of Granada at day's end and walk to the *capilla real.* An oblique ray of light from the Gothic window, over which hangs the escutcheon of the Catholic sovereigns—spires and Gordian knot—falls upon Isabella's rounded forehead and Ferdinand's gorget, lending a lifelike quality. So real are these figures sculptured in wood by Philip of Bourbon that it almost seems that they might rise from their prie-dieu and walk toward us.

Isabella was a striking blonde, with blue, almost green, eyes that recalled her English antecedents. She was altogether beautiful in both face and figure. Vigorous and athletic, she rode high-spirited horses, hunted deer, and even killed with her own spear a boar considerably larger than a man. Blessed with a virile mind and an energetic nature, she worked at affairs of state until late at night. Ferdinand was less industrious, but possessed of a quick mind. This lively and handsome cavalier, an excellent swordsman, was most seductive, and he knew how to make use of his charms. A face tanned by the sun, an abundant and glistening head of hair, wide shoulders, and manners of great distinction— such was the prince that Castile was proud to claim. It was he, of the two, who had a true sense of politics. Indeed, Isabella was never more than her husband's collaborator, and when she advised Ferdinand it was more as an impassioned princess than as a ruler. Often her influence was unfortunate. An example of this was her fanatical clericalism, which, in the end, proved harmful to Spain. Her boundless pride would not countenance contradiction, even when offered by her husband or Cardinal Mendoza.

A conference of jurists fixed the conditions under which Isabella and Ferdinand were to exercise their authority. It decreed that the couple would govern together, that the king's name would precede the queen's on all documents, but that the same seal and both coats of arms would be used. Actually, it had been necessary to deal gently with the hot-headed Aragonese, who at first wanted to have the Castilian throne all to himself. "By caresses and words of reason" Isabella was able to persuade him. Although shrewd, she was also in love and convinced her husband "that it did not matter which of the two had the greatest right to the throne, that he would lose no authority, and that she would always be submissive to the will of her lord." One can almost see the coaxing kitten, her arms entwined around her royal spouse, and one can almost hear the honeyed tones. Had she not told the general of the Franciscans: "Of all the blessings that God has seen fit to bestow upon me, the greatest is the fine husband He has given me." But she was not so blinded by love as to neglect her rights. Moreover, she knew how to deceive and to feign innocence. The crown of Castile, which had been destined for another and which she had acquired by patience and cunning, was much too important to her to be relinquished to her husband. This pious woman would not hesitate to use any weapon to keep her throne— including coquetry, of course, and lies.

"*Tanto monta, monta tanto Isabel como Fernando*"—"Isabella and Ferdinand are equals"—this was the motto of the royal couple. Throughout their close association, they signed the edicts of Castile jointly: "*Yo el rey, Yo la reina.*"

Te Deum *at Granada*

The Catholic Kings had an ambitious program, but first they had to complete the Reconquest. For over two centuries the kings of Spain had abandoned the crusade either because of internal dissension or because they were looking toward Europe. Moreover, the Moors had gradually grown less combative. Little by little they had fallen back to Granada, taking with them all the enemies of Christian Spain. Their territory stretched along the Mediterranean from Gibraltar to Almería, and, at the northern end, reached the source of the Guadalquivir.

Theirs was a precarious and wonderful kingdom, fit for the sultans who succeeded one another at the Alhambra. There was one among them whose exploits were legion— Ottoman ben Abi Ola, "the Sheik of the Volunteers of the Faith, leader of the Zegri princes." He was the direct descendant of Abdul Akk, founder of the Merinid dynasty of the Maghreb. "Standing at the portals of Paradise, in the shadow of swords, fighter of the Holy War, destroyer of enemies, staunch and unyielding lion of lions, forever blessed." Others followed him, Abu Hadjaj Yusuf, the builder of the Alhambra, Mohammed V, "powerful amid luxury and pleasures," and finally the Abencerrages. But the position of Granada grew increasingly precarious. "The Moslem empire, at one time so extensive, began to shrink, and the enemy serpent devoured here a city, there a fortress, and gnawed away at a branch of the national tree."

The last counterforts of the Sierra Nevada ended on three

hills. Upon them the city of Granada rose in graded steps: the Crimson Towers, the Alhambra, and the Alcazaba. All around, irrigated by the Genil, extended the grenadine *vega*. Not far away were Almería and Málaga, junctions of Arab Spain and the Barbary empire. Figs and wines of Málaga, Santa Fé almonds, oranges of Almería, spreading holm oaks and arbutus, the pungent aroma of lavender baked by the sun, the unending whisper of rivers—who can forget the undying fascination of the Andalusian *huertas?* Overhanging this shaded oasis, dotted with villas and windmills, was the Alhambra, the residence of the Moorish kings. Here and there in the Hall of the Ambassadors, the motto of the Nasrid kings was engraved: "God alone is victor." In the doorway an inscription below an urn welcomed the visitor: "The hand of the sculptor has woven me like silk cloth. I shed a blazing light. To him who comes here thirsty I offer as refreshment a pure and limpid drink. I am likened to the sparkling rainbow and the sun. May heavenly blessings descend on the balconies of this palace so long as caravans of pilgrims voyage to the sanctuary of Mecca." This was the "castle ablaze with splendor and beauty," the summer residence of Arab sovereigns. And here was Boabdil, the last of the Abencerrages.

For the last ten years the two leading families of Granada were locked in a struggle to the death. Women led the feud: the beautiful Zoraya, "Star of the Dawn," a Christian converted to Islam, mistress of the sultan Muley Hassan, and his haughty wife, Ayesha. The Abencerrages sided with the favorite, the Zegris with the queen. When the sultan installed the Spanish woman in the Alhambra, Ayesha retreated to the hill of the Albaicín and awaited her chance to strike.

Ferdinand and Hassan, who had been friendly for a time, broke their truce. A bitter battle between Christians and Moslems ensued. Defeated at Zahara, the sultan took his revenge at Loja. At the same time, a political crisis beset the Moors. Ayesha, the repudiated queen, fled to Guadix and there had the Infante Boabdil, *el rey chico*, crowned King of Granada. She raised an army to fight her husband, chased him from Granada, and there established her son. Disorder reached its peak.

The Catholic Kings watched the final convulsion of Arab power and prepared to pounce upon their exhausted prey. From the Cortes they obtained funds for a lightning campaign which cost almost a million silver ducats. Pope Sixtus IV issued a papal bull sanctioning the crusade and sent a silver cross to the armies. A hundred thousand Spanish soldiers converged on Granada.

Málaga, Almería, and Guadix fell into their hands. But Granada—that thorn in the side of Christian Spain—stood firm. Realizing their common danger, the Abencerrages and Zegris quickly made peace. "Down with the Infidels!" was the order of the day.

Granada was beleaguered. The Spanish camp at Santa Fé was so close to the walls of the city that Christian horsemen and Moors could take one another's measure and exchange insults. Here and there on the plains they engaged in hand-to-hand combat, sword against scimitar. One night Pérez del Pugar crossed the Arab trenches, stuck his dagger in a parchment on which was written the *Ave Maria*, and affixed it to the door of the mosque. Both sides displayed enormous courage, to say nothing of religious fervor.

Isabella stayed at the camp with the soldiers. A tent was pitched for her near Ferdinand's and her mere presence served to hearten the Castilians. One morning she climbed the Zubia, a mountain in the Sierra Nevada, for a full view of the beleaguered city. Granada lay at her feet, "resplendent like a fiancée dressed in her holiday best." The three fabulous hills resembled sections of a pomegranate split open, between which ran the waters of the Darro and "the river of snow called the Genil, for its source is in the Cholaïr, or snow mountains!" On the highest hill, the Alhambra stood out like a flaming torch. In the hollow of the shadows, parts of the Moorish city emerged clearly. She could see the Court of Lions, with its marble portico and yellow-and-blue-tiled walls, and the twelve stone lions poised to spring. The Court of Myrtle was here too, with its mirror of water, and the Abencerrages' Hall of the Ambassadors, where, not so long ago, thirty-six of their noblest cavalrymen were traitorously beheaded. All around was the poignant Oriental country-side—the pale green of the campaniles fused with the darker, almost black shades of cypresses. The mountains were barren, the sky in flames, and a tawny luminosity flooded the vast silver bowl—the colors and brightness of Africa rather than Spain. The princess of the *meseta* was overcome by all this beauty. Was she not a native of Madrigal de las Altas Torres, on the black soil of Old Castile? And now Africa flung this bouquet of fragrance, this shower of blazing lights, straight at her face, her heart. "If I just stretch out my hand Africa will be mine," the dazzled Isabella told herself.

But events moved quickly. Boabdil's vizier negotiated secretly with the Spanish generals. The last Moorish king was about to surrender. The conditions imposed by the victors were not harsh. The lives of all Moors would be safe and they would be allowed to practice their religion, maintain their mosques, and keep their property. Their own cadis and their own laws would govern them. Nor would they be subject to military service. Naturally, anyone who wished could embrace the Catholic faith. There would be no restrictions on travel or business transactions. "The Moors will be favored and treated well, as good vassals and subjects, by their Highnesses and their honorable administrators." Thus, by offering the defeated emir acceptable conditions, Ferdinand and Isabella deliberately displayed an evangelical tolerance that contrasted with Moslem fanaticism. The document they drew up ended as follows: "We declare, promise, and swear on our royal oath that we will observe and implement everything herein stated, each item and section, now and forever." *Siempre y siempre* . . . The ink was hardly dry on the treaty when tolerance became intolerance and the Court of Myrtle was transformed into a pool of blood.

At dawn on January 2, 1492, the Catholic Kings emerged from their camp at Santa Fé, preceded by the banners of Santiago and the Virgin. The great Spanish cardinal, González de Mendoza, rode beside them, followed by nobles of Aragon and Castile, bishops and deacons. Boabdil, accompanied by fifty horsemen, went to meet the victors. Reaching the banks of the Genil, where Ferdinand awaited him, the Moor descended from his horse and handed Ferdinand the keys of the Alcazar; he gave the seal of the city to the new governor, the Count of Tendilla. While Isabella and Ferdinand exchanged amenities with Boabdil, the Spanish advance guard entered Granada. Cardinal Mendoza hung the pontiff's silver cross and the standard of Castile on the tower of Comares. From the top of the tower of Vela a herald proclaimed: "Granada belongs to the Catholic Kings!" A few hours later the Spanish sovereigns solemnly entered the Alhambra.

"Come to Valladolid with me," Ferdinand suggested to Boabdil. "You will be treated like my own brother." But *el rey chico* shook his head. He pointed to his family, waiting to go into exile. His place was with them. Followed by his aging mother, Ayesha, and all his women and servants, Boabdil headed for the Sierras. Before entering the mountains he turned around for a last glimpse of the minarets of Granada. He could not hold back his tears. Dry-eyed, Ayesha gnashed her teeth. "Cry like a woman for the kingdom you could not protect like a man." Then the last Moorish king, the dark, baneful sultana, and the sorry procession moved into the wild Alpujarra Mountains.

A few days later, in the Alhambra, the Catholic Kings celebrated the successful termination of the Reconquest. Arab domination, which had lasted for eight centuries, was finally destroyed. The Moslem empire no longer existed.

While in the vast turquoise sky of Granada trumpet blasts sounded the *Te Deum*, from the Darro, swollen with corpses, a sweetish odor of carrion mingled with the scent of triumphal incense and Andalusian carnations.

La Limpia Sangre

Moderation comes easily to the victor in the first flush of success. Yet the extraordinary clemency shown by the Catholic Kings to the Moors was nonetheless surprising. Actually, it concealed a political motive, stemming from the determination to end a ruinous war, even at the cost of mercy. In any event, the Spanish sovereigns could not assume that the Moslem danger had ended with the destruction of the Moslem state. Moors who had gone to Africa lent their support to the enemies of Spain. Feigning submission, Moriscos who had chosen to remain under the new rulers bided their time, awaiting a chance for revenge. Both groups hated the country with which they had never completely identified themselves. Besides, how could faithful disciples of Mohammed forgive Christians for hanging crosses from the cupolas of their mosques?

Soon after the Moors of Granada had been defeated, the Catholic Kings realized the danger posed by this "fifth column" which was obedient to the Sultan of Constantinople. Isabella, who represented Christian orthodoxy far more than did Ferdinand, foresaw the peril with particular clarity. The Moor was a heretic, to be converted or destroyed. And so the intolerant Isabella, following the advice of her spiritual counselor, Jiménez de Cisneros, opened a campaign against the Moors.

The order was given to burn Arab manuscripts and to harass Moorish peasants and merchants until they had no choice but to flee or embrace Christianity. Many chose baptism in order to keep their property, for, after all, they had to live. They remained in Spain, but of course were never good Christians. The majority preferred to cross the sea, and a few, the most recalcitrant, chose rebellion. On the hill of the Albaicín in the Alpujarras, they organized nuclei of resistance which survived for years.

The Jews' turn came next. Ferdinand and Isabella never forgot their role in the Arab invasion. Closing their eyes to the incomparable service that the Jews had rendered since then to Spanish civilization—so many of them were doctors, scholars, and philosophers—the two sovereigns remembered them only as former allies of the Moors. An edict issued by the king and queen, which was supplemented by one of Torquemada's, gave the Jews three months to leave Spain.

Preceded by violinists and accompanied by their rabbis, almost 200,000 Jews, who had liquidated their affairs as best they could, streamed toward the southern ports. For many centuries, in Africa and in the Balkans, their descendants spoke the Spanish tongue.

The Jews were gone, and the Moriscos soon followed. Jewish converts, called *marranes*, remained, as did Moslems who had become Christian. These were called *conversos*, and they adhered secretly to the faith of their fathers. Religious and political factors became intermingled. Fundamentally hostile to Christianity, most of the *conversos* were even more unfriendly to Spain. To eliminate this danger, Isabella relied upon the terrible arm of the Inquisition. Torquemada resorted to torture by fire, and in Seville the pyres began to blaze.

How can one explain such savage violence and such religious bigotry? Many members of the Spanish clergy, and not the least distinguished, were reluctant to be associated with the movement. Isabella was chiefly responsible. One must also remember that fifteenth-century Spain, after the Reconquest, was still permeated with Jewish and Arab influence. In the opinion of the queen, territorial unity had to be supplemented by ethnic unity. Only a radical purge, odious as it was, could eradicate the past and safeguard the future from the threat of Lutheranism. Such was Isabella's way of thinking, and her uncompromising piety did not blind her very keen sense of reality. By rallying the energies of the Spaniards around two overriding ideas—race and faith—a way was cleared for the coming of the Golden Century. Everything was expected of the pure in blood, *la limpia sangre*, provided they also believed in Jesus Christ. All the others were exiled or looked upon with suspicion. But neither reasons of state nor the notion—a new one in Spain—of imposing on the people the religion of their princes adequately accounts for the pitiless deeds of the Catholic Kings. One must look elsewhere, in a quasi-mystical domain, for an explanation. Indeed, Spain's fundamental tendency to identify with Catholicism had already begun to be apparent. Every war became a crusade; every quarrel was tinged with dogmatism. Royalty acknowledged its role as defender of the faith and gloried in it. Was this racism and fanaticism? It probably was. In any case, that tough, militant country which the Catholic sovereigns fashioned, and which was to have an amazing career in the sixteenth century, pulsated with the religious fervor of a neophyte. It was nourished by God and that was enough.

The New Spain

To the detriment of the national interest, Jews and Moslems were now either banished from Spain or assimilated. Political and religious unity was an accomplished fact. There remained but to marshal the royal authority and to re-establish order. In a few years this was done, and by means of the iron fist. The nobility, which had fallen into disrepute after the civil war in Castile, resumed its former position, and the military orders were attached to the crown. Hereafter there was but one militia, that of the kings: the *Santa Hermandad*.

The need for a strong militia had made itself felt long before Ferdinand and Isabella; consequently, a Holy Brotherhood, the *Hermandad*, was created. It consisted of all the forces of law and order responsible for preventing local disturbances, such as plunder or robbery. The *Hermandad* was strictly a military organization. To keep it from overstepping its authority, the Catholic Kings from the very first fixed its duties clearly: "Should malefactors commit a felony in a populated area and flee to the country, carrying off stolen property, or kidnap women they have raped, the *Hermandad* should be summoned. . . . It should also be called in case of highway robbery, assault and battery . . . and rape if the woman is not a prostitute." The officers of the *Hermandad* were called *quadrilleros*. They were dispersed throughout the villages, their number varying according to the size of the population. In every village of three hundred or more, two alcaldes to serve the *Hermandad* were elected, one from the equerry, the other from the plebs. Whenever a misdemeanor was reported to the *quadrilleros*, bells were rung in all the parishes and everyone was expected to join the chase. Sancho Panza spoke of this when, deploring Don Quixote's freeing of the galley slaves, he "thought to himself that the runaways would alert the *Santa Hermandad*, who would rush about amidst a great ringing of bells in search of the offender." Should a malefactor, fleeing the *Hermandad*, seek refuge in a castle, and should his protectors refuse to give him up, the *quadrilleros* were required to besiege the castle and raze it to the ground. The *Hermandad* had its own penal code; penalties ranged from a mere fine to capital punishment, but torture was allowed in all cases, regardless of the nature of the offense. People were whipped, their ears were cut off or their feet amputated, and, cruelest of all, some were subjected to a slow death from arrow wounds. In short, the *Santa Hermandad* was a state police, a constabulary with its own tribunal. Not only bandits but noblemen and prelates had cause to fear it, for it interfered with their control of the people. For this reason the Archbishop of Toledo wrote to the Catholic monarchs: "The newly established *Hermandad* must be abolished. It is a burden upon the people and an abomination to the great." The sovereigns quite rightly disregarded this piece of advice.

While the *quadrilleros* continued to track down criminals and thieves, the Catholic Kings set the affairs of the state in order. The various cortes were consulted, but the principal instrument of the royal authority was the Council of Castile. Furthermore, local assemblies of the crown's delegates, the *corregidores*, controlled and supervised the courts and the administration. Communication between the various branches of government improved. In fact, the domestic business of the kingdom had never been so well organized. To be sure, although the policies of the monarchs played a part in the establishment of internal order, the nobility unwittingly facilitated their task by engaging in quarrels that lasted a half century. Feudal rebels, weary and divided, proved easy prey for the Catholic Kings, and those who resisted felt the full force of the kingdom's machinery of war.

The Armada, extremely powerful on land and sea, was commanded by Generalissimo Gonzalo de Córdoba, the "Great Captain" and conqueror of Granada. Since there was no treasurer, Hernando de Talavero, the queen's confessor, served for a time as Minister of Finance. Strong personalities appeared in the wake of the new monarchs, smoothing the path for the clergy, just as similar figures had done under the Visigoths. Ferdinand and Isabella obtained from the Holy See permission to choose their own bishops, and they used it with keen discrimination. Never before had Spain known so brilliant an ecclesiastical elite. Three outstanding prelates succeeded one another on the episcopal throne of Toledo: Carrillo de Acuña, Gonzales de Mendoza, and Jiménez de Cisneros. The last two, although very different in temperament, helped significantly to build the new Spain.

The scion of a fine old Guadalajara family, Mendoza became a bishop at the age of twenty-six. He had fought the partisans of the Beltraneja at Toro. General of the Christian army that besieged Granada, he was the first to enter the Alhambra and receive the homage of Boabdil. In his feudal castle at Calahorra, on the slopes of Aldeire, the brilliant prelate lived like a Renaissance prince. He erected hospitals, convents, and basilicas. A great lord and poet, he was born on the day of the Invention of the Cross, the very cross that he had affixed to the tower of Comares. Three years after this happy occasion he died, his hand clasped in Isabella's. To the very last, Mendoza was preoccupied with the affairs of the kingdom. On his deathbed he urged the Catholic Kings to indemnify the Beltraneja for her lost legacy by marrying their son Juan to her. Isabella gently shook her head and sighed: "The cardinal is delirious."

Jiménez de Cisneros, the Third King

Francisco Jiménez de Cisneros was born at Torrelaguna at the foot of the Guadarramas, twenty-five miles north of Madrid. He was the son of a tax collector. At a very early age he showed so much aptitude for study that he was sent to Alcalá de Henares, and then to the University of Salamanca. He chose an ecclesiastical career and became an ordained priest. Then, barely twenty-three, he left for Rome, where he was employed in the papal consistory.

After fourteen years in the Eternal City, Cisneros returned to Spain, determined to live the life of a penitent. He had accomplished his earthly tasks and now prepared to withdraw from the world. He donned the robe of the Franciscans and retreated to a monastery, El Castañar, not far from Toledo. On an isolated hillside he built a wooden cabin and there he lived, devoting his time to prayer and to the Scriptures.

It was at this time that Cardinal Mendoza died, and there seemed to be no suitable successor. Isabella was perplexed, remembering the dying words of Mendoza: "Keep eminent people away from the archbishopric of Toledo." The sixty-year-old Franciscan, who during Lent in 1495 had had charge of the court's retreat, appeared to be the most appropriate candidate. But would he accept? At first Cisneros replied indignantly: "Only a woman would entertain such absurd ideas!" But Rome ordered him to say yes, and so Cisneros became an archbishop. His life changed radically. He lived in a palace and wore purple and furs. But he slept on a board, adhered to his self-imposed discipline, wore the Franciscan frock beneath his fine clothing, and never touched the delicacies he was obliged to offer his guests. The people of Toledo would always remember his arrival. The brilliant dignitaries and lords who had assembled at the gates of the city to welcome Cisneros were astounded. Could this be the new prelate, this monk in a coarse robe of brown wool, his bare feet in sandals, slowly riding toward them on his mule?

Cisneros had been most reluctant to accept the high office, but now that it was his, he resolved to make full use of his prerogatives. His first act was to establish order among the clergy. And it was high time, for it had fallen into disrepute. The majority of its members looked upon their calling as a convenient means of avoiding taxes and acquiring secure positions and sinecures. Too many priests were ignorant and

uninspired. Cisneros had convents, monasteries, and seminaries built to house and instruct this frivolous, illiterate
clergy. But he did not forget that a house of God must, by its
magnificence, symbolize the glory of the divine. He devised
a type of architecture upon which he left his own indelible
imprint. Cleverly combining cathedral and mosque, he originated a Gothic-Arab style which harmonized purity of line
with splendor of material.

Cardinal and leader of the Spanish Church, Cisneros was
also the Great Inquisitor. He accompanied Ferdinand and
Isabella to Granada, sprinkled baptismal water on the
crowds to obliterate any vestiges of heresy, and burned all
Arab manuscripts except those that dealt with medical
science. Nor was war distasteful to him. He accompanied the
army to Mers-el-Kebir and confronted the Arab lines, which
extended from Oran to Tlemcen. Dressed in his episcopal
robes and preceded by an enormous Franciscan who carried
the cross of the Spanish primate, the old man cried out:
"That long-awaited hour has struck. Look at this accursed
land and at the insolent and hateful enemy, thirsting for
your blood!" If anyone had told him, in his cabin at El
Castañar, that he would one day be issuing military proclamations, he would probably have been astounded. The tall,
red-gowned figure, walking among the soldiers and stopping
to inspect cannons and blunderbusses, seemed a far cry from
the anchorite he had been. Occasionally he would pick up a
gun and ask to be shown how it worked. Still vigorous at the
age of seventy, the erstwhile monk discovered that he had
an aptitude for the art of war. "The smell of gunpowder is
as pleasing to me as incense," he confessed with mischievous
artlessness.

Ferdinand had begun to show symptoms of the strange
ailment that was to end his life. Suffering from a nervous
melancholia, he suspected his enemies of poisoning his food
and went about consulting sorcerers. Yet his mind remained
quite lucid. On the day of his death, he wrote his grandson
Charles a letter of farewell: "Most illustrious Prince, our beloved son, it has pleased the Lord our God to reduce us to

such a state that we are obliged to behave more like the dead than the living." After Ferdinand's death, Cardinal Cisneros became the real ruler of Spain, and it was he who protected the regency until Charles came of age.

Cisneros never forgot that he was primarily a man of God. His brilliant career did not deflect him from his religious vocation. Having established order among the clergy, he founded the famous University of Alcalá de Henares, which rivaled the University of Salamanca. Twelve thousand students, the future elite of Spain, studied science, literature, every discipline from Hebrew to anatomy, with the exception of civil law. Cisneros was somewhat hostile to lawyers, whom he considered chatterboxes and parasites. The students worked hard at Alcalá, but they ate well, for Cisneros's motto was: "Empty stomach, empty head." It was here that the famous six-volume Bible, the Complutensian Polyglot, was published. For the first time the Bible was printed simultaneously in Hebrew, Chaldean, Greek, and Latin. "This was done to revive the study of the Holy Scriptures, dead or somnolent until now." Of course, the preparation of so monumental a work, to which the most eminent men of the time, including Erasmus and the famous Nebrissensis, contributed, was not accomplished without passionate controversy. One day Nebrissensis left the University of Alcalá, slamming the door behind him, and returned to Salamanca. "What is to prevent me from circulating among carpenters, blacksmiths, tailors, and shoemakers and join them in deriding those who wear the robe and who claim to be men of letters and sincerely believe that their interpretation of whatever they read is the only correct one? . . . And if nobody wants to heed me, I can always go off in a corner or dig a hole in the desert. . . . For I can think of nothing more amusing than to hear honored and authoritative men utter the kind of rubbish that would make children and even fools laugh." Fractious college professors never die.

Cisneros was now eighty. Everyone insisted that he allow himself some rest; Leo X ordered him to eat meat and follow the doctors' orders. But the venerable old prelate only

laughed. Never had his activities been more varied and effective. France was attempting to conquer Navarre and was
providing arms to the pretenders. Cisneros crushed them
and had the Navarrese fortresses razed. He organized a
professional army, established a flotilla, and attacked Barbarossa, but there he failed. Everything was grist for his
mill: he gave advice on how to cast cannon and manufacture
powder; he drafted a set of laws for the administration of
the New World and sliced unnecessary expenditures from
the government's budget. "I am working like a fiend and
manage very well. I will not give up."

But he eagerly awaited the end of the regency. It seemed
to take a long time for the prince to come of age! Exhausted,
the cardinal sought escape in a monastery, La Anguilera.
Would he live long enough to hand over the reins to young
Charles and give him some final advice? The young Flemish
king eventually landed at Villaviciosa in the Asturias. Cisneros set out to meet him but died on the way. Thus there
was no chance for a last conversation between the monk who
had become a cardinal and the emperor who was to end his
days as a hermit.

Alexander VI (Rodrigo Borja), the Spanish pope, had bestowed the title of Catholic Kings on Ferdinand and Isabella. Thereafter they ranked with "the very Christian King
of France." But a "third king" deserved a place beside them
—Jiménez de Cisneros, the Spanish Richelieu.

Mendoza and Cisneros—magnificence and poverty—one
wearing the purple, the other the coarse brown robe of the
Franciscans, one astride his horse on the ramparts of Granada, the other kneeling in the dust. The earthly empire
and the Kingdom of God. . . . The fifteenth century ended
and the sixteenth began amid these contrasting symbols
of pride and humility.

THE AGE OF
El Greco

"It was he, the man from Crete, who gave us the
greatest understanding of the contemporaries
of Cervantes and Theresa of Ávila."
                                —MAURICE BARRÈS,
        El Greco, or the Secret of Toledo

PART·III

I

The Great Clerics

On November 24, 1504, Isabella died at Medina del Campo. Her daughter, Juana the Mad, was married to Archduke Philip, the son of Maximilian, emperor of Austria; she was the nominal heir to the throne of Castile. Very wisely, Ferdinand had entrusted Castile to the care of Cisneros until his grandson, Charles of Ghent, should be old enough to rule. Ferdinand died in 1516, and the following year Charles I of Spain landed at Villaviciosa. For the moment we will take leave of this adolescent—he was only seventeen!—and allow him to make his way along the roads of Asturias. Later we will retrace our steps and become better acquainted with the character and personality of the man.

The year of the future Charles V's birth, 1500, also marked the beginning of the Golden Century in Spain, a glorious era, an enormous blazing fire whose sparks still light up the Western skies.

Charles V and Philip II. . . . Let us briefly consider these impassive rulers as persons, apart from their empires. Naturally the two Habsburg princes played a role during this period. Like the great lords of El Greco, or the table-mates of Count Orgaz, they must certainly be placed in the foreground of a fresco depicting the Golden Century. Merciless fighters, they offended the religious convictions of many, but their autocratic rule never triumphed over the spirits of men. In spite of their resounding victories, the Golden Century was in nowise indebted to them. The Battle of Lepanto is inseparable from Cervantes, and the author of Don Quixote, the simple soldier, outlived Don Juan of Austria. The source of all this beauty sprang spontaneously from the very heart of the masses—Luis de Granada was the son of a washerwoman, Zurbarán the child of a peasant. And while the sovereigns of the House of Austria were attempting to build a powerful Iberian world in the image of the Holy Roman Empire, scholars, painters, and poets were constructing a colorful musical and spiritual universe of their own. The empire of Charles V crumbled, but that of Cervantes and El Greco is as young today as it was at the start.

The Precursors

The gold of the Golden Century lies in its soul, newly sprung from Christian thought and culture. It is hardly enough to say that this brilliant era, which began with Ferdinand and Isabella and continued until the middle of the seventeenth century, was fructified by the religious ideal. So close was the relationship between faith and genius that the age seemed to be nothing less than Christ's gift to Spain.

An ever-expanding culture had prepared the way for the Golden Century. Lower schools had been established in Spain as early as 900; universities followed a little later. The University of Coimbra, operated by the Augustinians, dated from Alfonso VI of Castile. At Palencia, Alfonso VIII founded a university directed by Bishop Don Tello Téllez de Meneses, the hero of Las Navas de Tolosa. Not long afterward, Alfonso IX of Leon and Ferdinand the Saint founded and developed the University of Salamanca.

In the heart of Leon, churches, houses, the palaces of Salamanca, built in beautiful shades of ocher, seemed to be strung along the three hills like the beads of a rosary. Below flowed the Tormes. So many historical memories were associated with this region—Hannibal had maintained one of his residences here—that Salamanca came to be called "Little Rome." But it was to its university that it owed the title of "mother of virtues, sciences, and arts," which it retained for several centuries. And indeed, like Paris, Oxford, and Bologna, it represented one of the spiritual capitals of the world. Here Christopher Columbus sought scientific advice before setting out for the New World. In the sixteenth century the University of Salamanca had almost 7,000 students. All the sciences were taught, even the Copernican system, which was considered heretical by all other universities. The influence of the great Salamancan school has steadily declined; today it ranks only eighth among Spanish universities. One can still see Fray Luis de Leon's chair in the old theological seminary and, on the wall of an ancient balcony, the diploma of doctor *honoris causa* awarded to St. Theresa of Ávila.

In addition to the universities of Salamanca, Palencia, and Alcalá de Henares, many secondary institutions of learning were established between the thirteenth and fifteenth centuries at Valladolid, Seville, Compostela, Granada, and Saragossa, to say nothing of valuable libraries. There were both masters and books—all that was needed to create the great family of Spanish humanists. Thus, long before the close of the Middle Ages, Spain had potent instruments of learning. Its kings imported books and the first printing presses, and the language began to be noted for its ever-richer nobility of expression. During this fertile period, which extended from the twilight of the Middle Ages to the dawn of modern times, Spain was learning and meditating.

A few precursors foreshadowed the philosophers of the Golden Century. Alfonso of Cartagena, bishop of Burgos, was a Latinist and Hellenist; Alfonso Tostado, bishop of Ávila, astounded his fellow clergymen with his enormous erudition; Juan of Segovia made a name for himself at the Council of Basel by defending the doctrine of the Immaculate Conception against a Dominican and by refuting the tenets of the Koran. Ferdinand of Cordova, a physician and theologian, stimulated controversy at the Sorbonne, while Alfonso Martínez de Toledo, the archpriest of Talavera, wrote a *Holy Life of Isidorus.* To be sure, most of these pious men were not exceptionally talented, and their works, although praiseworthy, lacked originality, being more in the nature of compilations than the products of profound reflection. Nonetheless, they paved the way for the great humanists of the sixteenth century.

The Great Clerics

Luis Vives was born in Valencia and died in Burgos; he taught at Louvain and Oxford and resided for a time at the court of Henry VIII, where he tutored Mary Tudor, the future wife of Philip II. Educator and moralist, Vives, long before Kant, distinguished the sensory perception of things, or *phenomena,* from their essence, or *noumena.* In the opinion of this outstanding Catholic philosopher, the coexistence in the minds of men of speculative and practical reason did not preclude belief in God and the eternal verities. Vives, who inspired both Kant and Descartes, was one of the great minds of the Golden Century.

Fray Luis de Leon was born in Belmonte, not far from the windmills of La Mancha. Of Jewish origin but converted to Catholicism, he attended the University of Salamanca, enrolled in the Augustinian Order, and finally returned to the university as a professor. He translated and expounded the Song of Songs, wrote the *Perfecta Casada,* and taught scholasticism. He was not only an exegete, theologian, and moralist but also one of Spain's greatest poets. To his friend the blind musician Salinas, he wrote: "The air grows more serene and fills with fresh beauty and light, Salinas, when that sublime musical phrase, yielding to your skillful hand, resounds. . . . At its heavenly sound, my soul returns from oblivion and recaptures the original feeling and memory it had lost. . . . It leaps over space to reach that supreme sphere where another harmony can be heard, attaining the eternal, which is the music of all musics. . . . Oh, ecstasy, oh, death which gives life!" This musicality, this glorification of mystical ecstasy and death, is certainly characteristic of the writings of St. Theresa. Yet Luis de Leon never knew St. Theresa. He did have some contact with St. John of the Cross, but we know nothing of the nature of this relationship. However, we do know that John of the Cross studied at the University of Salamanca when Luis de Leon taught theology there. What impression did the master, who had such an original mind, who cultivated music, astrology, and poetry, make on the student? Could it be that John of the Cross did not know the poems in which Luis sang of "the starry sky, the perfect image of Peace," of cosmic night, man's refuge in his search for God? Did he attend the organ concerts that Salinas gave in a small room at the university? Or did they walk past each other like strangers in the cloistered halls? After the death of Theresa, when persecution of the reformed Carmelite reached its height, Luis de Leon headed the revolt. Is it possible that, in this final phase of the struggle for reform of the order, Luis de Leon never met John of the Cross and never made common cause with him? Both men died the same year, and both bequeathed the same fragile theme and the same fresh view of the world.

Luis de Granada was the son of a poor washerwoman. He was born in Granada and died in Lisbon when he was almost ninety. Reared by the Dominicans, he soon joined their order and became one of their luminaries. Superior first of the Scala Coeli monastery in the Cordovan Sierras, then of the monasteries of Palma del Río and Badajoz, Luis de Granada became religious adviser to the Duke of Medina-Sidonia. Threatened by the Inquisition—in the sixteenth century, the slightest thing tended to arouse suspicion of Illuminism among the mystics!—Luis went on a mission to Portugal. He was provincial of his order, and Queen Catherine appointed him her confessor. Renouncing his intention of returning to Spain, he ended his days in Lisbon.

Luis de Granada wrote in Latin, Spanish, and Portuguese. His principal works in the Castilian language are: *The Book of Prayer and Meditation, A Guide for Sinners, A Memorial of Christian Life, An Introduction to the Symbol of Faith,* and *A Summary of Spiritual Doctrine*. Theologian and preacher of asceticism, he was also an outstanding writer, a virtuoso of the sonorous Castilian language. *"Oración es subir el ánima sobre si y sobre todo lo criado y juntarse con Dios y engolfarse en aquel piélago de infinita suavidad y amor."* He enjoyed—and still enjoys today—a very wide audience, and he influenced French thought and literature during the century of Louis XIV. His writings were in greater demand even than *Don Quixote*. And his sermons were apparently no less amazing and magnificent than his literary style. His prestige as a preacher was such that he was allowed to lecture everywhere in Spain, accompanied by a priest of his own choice. Yet this illustrious Spaniard elected to die in exile!

Francisco Suárez was likewise born in Granada and died in Lisbon. He was a member of the noble family of Suárez Vásquez, which had recently settled in Granada. He, too, studied at Salamanca and hoped to join the Society of Jesus. It required great effort on his part to realize his ambitions, for his health was delicate and his intellect seemed mediocre. After a lengthy novitiate, he became an ordained priest. It was at this juncture that he revealed his true genius, teaching theology and philosophy first in Segovia and Valladolid, then in Salamanca, Rome, Coimbra, and Paris. So daring were his ideas—he originated the theory of "congruism," which reconciled free will with God's foreknowledge—that he was suspected of unorthodoxy by some querulous scholars.

This frail and sickly man whose days seemed to be numbered—actually he lived to be seventy!—became one of the greatest spiritual leaders of his era. Popes consulted him. Thus Paul V asked him to mediate the quarrel between James I of England and his Catholic subjects who had been commanded to swear an oath of allegiance. Suárez immediately sent the Stuart monarch his famous *Defensio Fidei catholicae contra anglicanae sectorae errores*, in which he defended the supremacy of spiritual authority. James I's answer was to have the hangman of London burn the insolent priest's treatise. Had it not been for the Pope's protest to

Louis XIII, the Parlement of Paris would have done like-wise. What a thunderbolt in the royal firmament was this reprimand administered by the foolhardy Jesuit! One could almost hear the "Et nunc erudimini, principes!" which a cen-tury later chilled the court of France.

Suárez's only regret was that he himself had not been burned for defending the faith, for he, too, passionately yearned for martyrdom and death. "I would never have believed that it was so sweet to die," he said at the last.

His principal works were: *Commentaries on the Theology of the Incarnation in St. Thomas, De Sacramentis, Dispu-tationes Metaphysicae, De Religione*, and above all his im-portant treatise *De Legibus ac Deo Legislatore*. One en-counters passages that seem singularly spirited at a time when nationalism was rampant among the princes of the realm. "Although mankind is divided into different nations and kingdoms, it nonetheless possesses a certain unity, not only a specific unity but a quasi-political and ethical one as well, which stems from natural precepts of mutual love and charity and necessarily embraces everyone, even foreigners, of whatever nationality." The need for a Law of Nations, for an International Law based upon evangelical morality, and the primacy of the spiritual over the temporal—such were the ideas courageously expounded by Suárez, *doctor eximius et pius*.

Francisco de Vitoria, a Basque, was born in Vitoria and died in Salamanca. At Burgos he put on the Dominican robe, and then departed for Paris, where he studied and min-gled with the intellectual elite of France. After traveling for a while in Flanders, he returned to Spain and was offered the chair of theology—*la Cátedra de Prima!*—at the University of Salamanca. He has been compared to Socrates, perhaps because he revived the scholastic method. St. Thomas's *Summa Theologica* served as the basis for his doctrines. He stimulated a return to the study of the Scriptures and the Holy Fathers, and not the least of his accomplishments was that he was the first to teach students the habit of taking notes.

Vitoria participated in famous theological disputes, especially the one concerning Erasmus at Valladolid. Acknowledging that philosopher's genius but deploring his rashness, he displayed a moderate, almost benign attitude toward Erasmus. Equally fair and understanding was his position on Protestantism, for animosity played no part in his judgments of men.

Vitoria was essentially a professor of ethics, and his doctrines are contained in his lectures. *Relectiones*, a posthumous work, expresses his most progressive ideas, discussing the international community, the rights of the nation, colonial rule, the relationships between states, legitimacy, and rules of warfare. These were challenging and controversial topics, and the master of Salamanca never shrank from speaking on them *ex cathedra* at a time of vast colonial expansion and under the ever-vigilant eye of Charles V. What a blast he exploded in the cold and somber lecture hall when he said: "Even though they enjoy papal protection, Christian princes cannot prevent barbarians from committing sins against nature, nor can they punish them. . . . Even if an emperor conquered the world, he nevertheless would not be entitled to occupy the territory of the barbarians, substitute new masters for old, or levy taxes. . . ." Vitoria also had a word to say about religious and colonial wars: "Differences of religion do not justify war. . . . Nor does glorification of the prince. . . . War cannot affect the truth of one's beliefs. It cannot force barbarians to become believers; it merely obliges them to feign acceptance of Christian precepts, and this is inhuman and a sacrilege. . . . The expansion of an empire is no justification for war."

These dangerous words fell one by one like stones, and their echo reached the imperial palace. The solemn warning came on the very eve of the great Spanish conquests! Four centuries before the term "conscientious objector" had ever been heard, Vitoria, in order to give greater weight to his injunction, declared: "Even should the prince so order, his subjects must refuse to fight if they are convinced that the war is unjust."

Even as this implacable voice resounded in the sky of Salamanca, Charles V was waging war against the Lutheran princes, and Francisco Pizarro was conquering the fabulous Inca empire. Yet Vitoria's lectures did not go unheeded by sovereigns and conquistadors. Had he not publicly, and with all the authority he possessed, imposed limitations on Spain's military ventures, what excesses of fanaticism and cupidity might have been committed! Dreaming already of international morality and of a world of brotherhood, the brave Dominican reminded the princes of Christ's teachings. Although he was powerless to prevent abuses and crimes committed in the name of religion—the very worst crimes of all —he at least sounded the alarm at a propitious moment. From then on, neither the leaders of the Counter Reformation nor the colonizers in America could ignore the boundary where their rights ended and their duties began.

Ignatius Loyola and the Society of Jesus

Íñigo López de Recalde was born in the castle of Loyola near Azpeitia, in the province of Guipúzcoa, a year before Ferdinand and Isabella seized Granada. This stronghold, its enormous walls pierced with loopholes, overlooked the valley of Urola and was dominated by Mount Izarraits, where the soil is dry and barren. In the valley, on the other hand, the apple trees remind one of Normandy, and fields of corn extend as far as the eye can see. Such are the contrasts of the Basque countryside. But the climate, affected by the Gulf of Gascony thirty miles away, is mild.

The people of Loyola were noblemen, true to old traditions. In the evenings they often spoke of famous ancestors, especially of Juan Pérez, who "led his seven sons in combat against the Navarrese, the French, and the Moors." Ever since the days of Pérez, seven blood-stained stripes adorned their coat of arms. The Loyola family was well-to-do, owning livestock and farms. Nevertheless, life was not always easy for Ignatius, the youngest of four brothers in a brood that included eight sisters; there were quite a few mouths to feed.

At the age of fourteen Ignatius became an orphan and entered the service of Juan Velásquez de Cuellara, at Ferdinand's court. Here he learned the art of war and liked it. Are we to believe his sundry biographers who describe him either as a "vain and unruly soldier" or as a "traitorous, brutal and vindictive man"? In any event, he had two passions—horseback riding and novels of chivalry. Ignatius was a dashing rider. The slight, spare Basque, with well-developed muscles, was proud of his birth, his country, and his descent from the Iberians. Long, abundant curls fell to his shoulders, and he wore an open cape which revealed an embroidered jerkin slashed with silk. A satin cap sat jauntily on his head, and he bore a shining shield. The joy of living and a desire to please shone from his velvety eyes. He dreamed of leading a heroic and gallant life in imitation of the legendary Amadis of Gaul. Oh, if only the fairy magician Urganda would agree to protect him, giants would not intimidate him, nor tyrants, regardless of their weapons! But for the moment, he shared the fortunes of the viceroy of Aragon; diplomat and soldier in turn, sword in hand, he made his own way. One day he was summoned to intervene in Hernani, whose inhabitants were in a state of rebellion. Lacking troops, practically alone and confronted with an angry populace, he decided to parley. Choosing his words carefully, he convinced and calmed the irate throng. The revolt was over. This was his first encounter with mass emotions, and it was also his first triumph.

In 1521 the King of Navarre, Jean d'Albret, aided by the King of France, tried to recapture his capital, Pamplona, which Ferdinand and Isabella had seized. Ignatius, then a young man of thirty, followed Count André de Foix to fight the French on their own side; not long after, a cannon ball struck him. One leg was badly shattered and the other broken. The city fell and Ignatius was taken prisoner by the French. They treated him well and had him carried back to Loyola on a stretcher. He was so close to death when he arrived at the ancient Basque castle that the doctor shook his head, privately believing the case hopeless. However, Ignatius insisted that his bones be set regardless of the extreme pain, and thanks to his exceptional energy and determination, he recovered. His convalescence, which lasted several months and left him with a bad limp, proved a fruitful and enriching experience. Dragging himself along as best he could on his crutches, he went up and down the vast corridors, often visiting his father's library, where he would read novels of chivalry. Amadis of Gaul had also retreated to the rugged Basque coast. Since Ignatius was forced to lead a sedentary life, he could at least console himself with his favorite hero, and others such as Palmerin of England, Bernardo del Carpio, and Rinaldo de Montauban. On a dusty shelf he happened to see a well-worn volume of the life of Christ and a book entitled *A Life of the Saints*. He read them avidly and thus discovered a new kind of heroism, a heroism he had never dreamed of before. Was it then possible to live without the sword? As he meditated, a love of God welled up in him like the dawn of a new day. The crippled soldier discovered his true master and his real field of combat.

Ignatius left the castle with the intention of going to Jerusalem. He stopped for a moment at the sanctuary of Our Lady of Aránzazu, in the foothills of Mount Aitzgorri, then continued toward Montserrat. On his way he met a Moor who questioned the virginity of the Mother of God. Exasperated by his chance companion's incredulity, Ignatius left the decision of whether or not to slay him to the whim of his mule. For, as with the knights-errant, the honor of his fair lady demanded revenge. Fortunately for the Moor, they were approaching a crossroads and the mule began to trot, leaving the blasphemer far behind.

Ignatius had now reached Montserrat, the very heart of Catalonia. Above the Llobregat Valley rose a strange mountain, peopled with legends. Massively rooted in a ledge of red rocks, streaked in the center with parallel furrows and culminating in jagged stone ridges, it resembled a giant organ. The over-all coloration was pink and gray. Halfway to the top, on a terrace overlooking the valley, there was a monastery. In this sanctuary, built in honor of Our Lady of the Battles, future knights were to keep their vigils. His heart filled with God, but his imagination still stirred by romantic tales of chivalry, Ignatius, too, kept his vigil. He spent the night praying, placed his sword and dagger at the foot of the black Virgin, and swore he would conquer the enemies of his faith, not by the lance but by apostleship. Having made his confession to Jean Chanones, a French Benedictine monk, he exchanged his lordly jerkin for the rags of a mendicant.

His stay at Montserrat was brief. No sooner had he arrived than crowds of Navarrese noblemen, inquisitive about the extraordinary penance of this well-born young man, sought him out. He had become a curiosity. Seeking peace and quiet, he fled to another retreat at Manresa, not far from Montserrat. For a while he lived in a hospice; then he moved to a grotto on the banks of the Cardoner, where he had his first ascetic experience. Wrapped up in a sack, which explains why he has been described as "el pobre home del sac," he slept on the ground, fasted, and grew a beard. Considered mad by some, eccentric by others, he himself was occasionally assailed by doubts. But these he overcame. One day he was found unconscious and ill in his grotto and was hastily carried to the home of Don Andrés de Amigant, where he was cared for until he recovered. Ignatius concluded that he was not cut out to live the life of a hermit. Nonetheless, it was at Manresa that the Basque subjected his body to mortification and broke his last ties with the world of the flesh, just as John of the Cross was to do somewhat later. And it was here, too, that the first meeting between God and Loyola took place. Ecstasy and visions illuminated the cueva de San Ignacio; on this cold and remote rock Ignatius outlined his Spiritual Exercises.

He now felt strong enough to face the challenge of a visit to the Holy Land. He embarked at Barcelona, landed at Gaeta, walked to Rome and then to Venice, whence he sailed for Jerusalem, although he had again fallen ill. If we are to believe his biographer Ribadeneira, the sea voyage apparently cured him: "Seasickness purged him of physical impurities and restored him to health." After six weeks of rough weather, Ignatius landed at Jaffa. The hostility he encountered from both Turks and Franciscans did not encourage him to prolong his stay. Disappointed and displeased, he returned to Barcelona. His many trials and experiences had turned out badly! What would he need to succeed in his new vocation? Convinced that his failures were due in part to a lack of religious training, Ignatius now decided to become a priest. Although well past thirty, he began to study theology. At Barcelona he took courses in grammar, and then registered at the University of Alcalá, where he also preached. But his sermons were not at all to the liking of his teachers. He was harassed, reprimanded, even jailed, and finally forbidden to speak publicly. He left Alcalá to attend the rival University of Salamanca, only to encounter a similar mistrust. But even more serious was the criticism directed against him by the Inquisition. The time had come for Ignatius to leave a country that could not understand him. He took up his mendicant's stick and headed for Paris.

Determined to make a fresh start, he tried the humanities again. The former hero of Pamplona was now seated at the same ink-stained table as Montaigu's pupils—the "hencoop college," Rabelais called it. Would he be spared further humiliation? Apparently not, for he had to endure sarcastic remarks from regents as well as fellow students. This Spaniard, handicapped by lameness, ridiculed for his jarring accent, quietly accepted humiliation and mockery. He soon graduated, became a licentiate, and finally acquired a solid grounding in philosophy and theology.

But he was in great need of friends. A close-knit group, called "the inseparables," soon gathered around the intrepid Spaniard: Pierre Lefèvre, Francis Xavier, Diego Laynez, Alfonso Salmerón, Simón Rodríguez, Nicolas de Bobadilla, Claude LeJay, Pascal Broët, and Jean Godure. Sharing the same dream, the members of this talented and effervescent circle brought to maturity the bold project they had devised.

On the Feast of the Assumption, August 15, 1534, Ignatius and his companions performed an act that was to commit them for the rest of their lives. They went to the crypt of the Benedictine abbey of Montmartre and knelt on the flagstones. Pierre Lefèvre celebrated the Mass. When it came time for the Eucharist, Ignatius and his friends swore to serve their God by going to the Holy Land to convert the Infidels. They promised total submission to the authority of the Pope and made a vow of poverty, chastity, and obedience. On this beautiful summer morning in Montmartre—how tinged with blue was the hill overlooking the ramparts of Paris!—the Society of Jesus came into being. Then the Spanish and French brothers rushed out into the sunshine and romped like children. They played prisoner's base, shoved one another into ditches, and climbed, singing, to the top of Montmartre. The entire day was spent in gay companionship. Only occasionally was there a quick glance at the city below, shrouded in light mist. Indeed, within its walls Huguenots were being burned alive on the parvis of Notre-Dame, and the plague was rampant.

Ignatius visited Spain but found the same climate of opinion as before. He was not welcomed; in fact, people seemed to be lying in wait for him. Even his own family begged him to renounce his vow of poverty! No one, including relatives and compatriots, seemed to realize the tremendous effort his vocation demanded. He left Spain, never to return.

In Italy, on the contrary, he received a favorable response. Granted an audience by Pope Paul III, to whom he introduced his companions, he proceeded to explain their project. The sovereign pontiff, "the Pope of Reconciliation," immediately sensed the valuable assistance which this handful of determined men might give him in his efforts to combat the Reformation. He persuaded Ignatius that the spiritual reconquest of the Holy Land was less urgent than the struggle against the threat of Lutheranism. He bestowed official recognition on the Society of Jesus and approved its statutes.

Ignatius was elected general of the order. His companions were scattered to the four corners of the earth to "go . . . and teach all nations." Francis Xavier left for India while Ignatius remained in Rome. The battle had begun.

It was an arduous and unremitting struggle because the animosity directed against the nascent Society of Jesus came not only from heretics but also from within the Church itself. It took over ten years to complete the Constitutions of his order. Ignatius had to contend with innumerable difficulties, but his tenacity was proof against all obstacles. Temperamentally, he was well suited to daring ventures. As a foolish youth, he had coveted the widow of Ferdinand the Catholic, Germaine de Foix, and something of the swordsman and knight persisted in the heart of the apostle. Although he would not admit this to himself, Amadis of Gaul remained his ideal. He loved to fight, and he also loved discipline and its corollary, obedience. It was no accident that his Constitutions were named *Regimini Ecclesiae Militantis*—the military spirit in the service of God. Only the elite was admitted to the Society of Jesus, which demanded a fifteen-year probation. Such prolonged training was designed to strengthen a man's character and, at the same time, to break his will as an individual. Novices were taught the necessity of baring their souls to their superior. Their lives had to be an open book without any secrets or mystery, for their hearts belonged solely to God. Ignatius urged his novices to engage in methodical reflection, in constant and minute analyses of their sins. He wrote: "The first step is to review one's sins." His *Spiritual Exercises* is a manual for the practice of contemplation as well as asceticism. By dint of concentrated effort, the mind must discover Christ's humanity and construct themes for religious meditation. It would thus attain a conception of the essentials of eternal truths. The object so intensely contemplated would then become a tangible image. For example, the idea of Hell would be so deeply imprinted that the mind would eventually be able to perceive it. "Fires glimpsed, cries heard, tears and bitterness sensed, flames caressed." There is a similarity here between Loyola and Theresa of Ávila; we are also reminded of Ignatius' own ecstasy and his visions at Manresa. After undergoing this arduous training, the Jesuit is turned loose in the world. He preaches, teaches, and debates. Although he enjoys total freedom of action, he is nonetheless accountable in all things to his superior. The general heads the hierarchy. Elected by the Congregation, his authority is absolute. Only the Pope outranks him, and he, too, is the "servant of the servants of God." Total commitment of oneself to the pontiff, complete devotion to the Catholic cause, blind obedience to its leaders, discipline and fervor—these constitute the credo of the Society of Jesus.

So harsh a discipline, so tough and militant a conception of apostleship, startled the highly individualistic Spaniards of the sixteenth century. The introduction of the order in Spain met with stubborn resistance, whether declared or concealed. Melchor Cano, Vitoria's Dominican successor in the *Cátedra de Prima* of Salamanca, and Siliceo, the archbishop of Toledo, opposed the Society of Jesus with all their might. But Ignatius had powerful protectors: the Infante Don Philip, the Great Inquisitor Tavera, the nuncio Poggio. Somewhat later Don Francisco de Borgia, duke of Candia, heartbroken over the death of his wife, withdrew from the world and donned the robe of Loyola. This Valencian aristocrat became an ardent champion of the Society of Jesus in Castile and in Guipúzcoa. Later he was adviser to Theresa of Ávila and was named general of the order.

When Ignatius died in 1556, he left behind in his native land, which had been so unfaithful to him, sixteen colleges and three hundred Jesuits. Did he foresee the tremendous international influence the order was to exert in the centuries ahead? He died too soon to witness the close of the Council of Trent, which signalized the triumph of the Counter Reformation and revived Catholicism. However, such Jesuits as Diego Laynez, Alfonso Salmerón, Arias Montano, Pedro de Soto, and Diego de Covarrubias had already made major contributions. Ignatius barely lived long enough to have a glimmering of the role the order was to play in the evangelization of the New World. Nor did he receive during his lifetime his rightful reward for the enormous effort he had put forth. Practically alone when he died, he was given neither communion, extreme unction, nor papal benediction. There was not even a chance to say farewell to his own people; such is the solitude of the leader and the saint. A few months before, his Navarrese friend and one of the original pilgrims of Montmartre, Francis Xavier, also died alone off the coast of China. The Society of Jesus was less than fifteen years old! Loyola, Pamplona, Manresa, Rome, Canton . . . these marked the first stage of a spiritual and ultimately a political conquest of the world.

The Shadow and Light Erasmus Cast Over Spain

We cannot bid farewell to the great Spanish scholars without mentioning the sardonic and mighty shadow cast by that prince of humanists, the Dutchman Erasmus.

What a strange fate was his! The illegitimate son of Gérard Praet, he was brought up by tutors who thoroughly spoiled him. Induced to enter one of the orders, he was later released from his monastic vows by the Pope. He was at home in the great intellectual capitals of Europe—Paris, Oxford, and Bologna—and became an adviser to Charles V; later he moved to Basel, where he found the atmosphere of religious tolerance more to his liking. When Erasmus published his *Praise of Folly* in England, could he possibly have foreseen the emotional impact it would have and that it would provoke terrible religious reprisals?

Ten years later he wrote his *Novum Instrumentum*. Although it, too, was satirical, it dealt with major problems. "Christ's philosophy must be lived, not discussed," he wrote. The book was well received in Spain, especially in the intellectual circles of the cathedral of Palencia. Many people were greatly interested in meeting this daring and witty writer, who put humanism in the service of religion. He was invited to visit Spain by a variety of individuals. Cisneros himself, the regent of Castile, joined Spanish men of letters in requesting him to come; but Erasmus, recently named adviser to Charles of Ghent, hesitated. He was not drawn to the Spanish court, which he considered both supercilious and frivolous. Fernando Columbus, the son of the famous discoverer, went to see him at Louvain, but Erasmus said that he preferred to postpone the trip to Spain.

Ethusiasm for Erasmus was growing apace in the Spanish universities, particularly at Seville. The Dutchman became quite fashionable and his books had phenomenal sales. Apparently humanism was taking root in Spain. Then the Pope suddenly issued a bull excommunicating Luther. In the public square of Wittenberg the Augustinian monk burned the papal decree. Thus Lutheranism was born. Would the sacrilegious flames of this Prussian town scorch Erasmus?

What would happen to Erasmus' fervent disciples—Archbishop Fonseca, Friar Alonso de Virués, Juan de Vergara, and so many others? The Inquisition pursued well-known followers of Erasmus, and Diego de Zúñiga published his pamphlet *Blasphemy and Impiety*. Erasmus countered cleverly, displaying all his talents. Somewhat earlier he had published his *Enchiridion;* it was now translated into Spanish. Having had his say, he had nothing to add. The two weapons at the disposal of a Christian knight were prayer and knowledge of divine law. Prayer is an impulse of the heart, accompanied by acts of charity. Superstition is not religion. One must rise above the demands of the flesh and meditate upon spiritual matters, advancing from the tangible to the intangible. But bad priests were legion. In his *Colloquies*, which appeared at the height of the religious crisis, Erasmus vividly depicted the morals of the times. Not content merely to mock the German hostelries, he also attacked the mendicant monks, especially the Franciscans. Finally, his *Preparation for Death* disclosed his preoccupation with religious questions. Do not torment dying men by asking them for endless confessions! It is enough if they repeat the last words of Christ on the Cross: "*In manus tuas, Domine, commendo spiritum meum.*"

At first glance, none of this seemed to deviate from orthodoxy. Erasmus' philosophy would have remained a mere intellectual dispute if some of his friends had not drifted into heresy after the condemnation of Luther. Even more serious was the fact that the Alumbrados (later, when we deal with the mystics, we will explain the role this curious sect was to play) also claimed to have been inspired by Erasmus.

The matter became so grave that it was laid before a tribunal convoked at Valladolid especially for this purpose. After six weeks of deliberation, with Vitoria trying to exert a moderating influence, the tribunal condemned the Castilian editions of Erasmus' works and ordered that his Latin writings be expurgated.

For a long time after the death of Erasmus, controversy persisted between clerics who continued to admire him and monks who defended tradition—despite the vigilance of the Inquisition and some burnings at the stake. But in the interval between Charles V's going into seclusion in St. Yuste and the termination of the Council of Trent, Spain's spiritual climate underwent a change. The Spanish Caesar's dream —to reconcile Protestants and Catholics—was washed away by the blood of Mühlberg. Philip II mounted the throne and destroyed heresy. The name of Erasmus, if not his philosophy, was slowly effaced.

Yet so brilliant were the thoughts of this amazing man that even under Philip II his ideas survived him. The great clerics of the Counter Reformation could forget neither *Enchiridion* nor the *Colloquies*. Luis de Leon and perhaps John of the Cross—how caustically the Carmelite flayed sanctimonious sinners!—appreciated the writings of the Dutchman. The last sparks of Erasmian philosophy still shimmered on the porphyry tables of the Escorial library at the court of the "prudent king." And indeed, the Estremaduran Arias Montano was appointed by Philip II to translate the Polyglot Bible. Professor of Oriental languages at the royal monastery, Montano was already well known for his historical works as well as for his role at the Council of

Trent. He scorned the scholastics, adhered to the Old Testament, and, in his *Natural History*, did not hesitate to come to grips with pure science. A vast erudition, the application of new methods, an attempt to attain broader intellectual horizons, an almost religious espousal of humanism, a penchant for popularizing the Bible—all this bound him quite closely to Erasmus.

Erasmus never chose between Luther and Rome, for reasons of prudence or because of his scruples. His Christianity, based on salvation through faith in Jesus Christ, was obviously a departure from Spanish Catholicism. Freed from the formalism and the rigid framework of the Church, as he understood these, the religion of Erasmus was no more than an individual, anarchical process, a colloquy with God. Stripped of the universality and the hierarchical and communal nature which justified the Church's authority, Erasmus' credo, although seductive and not at all labored, was not to the liking of Catholic Spain, which was irresistibly attracted to a complex and tortuous form of worship.

Erasmus' spiritual presence in the peninsula for half a century coincided with the advent of Charles V. Only recently rid of the Moors, the new Spain at long last could turn away from Africa and look toward the north, from which its emperor came. His infatuation with Erasmus drew added attention to the philosopher. Moreover, individual piety and the inner life which the works of the Dutchman extolled were infinitely attractive to the first mystics. How enticing to the new *conversos*, who already leaned toward Illuminism, was this foreign philosophy that praised Christian freedom and surrender to divine inspiration! Of what use was moral discipline and dogma if one had but to pray in order to feel overwhelmed by the divine presence. Thus, the cold philosophy of the northerner was fused with very ancient Oriental modes of thought.

Erasmus rallied to his side the humanists, the men of culture, and the intellectuals. Against him were the scholastics, enamored of tradition, and the monks he derided—*"Monachatus non est pietas."* Yet this amazing scholar, who wrote equally well in Greek and Latin, and who esteemed the masterpieces of antiquity, this fascinating virtuoso so reminiscent of Priscillian, never succeeded in conquering Spain, although he exerted a strong influence on the artistic and literary tastes of northern Europe. Religious freedom would have destroyed completely the still somewhat fragile unity which Spain had forged with such difficulty and which Catholic orthodoxy served to cement. Besides, Erasmian ideas were unsuited to the mentality of the Spanish people, who were illiterate, but steeped in medieval traditions, faithful to the *cristiano viejo* that had become part of them; they were neither qualified nor inclined to take an interest in intellectual jousts. Finally, the caustic, bantering tone, the sparkling irony—two and a half centuries before Voltaire— the somewhat grating laughter that characterized Erasmus, struck a false note at a time when the taciturn king reigned at the Escorial. Irony had no chance of evoking a response in the fanatical Spain of the sixteenth century. Indeed, the revolutionaries of the Golden Century exerted themselves to effect a tightening of monastic discipline. If Erasmian ideas —those brilliant fireworks in the sky of Seville—were welcomed and savored by certain clever intellectuals, they failed altogether to deflect the great clerics of the Counter Reformation from the inexorable course already chosen.

Presumably, Erasmus foresaw all this and sensed the danger when he politely declined the invitation of Cardinal Cisneros, primate of Spain and Great Inquisitor.

2

God's Conquerors

CHARLES V dreamed of establishing a "world monarchy." His successor, the meticulous Philip II, toted up his kingdoms. Spanish caravels, loaded with gold and spices, cruised the waters of the Caribbean. Castilian pennons could be seen on virtually all the oceans. It seemed as if the Habsburgs were bent on world conquest.

Simultaneously, a race of adventurers sprang up who carried ambition even farther and built a world of unlimited possibilities. While the amazing Spanish empire was being forged, mystics were erecting and enlarging an inner empire that survived the more tangible one. Now more than ever, spiritual and historical events were connected. 1515 . . . Charles of Ghent was about to mount the throne of Castile, and Theresa of Cepeda was born in Ávila. 1542 . . . López de Villalobos named a Far Eastern archipelago after Philip II—the Philippines—and John of the Cross was born in Fontiveros. 1567 . . . the Flemings rebelled against their Spanish masters, and Theresa met John of the Cross at Medina del Campo. 1571 . . . The Battle of Lepanto and the "spiritual marriage" between Theresa and God. 1582 . . . Philip II seized Portugal and Theresa died. 1588 . . . Defeat of the "Invincible Armada," and John of the Cross became prior of Segovia. 1591 . . . Spain's political zenith and the death of John of the Cross. To be sure, the people of

the Golden Century—public opinion in Habsburg Spain—
were not preoccupied with the Carmelite revolution. The revolt and the writings of these obscure monks fascinated them
a good deal less than did the exploits of Don Juan of Austria. But any true historian who attempts to depict sixteenth-
century Spain must point out that spiritual and political
events were closely linked. Captains, conquerors, public figures, were imbued with the same mystic quality as El Greco,
even if they were not always aware of it. The actions, attitudes, and heroic outpourings of the protagonists of the
Golden Century do not emerge clearly until the searchlight
of mystical ecstasy plays upon them.

The Mystical Adventure

Christian mysticism is unintelligible without reference to the
concept of grace. To be sure, an important aspect, but probably not the most essential, can be perceived if one adopts
the clinical approach. After all, religious hysteria and the
nervous phenomena that accompany it are related to pathol-
ogy. Such disorders are treated medically, although, according to the most authoritative neurologists, a "psy-
choneurosis" is difficult to define; it cannot be viewed as an
illness, a disease, or a syndrome. In any case, it belongs to
the domain of physiology. Because the mystical process and
state defy medical analysis, they must be examined in the
light of faith. To avoid confusion, one must eliminate at the
very outset the hallucinated, the simulators, the definite
neuropaths—in short, all the false mystics—and consider
only the great masters. Of course, true mystics are not entirely free of morbid symptoms or nervous disorders, but
their genius resides precisely in their capacity to rise above
physical anomalies and attain the supreme sphere of the
spirit.

What then is mysticism and what does the word "mystical" imply? In the opinion of physicians, a mystic is a sick
person whose disorders are tinged with religion. Men of let-

ters regard him as an ardent idealist, incapable of clearly explaining the reasons for his feelings. According to philosophers, mystics are ascetics, Christian, Buddhist, or Moslem, who display strong religious emotions and a yearning to be one with God. Catholics see them as devotees of their faith and look upon mysticism as a doctrine and also as a personal experience that derives its substance from that very same doctrine as well as from life. To experience mysticism one must pass through three stages. The *purifying* stage tends to suppress external states of mind and requires a "purge" of emotions and feelings. One must discard every tie to earthly life, create a void within oneself, and obliterate both will and imagination. The *illuminative* way is narrow and brings one closer to the final objective, which is not only contemplation of God but also the process of uniting and identifying with Him *unitively*—a profound objective, which many attempt but few achieve! The true mystic transcends himself. He walks a long way in darkness and suppresses every sensation, every image. He renounces everything, even ecstasy, even visions. He is less obedient to the impulses of his heart than to that mysterious intuition—knowledge and certitude of God—which is totally unrelated to the insipid images of the merely pious. In order to realize his true purpose, a mystic must possess a spirit of conquest and a taste for it, a clear head and sound reason, wisdom, heroism, and strength. In the very depths of the "I," in the profound layers of the subconscious, he must uncover that inclination toward God, that hidden thread that will guide him to God. None of this has any connection with the questionable exaltation of pseudo mystics. For the inner experience of true mystics is based upon the moral personality, the "profound I" which the English psychologist Myers compared to an iceberg, most of which is submerged in the ocean of the unconscious, but whose upper portion, which becomes iridescent in the rays of the sun, corresponds to a clear conscience. This lucid "I," which one philosopher has spoken of as the "chiaroscuro of our ancestral emotivities," cannot be that of a madman.

Such is the lofty and solitary process, at once a full flowering and a withdrawal, an intelligent intuition that excludes
neither action nor awareness of the human nor generosity.
And the most accomplished mystics were Theresa of Ávila
and John of the Cross. What tender and occasionally
amused glances they cast at their fellow mortals! For them,
ecstasy was never limited to gentle languor. They developed with almost mathematical precision a method whose
purpose was essentially practical.

In order to realize the extent to which mystics harmonize
contemplation and action, we have but to observe their lives.

"Que Muero porque No Muero"

Let us look at Old Castile in the spring of the year. Ávila
. . . Already, between the rocks that only yesterday were
capped with snow, sumac has begun to grow. The rumbling
waters of the Adaja, less tumultuous at this season, were
singing. Ávila was emerging from winter. The March sun
sparkled coldly on the ramparts. Turrets with machicola-
tions, granite walls built by the Romans, Moorish battlements—it was as if each successive master of the ancient city
had added new stones to the forbidding ramparts. Inside
the walls, narrow, dark passageways intersected. Here was
the palace of the viceroy Núñez Vela, there the noble manor
house of the Duke de la Roca, and directly opposite was the
home of Alonso Sánchez de Cepeda, the father of the newborn child.

Theresa's parents were provincial lordlings who lived on
the scant revenue from their lands. Alonso de Cepeda was
austere and very pious. His second wife and Theresa's
mother, Beatrice de Ahumada, was quiet and unassuming.
She rarely went out, and although very young, dressed like
an old woman and surreptitiously read novels of chivalry.
There were twelve children at home! Six of the boys left for
India to wage war and seek their fortune. Rodríguez de
Cepeda, Theresa's favorite brother, was made a captain in

the royal army and shortly afterward was killed at Río de la Plato, when he was barely twenty-five. At the age of six, Theresa ran away with Rodríguez to convert the Moors, but an uncle they met accidentally brought them home. The escapade was quite understandable in view of the kind of conversation adults engaged in when Theresa was present. Their discussions revolved around the lives of saints, the prowess of the early conquistadors, and sometimes a point of theology. The odor of gunpowder and the aroma of incense. . . . In France it seemed that heresy was about to triumph. Would it spread to Spain? One can almost hear the close-knit family whispering in their house, built in the hollows of the ramparts. Alonso de Cepeda was an uncompromising Catholic who believed that it was not enough merely to be virtuous. One must set an example, perform acts of piety, carefully scrutinize one's slightest doubts. Children as well as parents sternly disciplined themselves and probed their every act. At a very early age Theresa was taught a relentless piety—prolonged prayer, endless litanies, recitation of the Holy Mysteries. There was little laughter or gaiety, only an atmosphere of saintliness.

The entire city of Ávila was one large monastery. When the Angelus sounded, thousands of church bells carried the message all the way to the Sierras. On the stony slopes, in the shade of rust-colored dungeons, monasteries abounded. The Dominicans at Santo Tomás and the Jesuits at San Gil fiercely defended Catholic orthodoxy. No sooner did the day dawn than the murmur of countless prayers could be heard issuing from the cathedral-fortress.

Each day the blazing Castilian sun scorched the slate and lead of churches on that rocky carapace of Ávila. It was in this oppressive moral climate, on this harsh and parched soil, that Theresa began to fashion her inner homeland.

When she was twenty she entered the Carmelite Convent of the Incarnation. She had hesitated for a long time; although inexorably drawn to the service of God, it was not easy for her to renounce worldly pleasures completely. She loved diversion, romantic tales of chivalry, compliments, nice clothes and perfumes, frivolous conversations with friends and younger cousins. These were innocent enough, and it was painful to give them up. Besides, she was beautiful. Everyone said so and she herself knew it. Her waist was slender, her hair quite dark, her eyes lively though not deep-set, her lips smiling and her complexion rosy. Her hands were small and plump and three beauty spots graced her left cheek. She was handsome, fiery, and graceful.

We next see her in the convent cell. She has not yet removed her orange-colored dress with the long velvet ribbons that trail to the ground. From her open window she can see Ávila, the thin, crenelated outline of the ramparts and a few patches of greenery on the banks of the Adaja. A purplish glimmer tinges with coral the summit of the Sierra de Malagón. It is twilight and Theresa can hear the windmills as her new companions intone psalms. She sighs.

The following year Theresa took her vows. The rule of the Convent of the Incarnation was that of St. Albert, but substantially modified by Pope Eugenius IV's so-called "bull of mitigation." Although the one hundred and eighty Carmelites of Ávila lived apart, they were not entirely cloistered, being permitted to receive visitors from the outside world. The parlor of the Incarnation was "the last salon where one conversed." Pretending moral self-improvement, tongues wagged; charity and piety were not always present among the *tertulias*. The muffled laughter, the childish chatter, seemed more appropriate to a school for debutantes than to a Carmelite convent administered in accordance with the rules of its founder.

Although Theresa appeared to be in good health, she fell seriously ill after taking her vows. Was this a recurrence of the mysterious ailment that had so worried her parents a few years before? Could her nervous disorders—sudden fainting spells, alternating moods of depression and elation, gastric pains, vomiting, temporary paralysis of the lower limbs—be the warning signs of the ecstasy she was later to experience? Today a neurologist would not find it difficult to make a diagnosis. Theresa's father removed her from the convent and took her to a healer at Becedas, where she remained for two months. But upon her return to Ávila, she had a relapse. Suffering terribly, she begged for extreme unction and lost consciousness. Everyone thought she was dying; she recovered and, after three years of convalescence, again took up her abode in the convent cell.

Now began what Theresa herself called her "period of infidelity." She was bored with religious practices and performed them halfheartedly. She gave up praying entirely. Her soul, once filled with fire, was indifferent, uncaring. On the other hand, she developed a passion for embroidery and spent most of her time in the parlor. Crowds of friends came to see her, mostly men, the cream of Ávila's nobility. Theresa was so witty, and how beautiful she looked in her woolen robe! Having just eluded death, Theresa wanted to enjoy life. She remembered that she was the daughter of a nobleman who belonged to one of the finest families of Castile. The King of Leon was among her ancestors! She and her friends pored over books of heraldry about Toledo and Ávila. Would the world with all its vanities claim Theresa de Ahumada? This seemed likely, judging by the mocking voice of the girl and the supercilious laughter of the *caballeros* that resounded in the parlor of the Incarnation.

When Theresa was twenty-eight her father died. Her grief was hard to bear, but it was salutary, for it marked the end of her frivolity. From then on idle chatter and daydreaming ceased. Immense sorrow enabled her to hear once again and more clearly than before the call of God. She consulted her father's confessor, the Dominican Vicente Barón, who taught her the technique of prayer which Angela de Foligno had discovered three centuries earlier. First comes *corporeal* prayer, comprising words and genuflections; then *mental* prayer, accompanied by an overwhelming sense of the presence of God; and finally *supernatural* prayer, in which the soul is "enraptured" by God's mercy and comprehends the incomprehensible. Theresa read the *Confessions* of St. Augustine, another professor of mysticism, who explains the three processes: *purification* by *virtus,*

illumination by *tranquilitas*, peace and *unitivity* by *lux*—
entry into and sojourn in light. One day, as she was entering
a private chapel, she noticed a statue of Christ that had been
placed there by chance. She was deeply moved by this likeness in multicolored woods—the open wounds, the long trail
of blood. What remorse she felt, how much time she had
wasted! Years passed. Theresa was reaching maturity. The
voice of Jesus grew more persistent, more imperious. She
realized that her life was just beginning, or rather God's
life within her heart. Already extraordinary visions came to
torment and delight her.

At the age of forty, Theresa entered the world of mysticism. At first intermittent and confused, her visions soon
multiplied and became clearer. Little by little Christ revealed Himself to her. She saw His hands, then His face.
She did not know what to make of such strange phenomena.
Was God truly manifesting His presence or was He merely
tempting her? She anxiously wondered whether she was not
simply a prey to physical disorders. A nobleman of Ávila,
Francis de Salcedo, to whom she confided her worries, advised her to consult her confessors. She placed herself successively under the spiritual guidance of two men: a Jesuit,
Juan de Pradanos, and Father Balthazar Álvarez. Everyone
badgered her and offered conflicting advice. Finally she met
Pedro de Alcántara and Francis Borgia and was reassured
by them. Asked to write the story of her life, she complied.
She said she did so out of obedience, but some vestige of
vanity still persisted; her style had often been praised. Every
intelligent woman, even one on the road to saintliness, has
something of the creative writer in her.

Contemplation alone was no longer enough for this soul
consumed with love. Pedro de Alcántara had taught her the
grandeur of Franciscan poverty, contending that only destitution could open the portals of heaven. Accompanied by
four nuns as weary as she of too lax an order, Theresa left
the Convent of the Incarnation and founded a "small and
poor" house, her first, which she called St. Joseph of Ávila.
At the same time she completed her autobiography and

began *The Road to Perfection*, intended for the guidance of her nuns.

Aiming to reinstate the original ideas of the Carmelite Order—poverty, penitence, and prayer—Theresa introduced a rigid discipline. The people of Ávila disapproved of the dissident nun. Municipal judges, bishops, and churchgoers were highly critical, to say nothing of the nuns at the Convent of the Incarnation, who felt deeply insulted. Utterly indifferent to public opinion, the determined reformer persisted. She was now forty-seven and believed that every day counted. Five years later, the general prior of the Carmelite Order, Father Rubeo, granted her permission to found more convents and even two monasteries for "contemplative Carmelite friars."

The second convent of Barefoot Carmelites was established at Medino del Campo, in a half-demolished hovel. But who would help in founding a monastery? A certain John de San Matíos was suggested. Recently graudated from the University of Salamanca and having renounced a promising career there, he had just celebrated his first Mass. He apparently intended to "give himself up to God" and withdraw to a Carthusian monastery. Here was an ideal helpmate! The first meeting between Theresa and the future John of the Cross took place at Medina del Campo, in a house that had just been converted into a convent. John was twenty-five and Theresa was fifty-two. The patrician nun of royal blood and the son of a humble weaver from Fontiveros quickly reached an understanding. The Mother Superior's arguments proved convincing. John agreed to reform the order "provided he would not have to wait long." Thirsting for God, he had looked forward to his solitary retreat, but since action was now required of him, he was eager to get on with the task.

While John of the Cross was finishing his last year of theological study at the University of Salamanca, Theresa was in Valladolid founding a third convent. She gave John his final instructions when he came to see her. One can almost imagine the conversation that occurred as Theresa super-

vised the work of the masons who were putting the finishing
touches to the convent wall. They discussed practical matters—the transformation of an attic into a dormitory, the
installation of a chapel in the barn. But what enthusiasm on
the round, friendly face of the little Castilian and in Theresa's large, dark eyes!

After Valladolid and Duruelo came Toledo, Pastrana,
Salamanca, Alba de Tormes. . . . One after the other
Theresa founded convents on the harsh Castilian plain. At
the same time she acquired new helpers. During one of her
many trips she met, at the Franciscan monastery of
Madrid, an Italian hermit and former diplomat, Mariano
d'Azzaro, and a peasant and sculptor from the Abruzzi,
Giovanni Narducci. Theresa sensed that these adventurers,
both recent penitents, could be of great help to her. She
urged them to serve God by working for the Carmelite Order. How could they resist the appeal of this determined
woman? They were given the robe of lay friars and adopted
the names of Ambrosio de San Benito and Juan del Misero.

A sudden decision of the apostolic vicar interrupted
Theresa's itinerant existence for a time. She was ordered to
go to the Convent of the Incarnation, where, at the age of
twenty-two, she had taken her vows, and to remain there for
three years as prioress. Was this an honor or a punishment?
Probably both. Theresa was overcome with grief. She
would have to abandon the work of reform to which she had
devoted the past ten years. The Convent of the Incarnation
acknowledged and practiced only the Mitigated rule. Before taking up her duties Theresa sought refuge in the little
convent of St. Joseph, the first she had founded. It was necessary, she felt, to make her position quite clear. Before the
entire community, she solemnly renounced the Mitigated
rule and vowed she would uphold the original rule of the
order until she died. Reassured now that she had publicly
declared her faith in the reformed order, Theresa crossed
the threshold of the Convent of the Incarnation with head
high.

To find herself once again in the place where, for over

twenty years, she had spun out her languor and her vague daydreams—what a trial for the saint she had become! The same parlor that had echoed with her idle chatter, the same cell still permeated with her boredom—nothing had changed! A taste of ashes was all that remained of youthful memories. Almost instinctively the new prioress approached the cell where she had spent so many hours of pleasant, pious torpor. She lowered her veil; her feet were bare in the hemp sandals. For a moment she felt weighed down by the unvoiced irritation of her former companions, who now had become her charges. They knew all too well that her arrival foreshadowed reform. She was greeted with icy silence, but soon the nuns rebelled openly, damning and slandering this madwoman who had come to upset their peaceful habits.

It took Theresa no more than six months to take hold of her recalcitrant flock. The nuns accepted not only her but the new rule as well. After completing this difficult task, she asked John of the Cross to serve as confessor of the community. For five years he remained at the Convent of the Incarnation, while Theresa, after serving three years as prioress, resumed her work of founding new convents. Very little is known about the relationship between Theresa and John of the Cross during this period, but everything suggests that these years of spiritual collaboration fructified their genius. No evidence whatever, not a single document or letter, is available to help one penetrate the secret of this extraordinary communion of souls. What did the two great mystics talk about, what books did they exchange? It is almost possible to visualize them walking slowly in the Ávila countryside, along the *camino de la Incarnación*, perhaps going all the way to the chapel of the *Cabeza*. In contrast to their meetings at Medino del Campo and Valladolid, this time John of the Cross did the talking while Theresa listened. Their fateful colloquies and the restrained warmth of their pious outpourings still echo in our minds. John was thirty and Theresa almost twice his age, but the world which they discovered together was that of eternal youth. Better than any document, two facts reveal the influence they exerted upon each other during their stay at the Convent of the Incarnation: six months after John of the Cross's arrival at Ávila, Theresa mentioned for the first time her "spiritual union" with God (before their meeting, she had not yet formulated her ideas); only now did either of them write a basic treatise. This would seem to indicate a mysterious attunement.

While Theresa joyously resumed her travels in Castile, John of the Cross, who remained at Ávila, gave himself up to meditation. Two years went by. Theresa founded more convents at Segovia and Beas and then started out for Madrid.

But a great gust of wind was to shake the young sapling of Carmelite Reform. The conflict between the Barefoot and Mitigated rules reached a more acute phase. The apostolic vicars sent by Pope Pius V to visit the Spanish Carmelites favored the Barefoot rule, thus overruling the instructions of the general of the order. Carmelites of the Mitigated rule used this as a pretext for intensifying their campaign against the reformed nuns, whom they accused of rebellion. Tempers flared. A general chapter of the order met at Plasencia to invoke sanctions against the Barefoot rule. Theresa herself was ordered to retire to a convent at Toledo and "forbidden to found new orders or to visit other convents."

Not at all daunted by this new test of strength, Theresa appealed to Philip II, imploring the sovereign to authorize the establishment of a separate order for Barefoot Carmelites. But the king did not answer. Meanwhile, a new prioress was elected at the Convent of the Incarnation. The election was presided over by the provincial of the Mitigated rule. The nuns who voted for Theresa—fifty-five in all—were "excommunicated and damned." The nun who had received the least number of votes was declared elected. Finally, to lend greater emphasis to the purge, the authorities moved against John of the Cross. He was arrested in the middle of the night and taken, "like a malefactor," to the monastery at Toledo, where the Mitigated rule was enforced.

More determined and energetic than ever, Theresa wrote Philip II that she would rather see John of the Cross in the hands of the Moors. "He would perhaps be treated with greater mercy." Although beginning to feel "old and tired," Theresa was still "young in her desires." She harassed the Spanish court with entreaties and finally got her way. Gregory XIII issued a bull legalizing the Reformed Carmelite Order. It was to have its own rule. Theresa again received permission to resume her visits and to create new convents.

But this was her swan song. For a short time the "restless vagabond" continued to roam Castile. Villanueva de la Jara, Palencia, Soria, Burgos—this was Theresa's heroic itinerary. Beneath the monumental gate of Santa María de Burgos, built in honor of Charles V, passed the wagons of the Reformed Carmelite Order. What endless waiting for permission to cross the bridges! How many accidents on the road—a wagon stuck in the mud or the sudden overflowing of a river! At night the nuns slept out in the open, beneath the arch of a bridge or in some sordid *posada*. Huddled together under a tarpaulin, the little sisters became a familiar sight. Their long, lowered veils and white woolen cloaks commanded respect. The irregular tinkling of mules' bells, the muffled tread of *alpargatas* on the dry soil of Old Castile, the jingling of rosary beads, the occasional strum of a guitar in the distance—such were the last sounds Theresa was to hear.

The chapter of Alcalá approved the constitutions of the Reformed Carmelite Order. Now, supremely satisfied, the *Santa Madre* could die. She finished her book *Foundations*, and traveled to Alba de Tormes. At nine o'clock on an October evening—it was the day of St. Francis—Theresa succumbed. Ever since the morning she had been softly moaning, "like the swan that sings more sweetly as it is about to die." Her murmurs were as gentle as those of the Tormes, which flowed, metallic, beneath the moon. Her face shone like a glowing sun. "It is time for me to meet my Beloved," she said. A final sigh and the *Mater spiritualium* was no more.

She was no more, but her experience and her doctrine remain forever fresh. She taught the essential role of prayer;

first mental prayer, then prayer for quietude, and finally prayer for union. One must create absolute silence within oneself, so that God can enter like water in a garden. By following these successive steps, Theresa reached a state of rapture. In the heaven of one's soul, "That Oriental pearl," make place for the Lord! Then followed undreamed-of spiritual delights. Theresa's heart, mystically wounded by the Seraphim's dart, both faltered and blazed. To make her meaning clearer, Theresa multiplied images and examples. The soul is not only a garden refreshed by water, but also a "castle within," possessing seven abodes: first a residence for preparatory prayers, then a place for the first summons, and then, successively, rooms for trials of strength, for contemplation of the divine, for ecstasy, visions, and, finally, union. The soul is also a silkworm that weaves the cocoon in which it must die before reanimating the butterfly. All these images of quasi-Oriental inspiration exemplify a rational and graduated practice of prayer, an intense concentration of thought which creates a state of receptivity to God. Thereupon one is *inhabited* by God, he is one's own prisoner, one can feel, see, and touch Him, not with one's eyes or bodily senses, but with one's spirit. This pure intuition, this intellectual vision, no human language, save perhaps that of the poet, can define or express. Theresian mysticism is incomprehensible when dissociated from the personality of Theresa herself. Her conduct, the various facets of her life, her work as a reformer, her writings, character, and physical disorders—which will someday be the subject of a neurological study—all these constitute a whole, an entity. The internal drama of the virgin of Ávila is best summed up in her long cry of love: "I am dying of not dying."

On the Mountain—Nothing

Between Salamanca and Ávila, on the plains of Old Castile, dotted with dark poplars, the small market town of Fontiveros casts its reflection on the blue lagoon. In one of the poorest houses, which had whitewashed walls and a low ceiling crisscrossed with brown wooden beams, Catalina de Yepes gave birth on St. John's day to the child that was later to become known as St. John of the Cross.

Not long after, Catalina's husband died. Seeking a better livelihood, Catalina moved with her three small sons first to Arévalo and then to Medino del Campo. At that time, Medino del Campo was a thriving feudal city. Throngs would gather in the *plaza mayor*—merchants, money changers, usurers, brigands, and beggars. During the season of large fairs, the principal cities of Europe would send their finest products to the Medina market: silks, earthenware, and precious stones. In this place, which looked like something out of *A Thousand and One Nights*, John of the Cross had his first glimpse of the world.

He attended a religious school, where he learned to read and write. Roaming the narrow, foul-smelling streets of the town with boys of his own age, he played around the moats of the Castillo de la Mota. Later he served as a male nurse at the Medina hospital, where he learned firsthand about physical misery. In his free time he took courses at the Jesuit school.

When he was twenty-one, John took his vows as a Carmelite *Observantine* at Santa Anna de Medina. Four years after donning the robe of the White Friars, he was sent by his superiors to the University of Salamanca to study theology. During his three years there he cultivated his skill as a writer and elaborated his aesthetic and philosophical views. He read a good deal, attended lectures—possibly those of Luis de Leon—made friends with fellow students and exchanged ideas with them. All this contributed to the development of his genius.

The brilliant young man might have had a fine future at the university, but he was not at all tempted because of a loftier ambition. Renouncing the pastoral ring and the square cap of the professor of theology, he left Salamanca, that rose-colored, stately city of one hundred escutcheon-filled palaces, to return to Medina del Campo. There he became an ordained priest and nourished his yearning for the cell, robe, and white hood of a Carthusian monk. But, instead, he met Theresa of Ávila.

From that decisive moment, John of the Cross dedicated himself to Carmelite reform. It was high time to cauterize the wounds. A century earlier, the Black Plague, which began in Asia, had spread to Europe and killed thousands. Is it possible that this experience caused the lassitude and general weakening of morale which contaminated even the Carmelites? Mercy was dying out in the cloisters, and prayer was giving way to bitter disputes. During the same period, the great Western Schism destroyed the unity of the Church. The antagonism of the rival popes was reflected in the religious orders, each of which had two generals, one claiming to represent Rome, the other the pontiff of Avignon. This intolerable situation forced Pope Eugenius IV, more than a century before the birth of John of the Cross, to promulgate a bull of mitigation which modified and softened the Carmelite rule. The wise holy father saw that it was necessary to adapt or risk being destroyed. Nevertheless, the order of St. Albert grew more and more decadent, so that in spite of a few isolated attempts at reform, every day brought the old Carmelite ship closer to foundering.

John of the Cross was probably thinking of this as he made his way to Duruelo, a small hamlet on the banks of the Almar River, approximately thirty miles from Ávila. There he donned the new robe of the Barefoot Carmelites, which Theresa of Jesus had cut and sewn herself: a coarse woolen gown and white hooded scapulary, encircled by a broad leather belt. A second convent was founded at Pastrana, in a large grotto of yellow ocher rock below the town, and a third at Alcalá, in a glacial plain exposed to all the winds. Finally, Theresa summoned him to help her at Ávila.

Five years went by, during which the reformed convents multiplied. The austerity and dignified way of life, together with the extraordinary fervor of the Barefoot Carmelites, attracted men of distinction and talent who admired the

evangelical nature and harsh grandeur of the order. Its
heroic efforts were inevitably contrasted with the laxity of
the Mitigated order. This irritated, then alarmed the gentlemen of the Mitigated order. Enough of rumors and scandal!
John of the Cross was seized, put in chains, and dragged to
Toledo.

This Carmelite monastery, which was situated at the eastern end of the city, looked out over the Alcántara Bridge.
The rumbling Tagus, like a yellow serpent, wound around
the Saracen fortress. Dark clouds drifted in the apocalyptic
sky. Did John remember Theresa's remark? "Never in my
life have I seen a place with such a flavor of aridity as Toledo." During his nine months of captivity John had plenty
of time to brood about this. Every day he would go to the
refectory to be disciplined. False promises accompanied the
blows and insults. "If you renounce the reformed rule we'll
make you prior." The priests queued up and took turns beating him. "Deaf bastard," they shouted, spurning Christian
charity. But bribes, calumny, and flagellation were thwarted
by his iron will and infinite gentleness. He would not yield an
inch "even if it cost him his life." It was, of course, quite obvious that the Mitigated order was less irate with the reform
movement than anxious to punish John of the Cross and,
indirectly, Theresa of Jesus—two souls possessed of divine
love. A shaft of light rose from the somber crypt. In his
prison cell, John composed the first lines of his *Spiritual
Canticle*. At the same time, not far from the monastery, El
Greco completed his painting "The Stripping of Christ before the Crucifixion"—a double burst of flame in the black
Toledan desert.

John of the Cross escaped from the monastery. A little
later, Philip II, finally realizing the plight of the Reformed
Carmelite Order, requested the nuncio to intervene. The reformed order thus obtained justice and was free to carry on
within its own framework. After his flight from Toledo,
John of the Cross was named prior of the Calvary monastery near the Guadalquivir. On the way to his new post, he

stopped near Beas de Segura. Here the poor martyr, "his face darkened," enjoyed for a moment the gentle Andalusian countryside. A soft wind was blowing from the chain of Sincola y Sincoluella. Feeling at one with the sonorous Sierra, he finished his *Canticle* and began his treatises. In the evening he followed the muledrivers' path to Beas and talked with his spiritual daughters about "the things of this world and the next." Here, too, he found silence, punctuated by the gentle murmur of flowing waters and the occasional sound of galloping horses.

A brief service as rector of Baeza was followed by appointment to the priorship of the Carmelite monastery at Granada. Now John completed *Climbing to Carmel* and *Dark Night* and began work on *The Living Flame of Love*. The monastery for martyrs was built on the heights. From his cell, John could see the darkling plain of Granada, traversed by the silvery thread of the Genil. In the distance was the Sierra Nevada, and near by, the red and gold Alhambra, the Mirador of the generals, its gardens luscious with fragrance. Around the Moorish city, prickly pears and myrtle grew in profusion. It was in this African setting that John waged his last battle against himself—inflicting severe punishment on his body—and worked for the triumph of the reform movement.

Theresa died and Father Doria was elected provincial of the Reformed Carmelite Order. The new vicar, a henchman of Philip II, swore he would destroy John of the Cross by any means at his disposal, nor did he balk at the meanest. Overburdened by responsibilities, physically weakened by acts of penitence, but at the height of his intellectual powers, John yet resisted. He left Granada for Segovia, which was to be his last priorship. He spent his nights in prayer, lying beneath a chestnut tree, his arms crossed on his chest. He could scarcely sleep, and he ate very sparingly. A tremendous yearning for death possessed the emaciated, worn, and ulcerated body. Like a spent, breathless deer, his heart was lacerated by joy. He had already reached a world where none could follow him. The cry of the jackdaws, the whispering river, harmonized with his vast Spanish dream of martyrdom and blood.

Pope Sixtus V's bull decided the question of reform. Although it conferred independence upon the Barefoot order, it nonetheless imposed so many restrictions that the spirit of St. Theresa in the end was destroyed. Both friars and nuns were placed under the jurisdiction of a religious council, which could assign them to monasteries and convents. A less rigid discipline replaced the iron one Theresa had espoused. Political organization was substituted for mystical dreams, almost as if the cold Doria—out of spiteful obstinacy or perhaps in compliance with orders from the Escorial—wanted to shatter the very memory of Theresa.

But John held out against the gathering storm. He preached piety above all, then penitence and love of God. His strong will, his spirit which could not be made to yield, irritated his persecutors. This little man who held reform, like the Eucharistic wafer, high above his head, must be crushed. What errors could be ascribed to him, with what crimes could he be charged? For he was the real enemy; he had to be overcome and condemned. This madman stationed at the head of his aging troops—an Anna of Jesus, an older Luis de Leon—who defied the order's rule, must be silenced. God so decreed.

A council met at Madrid and ordered John of the Cross to desist. He was stripped of all responsibility and position and commanded to retire to the desert of Peñuela. The grandiose drama was nearing its end. After a few days at Peñuela, John fell seriously ill. He was transferred to the San Salvador monastery at Úbeda, the ancient city of the Moors, where he was received with frigid hostility. Nobody wanted to be compromised by his presence, for this man was truly marked by persecution. The north wind attacked the portals of the monastery in great lashing gusts. Now and then a flash of lightning streaked the gloomy Andalusian sky. It was December at Úbeda! Gypsies in gay-colored wagons gathered around the sick man and sang, hoping to distract him from his sufferings. But John of the Cross brushed them aside with a gesture. "It would not be good to ward off with music the pain that God has seen fit to visit upon me." While heavy rains bent the slender bushes of the Sierra Morena, John's martyrdom drew to a close. Crowded around his wretched pallet, the prior and the entire community, their hearts finally moved, watched motionless. Like the lines of an engraving, the oblique light of a smoking candle etched these wooden-faced monks. Just as the matins sounded, John of the Cross, freed from his long night, welcomed the dawn of eternal love. His soul, finally at the end of its mystical flight, was sundered from the crucified body in one great wrench. God incorporated his spirit and became one with it.

A prince of solitude all his life, John of the Cross died alone—alone as he had been among his Carmelite friars, alone among men, and alone in the presence of his God. Like all those who are impelled by an overpowering ambition, he could expect help from no one. He trod his mysterious path in solitude, followed at a great distance by a hesitant flock, quick to tire and ready to break ranks at the first obstacle. The royal bearing, the princely gait, the sad and weary look with which he embraced the world—all this is familiar to us. Thus Jesus, that other solitary being, walked the road to Galilee.

But John of the Cross was not only a man of silence. Despite his inclinations, he had been forced to act. He originated a technique that permitted the soul to comprehend the divine. The method he taught and disseminated influenced all humanity. He trained "beginners," browbeat, bullied, and lashed out at recalcitrant souls. His iron discipline was often accompanied by harshness.

What was his aim? To create an inner void and, armed with ineffable love, to rise to the realm of the spirit. The soul, on its flight, will be plunged into the "active night," of the mind and the senses. Physical appetites will be destroyed and intellectual faculties stamped out. The soul will then forsake meditation for contemplation. The narrow door will be forced open and the mysterious threshold crossed. But hardly does the soul congratulate itself on its victory when once again it is plunged into a second night, far darker than the first—a "passive night." At the very moment God invades it, the soul feels forsaken. So near to the end of its search, it is overcome by depression and languor, and must begin anew! Old temptations, the impurest, assail it. God is not within reach, and the soul, faced with the terror of nothingness, is defenseless. There is nought but the spirit's abject "spiritual howling" in the silence of the dark night.

But moments of ecstasy intervene. The hour of the mystical betrothal is about to sound. Like the shaft of an arrow, the soul lunges at its divine prey. It demands and receives God's love. Better still, it becomes one with its Master and is identified with Him. It participates in Divinity. While the body is inert, confusedly longing for death, the soul is gathered in by God and God by the soul. John of the Cross chose to say nothing about the unfathomable aspiration to total fusion of God with the soul. "I can plainly see that I cannot describe it, and that, should I try, the thing itself would seem less than it is."

The solitary voyage of the soul toward God, as well as the dialectical progress of Johannine thought, culminates in a blazing trail, and in silence. Exhausted by joy, the soul is still. And the proscribed martyr of Úbeda, whose last song was sung in the fading glory of the Andalusian autumn— oh, if he were only alive, now that God besieges him on every side!—let fall his pen. One can scarcely hear the dying voice. But "the dazzling shadow of God," like the final ray of the setting sun, slowly covers the dead man, enveloped in his woolen robe. John of the Cross has ended his day. His soul has reached its destination.

Asceticism, Yoga, and Psychoneurosis

Although the Catholic Church treated John of the Cross quite badly during his lifetime, once he was dead it claimed him as its own. Moreover, the confessions of disciples of other reform movements revealed undeniable and profound affinities between his ideas and theirs. Protestant writers were the first to appreciate and understand Johannine thought. It not only fascinated the Christian elite and aroused the curiosity of lay philosophers; it also stimulated physicians and yogis.

Doctors have made a careful study of the mystic state, beginning with the *tepid state*, "which produces vomiting," and ending with *acedia*, which creeps into monasteries around the noon hour—"the noonday demon"—and consists in a melancholy torpor, described by Spanish mystics as "dullness." This prepares the way for obsessions—called temptations by some—which are accurately described in *The Imitation of Christ:* "First a simple thought occurs to the mind, then a fantasy, followed by delight and consent. Thus, if no resistance is encountered at the outset, the enemy gradually invades the soul." There follows a feeling of *strangeness*. The mystic feels light, immaterial; no longer feeling the ground under his feet, he floats. At times he seems to be rising above the earth. In addition, there is the illusion of *déjà vu*—of something not only already seen but heard. John of the Cross distinguished between external visions resulting from psycho-sensory hallucinations—groundless imaginary visions—and intellectual visions which represent intuitive knowledge of tangible forms. Similarly, he alerted his pupils to a danger "that does not dare to declare itself," the tendency to confuse mystical ecstasy with sensual desire. He was a confessor, and for several years had been a male nurse; this gave him the right to approach such problems with the authority of a priest as well as of a former hospital attendant. The crudeness of the terms he employed when addressing his novitiates leaves no room for doubt. "It often happens that in the midst of a spiritual exercise, bodily movements and shameful acts of sensuality unintentionally occur. Why? Because, as the spirit advances toward God, sensuality moves in the direction of physical pleasure." Moreover, the devil delights in undermining prayer and in tormenting us with "very ugly and shameful images." When somber natures are plagued by such tortures they become even more violent, just as the fear aroused in good people by these torments increases their impact. "Tender, delicate" natures are to be pitied, for often their emotions assume a sensuous form. Their prayers are dominated by a lust "which so intoxicates them" that occasionally "acts of turpitude and rebellion" have been noted. This did not surprise John of the Cross. He ascribed it to the "circulation of the blood and the body fluids." Long before modern theories explored the relationship between sensuality and anxiety, and long before anyone knew the connection between the vagus, a cranial nerve, and the sacrospinalis, the Carmelite of Segovia gave proof of amazing clinical acumen. He accepted the incidence of seminal emission, which he treated less as a priest than as a doctor, regarding it as a physical irregularity that required methodical care. For, in order to be receptive to God, total purification was necessary.

Even more surprising than the interest of doctors in John of the Cross was that of Hindu philosophers. Specialists in the religions of India have compared *Dark Night* with *Ashtamga-Yoga*, the work of Patanjali, originator of yoga. To illustrate the affinities between the two, and to dispel misconceptions about Christian asceticism and yoga, they cite the following passage from *Dark Night:* "Such is the spiritual night, which we call active, because the soul does everything to penetrate it." Despite original sin, the soul can escape, should it so desire, provided it quickly exchanges its active role for a passive one. Thus we arrive at total renunciation, the prelude to union with God which the yogis called the *savikalpa-samahdi.* Here we are reminded of the words of one of the spiritual leaders of southern India: "The soul must become like a block of marble in the hands of the sculptor." According to mystical theory, our spiritual life has three stages. The first, the purifying way, corresponds to *Yama-Niyama;* the second, the contemplative way, is equivalent to *Pratyahara Dharana;* while the third, the unitive way, is also the ultimate manifestation of yoga. To be sure,

Western theologians do not agree in their interpretation of
yoga. Does spiritual effort result solely in reducing "mental
concentration" to immobility? If so, what is the point of mental suicide? Actually, Patanjali's second *sutra* is not an end
in itself, but a path leading to the third *sutra*, which says:
"Then the traveler, the *puruscha*, inhabits his own condition." This signifies that the final stage of spiritual life—the
soul's union with God—is essentially active. In this, yogis
and Christian ascetics see eye to eye. The techniques are
similar and at times the translated vocabulary is also identical. This apparently unusual connection between Indian
yoga and Spanish mysticism led Asian philosophers to claim
that John of the Cross was the Patanjali of the West.

"Los Alumbrados"

The God of Theresa and John of the Cross is a deity of rational thought. Their lucid search for God, like Hinduism's
"avenue of approach," requires man's staunchest virtues:
absolute self-control, iron will, cool awareness of one's potentialities. One must be careful not to confuse true mystics
with the charmers and sorcerers who abounded in Spain under the first Habsburgs.

The "Illuminati," those impassioned brothers of the
mystics, deserve special mention because they probably gave
the Holy Office more trouble than did the Lutherans. Indeed, the Alumbrados, although claiming to be orthodox
Catholics, professed wild and revolutionary theories, varying with the individual. They included personalities as different from one another as Juan Valdes, who was first an
Erasmian, then a Lutheran, and finally a member of the Illuminati; Miguel Servet, humanist, geographer, therapist,
and discoverer long before Harvey of the circulation of the
blood; and, finally, Magdalena de la Cruz, the nun of St.
Clare who was possessed by the devil. It is said that the wife
of Charles V had great respect for the inspired sister, whose
portrait hung above the queen's desk. Magdalena was asked
to make the baptismal robe for the future Philip II. It was

also said that she foretold the battle of Pavia and the arrest of Francis I. But in a moment of honesty, she confessed that her visions and premonitions were merely tricks and that she had secretly made a pact with the devil. Illuminism of this sort was a pathological deviation of the religious sense, a hypertrophy of the mystical "I," complicated by mythomania. On the other hand there were Alumbrados such as Juan de Vergara, María Cazalla, and Cardinal Carranza, who had more in common with the Lutherans. Contempt for oral and prescribed prayer, indifference to traditional practices, a quasi-passive surrender to divine influence—all this separated them from orthodox Catholicism. "You will never make me believe that by dropping a coin in the plate, one can release a soul from purgatory," Vergara ironically told his judges. He was dragged to the scaffold. At the very last, yielding to force, he recanted. But María Cazella went even further. Speaking of Luther, she calmly declared: "I was told at first that he was a very virtuous and religious man. And if, on occasion, I felt that he was right, this was probably because the aberrations and vices of prelates and priests gave him cause to speak ill of them." More courageous than Vergara, she suffered cruel torture in silence and without recanting a single word of what the Holy Office termed "her errors."

With the exception of the Alumbrados, the magicians, and sorcerers, Illuminism ceased to be looked upon as a diabolical sect and had to be taken seriously as a new technique of inward contemplation, a spiritual exercise akin to asceticism. Yet there was something insipid and incomplete about it that left the great mystics dissatisfied. One can readily imagine John of the Cross, transported from the shores of contemplation to the very frontiers of Illuminism, hesitant, then, in a flash of lucidity, retreating from it but adapting what was best in its method. John of the Cross transcended Illuminism just as he went beyond the teachings of his Salamancan masters. Impervious to other influences, he rejected everything that seemed impure or questionable. He alone was the architect of his monolithic and rugged world.

3

Conquerors of Gold

Like the flight of falcons from their native nest,
Weary of winging their wretchedness on high,
From Palos de Moguer, travelers and captains
Departed, drunk with a heroic and brutal dream.
— JOSÉ MARÍA DE HEREDIA

THE CONQUISTADORS now came to the aid of the mystics! While the great Spanish humanists constructed the cathedral of knowledge, while John of the Cross and Theresa of Ávila slowly erected the tower that was to rise to the heavens, the soldiers and captains of Charles V expanded the temporal empire of the Spanish monarchs. If we were to use a geometric symbol to describe the simultaneous endeavors of mystics and conquistadors, we would draw a perpendicular line bisecting a horizontal one. The universe of the mystics was built in height—their thrust was skyward. Whether it be John of the Cross's mountain or the dungeon in Theresa of Ávila's inner castle, both suggested ascent, upward movement. The conquistadors built in breadth. Within a few years they extended the frontiers of Spain to the Amazon, conquering as they went "the peoples of the dawn and those of the twilight."

Everything has been said about the conquistadors—the best and the worst. At times they have been described as Christ's legions, at times as abominable bandits. Epic legend and "black" legend conflict—one excessive in praise, the other unjust in censure. The truth is that the two are unrelated. Conquistadors are one thing, the epic of conquest quite another.

Who made up the handful of sailors and soldiers that carved out an empire for Charles V "upon which the sun never set"? Members of good families who had cut loose from their moorings, career officers, including some who had been cashiered, functionaries guilty of minor indiscretions, noblemen with debts, poets, and adventurers. It was a motley crew; honest peasants rubbed shoulders with convicts. The majority were either Estremadurans or Andalusians. The event which had greatly impressed them was the fall of Granada. They were born at a time of euphoria— in the aftermath of victory over the Moors—and had seen the Jews flee. For them, to be a Spaniard meant first and foremost to be Catholic. Their intellectual horizon was limited to the *Santa Hermandad* and the Holy Office, their sole enemies, heretics and idolators. And so they went to confession before going to fight the Aztecs or the Incas. And with the greatest piety in the world they built altars to the Virgin on soil splattered with the blood of their victims. Their physical endurance and their courage commanded respect, for they experienced many things—the fathomless ocean, suffocating heights (the *soroche* of the Cordilleras and the Andes!), earthquakes, the bite of fearsome beasts—the velvety kiss of bloodsuckers—and the refined tortures of the Quetzalcoatl priests. But some rewarding moments punctuated their unimaginable sufferings—playing dice for the moon, sharing the all too brief tropical night with some musk-scented girl! The enchantment of the unknown, a longing for the miraculous, the lure of gold, the pursuit of exotic sensual delights—such were the incentives that sent men off to the West Indies. All in all, they were a simple lot, typical of their times, neither basically evil nor exceptionally virtuous, sufficiently devoid of scruples to disregard the rules of war in the face of a merciless enemy, yet convinced—so naïve was their Christian faith—that theirs was the side of justice.

From their varied ranks a true hero or a near saint emerged now and then; but for the most part they were ordinary Spaniards—strong and healthy.

How can we best describe the Conquest? It was not only epic in character but planetary, since it brought a widening of horizons—an ideal subject for dramatists and poets. Indeed, the epic of conquest had all the elements of great drama—a backdrop formed by the Sea of Darkness, the firmament with all the constellations reversed, a barbaric shimmering horde, and the discovery of a sparkling continent that smelled of frangipane. Heredia describes the sunset over the Andes:

> Straight ahead rose the Sierra, high and somber,
> But when the royal star in the waves was drowned,
> The mountain suddenly caught fire
> From the foot to the summit, and the shadows of the Andes,
> Reaching Cajamarca, loomed larger than ever.

Here, the Peruvian landscape was streaked with the victorious colors of Spain. A little further was the fragrant languor of the islands, the vast tropical horizon enveloping a slumbering city:

> Between the fiery sky and the foaming sea,
> In the slumbering sun of a monotonous noon,
> You dream, O warrior, of the ancient conquistadors . . .

Other poets were inspired to describe the American ocean —that "ancient sea of crystal waves"—and the Cordilleras— "cities pressed against a crater of clouds," "the opium of high altitudes." Paul Claudel is the writer who best knew how to portray the "cosmic" magnitude of this epic, its everlasting significance. Out of this bugle blast he composed a symphony. He found the right words to express the flowering of this sonorous, colorful New World, symbol of all the new worlds yet to be conquered. "World of fire and snow— cornucopia—chalice of silence—planetary fragment." His admirable prose includes such phrases as: "The sea has lost

its terror, retaining only its wonder. . . . Its propulsive
waves scarcely alter the course of that long route to gold that
connects one Castile with another." In conclusion, Claudel
says of the epic and its excitement: "Thanks to thee, son of
the columbine, my kingdom has become like the heart of man
. . . one part of it belongs to its bodily presence, the other
has found its home beyond the seas. . . . Its anchors are
forever moist in that part of the world which is brightened
by the stars."

Christopher Columbus Unwittingly Discovers America

Before the New World could be conquered, someone had to
discover it. And this Christopher Columbus did, albeit unintentionally. In the camp at Santa Fé before Granada, only
recently become Christian, one of the most mysterious men
of history made the acquaintance of Queen Isabella—mysterious because nothing is known about his nationality, race,
family, or religion. Was he a Genoese? In his last will he so
claimed, but the document may well be spurious. Was he
Italian? If so, he never spoke his native tongue. Rumor had it
that he first experienced war as a pirate. Actually, his civil
status and *curriculum vitae* were a matter of indifference to
Isabella. All she cared about were his plans.

What did he propose? Columbus claimed that, instead of
going around Africa, he could get to the Indies by sailing
directly west. He uttered the magic words "gold, spices,
and silk." But even more important in the eyes of Isabella,
the ardent Catholic, was the vast and new opportunity to
spread the Gospel. And what a clever trick to play on the
Moslems of North Africa and Arabia, who would be attacked from the rear and forced to return the Holy Sepulcher to Christendom! While the queen thus acted out of
piety, the king was swayed by his passion for gold. But
Columbus made exorbitant demands: two million maravedi,
one tenth of all the precious metals and stones he might discover, one eighth of every commercial transaction concluded,

the vice royalty of the new territory, and the title of admiral.
The Catholic Kings hesitated. It took all the eloquence of the
Dominican Diego de Deza and the Franciscans Marchena
and Juan Pérez, Columbus's supporters, to convince Ferdinand and Isabella. After all, the capture of Granada was but
a beginning. The crusade must be continued and the Moor
pursued all the way to Constantinople. All this would be possible if one had enough gold and a strong strategic base
against Islam, both of which the West Indies could provide.

Finally won over, Isabella gave her consent. The Capitula-
tions of Sante Fé were signed, guaranteeing the explorer
the privileges and titles he had requested. The crown, the
Santa Hermandad, and a few benevolent moneylenders
financed the expedition.

The three ships were docked at the quay of Palos de
Moguer. The *Santa Maria* was the admiral's ship; the
Pinzón brothers were in command of the *Niña* and the
Pinta. It was Columbus's great good luck to have come
across the Pinzón brothers, who guaranteed the undertaking, provided the crew, loaned one of the vessels, and—most
important of all—gave the new admiral the benefit of their
maritime experience. When complete, the crew numbered
120, including one Englishman and one Irishman. Virtually
all the rest had been released from prison on orders from the
governor of the province of Huelva. The men preferred the
risk of drowning to the certainty of the gallows. The ships
took on their cargo, half of which consisted of trinkets for the
savages. Columbus had armed himself with a letter of introduction to the great Khan, a somewhat legendary figure
whose assistance the Catholic Kings had solicited. On the
evening of August 3, 1492, after celebrating the Lord's
Supper, the crew raised anchor. The flotilla, lateen sails
facing windward, headed for the Canary Islands.

The crossing began auspiciously. The sea was calm and
the crew full of hope. Every morning and evening Columbus
took his bearings, believing each day was bringing him closer
to China, whereas actually he was sailing further and further away from it. Weeks passed. One morning the stern of

the ship scraped enormous clumps of grass. "At times they took heart because of the grass, believing that it meant land was near. Then their hopes would change to fear, for the thick grass was slowing the ships down." This was the Sargasso Sea. They had been gone more than two months and land was not yet in sight. However, certain indications persuaded them that it was not far away. They saw a whale, a pelican, a tortoise, and five birds. The day was fine. "The air is so mild and pleasant that one almost expects to hear the song of a nightingale," the admiral noted in his logbook. But after a while the crew again grew anxious. Columbus had difficulty calming them. He was reassuring yet firm, "determined to continue the voyage and, with God's help, not to stop until he had succeeded in reaching the Indies."

On October 11, sailors on the *Pinta* saw some objects floating in the sea: a strip of bamboo, a plank, and a piece of carved wood. The crew of the *Niña* plucked out of the water a thorny bush full of red fruit. Land was now near. On the night of October 11, a beautiful moonlit evening, Juan Rodrigo Bermejo, a Sevillian, fired a shell and shouted: "Land!" While the men sang *Salve Regina*, Columbus, clutching the royal banner, and two of the Pinzón brothers, each carrying a standard with the green cross and initials of Ferdinand and Isabella, took possession in the name of the Catholic Kings. What they believed to be a projection of land on the Asiatic continent was really Watling Island in the archipelago of the Bahamas, in the British Antilles. The Indians called it Guanahani. Upon his return to the *Santa Maria*, Columbus made the following notation about the island people who had run up to greet them: "They carry no weapons and are not even familiar with them. I showed them swords; in their ignorance, they seized them by the blade and cut themselves. . . . Generally speaking, they are quite tall, move with grace, and have fine figures."

After claiming several islands in the Antilles and effecting landings in Cuba and Haiti, which he named L'Española, Columbus headed back for Europe. The voyage turned out to be difficult. The *Santa Maria* sank on the way, but the two

other half-dismembered ships—the *Niña* commanded by
Columbus and the *Pinta* piloted by Alfonso Pinzón—
reached the port of Palos. Columbus hastened to Barcelona,
where the sovereigns were residing. Six tattooed Indians,
shivering with the cold, whom he had captured in Cuba,
proved the existence of the West Indies. They wore gold
rings on their wrists and ankles. The chattering of green and
red parrots, the peppery scent of spices, and a few samples of
exotic fruits and vegetables further authenticated the marvelous voyage. "I lay the Spanish Indies at the feet of Your
Majesties," the *Almirante Mayor de la Mar Océana* announced with a flourish. Isabella placed the collar of her own
order around his neck. Christopher Columbus had won the
first round.

Scarcely had the New World been, if not discovered, at
least approached, when both the papacy and the crown took
a stand. The leaders of the temporal and spiritual world
wasted no time. To calm the fears of Portugal, which
claimed its rights as the first occupier of transatlantic territory, Pope Alexander VI, a Spaniard, promulgated his famous bull. It assigned to Spain all the land one hundred
leagues west of the Azores, to Portugal the territory that had
been, or still remained to be, discovered east of this line. In
return for this favor, Ferdinand and Isabella were to assume
full responsibility for disseminating the Catholic religion
among the conquered peoples. Neither they nor their successors failed to keep this promise.

Columbus's second trip to the West Indies was a real
colonial expedition. This time his flotilla comprised fourteen
vessels and three smaller craft. Fifteen hundred men, representing all the professions, were aboard: doctors, geogra-
phers, priests, historians, and sundry technicians. The cargo
was almost as diversified as the crew, consisting of farming
implements, religious objects, and kitchen utensils. For three
years the expeditionaries cruised the waters of the Antilles
and founded cities with such melodious names as La Dese-
ada, Santa María la Redonda, Marigalante, Once Mil Vír-
genes. Columbus tried his hand at governing but met with

little success. He was greatly disliked for his harshness. Moreover, he was very anxious to obtain, at all costs, a sizable yield from the newly discovered lands. The Indians were easygoing and reluctant to work; they had to be coerced. Slavery began.

After a three-year absence, Columbus returned to Spain, but this time he was received coolly at Burgos by the Catholic Kings. So far his discoveries had produced little for the royal exchequer. Nevertheless, he managed to win support for a third voyage. In Haiti he encountered anarchy and confusion. He tried in vain to impose his rule upon both the Spaniards and the Indians, who united in waging an underhanded and merciless war against him. At the command of the visitor-general, he was brought back to Spain in chains like a criminal.

After Barcelona and Burgos, Granada. . . . Columbus, his beard grown long, his feet in chains, a woolen robe over his shoulders, threw himself at the feet of Ferdinand and Isabella. The dramatic gesture was accompanied by great eloquence. The Catholic Kings drew the admiral to his feet, forgave him, and reinstated him in his offices.

Apparently the old sailor could not live without the sea. With only four vessels, one more than he had on his first voyage, he headed westward. He arrived at Nicaragua and spent several months exploring the Isthmus of Panama, in search of what he believed to be the mouth of the Ganges. He stopped at the Gulf of Darien, was within a cable's length of the Pacific Ocean—which Balboa was to discover eleven years later—cruised past Haiti, where he was denied entry, and sailed back to Spain. Of his four ships, only two were left, "as full of holes as a honeycomb." Landing at the docks of Sanlúcar de Barrameda, Columbus walked off toward the city, his tall body stooped, his beard grown white, his eyes dimmed. Thinking he had returned from the China Sea, he never realized that he had discovered America. Not long after, he died at Valladolid in solitude. The local chronicler did not even mention his death.

Hernando Cortes Smothers the Plumed Serpent and Founds "New Spain"

While Christopher Columbus, amid general indifference, was breathing his last at Valladolid, Hernando Cortes landed in Haiti. Young, brilliant, and handsome, as agile with a sword as in turning a compliment, sentimental, practical, enamored of gold, women, and his country (but possibly not in that exact order), Cortes was the perfect conquistador, superior to other explorers in education, political acumen, and ability to handle men. A native of Estremadura and scion of a distinguished family, he was drawn at an early age to a life of adventure. Through the good offices of the governor of Cuba, Diego Velásquez, he obtained a position in the Antilles and there he marked time, awaiting a propitious moment.

It was not long in coming. Some venturesome explorers had gone off to reconnoiter the coast of Yucatán, opposite Cuba, and they came back with extraordinary information, whereupon Diego Velásquez sent Cortes on a reconnoitering expedition. The young Estremaduran joyfully gathered together a small army and set sail for parts unknown. He had a standard embroidered with the motto of Constantine: "Friends, let us follow the cross and, if we have faith, by this sign we will conquer." A chaplain, Father de Olmedo, accompanied him.

Around the bend of the Gulf of Mexico, at San Juan de Ulúa, the young captain encountered the Aztecs for the first time. They approached him as ambassadors of Montezuma, the emperor of an immense territory whose capital was called Mexico. Heedless of the warning of the Aztecs, Cortes decided to seek out Montezuma. He wanted to see and judge this red-skinned chief. From the people who resided along the coast, the Totonacs, he recruited an army and began his march on the Mexican plain, taking the Jalapa road.

He went through the city of Tlaxcala, dispersing the natives after a stubborn battle and then adding them to his army. He followed a path between two volcanoes, Ixtaccihuatl and Popocatepetl, whose enormous snow-laden crests rose to an altitude of over 17,000 feet. A halt was called at Cholula, the holy city of the Aztecs. Finally the conquerors came to the valley of Anahuac, a sensuous and gentle land. This was on November 8, 1519, the Catholic's feast day of the Four Crowned Saints and the Aztecs' Festival of Love.

Followed by his regimental staff and his army, Cortes started out on the Ixtapalapa causeway. A magnificent procession came to meet him; at its head was Montezuma, borne in a chair with a canopy of green plumes. Princes of his family and the priests of Huitzilopochtli accompanied the Indian emperor. Both armies halted while Cortes and Montezuma alighted. Bowing to each other, they exchanged gifts. Two different worlds were meeting.

But gestures of courtesy were soon followed by acts of aggression. Dazzled by Mexico's wealth, Cortes took possession of the city in the name of the King of Spain and clapped Montezuma into prison. During his internment, Father de Olmedo undertook to convert him, but the task was far from easy. "We have our own gods here, and we have worshipped them for a long time because we believe them to be good. Yours, too, are probably good." Such was Montezuma's judicious response to the homilies of the Spanish priest. And, indeed, there was no lack of gods in the Aztec pantheon. Some were evil and greatly feared, like Mictlantecuhtli, the god of death, and Tezatlipoca, "the smoking mirror," god of the sun. Others were benevolent; these included Tlaloc, god of rain, and Coatlicue, goddess of the earth and mother of the gods. There was also Quetzalcoatl, the "Plumed Serpent," priest, thaumaturge, and prophet. But the rites of the Aztecs were unbelievably fierce. One day Cortes went to the great temple of Tenochtitlán. High above a pyramid of 114 steps, stone gods presided over human sacrifices. To the beat of tom-toms, accompanied by nauseating streams of burning copal, priests cut open the chests of their intended victims, all adolescents, tore out their hearts, and shoved the still palpitating bodies down the temple steps. Wild with rage, Cortes destroyed the pyramid and killed the priests.

Although Montezuma accepted Spanish rule as imposed by Cortes, the same was not true of other, more combative tribes. Taking advantage of Cortes's temporary absence, an Aztec army besieged the palace of Axayacatl, where Spanish soldiers were bivouacked. Alvarado, Cortes's lieutenant, succeeded in staying the attack. But, unwilling to accept defeat, the enemy laid siege to Mexico City, and their pressure increased from day to day. Cortes tried to use Montezuma as a hostage, but the emperor no longer enjoyed prestige in the eyes of the people. Jeers drowned out his faltering voice and in the end he was stoned to death. Finally the Spaniards were able to force a way through the blockade. But it was a sorry group of men that camped on the hill of Los Remedios, at the gates of the city, which the Aztecs had captured. Beneath a cypress tree, Cortes wept . . . *El Árbol de la Noche Triste.*

Weeks passed. Cortes reorganized his army and launched a fierce counteroffensive. After seventy-five days of fighting, and despite the heroism of the last Indian leader, Cuauhtemoc, Mexico surrendered. The Aztec empire was no more. Spain's hour had struck. Charles V named Cortes governor and captain-general of "New Spain." An era of construction and colonization began. While Cortes was building a new city over the ruins of Tenochtitlán, his lieutenants were dispatched to the Gulf of Mexico—to the Pánuco River in Yucatán—and to the Pacific coast. Then he made his way to Lower California and explored the area around the 30th parallel. Traveling south, he reached Honduras. But his fabulous success had only irritated the court of Spain, and a viceroy was appointed to take his place. Cortes was assigned to a residence in Oaxaca. It was considerably larger than a county in France, but nonetheless the explorer felt hemmed in. He returned to Spain as Marquis of the Valley of Oaxaca. Having enriched the royal treasury and given Charles V, according to his own statement, "provinces more numerous than the cities he had inherited from his relatives and ancestors," he died practically a poor man.

Francisco Pizarro Strangles the Last of the Incas and Builds the City of Kings

The illegitimate son of an Estremaduran army officer, Francisco Pizarro began his career after he was fifty. The antithesis of Cortes, this almost illiterate peasant was equally energetic. After several reconnaissances along the Peruvian coast in the company of twelve friends—the Thirteen Companions of Glory—Pizarro decided to venture a little farther. To the strains of the *Ave Maris Stella*, he set sail from Panama with a hundred men and landed at Tumbes. He knew nothing about the empire he was to struggle with save the rumors he had heard. Actually, it was a powerful administrative and religious organization, established by Inca conquerors who had united almost all the peoples of South America. Explorers of Panama and Colombia had for long been aware of the fabulous wealth of this empire, called the "empire of the Sun" because the sun was its supreme deity. The religion of the Incas was not a whit less ferocious than that of the Aztecs. "They sacrifice men, children, and wild beasts, examine the victims' hearts, for omens, and with loud cries, invoke demons by sprinkling the faces of their gods with blood." As God and master, the Inca exerted absolute authority over his terrified subjects.

Just as the Spaniards landed at Tumbes, a dynastic crisis erupted between competing brothers, Huascar and Atahualpa. Pizarro and his small band crossed the Cordilleros of the Andes and reached Cajamarca, where Atahualpa resided. Stupefied, the Peruvians watched the advance of the Spanish cavalry, believing them to be four-legged monsters: never before had they seen horses. Pizarro decided to exploit the element of surprise and seize Atahualpa. First he requested a meeting, and the Inca complied. On the appointed day, the chaplain of the expedition, Father Valverde, approached Atahualpa, a cross and a Bible in his hands. He began the customary harangue to win the pagan over. Aided by an interpreter, he explained Charles V's claim to Peru and the benefits of Christian baptism. But the Indian could not make head or tail of the argument. What did he care about Pope Alexander V's bull or the Catholic catechism? The Dominican held out the Bible. Greatly astonished, Atahualpa took it in his hand, then let it fall. "Sacrilege!" cried the priest. "Santiago!" replied the Spanish soldiers, lying in wait behind the palace. A fierce battle ensued. The Indian warriors, taken by surprise, were soon dispersed. Atahualpa was taken prisoner and within a few minutes a political structure that had lasted several centuries collapsed.

But Pizarro was not satisfied. What was the point of ruling with an empty treasury? Atahualpa was promised his liberty if he would fill a room with gold and silver—coins, vases, and jewelry. Two months later the fantastic bargain was consummated. Pizarro found himself in possession of a treasure equivalent to three million dollars in today's money. But this did not soften the heart of the Spanish chief. After robbing the Inca, he dishonored him in the eyes of his subjects. Accused of high treason, polygamy, and idolatry, Atahualpa was condemned to be burned alive. But in exchange for his willingness to be baptized, the sentence was commuted to death by strangulation. The Inca empire was no more. A few months later, the conquistadors seized Cuzco and founded the *Ciudad de los Reyes* in the valley of Rimac, which later became Lima, the capital of Peru.

Civilians Succeed the Military, and Organization Follows Conquest

Christopher Columbus discovered the New World. Cortes and Pizarro captured two great empires. The three men played a leading part in the drama of conquest.

Others were to follow: Núñez de Balboa, who discovered the "sea to the south," the Pacific, and whose successors oc-

cupied the Isthmus of Panama; Valdivia, Pizarro's lieutenant, who conquered Chile; Sebastian Cabot, "grand pilot of
Castile and lifelong governor of the Company of Merchant
Adventurers," discoverer of La Plata; Pedro de Mendoza,
founder of Buenos Aires; Ponce de Leon, who conquered
Venezuela. By the middle of the sixteenth century, the Spanish empire was fixed on the map of the world and remained
unchanged for three centuries. It extended from California
to Chile, from the Antilles to Patagonia, embracing all of
Central America. Over 6,000 miles long, it stretched over
sixty-seven degrees of latitude, with an area of about 10,-
000,000 square miles.

The era of conquest was followed by a period of colonization. The crown quickly realized the need to tighten its
control over these vast territorities, which included two
viceroyalties: Mexico, including the Antilles and the island
of Leyte (called the Philippines), and Peru, including La
Plata, Chile, Colombia, and Venezuela, and finally three
captain-generalcies: Guatemala, Puerto Rico, and Manila.
Furthermore, Ferdinand the Catholic established the Council of the Indies, which had jurisdiction over all commercial,
civil, religious, and military matters. The *Casa de Contrata-
ción* was an office created especially for the regulation of
commercial and maritime relations between Spain and the
Indies.

The conquest of America opened up enormous economic
possibilities. From the end of the sixteenth century, Spain
received from its colonies large quantities of precious metals,
jewels, dyewoods, tobacco, and animal pelts, to say nothing
of spices, vanilla, cocoa, and indigo. For over three hundred
years, galleons of the Spanish kings continuously plied the
Atlantic Ocean and the Caribbean Sea, carrying Cordovan
leather, Málagan wines, Murcian silks, and Toledan steel to
America and bringing back Peruvian gold and Mexican
silver. The sudden commercial boom had curious consequences. The rise of prices in metropolitan areas brought
about by the influx of precious metals so depressed the market that in the end people found themselves poorer than they
had been before Columbus's voyage.

As soon as the American colonies had been pacified, the crown began to concern itself with the dissemination of the Gospel. Ecclesiastical missions were sent to the new Spanish provinces with this in mind. Although the methods of conversion depended on the nature of the country and varied according to the religious order involved, the same techniques were generally employed. After a summary instruction and baptism, the natives were taught to live like Christians; that is, they were expected to follow the precepts of the Gospel. In Mexico, missionaries summoned leading citizens and Indian priests, who were "overcome by sadness and also great fear" when they were urged to renounce their gods. In order to convince them of the need to abandon their form of worship, which had been handed down to them from their ancestors, the Catholic clergy had first to get to know the people well, to speak to them in their own language, and to share their lives and concerns. To the indignation Spaniards expressed at the sight of the Bishop of Mexico, Juan de Zumárraga, rubbing shoulders with his dirty and malodorous Indian neophytes, the bishop replied: "In my opinion, you are the ones who smell badly because you have nought in your heads save vanity, because you live as sensuously as if you were not Christians. A heavenly fragrance seems to emanate from these poor Indians. They console me as if they were mirrors of the hard life, of the penitence in which I must seek refuge if I wish to be saved."

To establish contact with the Indians, it was therefore necessary to try to understand them. Once a feeling of mutual trust had been established, these "savages," not all of whom were "good savages," showed a greater inclination to heed the words of Christ. But the hardest task of the missionaries was to rid the natives of old habits—cannibalism, polygamy, sodomy. Moreover, as primitive people, drawn to the spectacular, they missed the barbaric sumptuousness of human sacrifice. The Church of Mexico soon learned to gratify this thirst for the dramatic. On religious holidays, majestic processions descended from monasteries built on high, above ancient pyramids that had once been teocallis. Three thousand crucifixes blazed in the hot sun of New Spain. At the

head of the processions were *pasos*, representing scenes from
the New Testament and impersonated by Indians. Graceful
natives danced on paths strewn with iris and mint. The Indians' plain-song, now glorifying the true God, mingled with
the hoarse voices of the Spanish soldiers. Fifes, woodwinds,
trumpets, the persistent sweetness of the Moorish *jábega*,
and the drumming of the atabal swelled this prodigious hal-
lelujah. Far better than any intellectual argument were ceremonies such as these; they impressed the Indians, who still
yearned for their old idolatrous rites. The pomp of Catholic
liturgy eventually destroyed all remembrance of the bloody
banquets offered to Huitzilopochtli.

Francis Xavier, Conquistador of Cipango

The sixteenth century was a century of movement. If the
word "dynamic" has any meaning at all, it correctly describes the activities of Spain's kings, clerics, mystics, and
conquistadors. To move about over vast stretches of almost
limitless land or among the unfathomable reaches of pure
thought—such was the lot of these wonderfully ignorant
men. Christopher Columbus sailed to the Antilles believing
he was headed for Cipango. Fifty years later a Spaniard,
Francis de Jassu, born at Xavier in Navarre, actually did
reach Cipango.

Francis was the sixth son of Juan de Jassu and María de
Azpilcueta. The family atmosphere was austere, resembling
the paternal castle over whose portals hung the escutcheon
of Xavier noblemen, "a checkered black-and-white crescent."
Francis was fifteen at the time of the Battle of Pamplona.
His two brothers sided with France, for the kingdom of
Navarre, although independent, had been claimed by the
French crown ever since the days of Charles the Bold.
Among the Spaniards, Ignatius Loyola fought like a lion.
Soon he and Francis were to meet.

When Francis was eighteen he left the castle of Xavier to
go to Paris. He registered at the Collège de Sainte-Barbe
and took courses at the Sorbonne, which already enjoyed a

world-wide reputation. There he made the acquaintance of Ignatius, and they took their vows together at Montmartre. Francis was ordained a priest. Answering an appeal from the King of Portugal, he set sail for India. The night before he left Lisbon, he received a brief from Pope Paul III accrediting him as apostolic nuncio "in the islands of the Red Sea, the Persian Gulf, the Ocean, and regions situated on either side of the Cape of Good Hope." This was a large area, but Francis headed specifically for Goa, the capital of Portuguese India, off the western coast of Hindustan.

He reached Goa, called by Camões a "Babylon of iniquity," and his shabby cotton garb made him conspicuous among the richly clothed Portuguese, whose wives wore heavy make-up and were covered with jewelry. As he mingled with this glittering crowd its glamour was somewhat marred by the distressing spectacle of slaves in chains and Indian neophytes in tatters. He played dice with hangers-on at the port or invited himself into the homes of poor fishermen, much to the indignation of the local churchgoers. But he had crossed the ocean for better things. Boarding a ship again, he sailed down the western coast of India. He skirted the Malabar Coast, passed Calcutta, glimpsed Cochin China, land of cinammon and spices, and landed at Cape Comorin, in the kingdom of Travancore, where pearl fishermen lived.

Francis now found himself among the Paravas, not far from the holy pagoda of Ramanancore, which rivaled Benares. On clear days one could see the shores of Ceylon, the sacred island where Vishnu, the incarnation of Brahma, dwelt. The coast of the Pescadores was one of the most inhospitable in the world. The only shade was provided by coconut trees, which the monsoon, sweeping in from the Gulf of Bengal, occasionally uprooted. The children were emaciated, the slaves wore iron rings in their ears, and the silence was oppressive, broken now and then by the scraping sound of nets on the beach. Fanning themselves with palm leaves, the Brahmans stared at this white man who wore a rosary around his waist. For two years Francis lived among the Paravas. He tramped the beaches, slept under palm trees, fed on a handful of rice seasoned with peppered water.

Having learned to speak Malabar, he went from one straw hut to another, teaching the catechism, administering the sacraments, trying to convert. His destitution was even greater than that of the Hindu penitents, who at least wore khaki linen, were shod with clogs, and carried bamboo sticks. But the Brahmans respected him.

Francis bid the Paravas farewell and left for Malacca and the Moluccas. Arriving in Malaya, he traveled from island to island, went through the straits, skirted Sumatra and Java, passed Macassar and Celebes on his left, breathed the hot air of the Moluccas, and returned to Malacca. Standing in the prow of the vessel, he sprinkled purifying waters over these fragrant islands. "Not far from Tidore, Ternate appeared, with volcanoes that belch forth flowers." An elderly queen, Neachila Pocaragua, governed Ternate. Francis baptized her, naming her Isabella. After three months the entire population was converted to Christianity; Malayan stevedores intoned the *Credo* as they loaded the ships. Etched against the green almond sky was "the dazzling plumage of birds whose beaks shred the sweet-scented nut from the nutmeg tree." And Francis himself, that fleet pilgrim of the South Seas, flew from island to island like "a flaming bird that touches earth only at the moment when life leaves its body."

Before coming to earth for the last time, Francis set out on his great adventure. For a long time he had been thinking about Japan, not in order to annex it to the Spanish empire, but because he longed to make it another outpost of Christianity. The man on the bridge of the *Santa Maria* who dreamed of Cipango was not very different in spirit from Francis, who now, fourteen years to the day since he had made his vows in Montmartre, was entering Kagoshima Bay. The Japanese welcomed him and he responded. "One finds among them what is often lacking in Christendom: a nobleman may be impoverished while ordinary folk are quite wealthy, but he will be as honored as if he still possessed a great fortune. . . . The Japanese have a fine attitude toward progress in religious matters." Francis spent a year in Kagoshima. His first visit was to the daimio, who granted him the right to instruct the people provided he abstained from moral coercion, and this more than satisfied the priest. He asked permission to call on the emperor "of sixty-six provinces," but his request was denied. Francis and his two companions set themselves up in a small wooden house covered with rice paper, and here they attempted to draft in the Japanese language a précis of the Catholic religion; it abounded in "moving solecisms." Although certain things about them surprised the natives, the missionaries were far more bewildered by the Japanese. Twenty-five years later a Jesuit visitor described this bewilderment: "A world in reverse, the very opposite of our European world, where white, which is our symbol of joy, denotes mourning, where women dye their teeth black, bind themselves tightly when they are pregnant, and men bow, eat, and ride horseback altogether differently than we do." Although strange, it was part of God's universe, the persistent Basque told himself.

After an unprofitable sojourn in Kyoto, the political capital of Japan, Francis settled in Yamaguchi. At that time it was a prosperous and populous city, a center of art, literature, and fashion, well known for its competitions in poetry and its dance festivals, which attracted large crowds. To spread his message to the people of Yamaguchi, Francis decided to preach in the streets. But this attempt at direct communication, which had brought good results in the small fishing villages, failed utterly in this city of skeptics. His sweeping gestures and halting use of the language aroused mirth; such articles of faith as the immortality of man and the suicide of a god turned man shocked the Japanese. Outdoor discussions having proved unsuccessful, Francis changed his tactics. After all, as the pontiff's legate, he enjoyed all the prerogatives of an ambassador; he might as well make use of them. Tossing a magnificent cloak over his shabby frock, he appeared before the daimio and presented his credentials. Servants placed the Spaniard's thirteen gifts at the feet of the Japanese prince: a clock with wheels that struck the hour, a crossbow inlaid with stones that could be used three times in succession, pitchers of cut crystal, a music box, mirrors, lengths of brocade, and, wonder of wonders, eyeglasses with which the elderly samurai could read as easily as if they were eighteen again! Filled with enthusiasm for Francis and delighted by his gifts, the daimio granted him permission to preach, a residence in the pagoda, and a vast tract of land on which to erect a church. These privileges made it plain that the Jesuits were "bigwigs from the West who came to preach the doctrine of salvation that would lead to deliverance."

From then on strange controversies were politely aired in Francis's antechamber. The Basque expounded the Gospel in halting Japanese. Noblemen, bigwigs, and shopkeepers, squatting on their heels, listened for hours to the hoarse Navarrese inflection. They asked questions, some quite unusual ones, and were surprised to learn that the earth was round. They knew nothing about rain, lightning, or astronomy. Then it was the turn of Buddhist priests. They stressed the similarities between the teachings of Jesus and those of the sage of the Shaktis who, five centuries before Christ, preached self-abnegation. The Shintoists—for a schism beset the empire of the Rising Sun—compared both deities to their goddess, Amaterasu. When long silences punctuated the discussions, only the waving fans and the rustle of swords against the silk belts of the samurai could be heard.

After Japan, China. Francis charged his companions, Juan Fernández and Cosme de Forres, with the task of continuing the work in Japan, and then made ready to return to Goa. But he was tired. On board ship he fell ill. The boat docked at the island of Shang Chu'an, opposite Canton. There he lay down on the threshold of a miserable straw hut, his only companions a Portuguese and a Malabar, and waited anxiously for ship that would take him the rest of the way. Boats appeared, their sails lowered, then grew blurred and vanished. Days passed. "Your Reverence is very ill," the Portuguese sighed, placing a candle in Francis's hand. So ill, indeed, that he died, his eyes fixed on China, near yet so inaccessible.

4

The Masters

THE CLERICS carved out a
spiritual empire befitting Spain, while the conquistadors not
only sought the gold required by the Habsburgs but also
added to the Spanish robe of state an enormous train. Francis
Xavier, that captor of souls, conquered Cipango, whose
glamour Christopher Columbus had dreamed about. And
now, taking their places beside the heroic figures of Theresa
of Ávila, Cortes, and Pizarro were the immortal Don Quixote,
Don Juan, and the companions of the Count of Orgaz—all so
lifelike that they became confused with them. Both real and
imaginary characters were part of the Golden Century; their
fortunes, like their personalities, represented the varied
shades of the Spanish gold that was fashioned by so many
craftsmen. Indeed, it can be said that this century—beginning with the birth of Charles V in 1500 and ending with the
death of Philip II in 1598—suddenly emerged from the
shades of history, although the way had long been prepared.
The Castilian language had gradually acquired a certain
polish and nobility of expression. Isabella and Cisneros
worked diligently to endow Spain with a superior culture
and a plateresque art, while the profusion of literary styles
foreshadowed the rich harvest of the sixteenth century. During the reign of the Catholic Kings and even for a while
after the death of Philip II, art and philosophy flourished.
They were nourished and permeated by a lofty inspiration,

whose wellsprings were as varied as the humanism of Luis de Vives, the fiery spirit of Ariosto, and the ironic mirth of Erasmus. But the Golden Century did not belong solely to the elite; the people also played a part. Cervantes, El Greco, and Lope de Vega were men of the towns and fields. Better still, the writers and artists of the sixteenth century were the historians of Spain, whose reality they felt in their very flesh and bones.

Don Quixote, Knight of the Golden Century

Miguel de Cervantes was born in Alcalá de Henares. His grandfather was a university graduate and a magistrate. However, his father did not have the intellectual ability to pass the examinations leading to a medical degree. Although he had studied surgery he was only called upon to bleed a patient or bandage wounds. Moreover, he was very unstable. Miguel's childhood was spent moving from city to city with a father eternally dissatisfied with his lot. As a consequence, his studies suffered. Cervantes was not cut out to be a humanist or scholar, but he knew how to make marvelous fun of such people. Adventure attracted the young man. He set sail on the *Marquesa*, joined the Spanish army that was fighting in Italy, and took part in the Battle of Lepanto. A bullet shattered his left arm, and he became known as the One-Armed Man of Lepanto. Extremely proud of the injury, he reacted sharply when Avellaneda, who wrote a spurious version of *Don Quixote*, mocked Cervantes's age and infirmity. "I cannot help resenting his reference to me as old and one-armed, as if I had the power to stay the course of time or to prevent its passage, and as if I had lost my arm in a tavern instead of in the most exciting battle that past or present centuries have ever witnessed." Don Juan of Austria sought him out to shake his hand.

Although now unfit for service, Cervantes participated in the Tunis expedition against the Turks. Captured by Barbary pirates and taken to Algeria, he was imprisoned there for five years. Later, in his book a captive was made to say: "Every day the King ordered a man to be hanged or impaled, or that someone's ears be cut off, and all this with so little cause that even the Turks admitted he performed evil deeds for the sheer joy of it, being by nature a murderer of the entire human race." Actually, Cervantes was treated with relative consideration because it was expected that he would be ransomed. In the end the ransom was paid and the prisoner freed.

Cervantes was now thirty-three and in need of work. After a thousand humiliating experiences he finally obtained a lowly position as a steward: "One of those birds of ill omen, abandoned by fortune, shipwrecked in the sea of the world, with not even a cape to throw over his shoulders, who plunders cities and villages, costing more than his wages and upkeep because of the produce he pilfers." And so it was with Cervantes. "Perched on a hired mule, a stick in his hand," he galloped from village to village in search of food for the Armada that Philip II planned to launch against England. It was a thankless and sorry occupation, and Cervantes had not had it long when he accidentally became involved in a shady affair, lost his job, and was imprisoned for his debts.

Cervantes moved his household of four women to Valladolid. He had two sisters, Magdalena and Andrea, a niece, Constanza, and an illegitimate daughter, Isabel de Saavedra. His wife, a worthy but unpleasant lady, lived elsewhere. Two churlish sisters, a wife who only came to quarrel, a scatterbrained daughter, and a niece who was indifferent to him—such was the atmosphere in which the soldier-poet began writing *Don Quixote*. His family did not take him seriously; they scolded and nagged him. Yet to everyone's surprise he proved that a man could earn a living as a writer. Encouraged by the success of *Don Quixote*, Cervantes moved to Madrid with his cantankerous crew. There he published *Twelve Instructive or Moral Tales*, which won some acclaim but no fortune. To play a trick on the author of the spurious version of *Don Quixote*, Cervantes wrote the second part of the novel. He also wrote *Pérsiles and Sigismunda*, *a Northern Romance*. The appearance of this work marked the end of his literary career.

He was now sixty-eight and tired, but his mind was still lively. Although his financial situation was not good at this time—and never really had been—he did have some security as he neared the end of his life. Cervantes knew his days were numbered. But this did not bother him. Parodying an old popular song, he wrote to Count de Lemos: "My foot already in the stirrup, a prey to death's agonies, great Lord, I still have this to say to you." And he concluded: "Farewell to wit, pleasures, and joyous companions, for I am going to die and hope to see you soon in a different life." He prepared his will, died almost alone, and was buried like a pauper, his face uncovered, in accordance with the rules of the Third Order of St. Francis, of which he was a member.

Begun when Cervantes was sixty, *Don Quixote* is the immortal product of his profound experience of life and men. The story is familiar. An impoverished country gentleman of La Mancha becomes so imbued with tales of chivalry that he is crazed by them. Believing himself to be a knight-errant, he sets forth in search of adventure, sword and shield in hand, accompanied by his squire, Sancho Panza. He returns to his native village, recovers his sanity, and dies happy. This is a brief summary of the simple farce, a humorous satire written in the literary style that was then quite popular in Spain. But the tale surpassed the author's original intention. The contrast between Don Quixote and Sancho Panza is also the contrast between man and society in sixteenth-century Spain. Don Quixote offers medieval solutions to modern problems. He is both anachronistic and full of common sense. Advocating independence, loyal to his ideals, and refusing to become respectable, the Knight of La Mancha is the incarnation of the free man; his battered armor has a curious affinity with Charlie Chaplin's coat and its shiny elbows. The Spaniard brandishes his sword, the American twirls his cane—the shaving mug Don Quixote uses for a hat is not a far cry from the derby retrieved from a New York gutter. The Golden Rule of Don Quixote is respect for a promise given, but it is also the sense of duty; Don Quixote will never be tranquil until his obligations are fulfilled, no matter how dangerous they might be. With an intrepidity like Charlie Chaplin's, who does not hesitate to brave the rage of huge policemen or the brutality of powerful young hoodlums to save a poor girl's honor, Don Quixote lunges at windmills, mistaking them for giants. Thus, this stoical madman, spurring the raw-boned flanks of his old nag in pursuit of injustice, is not merely the temporal symbol of the Spain of Philip II, involved as it was in exhausting battles; he also represents the eternal drama of man and his environment. John of the Cross faced his God alone; Don Quixote faces the world alone. When he roams the plains of Montiel, shield in hand, the contrast between the weak and naked hero and the flaming desert, devoid of shade and water, is striking. Man's unfitness for his environment, the discord that exists between the protagonist and his setting, between the material and spiritual world—all this is an essential part of the story. Will the hero adapt himself to the world, or the world to the hero? The free man never adapts himself. "Let me return to my former liberty," Sancho Panza tearfully exclaims as he embraces his donkey. And Don Quixote echoes him when he gravely utters the words that sum up his philosophy and his mysterious grandeur: "Freedom, Sancho, is one of the most precious boons that the heavens bestow upon man. All the treasures hidden in land or sea cannot equal it." And we watch the immortal figure of the master and his squire grow smaller and merge with the night sky, where the headdress of princesses and the dark outline of enchanted castles begin to appear.

Don Juan, the Man Who Played the Devil

In Spain as in France, the theater started in the churches. From the end of the eleventh century through the twelfth,

religious dramas called *Juegos escolares* made their debut.
Soon they were staged in convents and cemeteries as well
as in churches. At first the dialogue was in Latin, but as the
popular language gradually developed, Latin was dropped,
and by the end of the thirteenth century a Spanish theater
came into being. "Mysteries," or sacred pieces called *autos
sacramentales*, were performed on stages set up in churches
or public squares. Occasionally itinerant players in chara-
bancs drove through the streets, stopping at the crossroads.
The theme was not always religious, and consequently the
clergy was forbidden to take part. Mimes and jugglers recited comical, and often obscene, *decires* and *disputas*, gesticulating wildly and burlesquing. From these primitive beginnings the theater gradually evolved until it reached its
zenith with the three great masters of the Golden Century:
Lope de Vega, Tirso de Molina, and Calderón.

"Thereupon that monster of nature, the great Lope de
Vega, appeared," Cervantes commented. Monstrous indeed
was the copiousness of his output—1,800 plays—as well as
his superhuman energy and the almost universal range of his
knowledge. He drew his inspiration from the Bible, ancient
history, classical poetry, Italian novelists, and, naturally,
from Spanish writers; he could recite by heart long passages
from Herodotus, Ovid, Anacreon, Boccaccio, and the *Romancero*. But his studies did not preclude a full and varied
life. The son of an embroiderer, a pupil of the Theatines, an
ecclesiastical and lay order, he began his career as secretary
to the Bishop of Ávila. After four years of study at the University of Alcalá, he went on an expedition to Terceira Island in the Azores, where he met his first love, Elena Osorio,
the daughter of a theatrical director. The affair lasted five
years and inspired his novel *La Dorotea*. Scarcely had he
broken with his first mistress and finished writing the book
when he met and ran off with Isabel de Urbina, the daughter of Philip II's sergeant-at-arms. To avoid a scandal, her
father consented to the marriage. Lope joined the Invincible
Armada, then returned to Spain and settled in Valencia with
his young wife. Later he moved to Toledo and entered the

service of the young Duke of Alva. Upon the death of his
wife and his two young daughters, Lope moved to Madrid,
where he became the secretary of the future Count of Lemos.
He married the daughter of a butcher, Juana de Guardo,
and soon took a mistress, Micaela de Luján, who bore him
seven children, only two of whom survived. His second wife
died shortly after the death of their son. Was it the dismal
atmosphere in which he lived that caused so many deaths
around him? He decided to take holy orders and seek the
path to God. But actresses continued to attract him and he
gathered a few rosebuds on the way. The belatedly ordained priest did not disdain the favors of Jerónima de
Burgos, nor those of Lucía de Salcedo, both comediennes.
Finally he met his last great love, Marta de Nevares San-
toyo, who gave him a daughter, Antonia Clara.

Lope's fame was now at its height. He was present at the
beatification ceremonies for Theresa of Ávila and presided
in Burgos over the festivities that marked the marriage of
Anne of Austria. This aging lover, this priest, was the great
man of Spain. Both good fortune and bad had pursued him
throughout his stormy career. Marta de Nevares died, and
one daughter took the veil while another ran off with a seducer; his son, Felix, perished on an expedition to India,
and Antonia Clara, the comfort of his old age, succumbed
to a mysterious ailment. Lope was left alone in the world
with no other resource save the life of a penitent. And so,
with the same fervor with which he had written his plays
and made love, he steeped himself in piety. He had become a
familiar figure of the Inquisition and a member of the Third
Order of St. Francis. Sensing the approach of death, he
wrote: "Already the dismal cypress entwines its branches
with those of the heavenly laurel." He subjected his body,
which had known the joys of love, to such severe treatment
that the walls of his room were spattered with blood from
his self-flagellations. He died at the age of seventy-three.
An impressive procession followed his coffin to the grave;
many of the good people of Madrid were in tears. But
when it was learned that his tomb had not been paid for, the

remains of this Prince of Geniuses were exhumed and tossed into the public burial ditch.

Husband, lover, soldier, priest, wonderful father to his many children, when did Lope find the time to write? With equal success he tried every medium—didactic works, novels, various dramatic forms from pastoral comedy and *autos sacramentales* to dramas and mythological evocations; he experimented with every style of meter, struck every note, running the gamut from the amusing to the severe, from the sublime to the prosaic. His theater was a world in itself, portraying the men of Spain in all their naked reality, from medieval times to Habsburg rule: washerwomen jostling one another on the banks of the Manzanares, a meeting of poets on the Night of St. John, a commanding officer subjected to torture. Lope de Vega excelled in his sense of the dramatic, whether in *The Star of Seville*, *The Certain for the Doubtful*, *Peribañez*, or *Fuente Ovejuna*. He would have made a wonderful film director today; his gift for dialogue and his skillful delineation of plot were especially noteworthy. What a strange destiny was his—this Don Juan born before the real one—touched as he was by grace *in extremis*, yet so reluctant to renounce love!

Calderón de la Barca was also a priest and a soldier. His career, which was momentarily interrupted by a campaign in Catalonia, unfolded smoothly enough. He was named chaplain of the Reyes Nuevos at Toledo, then first chaplain of the congregation of priests in Madrid. He lived to the ripe age of eighty, greatly honored and respected. His plays were highly dramatic and for the most part dealt with philosophical and moral themes. Although not as prolific as Lope de Vega, he wrote 120 plays, and almost 100 *autos sacramentales*. Among his most famous were *The Governor of Salamea*, *The Wonder-Working Magician*, and *Life Is a Dream*. Certain events in the last play seemed to be inspired by *The Thousand and One Nights:* a beggar is put to sleep and awakens to find himself a king; falling asleep again, he reawakens a beggar. Actually, the hero, Segismundo, symbolizes the prehistoric man who, clothed in animal pelts, breaks his chains and emerges from the dark cave, opening his eyes to the light of wisdom. Similarly, when he awakes in chains, he expresses man's disillusion with earthly life: *"Que toda la vida es sueño Y los sueños sueños son."*

The man who created the immortal Don Juan was Fray Gabriel Téllez, who wrote under the *nom de plume* of Tirso de Molina. He belonged to the Order of Mercy. Almost as productive as Lope de Vega, Tirso was primarily famous for his dramas *El Condenado por Desconfiado* and *The Sevillian Deceiver*. The first was inspired by a Hindu tale: the Brahman and hunter demonstrate that a criminal who has not lost his faith in God is more certain of salvation than an arrogant Brahman. The second play is about Don Juan, who after a thousand immoral and deceitful deeds, enters a chapel in Seville. There he sees the marble tomb upon which lies the stone statue of the commander of Ulúa, killed by him after he had seduced his wife. Jokingly, he invites him to dine at the inn. When evening comes, the statue knocks and enters. Don Juan remains impassive, but the servants tremble with fear. He urges the commander to be seated, mocks him, and asks him to fix a meeting in the chapel. Despite many warnings and the shadows that darken the room, Don Juan will not be deterred from his foolhardy plan. A libertine, he is nonetheless a brave man. We next see him beside the tomb, feasting with the commander. When the meal is finished, the stone statue holds out a hand to Don Juan, who clasps it, only to scream with pain. "Call a priest so that I can confess and be absolved of my sins," Don Juan cries out, while the fiery hand of the funereal guest hurls him into hell. Thus expires the cynical cavalier who all his life answered those who begged him to mend his ways by saying: "I have plenty of time!" The man who never loved anyone— neither the Duchess Isabella at the court of Naples, the fisherwoman hauling in her nets on the beach of Tarragona, nor Aminta, the young bride of Dos Hermanas—from now on he is at the mercy of Satan. Such is the Deceiver of Seville, whose tall and haughty figure we encounter even in Philip II's antechamber, pale in his black velvet doublet, a rapier concealed under his arm.

El Greco, Artist of the Soul
Velázquez, Portrayer of Man
Zurbarán, Religious Painter

Góngora wrote the following epitaph: "Here lies El Greco. If study won him the secrets of his art, art revealed to him the secrets of nature. Iris bequeathed him his colors, Phoebus his light, Morpheus his shadows. May this urn, funeral bark of the palmetto tree, drink in our tears and, despite its hardness, exude all the more flavor." Color, light, shadow, perfume, and tears—such was El Greco's palette.

This greatest of Spanish painters, Domenico Theotocópuli, was born at Candia in Crete. At an early age he went to Venice to study under Titian. When he was thirty-six he moved to Castile and settled in Toledo. But his fiery and tempestuous style was not at all to the liking of Philip II. One day the king commissioned a painting of the martyrdom of St. Maurice, to be hung in the monastry of San Lorenzo del Escorial. When the painting was finished Philip II took one look and frowned. Such emphasis of line and color was not suitable for God's altar. The mediocre work of a Florentine painter finally graced the tabernacle. On another occasion, El Greco clashed with the Inquisition, which reproached him for having violated in his paintings certain canonical rules. Had he not allowed himself to paint angel's wings whose excessive dimensions bordered on heresy? His habits perplexed the Toledans. At mealtime he liked to listen to Oriental melodies, airs so melancholy and harsh they seemed to spring from the pebbly soil. He painted to music, why not to the dance? El Greco was not cut out to be the official painter of the state; he had a fine clientele and no need of an official status. Not far from the Tagus, in his

small country house, Buena Vista, he would meet his many
friends, the finest minds of Toledo: Tirso de Molina, Lope
de Vega, the poet-conquistador Ercilla, Góngora, and even
Cervantes. They would stroll about gardens filled with orange trees, among statues of nymphs, and around pools
where deer came to drink. He died quietly at the age of
seventy-six, leaving no will, since he had neither fortune nor
family. His only possessions were two hundred rough
sketches of paintings.

Much has been said about El Greco's work. "Blazing furnaces rather than drawings of bodies," René Schwob concludes. "His genius plunges into the hard Toledan plain
like a knife, and brings to flower a tree struck by lightning,"
according to Jean Cocteau. Maurice Barrès suggests an explanation of El Greco's genius. Perhaps it was his early Byzantine training or his Hellenic origins that made him so sen-
sitive to the Semitic streak in the Spanish soul. In any case,
it is obvious that El Greco, "who had just arrived from Italy,
became, in a very short space of time, the most perceptive
delineator of the Castilian spirit. It is he, this man from
Crete, who best portrays the contemporaries of Cervantes
and St. Theresa." And yet, for a long time, his Spanish contemporaries thought him insane. Everything about him startled them, primarily his choice of colors. White, black, crimson, yellow ocher, and madder red were the only colors of
his palette, but he combined them in such a way as to obtain new shades—carmine with ash gray, yellow sulfurs,
cadaverous whites, and almost black reds. Phosphorescent
clouds streaked greenish skies. And how strange were his
drawings and his composition of groups! At times Christ on
the Cross is portrayed alone, abandoned by everyone, even
his executioners, who flee under an apocalyptic sky; at others,
the Virgin or St. John writhe in agony at the foot of the gallows. Or else two noblemen calmly stare at the contorted
body. The twenty-four Toledans with long, grave faces are
the same who intoned the *Requiem* at the funeral of Don
Gonzalo Ruiz, a nobleman of Orgaz. A mitered bishop leans
his head against the head of the deceased. "An atmosphere

of solemn grief pervades and brings peace to the beautiful
service for the dead." Upon the ivory-toned foreheads one
senses the presence of holy thoughts. The figures stretch so
poignantly toward the heavens that they almost seem to rise
up from the ground. Perhaps more than any other of El
Greco's paintings, the "Burial of Count Orgaz" reveals the
secret of his art—his tendency to elongate his figures, which
creates a feeling of spirituality. Some have attributed this
manner of painting to an anomaly of the artist's vision, as if
astigmatism alone could account for his style. Whether El
Greco painted people and things as he saw them or whether
he deliberately distorted is far less important than the striking results be achieved. His heroes respond to a lofty summons, to an inspiration of the same order as that of the soul
in "God's bottomless abyss," which John of the Cross felt he
could not describe. . . . "Should I try, the thing itself
would seem less than it is." The painter portrays precisely
that which the writer admits he cannot express because it is
indescribable. Arms crossed, elongated face, lines that van-
ish—and the world of the mystics becomes palpable; it is
perceptible in the parting of a cloud, in the fold of a silk
robe, in the reflection of light on the polished surface of rock.
El Greco's work is an introduction to metaphysical life. But
this artist of the supernatural is also a portraitist of his times.
"The Dream of Philip II," halfway between heaven and hell,
Cardinal Tavera, the Dominican of the Prado, "The Knight
with His Hand on His Heart"—such are the figures of sixteenth-century Spain, epitomized by "Captain Julian Ro-
mero," whose ample cape is blown toward some vague and
dismal kingdom, less dismal, however, than the sky of Toledo. The palace is mirrored lugubriously in the chalk-
colored Tagus, phosphorescent clouds float in the gloomy
heavens where a Biblical flash of lightning will soon appear;
it is a landscape that offers no hope. But in the "Burial of
Count Orgaz," the delicate hands of the Spanish hidalgos,
with their lace-ruffled cuffs, are so many white splashes on
the canvas. One such hand, almost winged, is raised over
the dead man in blessing, symbolizing the mystical dove.

What fascinates this "hallucinated Tintoretto" is not so much Toledo as an intellectual Paradise which he conceives with his blood.

Diego Rodríguez de Silva y Velázquez pursued two careers simultaneously: he was Philip IV's quartermaster general and official court painter. IIe, too, studied in Italy, but when he was thirty he turned his back on the Venetian masters and developed a style all his own. Where did he find his models? Nothing could have been easier; he had but to select them from his surroundings. For thirty-seven years, he served as the royal portraitist. He painted not only the king but the Infante Don Carlos, the Infante-Cardinal Fernando, the king's sister María, his first wife, Elizabeth of Bourbon, and his son Baltasar Carlos. All the models died, and the king remarried. Velázquez painted Philip's second wife, Mariana of Austria, and her daughter the Infanta Margarita. But the demands of his art did not distract him from his duties as quartermaster general. It was he who arranged the meeting between the royal families of France and Spain after the Treaty of the Pyrenees and prepared the way for the marriage of Louis XIV and the Infanta Maria Theresa of Austria. Cold, formal, reserved, he was a courtier who attended every festivity and whose elegant attire won the praise of princes. "His clothes were adorned with Milanese lace. . . . He wore the red cross of his order and an engraved silver badge, and carried a very handsome short sword of state. . . . A small diamond-encrusted coat-of-arms with the habit of Santiago in inlaid enamel hung from a heavy gold chain which he wore around his neck." Such was Velázquez when he lived at close quarters with the royal couple on the Island of Pheasants in the Bidassoa. He also had more prosaic duties—paying for the firewood and the services of chimney sweeps, supervising the maintenance of lamps, the setting of tables, the preparation of guest rooms, seeing to the last details, even to the placing of chamber pots in the bedrooms. Both steward and major-domo, Velázquez could hardly fail to profit by this unique opportunity to live with his models. In the corridors of the

Buenretiro, which courtesans and ambassadors crossed several times a day, the quartermaster general would meet his protector, Don Gaspar de Guzmán, duke of Olivarez. He exchanged pleasantries with the court jester, Pablo de Valladolid, played with the cardinal's dog, and pinched the ear of the little prince Baltasar. Withdrawing to his studio, he merely reproduced on canvas the traits and gestures of his hosts. His tremendous facility as a painter may be explained in part by this familiarity with the notables of the day.

He relied on a single stroke of the brush, using very simple techniques and few colors. Whereas El Greco portrayed supernatural man, Velázquez, on the other hand, painted human beings in their natural condition, giving them a lifelike quality. Described by some as a "psychoanalyst," he shows quite clearly the Infanta Margarita tired of holding her bouquet of flowers, the Infante Don Baltasar afraid of falling off his horse, Doña Margarita uneasy on her chestnut-and-white palfrey. In this half-Burgundian, half-Spanish court which was insatiably devouring Charles V's legacy, among the declining Habsburgs, to say nothing of Quevado, "the secretary without secrets," and the chaplain Góngora, it was Velázquez who had the bearing of a sovereign: one has but to look at his self-portrait in *Las Meninas*. Doña Agustina Sarmiento offering a jar of water to the Infanta, Nicolas de Pertusato teasing a dog, the duenna and her equerry, and in the background, the *aposentador* of the queen—although these are his models, they seem instead to be his subjects.

Velázquez did not confine himself to painting court notables. After a time he probably grew weary of children, buffoons, and queens, to say nothing of the arrogant grandees who looked upon him as a subordinate and whose patronizing attitude he must have resented.

Many of these aristocrats regarded Velázquez as being on a par with the child of Vallecas, the Infante Baltasar's favorite dwarf, a melancholy hydrocephalic nicknamed in turn Little Wind, Calabash, and Christopher the Blind. But the friendship of Philip IV made up for the contempt of the nobles. The Habsburg ruler was not a happy man; not he but another was in command, and everyone knew it. Often he would slip away and traverse the secret corridors that led to Velázquez's studio, eager not so much to converse with the artist as to watch the striking progress of life's hues on canvas.

The masses appealed to Velázquez. Drunkards and black-smiths, beggars and spinners, seemed as true to life as princes, and more human, perhaps, because they did not pose for him. "The Water Vendor," "The Drinkers," "Forge of Vulcan," "Buffoon of Valladolid," are all masterpieces, depicting man's experience of familiar enemies—envy, lust, pride, intemperance, and also misfortune. A black coat thrown across his shoulders, "Menippe," "crazed by total freedom," smiles cynically. And soon the official court painter, portrayer of the masses, became a marvelous artist of love. Defying the Inquisition, which excommunicated, fined, and exiled painters of "indecent" pictures, Velázquez was the first to draw a nude—his admirable "Venus" for whom Cupid holds a mirror. Although the body of the Andalusian is reminiscent of some of Titian's paintings in its purity of line and style, it differs in one respect: Velázquez's Venus is a brunette and the curves of this high-spirited beauty, the softness of her boldly nuanced flesh, are less sat-isfying to the aesthete than they are exciting to the lover. Velázquez's sensuality is sometimes ambivalent, as, for ex-ample, in "The Drinkers," where el Borracho, his torso bared, gazes tenderly at the effeminate statue of Bacchus, crowned with vine leaves. Will he touch the soft shoulder?

Zurbarán was a religious painter. The son of a peasant, he came to Seville from his native village in Estremadura at the age of fifteen. By the time he was thirty he had achieved fame. Although his saints, nuns, and monks have the honest look of peasants, he enveloped them in a regal light. Celes-tial shades depict "The Vision of St. Peter Nolasque"—creamy white the woolen frock, pink and green the angelical robe. St. Thomas of Aquinas in his chapel, St. Bonaventura

receiving the envoys of Emperor Palaeologus, St. Bruno
visiting Pope Urban II—faces that reflect the supernatural,
while the folds of their robes catch the flames of the earth
and "sing, in varied tones, the glory of the sun on snow, the
iridescence of glaciers." A painter of the Holy Orders, Zurbarán endowed the monastery of Guadalupe with pictures
that exalt faith and prayer—"The Temptation," "The
Flagellations," "The Apotheosis." Tall white monks that
seem to glide noiselessly over the flagstones of churches,
cardinals at prayer, even the arrogant conquistador of "The
Adoration of the Magi"—all represent a saintly fervor.

The last years of Zurbarán's life were darkened by the
fame of Murillo, who was also of modest origin but was an
opportunist. He initiated a style that combined Flemish and
Italian techniques and fused them with Spanish mysticism.
"The Marriage of St. Catherine," "The Death of St. Claire,"
"Holy Family," "Adoration of the Shepherds," convey religious sentiment in all its tenderness. Murillo's paintings em-
body neither the ecstasy nor the tenseness of El Greco, nor
the grave introspection of Zurbarán, but rather a tranquil
piety. However, fame spoiled this meticulous artist. As orders began to pour in, his work became repetitive. Many of
his pictures were mere stereotypes of piety. So virginal were
the Sevillian women whom he chose as his models that one
critic remarked: "One would think they were painted in
Paradise!" He used too much light pink, tender blue, and
pale gold; yet he did have the ability to portray life in all
its crudeness. The little lice-infested beggar scratching himself is perhaps Murillo's masterpiece.

Ribera also broke down the doors of the supernatural with
his extraordinary "Martyrdom of St. Bartholemew." As the
executioners drag their unhappy victim to the gallows, his
waxlike face depicted against a greenish sky expresses both
terror and determination. The originator of "tenebrosi,"
Ribera used his brush strokes to produce a blinding light in
the foreground while shadows shroud the distant horizon.
He was known not only for "Jacob's Dream," "St. Anthony,"
"St. Jerome," and "Magdalen in the Desert," but also for

his paintings of Diogenes, lantern in hand, Cato of Utica, pointing to his wounds, and Archimedes, brandishing his compass, and for perhaps the most beautiful of all his works, the painting of Prometheus, his liver consumed by the eagle of Jupiter.

What better place is there than Seville on Holy Thursday to take leave of the masters of the Golden Century? Long lines of penitents wended their way toward the cathedral. Some wore red cowls over lavender robes, others were dressed in satin as if for a masked ball, and a few carried wax torches. These were the brotherhoods, each honoring the Virgin it revered—Virgin of Sorrow, Virgin of Bitterness, Virgin of Agony. . . . Resting firmly on the shoulders of the bearers, the *pasos* paraded by, representing episodes of the Passion—the Last Supper, the Mount of Olives, Mount Calvary. The streets were narrow, and the crossroads were full of people in a state of intense religious fervor. Now and then a bearer would stumble, and the wooden statues would sway—statues carved, painted, gilded, and clothed by the *escultores*, the *encarnadores*, the *doradores*, and the *imagineros*. All this agitation seemed to bring them to life. The flickering candles were reflected in the large baroque mirrors that hung from the miradors, while the boldness of the polychromatic statuary reinforced the inventiveness of the painters. Long streams of blood streaked the Christ of Montañez, and the heart of the Virgin, *la Purísima*, sculptured by Cano, bled profusely. Bleeding, too, were the wooden torsos of martyrs, the lacerated bodies of the flagellants. The crimson blood of Holy Week mixed with the black blood dripping from the flank of the crucified Christ by El Greco; blood shed by Spanish soldiers on battlefields from Metz to Cajamarca. *Oro y sangre!*—the colors of the Spanish banner, of the Golden Century, too, splattered with the blood of victory.

5

Charles V
and His Disloyal Empire

ETTER THAN a thousand
books perhaps, two portraits by Titian give an understanding of the personality of Charles V. Although painted approximately during the same period, they reveal two essentially different aspects of the emperor. One shows the incredible horseman in shining armor, astride his mount, wearing plumed helmet and sword—the victor of Mühlberg. A vermilion taffeta scarf, fringed with gold, is slung across his shield. He advances in the glorious dusk just as, thirty years before, when he was an impetuous young prince, he rushed down the Asturian highway to conquer his Spanish kingdom. The sky is stormy, like his destiny. And the boundaries of his empire, "upon which the sun never sets," disappear in the melancholy stretches of the Saxony landscape. The picture "Charles V Seated," painted the following year, is altogether different. Eyes pensive, countenance gloomy, he can scarcely conceal his weariness and infirmities; yet the set jaw betokens unshakable will. He is still the emperor and intends to remain so, even among the Hieronymites of Yuste. Nonetheless, he is tired, spent, as shown by the nervous tension of his features, the sagging shoulders. And so we have two dif-

ferent likenesses of the monarch who, unable to become a Caesar, wanted to die like Scylla.

His strange personality can perhaps be explained by the contradictory strains he inherited. He was the son of Philip the Fair and Juana the Mad, and the paternal grandson of Maximilian I, the German emperor, and Marie of Burgundy; on his mother's side, he was the grandson of Ferdinand and Isabella, the Catholic Kings, and the great-grandson of Charles the Bold, the last Duke of Burgundy. Born at Ghent in 1500, Charles was not at all like his maternal grandparents, either physically or morally. Nor did he take after his mother, Juana the Mad. On the other hand, although he resembled the Habsburgs physically, he had the temperament of his Burgundian ancestors. However, instead of inheriting the famous "Habsburg lower lip," he had the mouth of his Burgundian relatives. Moreover, Charles was brought up in Brussels and received an intensely Flemish education, while his brother Ferdinand, who had been turned over to Ferdinand the Catholic, was raised in Spain. The Flemings were quick to gather around the blond, fair-skinned child, and they were his first teachers—Adrian of Utrecht, dean of Louvain, William of Croy, nobleman of Chièvres, and Charles de la Chaux. The Spanish soul and its culture and history were entirely unfamiliar to the future King Charles. There was nothing of the Spaniard about him, but a good deal of the Fleming and even more of the Burgundian.

Whoever mentions heredity must also discuss legacies, and Charles had more than his share. He inherited from both Burgundy and Spain. But he intended to pursue the policies of his Burgundian ancestors—John the Fearless, Charles the Bold, Philip the Good. When the French spoke of their enemies—Spaniards, Imperials, and Flemings—they said: "the Burgundians." The Burgundian problem was to obsess Charles V until the Ladies' Peace. Spanish affairs, which he never really understood, were merely an additional concern. Yet he elected to die in Spain.

Actually, he inherited legacies from everywhere. To begin

with those from Spain: Old and New Castile, Asturias, Leon, Galicia, Estremadura, Andalusia, Murcia, and Biscay came to him from Isabella; from Ferdinand he received Aragon, Catalonia, Valencia, Majorca, Sardinia, and Sicily, not to mention such newly acquired territories as Granada and Roussillon, Naples, Navarre, and the vast New World, discovered not long ago and now completely under Spanish control. When he became Emperor Charles V, he inherited from the Dukes of Burgundy the Netherlands, Luxembourg, Lorraine, Franche-Comté, Austria, and Germany. The Holy Roman Empire extended from the Pomeranian coast to Holstein and Gravelines, and it also reached beyond the Alps, embracing most of Italy, the Swiss cantons, Savoy, and the shores of the Danube. But this empire was more theoretical than real, "the shadow of what it had been," as Charles himself admitted at the Diet of Worms. A sumptuous mosaic whose poorly joined pieces gave way beneath the emperor's tread.

Charles's baptism occasioned almost as much pomp as did his coronation somewhat later. The entire city of Ghent turned out. At the head of the procession that made its way from the archduke's palace to the Church of St. John were the burgomasters and seventy noblemen of the court, each carrying a lighted torch; following them came the Knights of the Golden Fleece and seventeen prelates in silk vestments. Bringing up the rear were the lords, devoutly bearing the baptismal accouterments: a pearl-embroidered bonnet, silver oil containers, a shaker for the liturgical salt, and a white wax candle weighing one and a half pounds. The child was wrapped in a blanket of brocade lined with ermine. He was called the Duke of Luxembourg. Sixteen years later Charles was proclaimed King of Spain at a Requiem Mass celebrated in the Brussels church of St. Gudule in memory of Ferdinand, his grandfather. Five years later he was consecrated emperor at Aix-la-Chapelle, where another incredible procession honored him: three thousand German foot soldiers in red-and-yellow uniforms, one hundred and fifty cavalrymen of the empire dressed in black,

Flemish, Burgundian, and German lords in gold and silver brocade, pages in crimson satin livery—all this to the accompaniment of a deafening fanfare from the electors. From the time he lived in the palace at Ghent until his retirement to the monastery of Yuste fifty-eight years later, Charles V never went unescorted. There was to be no solitude for this "captive of power."

No sooner did he put on the crown of Spain than he made every effort to win acceptance from his new subjects. The first impression was not unfavorable. He was admired for the way he sat a horse and for his strength in tournaments. But he soon lost whatever popularity he enjoyed. The people resented the many Flemings who occupied positions of importance. And the king's lack of gaiety was disappointing in a man so young—he was only twenty! Above all, he was reproached for his lack of zeal in learning the Castilian language. Furthermore, his position was awkward. Everyone knew that Ferdinand of Aragon would have preferred to bequeath the kingdom to his favorite grandson, Ferdinand, Charles's younger brother. And everyone also knew that the rightful heir to the throne was Juana the Mad, who was still alive and had many partisans, although she was still locked up in the castle of Tordesillas. Thus, in the eyes of some, Charles was looked upon as both a foreigner and a usurper.

While the young king was trying as best he could to win the favor of his subjects, he learned of the death of his grandfather, Maximilian. Six months later, a Flemish courier brought him the news that he had been elected emperor. The seven electors—the Archbishops of Mainz, Cologne, and Trier, the King of Bohemia, the Duke of Saxony, the Count Palatine, and the Margrave of Brandenburg—had had to choose between two favorites: Francis of Valois and Charles of Ghent, and had selected Charles. The new emperor hastily prepared to depart, but was reluctant to meet his electors empty-handed. Pressed by the procurators, the Spanish municipalities contributed to the imperial treasury. A mass of gold—some said one million ducats—was sent to the port of La Coruña, where, accompanied by his small Flemish court,

Charles embarked to receive Charlemagne's sword and a globe of the world.

His mind inflamed by Caesarean visions, Charles V gave little thought to Spain, which he now regarded as simply one of many kingdoms. Refusing to be treated like a poor relative, Spain rebelled against its absent master. The *comunidades* seized arms and marched against the regular troops of the regent, Adrian of Utrecht. The revolution of the *comuneros*, like many similar movements, was symbolized by a hero, Juan de Padilla, a nobleman of Toledo. A courageous fighter, he already saw himself as the first minister of Queen Juana the Mad. Leading his army, he seized Tordesillas and broke down the doors of the palace where Juana was kept in seclusion. Flinging himself at her feet, he managed to convey to her feeble mind a glimmer of light. What, she might be Queen of Castile? For several months the *comuneros* and the Imperials fought fierce battles. From Worms, Charles V tried to effect a compromise; promising to reduce taxes, he urged peace. But the civil war continued unabated until the Imperials finally captured Juan de Padilla. The *comuneros* made their last stand on the outskirts of the tiny village of Villalar. Their small army was no match for the royalists. Realizing that defeat was imminent, Padilla's soldiers quickly removed their emblem, a red cross, and replaced it with the white cross of the regular army. "St. John and liberty!" shouted Padilla, charging at the enemy like a madman, his sword held high, his visor raised. Wounded, he surrendered and was condemned to death. Before going to the gallows he wrote two letters. One was to his native city, Toledo: "To thee, crown of Spain and light of the world, free since the days of the Goths . . ." The other was addressed to his wife: "I bequeath to you my soul, which is all I have left." The hangman put an end to his life just as the civil war ended.

Charles V returned to Spain, having learned his lesson. He promised to respect the Spanish *fueros*, and he kept his word. As for the Flemings, they were obliged, at least for the time being, to curb their thirst for power and wealth.

After the revolt was liquidated and the leaders executed, Charles V fought France over Milan. The fruitless struggle was marked by constantly shifting alliances. Charles emerged victorious but failed to weaken French power to any great extent. However, his most stubborn enemies were Suleiman, Luther, and possibly the Popes, rather than Francis I and the French. For the Habsburg emperor deliberately confused empire with Christianity. He intended to make himself the Catholic emperor *par excellence*, and opposed with equal violence Islam, the Reformation, and—in an oblique fashion—the papacy.

Luther's Defiance

The following scene was enacted on the first floor of the archiepiscopal palace at Worms. At four in the afternoon, Luther appeared before the emperor. Was his the countenance of Satan or saint, this strong, fleshy face with its large straight nose and sensuous lips? A grave voice put the question: "Can the councils of the Church be mistaken?" "Yes," the heretic answered resolutely. Without a word, Charles departed. A few days later the sovereign signed the edict of proscription. Under the surveillance of a herald, Luther was escorted to the border. But on the way he was freed by friends who pretended to kidnap him; they took him to the Wartburg castle, residence of the Elector of Saxony. Charles's brief encounter with the rebellious monk was decisive. In the statement that he himself drafted and read the next day before the imperial Diet, he recalled that his ancestors—German emperors, kings of Spain, archdukes of Austria, dukes of Burgundy—all had been faithful sons of the Roman Church. He added: "It is clear that an individual monk is in error when he contradicts the opinion of all Christendom; otherwise Christendom would have been in error for a thousand years and more. Therefore, I am resolved to commit my kingdom, my possessions, my friends, my body, my blood, my life, and my soul. For it would be a disgrace for you as well as for us if, during our time and because of our negligence, the merest semblance of heresy entered the hearts of men." He could hardly have been more explicit about his determination to combat the Reformation. The Lutheran princes took him at his word. But no sooner had he condemned heresy at Worms than he returned to Spain, where he remained for seven years. During this excessively long absence neither his brother nor the Council of the Regency fought heresy resolutely.

Charles V showed courage in opposing the Reformation, which started in Saxony and spread as far as the Baltic. Luther's message, influenced by the intellectualism of the Renaissance, and aided by the recent invention of the printing press, a powerful means of dissemination, won the support of the German nobility. The truly pious, justifiably troubled by the shortcomings of the Roman Church, were more than ready to accept a doctrine that preached a return to the original purity of Christianity, that cited the Scriptures, promised eternal salvation not for good works but for faith, and, above all, advocated ecclesiastical reform. Moreover, a highly realistic motive insinuated itself into this saintly enthusiasm. The dismantling of the ecclesiastical hierarchy would inevitably result in the secularization of Church properties. Thus, the princes had everything to gain.

While Charles was urging Pope Clement VII to convoke a council in order to avert civil war, peasants were fighting in the Black Forest and princes were marshaling their forces. The so-called League of Smalkald, comprised of nobles, bourgeois, and commoners, was organized to "defend the Gospel." The Catholic princes retaliated by creating the League of Nuremberg, which, unfortunately, the Pope refused to support. A league can easily develop into a military alliance, and this is exactly what happened. The Protestants, preparing for all eventualities, organized an army of considerable strength under the command of John Frederick, Elector of Saxony, and Landgrave Philip of Hesse.

Charles V hoped it would not be necessary to fight, particularly since he was not at all certain of winning. His confessor, Loaysa, admitted this frankly: "We must content ourselves with the loyalty of heretics, although in God's eyes they are worse than the devil. But even if they were dogs, His Majesty would still have to close his eyes because he is no position to cut them down." Meanwhile, the Council of Trent, which was finally convoked in 1545, did nothing to reassure the emperor, as he had hoped it would. War was inevitable. It began at Ingolstadt, where Charles V received an insolent challenge from the Protestant princes, delivered by a young man accompanied by his trumpet-major. A decisive battle was fought at Mühlberg, on the banks of the Elbe. Despite a painful attack of gout, Charles, riding his big black charger, led the assault for twenty-one long hours. Victory was finally his. Philip of Hesse surrendered, and the Elector of Saxony was taken prisoner. His wife threw herself at the feet of the emperor. Since the rebels had lost, Charles could afford to show mercy. At the Interim of Augsburg he agreed to accept the Protestant demand that priests be allowed to marry; he also assented to two kinds of communion. On the other hand, the Protestants were expected to accept almost all of the Catholic ritual. This tolerant attitude was not at all to the liking of the Catholics and greatly displeased the Pope. The victor over the Protestants was in danger of being branded a heretic.

Charles V seemed to have reached his zenith. The German princes had been defeated. Luther had just breathed his last, after uttering a few pessimistic words: "Nothing good is in store for the world. Germany is what it is." Francis I, too, was dead. Thus, Charles was rid of his principal enemies. But the Protestants had not disarmed. Their uncompromising attitude at the Second Council of Trent, convened by Pope Julius III, showed that no reconciliation between them and the Catholics was possible. They reorganized their league and obtained help from the King of France, Henry II. Maurice of Saxony, who had fought and lost at Mühlberg, reassembled 30,000 Lutheran rebels and marched on Innsbruck. "The Holy Evangelical War" was very popular; everywhere "fire, that favorite offspring of war," cavorted gaily. Charles's life was endangered, and he had to flee

Innsbruck in disguise, his beard dyed black. Negotiations were opened at Passau between the Catholic emperor and the Protestant princes. The outcome was the Religious Peace of Augsburg, which stipulated that Charles V would abstain from punitive action and guaranteed equality of rights in Germany for Catholics and Protestants alike. The Interim of Augsburg had been nullified. *Cujus regio, ejus religio.* . . . To be sure, it was wise to compromise, but what had become of Charles V's dream of complete religious unity throughout the empire? He now realized that, thanks to Luther, he would never be another Charlemagne.

The Distrustful Popes

Had it not been for Luther, Maximilian's grandson would not have been obliged to wage war against the Germans; Catholicism might have served to unite the empire; hence Charles V's hatred of heresy, which perhaps stemmed more from pique than from piety. At Mühlberg he had seen himself as master of the universe; Innsbruck shattered his dream. Nevertheless, he was always a faithful supporter of the Catholic church, although not its most obedient son.

Seven Popes succeeded one another at St. Peter's during Charles V's reign. Not one of them accepted unreservedly the emperor's collaboration with the Catholic Church. Some considered him a rival, or, even worse, an enemy. The Popes did not forget that they were Italian princes and that Italy was being used as a battlefield by Charles V and Francis I, two "very Christian kings." The empire represented a perennial threat to the papacy's temporal power. Moreover, the Roman Church harbored unpleasant memories of imperial protection. During the forty years of their relationship, Charles and the Popes, sometimes at each other's throats, sometimes in fond embrace, never achieved the kind of true and complete harmony which would have benefited both Catholicism and Spain.

And yet, at the beginning of Charles's reign, everything

should have drawn the emperor and the papacy closer together. Charles's teacher, Adrian VI, was Pope, and he
owed his position to the influence of his former pupil. However, the man lacked both competence and character. His
successor, Clement VII, was irritated by Charles's triumphs
and wanted a few for himself. Meanwhile, Luther unleashed
his fury against the papacy, "founded in Rome by the devil."
Lampoons were circulated in which the "Roman hermaphro-
dite and its partisans" were portrayed as living and dying
"like cows and pigs." Luther threatened to apprehend Popes
and cardinals and "tear their tongues from their throats and
nail them in a row to the gallows in imitation of the way they
hung the seals of their sacred bulls." Caricatures depicted
the Pope with donkey's ears, surrounded by devils who
crowned him with a tub of garbage and pulled him toward
hell. But even this outburst of verbal violence was less up-
setting to the papacy than was the rise of Charles V. Clement
VII concluded a military alliance with Francis I and the
Italian princes, which resulted in the Sack of Rome. The
Duke of Bourbon, in command of mercenary infantrymen,
did not hesitate to attack the Holy City. Spaniards and Germans vied in cruelty, and churches were pillaged. Daughters
of leading citizens were seized and cardinals were dragged
into the streets and trampled. Coffers containing the Eucharistic wafers were used as chamber pots, crucifixes became
targets of attack, and convents were converted into brothels.
With equal frenzy, Lutheran cavalrymen and Spanish infantrymen, their red beards and doublets blackened by
powder burns, danced a "carnival of death." Revelry,
orgies, and drinking bouts—nothing could halt the rage for
slaughter and pleasure, not even the "French evil," as syphi-
lis was then called.

The Duke of Bourbon, hit by a musket shot, died of his
wounds. Just in time, Clement VII took refuge in the castle
of St. Angelo. Six months elapsed. During this time
Charles V was at Valladolid, calmly waiting for his wife,
Isabella of Portugal, to give birth. He hoped for a son, and a
son it was, the future Philip II. Great were the festivities in

honor of his baptism; there was even a *corrida*, with Charles trying his hand as a toreador. Did he give Rome a thought? The Spanish Grandees, the Duke of Alva, the Archbishop of Toledo, could not conceal their indignation. While the emperor was dandling his infant and incense rose from the central altar of the Church of San Pablo, the Pope was "buried alive" in a small room of the castle of St. Angelo, and Roman prelates were being sold in the market place. "Free the Pope!" Charles V finally ordered the release of the Pope, but only in return for a promise of good behavior. The Pope agreed to this with ill grace; anxious not to fall into the hands of the Germans, he fled the castle of St. Angelo disguised as a valet. Not long after, Charles V and Francis I signed the Peace of Cambrai, which recognized France's claim to the Duchy of Burgundy and granted the emperor Naples and Milan. Clement VII ratified the treaty and promised to restore the imperial crown to Charles V.

Emperor and Pope met in Bologna. Charles cut a fine figure on his small Spanish horse, dressed in a coat of gold and carrying a scepter; around him were a thousand horsemen, swords lowered. His pages, dressed in yellow, gray, and lavender velvet, dutifully waited. Charles approached Clement VII, who was wearing a tiara, dismounted, and knelt. This was the first time the two had met. Charles asked forgiveness for the Roman affair. The Pope, who harbored no resentment, gave him the kiss of peace and granted forgiveness. Three months later, Charles received the gold crown of the Holy Roman Empire and the iron crown of the kingdom of Lombardy from the Pope's own hands. As they left the church of the San Petronio and the pontiff prepared to mount his horse, Charles insisted on holding the stirrup; the gesture symbolized his spiritual obedience to the papacy.

Hostilities between France and the empire were renewed upon the death of the Duke of Milan, who left no heirs. Francis I and Charles both claimed the duchy. Pope Paul III had succeeded Pope Clement VII. A brother of the beautiful Giulia Farnese, favorite of Pope Alexander VI (Rodrigo Borgia), the new pontiff owed his rise to her. This was why he was called "the cardinal of the skirt." A gifted and adroit politician, Pope Paul III was "as slippery as a fox." Upon his offer to serve as a mediator, the two princes met at Aiguesmortes and concluded a ten-year truce. Although the Pope frequently expressed a sincere desire to reconcile the two sovereigns, he disliked Charles, not only because he had inherited from his predecessor Rome's traditional mistrust of the empire, but also because the emperor's personality was distasteful to him. And although, after the victory of Mühlberg, he conferred the title of *Maximus Fortissimus* upon Charles, it was the military leader rather than the Catholic king whom he honored.

Revival of the Crusade

As King of Spain, Charles could not ignore the crusade. To be sure, his grandmother Isabella had driven the Moors from Spain a half century before; but the Moriscos remained, and they kept looking toward the African coast, while the Moors still fixed their gaze on Spain. Moreover, he was the Roman emperor and consequently the natural protector of Christianity against Islam. Finally, the German empire, which belonged to him, was being threatened along the Danube by the Turks. For these three excellent reasons he felt it his duty to intervene in North Africa.

Islam had undergone radical changes since the reign of the Catholic Kings. No longer could the Turks be considered barbarians. Their government, administered by renegade or assimilated Europeans, was one of the best in the world, and many European states might well envy them the stability of their finances—the Turkish sultanin was equal to the Venetian ducat—the discipline of their army, and the excellence of their military equipment. The empire of the Osmanlis, ruled by Suleiman the Magnificent, Commander of the Faithful, was a great power with which the European states had to reckon. Consequently, Francis I treated the Turks with great consideration and made alliances with them, as did the German and Italian princes and even the Popes. Charles V was alone in his plan—as daring as it was fool-hardy—to defeat Suleiman. He had no intention of launch-ing a direct attack. Rather, he waited for a propitious mo-ment, which was not long in coming. Mouley Hassan, the sultan of Tunis, had just been banished by the well-known corsair Khair-ed-din, son of a Christian mother and a Greek apostate. Owing to his bushy red eyebrows and beard, he was called Barbarossa. The deposed sultan sent his ambassa-dor to Charles V, asking him to intervene and promising perpetual vassalship in exchange. Charles decided to act. He assembled three hundred ships at Barcelona, boarded a magnificent vessel flying twenty-four golden banners, and gave the order to set sail for the Tunisian coast. Thirty thou-sand men disembarked near the ruins of Carthage. They in-cluded Italians, Germans, and Spaniards, who naturally quarreled among themselves but displayed bravery in bat-tle. The fort of La Goulette was attacked. The Turks sur-rendered it and fled in haste. In this engagement the great courage of Garcilaso de la Vega, the soldier-poet, stood out. In a fury, Barbarossa hurried to Tunis, stopping just long enough to assemble a few thousand men as well as his treas-ures. Rushing on to Bône, where fourteen galleys awaited him, he quickly set sail for Algiers. Meanwhile, Charles re-stored Mouley Hassan to the throne of Tunis and received in exchange Bône, Bizerte, and La Goulette. Twenty thou-sand Christian slaves were freed. Charles's return trip was triumphant; stopping at Palermo, Messina, and Naples, he was acclaimed by enthusiastic crowds as "the savior of Eu-rope, Africa, and Asia." At the gates of the cities there were streamers bearing the words: "From sunrise to sunset."

The dramatic victory of the Cross over the Crescent proved short-lived. Emboldened by success, Charles de-cided to take punitive action against Algeria, the capital of the Barbary pirates. An imperial flotilla of sixty galleys and two hundred smaller craft set out. But a terrible storm came up, fourteen galleys were shattered against the rocks and a hundred other vessels were completely destroyed.

Meanwhile, the army managed to land at Cape Matifou, twelve miles from Algiers. For several hours, Charles's soldiers, blinded by heavy sprays of water and sunk in mire, tried to fend off the Arabs, who surrounded them like swarms of bees. They finally retreated to Bougie, where they awaited the arrival of the ships that had not foundered. Not all of them reached Cartagena. At Charles V's side, prostrate in the bow of the flagship, lay Hernando Cortes, of the *Noche Triste*. Just as at Tlaxcala, heavy rains beat down on the defeated men. That very year Suleiman invaded Hungary and converted the cathedral of Buda into a mosque. Two years later, the Turkish flotilla bombarded Nice, and Barbarossa's Janissaries took up their winter quarters at Toulon. Charles V had lost his battle against Islam.

Retreat to Yuste

At fifty-six Charles V was tired and ill, but his mind was clear. It was time, he felt, to look back on his life, to assess his accomplishments and failures. Had he conquered the infidels? Barbarossa had died, but his successor continued with a firm hand to hold high the red-and-white banner with its blue crescent. Turkish rule extended from Gibraltar to Constantinople. The Lutheran princes, like birds of prey, were fighting over Germany. Only Flanders prospered, but at the expense of the Spaniards, who were wont to say: "Spain is devouring the New World, but it is the Netherlands that grows fat." As for the papacy, it had never shown any true friendliness to Charles. At that very moment, Paul IV was planning with the help of France to drive the Spaniards from Italy. And the French . . . Had it not been for them, Charles might have been the absolute ruler, if not of the world, at least of Europe. His eternal, almost monotonous rivalry with Francis I, that dear enemy, their disputes and reconciliations—they hated each other before Frankfurt, embraced after Pavia, became partners at Aiguesmortes —shattered his dream of a universal monarchy more surely than did his quarrels with the Protestants. Henry II, Francis I's successor, had also slipped between his fingers. France was wounded, but still on its feet, able to cope with its difficulties.

All this was perhaps on Charles's mind as he made his way to the monastery of Yuste, in a remote and wild region of Estremadura, beyond the Batuecas. The road from Jarandilla to Yuste was a difficult one, and the soldiers, carrying torches, were having a hard time keeping the emperor's stretcher in a horizontal position. The horses slipped on the soft ground, and the infantrymen, their muskets cocked, stumbled over the stones. Several months before, Charles V had abdicated in favor of his son, Philip II. He gave him Spain, the Netherlands, Franche-Comté, Milan, Naples, and the vast New World. But the German empire, his legacy from the Habsburgs, went to his brother Ferdinand. Suffering from an infirmity, this creature dressed in black had to be carefully helped down from the stretcher; he was no longer the man he had been. Hemming and hawing, not knowing how to address him, the prior stammered: "Our Father." "Your Majesty," a monk hastened to correct him. The bells of the monastery pealed. Charles asked to be carried to the central altar, where the *Te Deum* was being celebrated. The pale winter sun sank behind the Guadalupe Sierras, causing them to resemble the Golden Fleece, whose insignia Charles hung above his bed. One more battle, perhaps the hardest, remained to be fought, a battle against himself.

Charles had withdrawn from the world, but the world still interested him. He wrote to his sisters, to his son, and, above all, to his daughter, Juana. Heretics still drew his ire. In his cramped handwriting he scribbled to Juana: "One must see if it is possible to proceed against them on the grounds of sedition, as fomenters of scandal, disturbers of the peace, and agitators for a republic; then they would have no claim to mercy." His hatred of Protestants had not abated since Mühlberg; if anything, it had grown more intense, for he realized how much he had lost because of them. But the pen that trembled with anger against his enemies wrote in a different vein when he mentioned his son: "Although death has me by the throat, if I can help him in any way, I will do my utmost." His love apparently was not reciprocated.

Was he bored among the Hieronymites? Somewhat. The monks were good souls but limited. His physician and his reader were Flemish, and he made them his confidants; at times he still thought of himself as the emperor. However, as soon as Ferdinand mounted the German throne he ordered the removal of the imperial eagle from all his seals. No longer would the proud signature *Carolus Rex Catolicus* appear. Nor would Titian ever again address him as *Sacratissima Cesarea Maesta*. One by one, from the Danube to the islands and lands of the South Seas, kingdoms fell from him like scales. He stood stripped before God, yearning to return to the earth as naked as he was at birth. The last lines he wrote expressed penitence: "Forgive me, my Guardian Angel, heaven's messenger, for ugly actions and for shameful deeds." His final words were those of a soldier about to wage his last battle: *"Ya es tiempo"*—"Now it is time."

"He is mad," Pope Paul IV exclaimed when he learned of Charles V's departure for Yuste. Actually, he was completely lucid and reasonable. Nor was he the only king of Spain to die in a monk's garb. The Gothic sovereigns Andeca and Wamba, the kings of the Reconquest—Bermudo I, Alfonso IV, and Ramiro II—did likewise. After long deliberation—he first toyed with the idea at Aix-la-Chapelle—and of his own free will, the disillusioned emperor decided to sever all earthly ties. His withdrawal was due not to discouragement nor even to physical fatigue, but rather, in large measure, to repeated failures. Not despair, bitterness, or the slightest trace of romanticism influenced his decision; he merely gave up his post. Unfortunately, the fact that he was no longer emperor did not lessen his enormous appetite, to the great detriment of his health. His menus were the despair of his doctors. Anchovies, omelettes, sardines, crayfish soups, frog's legs, eel, deer, fried ham—was this a suitable diet for a man suffering from gout? At every meal he ate thirty different dishes and washed them down with cold beer or heavy wine. But how could one reason with this gourmet for whom the arrival of a crate of sausages from Tordesillas was almost as important as the visit of a diplomatic envoy?

Yet, by retiring to Yuste, Charles V was not merely seeking a quiet and comfortable way to end his career. A loftier ambition inspired his tormented spirit: to do penance. When he confessed his sins in the presence of princes, Knights of the Golden Fleece, members of the Estates-General of the empire, and the crowd that gathered at the Brussels palace of Coudenberg, he deliberately meant to humiliate himself publicly. "I know all too well, gentlemen, that in my time I have committed grave sins," he murmured in a broken voice. The people burst into tears. What were these sins? His attitude toward his mother, the blood of German and Spanish subjects shed fruitlessly, the Sack of Rome . . . He was filled with remorse; until his death, tangible evidence of his last sinful deed remained with him: a blond, blue-eyed lad who practiced on a harquebus in the garden of the monastery. The boy knew that his mother was Barbara Blomberg, but he was not aware that the broken old man who watched him pensively was his father. Called Gerónimo, he achieved fame as Don Juan of Austria, victor over the Turks at Lepanto. A glutton, sensuous, miserly, vindictive, often petty, occasionally hypocritical, Charles V had the same faults as many other men, but his pride was so obsessive that it blinded him to reality. One after another, crowns were placed on his head while his empire was slipping away from him; and as he stared fixedly at the distant New World, disloyal princes were plotting his ruin under his nose. All this he failed to perceive because of his excessive pride. And when suddenly he realized what was happening, his only recourse was to hasten to this retreat, a fitting finale to the life of any wise monarch. Francis Borgia, who delivered the funeral oration, developed a theme from the Psalms: "Who will give me wings like a dove, and I will fly away and be at rest? Lo, I have gone far off flying away; and I abide in the wilderness." And, indeed, it would seem that Charles was less "the divine eagle who, in its tireless, inimitable flight holds the world under its wings" (Calderón) than the dove in the Psalms. Yearning for powerful wings, he had flown so high and gone so far that he found himself alone. On the very day of his death, a lily bulb he had himself planted suddenly bloomed. "A miracle!" the Hieronymites exclaimed, and they tied the miraculous flower to the black crepe that draped the central altar. The contrast between the fate of Charles V and the purity of his motives could not have been more appropriately symbolized than by the lost dove and the posthumously flowering lily.

6

Philip II,
Neither the Noon Demon
Nor the Prudent King

T HE YEAR 1557, on the day of
St. Lawrence . . . A Spanish horseman emerged from the
sloping forest into the sun-filled plain, skirted the Somme,
and dashed up the hillside to St.-Quentin. In spite of the
heroic efforts of Admiral Gaspard de Coligny to defend the
city, it had just fallen into the hands of Philibert of Savoy,
known as Ironhead. Henry II of France was defeated. The
horseman hurried through the Spanish camp, shoving aside
French prisoners, who were guarded by butchers' dogs, and
German mercenaries sentenced to penal servitude. "Go to the
devil, Antichrist!" shouted Marshal Montmorency, who had
been gravely wounded. The nobleman riding at full gallop
among the multicolored tents was Philip II; and the precious
stones in his armor, the red satin slashes of his breeches, his
golden helmet, all gleamed in the sun. Absent during the battle, he wanted to be present at the moment of triumph. Occasionally his horse stumbled over a French flag, lying forgotten in the dust. Philip was young and almost handsome.

This victory created the first image of the king whose reign had just begun.

The following year Charles V died in Brussels. Three thousand monks carrying torches and intoning the burial hymn preceded the coffin, and they were followed by the princes of the Church and the lords of Spain and the Netherlands. Twenty-four horses, their stirrups dangling, were accoutered with the coats-of-arms of the emperor's kingdoms. The doors of St. Gudule were thrown wide open. The crown, scepter, sword, and globe of the world had been placed upon the sarcophagus, which was covered with a black cloth. William of Orange brandished the heavy sword, then put it back on the coffin, and in a booming voice that rose to the vault, called out: "He is dead." A monk standing next to William the Silent lowered his hood. Philip II, the recent victor, was now in mourning, his face drained of color. This was the second image he created, thus foreshadowing the ascetic, somber, and uncompromising king he was to become, the servant of Catholicism.

Another year passed. Philip, now thirty-two, signed the Treaty of Cateau-Cambrésis, which allowed Spain to retain Italy, the Netherlands, Artois, and Franche-Comté, but gave France the three bishoprics of Lorraine: Metz, Toul, and Verdun. This compromise peace was sealed by marriage: Philip II, widowed by the death of Mary Tudor, took as his wife Isabelle of France, daughter of Catherine de Médicis and Henry II. From St.-Quentin to Cateau-Cambrésis— what a long road he had traveled in less than two years! But a danger far greater than rivalry with France threatened the Spanish monarchy—the growth of Protestantism. Indeed, no sooner had Philip mounted the throne than he found himself involved in the religious struggle. Spiritual and temporal affairs came to be so intertwined that he tended to look upon all Moslems, Jews, and Protestants as major enemies of the Catholic faith. Very methodically, he planned their destruction, and mustered for this enterprise all his powerful and mysterious talents.

The Battle of Lepanto

Ever since the banishment of the Moors from Spain, there remained only the Moriscos and the Mudejares, the recently converted Moslems. Descendants of the Moors, the Mudejares had embraced Catholicism and seemed to be sincere believers. The same cannot be said of the Moriscos. As their conversion had been obtained by force, most of them continued to practice Mohammedanism secretly. When tracked down by Philip II's police force, the most fanatical took to the mountains or allied themselves with bandits in order to subsist. These fugitives came to be called *Monfies*, after the highwaymen they had joined. As their number was increasing daily, Philip signed a Pragmatic Sanction reinforcing the measures against Moriscos which his predecessors had taken. It forbade them to speak Arabic and proscribed their national songs, dances, and ceremonies. They were ordered to leave the doors of their houses open on Fridays, and women were forbidden to wear the veil. Angered by these measures, the Moriscos decided to stage an uprising. Fierce battles ensued in the Alpujarras between the Moriscos of Andalusia and the troops of Marquis de Mondéjar, governor of the province. Since no decisive victory seemed imminent, the king asked his half brother to smash the revolt. He did so, but not without great difficulty. Thereupon, Don Juan resorted to extreme measures. At the behest of the king, he rounded up the Moriscos and told them they would be deported. With ropes around their necks and chained together like animals, they were taken from Andalusia to the frontier of Castile. On the way some died of thirst or were beaten to death; others were hanged from olive trees. And above the gates of Granada, which led to the Alpujarras, the severed head of their leader, Aben-Abu, was nailed to a cage and strung up for all to see. Sickened by his task, Juan begged his brother to send him to war. "You must be a leader, not a swashbuckling soldier," was Philip II's reply.

But the problem of the Mohammedans extended beyond the frontiers of the peninsula. Troubled by the constant presence of the sultan's flotilla in the basin of the Mediterranean, Philip formed an alliance with Pope Pius V and the Venetian Republic, and then launched a powerful expedition against the Ottoman navy. It was headed by Don Juan of Austria, who had just won his stripes at Granada. Two hundred Spanish vessels met three hundred Turkish ships in the Gulf of Lepanto, near Cephalonia, not far from the promontory of Actium, which had witnessed Octavius' victory over Antony. The death of Ali Pasha, felled by a shot from a harquebus, led to the rout of the Turks. While thirty enemy galleys sank and twenty-five burned, a Spanish soldier on the *Marquesa* was wounded in the chest and in the left arm. "The scars on the face and chest of this man are the stars that guide others to the glorious heavens," the soldier, Miguel de Cervantes, was to declare later.

When Philip II learned of the Ottoman defeat he made light of the praise bestowed upon Don Juan. "The honor and glory of such a memorable event," he said, "should be attributed to God." But the Pope was more enthusiastic. Quoting from the Gospel, he declared: "There was a man, one sent from God, whose name was John." But the victory of Lepanto, like that of Charles V over Barbarossa, proved fruitless. The following year the Turks launched a counteroffensive and Philip was forced to conclude a truce. Nonetheless, the Battle of Lepanto had enormous repercussions throughout Christendom. It had now been demonstrated that any attempt by Islam to invade the western coast of the Mediterranean was doomed to failure—unless, of course, there was a change in the balance of power, which only the future would reveal.

Trial by Fire

Virtually all the impenitent Moors were gone and their faithful allies, the Jews, were no longer a threat, but Philip still had to contend with his most dangerous foes, the Protestants. Charles V had begun the fight against Luther and lost it. Determined to win, Philip II was prepared to use every means, including the Inquisition.

The origins of this institution go back to the Middle Ages. It began to gain ascendancy during the period of the Albigensian heresy. The Lateran Council in 1179, and the Council of Verona five years later, ruled that bishops must visit their dioceses at least once a year in order to insure that their flocks remained pure in faith; should they find any heresy, it was their duty to apprise the secular authorities. These injunctions were subsequently reinforced; and Simon de Montfort, using orthodoxy as a smoke screen, pillaged the counties of Toulouse, Béziers, Foix, and Comminges. To a soldier who asked how to distinguish Catholics from Albigenses, the Abbé of Cîteaux replied: "Kill, always kill. God will recognize his own." The Fourth Lateran Council organized the Inquisition down to the last detail. Four years later, Dominic de Guzmán founded the Militia of Christ, a religious police force whose members became important in the Inquisition. Thus, as early as the twelfth century, bishops could bring recalcitrant heretics to justice.

The new ruling, introduced in Spain at the end of the fifteenth century by Sixtus IV at the request of the Catholic Kings, was applied first in Aragon, then in Castile, and finally throughout the entire country. Tribunals were established in all the large Spanish cities, and they were controlled by a Supreme Council headed by Torquemada, the famous Dominican. The first document of any dossier was almost always an accusation, whether anonymous or signed, written or oral. It was the duty of every good Catholic to denounce suspects to the Holy Office of the Inquisition. The penalty for failure to do so was excommunication. The list of offenses was a long one, and Jewish customs were the primary target. To wear a white shirt on Saturday, to recite the Psalm of David without first pronouncing the *Gloria Patri*, to have one's children's horoscopes drawn, to wash a corpse in warm water, to remove fat from meat—these were crimes against faith. Once the accusation reached the Inquisitor he would hear the testimony of witnesses, who sometimes turned out to be heretics themselves. Should memory falter or fail, torture was applied. The dossier was then turned over to theologians, who were called "qualificators of the Holy Office," and it was they who decided the next move. If the charges were sustained, the public prosecutor decreed the arrest of the accused and the constable carried out the order. The culprit was put in jail, and was likely to remain there for a long time while his case was being investigated. He would appear three times before the tribunal; these appearances were called "monitions," or summonses. It would be made plain to him that the tribunal would very much appreciate a spontaneous acknowledgment of guilt. A thousand times the accused was interrogated about the same incident. Completely exhausted, he could almost always be trapped in some inconsistency. "He has lied!" the judges would exclaim triumphantly. The sentences varied according to the seriousness of the crime. If the culprit showed signs of repentance, he would be excused from excommunication and canonical censure; occasionally he would even be "reconciled" then and there. Should he persist in heresy, he would be declared "impenitent." If, after being "reconciled," he again showed signs of heresy, he would be pronounced an apostate or a "relapsed heretic." In either case he would be handed over to the secular authorities and made to expiate his crime publicly. His head bared, clothed in a sanbenito, he would recant and then suffer the auto-da-fé.

The following scene is that of an auto-da-fé at Toledo. Since dawn the Zocodover square has been black with people. The platform is ready. From the Arch of Blood all the way to the cathedral the crowd mills about, filled with an unsavory impatience. At the appointed hour the sinister procession begins, headed by well-known figures of the Inquisition carrying ebony-and-silver staffs; then come the soldiers of the *Santa Hermandad*, their visorless helmets reaching down to their necks. Friars Hospitalers follow, then the Grandees of Spain, carrying the cords of the Standard of the Faith; the brotherhoods come next with the Dominican prior himself in the van, holding in both hands a cross covered with a black cloth. The condemned are last. Each wears a sanbenito, a yellow dalmatic split open at the sides and reaching down to the knees, as well as a grotesque bonnet (*coroza*) adorned with flames and demoniacal figures. Those who have been "reconciled" will get only life imprisonment. The others will either be strangled—*agarrotados*—or burned alive. Preceded by the Inquisitorial banner, which reads: *Exsurge, Domine, et judica causam tuam*, the Great Inquisitor comes into view. His cassock, belt, cape, and mantelet are all a dazzling purple, as are the trappings of his black horse. The procession halts and a Mass is celebrated on a raised altar not far from the platform. A sermon follows. Then, one after the other, the condemned mount the platform as their sentences are read aloud. At this point the clergy withdraw, having implored mercy and solemnly deferred to the secular authorities. The Church gives way to the executioner. Night falls. The condemned are placed on mules and taken to some spot along the banks of the Tagus. Only the Inquisitors, constables, and halberdiers remain with the apostates and impenitents. Stakes are driven into the ground and, in the gathering dusk, one can hear the clink of iron collars. The pyre near by is ready, waiting to be lit. Soon, horrible smoke obscures the pink Toledan sky and one can hear the screams of the victims, the crackling of wood, the sizzling of flesh. Then all is still.

The acrid smoke drifts away, carrying off the nightmare. The sky grows clear again and the Zocodover square is deserted. Perhaps this was only a bad dream that faded away beyond the stony wasteland of the Toledan hills; perhaps the square has always been deserted. . . . But no, the Inquisition did of course exist. There actually were burnings at the stake. Some were very famous: in 1559 five consecutive auto-da-fés took place, and the third was presided over by Philip II himself, surrounded by ambassadors and princes. And there were less spectacular ones, but not very many. Unfortunately, a lurid literature has exaggerated the horrors of an institution in itself horrible enough. Many tales have

been told about burnings at the stake in Seville and Valladolid. According to some, the Catholic Kings, concealed in
one of the rooms of the Inquisition palace, feast and occasionally stare curiously out the window to watch heretics
being burned; according to others, Philip II shrieks hysteri-
cally to the executioner as he tears his black gloves to shreds:
"Put sulfur under their nails!" The statistics that have been
compiled are really fantastic: 35,000 burned alive, 19,000
tortured, 290,000 condemned to be galley slaves, 200,000
deprived of their rights, 5,000,000 exiled—a total of around
5,500,000! More moderate figures are closer to the truth.
Without going to the opposite extreme, careful examination
of the Holy Office's files would reduce the number of victims
to fifty-six in all, twenty-four by fire and thirty-two by
strangling, or at the most to not more than a hundred. But is
this a reliable figure, or should it be multiplied by ten or a
hundred? Actually, the odious nature of the Inquisition lies
less in the number of its unhappy victims than in the system
itself, based on spying, informing, and physical and moral
coercion. Self-incrimination under torture was an invention
of the Inquisition. It goes without saying that the Spaniards'
hatred of Moors and Jews, their accumulation of grievances
and bitter memories, neither justifies nor excuses the abomi-
nations committed by the Holy Office. But it is also unfair to
place the entire blame on the Church and the Spanish monarchy. All the people were in favor of the Inquisition; there
was no Spaniard who was not proud to be the unpaid assist-
ant of the Holy Office. No sooner arrived at his mission's
headquarters than an itinerant Inquisitor would find his
antechamber crowded with would-be informers and his desk
piled high with accusations. People vied for the distinction of
denouncing the most flagrant infractions. For more than
eight centuries Spaniards had been bullied by Moors and
plundered by Jews. They now had a chance for revenge, all
the more tempting since, in appeasing their rancor, they were
complying with directives from the crown. Had they not
been told that religious unity was inseparable from political
unity, that to prevent civil war it was necessary to destroy

heresy in Spain as well as abroad? The fervent masses that crowded around the gallows never doubted that both king and Church were right; and this conviction was proof against possible remorse. They could give themselves up to the pleasure of watching the dramatic spectacle—the hushed and funereal *corrida*—with complete peace of mind, and even a sense of righteousness. For every soul put to death increased the chances of salvation for Catholic Spain.

The "Invincible Armada"

The Council of Trent and the Inquisition accomplished their objective in Spain. The Protestant was crushed. But Philip II proposed to track him down in France, England, and the Netherlands as well. The costly wars he waged against Henry IV, William the Silent, and Elizabeth were merely different phases of a single, identical struggle, a religious war against heresy.

The victory of St.-Quentin did not confirm the hopes of Philip II; the French recovered and won back the territory Spain had captured. The Peace of Cateau-Cambrésis ended the Franco-Spanish war and sanctioned the marriage of Isabelle of France to Philip. She was only fourteen and looked like a child beside her thin, severe, and already graying husband, whom she obeyed without loving. Philip would leave her for weeks at a time, only to return late at night, arousing her from deep slumber. He would hasten through the corridors of the palace, accompanied by his chamberlains and followed by his guardsmen, and fling open the door so suddenly that the flames of the torches would flicker, arousing his terrified wife. He would then stare at her pensively.

Because she had served to reconcile Spaniards with Frenchmen, Isabelle was called the "Princess of Peace." A few years later, however, when the Protestant Henry of Navarre attacked Paris, hostilities were resumed. This was a fine opportunity for Philip to assert his position as Defender of the Faith by coming to the aid of the League with money

and weapons. But Henry's conversion to Catholicism sealed
the defeat of French Protestantism and, at the same time,
dashed the political ambitions of Philip. He was obliged to
renounce all hope of seeing his daughter ascend the throne
of the Valois; but it was thanks to his intervention that the
French religious crisis ended in a victory for Catholicism.

In the Netherlands the struggle was more bitter because it
was fought for both religious and political unity. The Dutch
had every intention of remaining Lutherans and preserving their sovereignty. Philip, on the other hand, could not
tolerate the thought of permitting one section of his empire,
the most important from an economic and military point of
view, to slip not only from his grasp but from that of the
Church as well—hence an unremitting conflict that was to
last twenty years.

In this frightful and monotonous succession of intrigues,
plots, and revolts, strong personalities stood out. On the
Dutch side were the Count of Egmont, bombastic and arrogant, and William of Nassau, known as William the Silent,
a great beer drinker and a gloomy companion; the Spaniards
boasted the Duke of Alva, Luis de Requeséns, and Don Juan
of Austria. Dramatic incidents broke the monotony of the
struggle. The nobility of the Netherlands, headed by Egmont, presented a petition to Margaret of Parma—Philip's
sister and his representative in Holland—requesting a
milder policy toward heretics. They were the leaders of the
Revolt of the Beggars. First the regent, then Alva, tried to
liquidate them. A special tribunal—the Council of Blood—
condemned 1,800 Protestants, including Egmont, to death,
for Philip was without mercy. He wrote the Pope: "Rather
than make the slightest concession to the detriment of religion, I would prefer to lose a hundred lives if I had them. I
do not care to rule over heretics." Alva, the king's ferocious
executioner, spoke in the same vein: "It would be better to
preserve by war, for God and the king, an impoverished and
blighted kingdom than to maintain it intact for the benefit of
the devil and his satellites, the heretics." It would be idle to
expect even a mite of charity from men who were capable of

such language. Only force could turn the scales in favor of their adversaries. William the Silent, for example, broke through the Dutch dikes in order to force Spanish troops to raise the siege of Leiden. Finally, at death's door, Philip gave up the struggle. Seven northern provinces of the Netherlands set themselves up as an independent Protestant state, under the nominal protection of Spain. Only Belgium remained both Catholic and Spanish. The Flemish war ended in failure for Philip II.

It was at sea that England and Spain first came to grips. The expeditions of Drake along the Andalusian coast gave Philip a pretext for invading England. A large fleet was assembled in Lisbon. It comprised more than 2,500 pieces of artillery and 20,000 sailors especially trained for landing operations. This was the "Invincible Armada," "the most powerful ocean fleet since the beginning of the world," according to one ambassador. One fine morning it set out under the command of the Duke of Medina-Sidonia, whose forte was administration rather than seamanship. It had scarcely rounded Cape Finisterre when a terrible storm struck. Was this an omen? The fleet sought refuge in Asturian and Basque ports, then set sail again only to meet the full force of the storm off the Dutch coast. At this point, the English and Dutch navies bore down on it simultaneously, moving faster because their ships were lighter. Decimated by cannon fire and tossed about by the tempest, the Armada made its way through the North Sea, had trouble rounding the northern coast of Scotland, and finally limped home, its forces reduced by half. What the Spanish king had hoped would be another Lepanto proved one of history's greatest naval fiascoes. To make matters worse, another defeat was in store for Catholicism with which Philip II was identified. In the meantime, English naval power remained intact and the citadel of Protestantism became stronger than ever. The king, however, took the loss of his vessels philosophically: "I sent them to fight the English, not storms," he remarked. But poor Mary Stuart was not avenged.

The Prince of God

The newborn child at Valladolid, the horseman of St.-Quentin, the orphan of Brussels, the impassive spectator of auto-da-fés, the young bridegroom of Guadarrama—these different images of Philip II follow one another like yellowed reproductions of great paintings. But they are merely likenesses; the real Philip was the man who resided in the Escorial.

The monarch chose to live and die in this arid mineral region of New Castile, in the heart of the Sierras. He wanted the Escorial to resemble the rack upon which St. Lawrence was martyred, to commemorate the battle of St.-Quentin, where his cannon had bombarded the church of St. Lawrence. The architecture and location of the edifice, which was more like a monastery than a palace, symbolized the reign of Philip II: materials of high quality—granite, porphyry, bronze, and gold marble—the use of straight lines, and a majestic, barren landscape. Long, bare façades, colors without any embellishments, the absence of sculpture in the choir stalls—all these were in perfect harmony with the desolate plain, surrounded by wild mountains that seemed worn and cracked by the passage of time. The stone itself, wrested from the quarries of Guadarrama, was hard and gray, like the heart and countenance of the king.

A royal residence, a monument to merciful deeds, the Escorial was also a necropolis. The central altar of the basilica was placed over the vault of the crypt where the kings of Spain lay buried, according to the wishes of Philip II, for he was obsessed with death and communed with his interred ancestors. There were seventeen coffins arranged in tiers. Here was his father, Charles V, there Don Juan of Austria and Don Carlos. Philip's wives were neatly aligned: Maria of Portugal, Isabelle of France, and Anne of Austria. Mary Tudor of England was missing; she was buried in London.

Impassive before the coffins of his father and his wives,
Philip could not restrain his tears in front of the huge sarcophagus of the children—*los párvulos*. A last satisfied
glance at one still empty coffin, his own, and then Philip returned to his apartments, which were almost as dismal as the
Pantheon of Kings. To get to his bedroom and private
chapel, he had to pass through a chamber with bare, whitewashed walls—the Hall of the Ambassadors. A peephole
enabled him to follow the services in the basilica without
being seen. From his window he could gaze at the Castilian
plain and watch the herds of deer as they trampled the blue
heather; he took a last look at nature while he listened to the
muffled sound of psalms intoned by seventy monks, praying
day and night for the peace of his soul. He never tired of
hearing the *De Profundis*, enamored as he was of death.

While Philip sat in his room, his gouty leg stretched out
on a footstool, his elbows leaning on an oak table covered
with reams of paper which his valet had sprinkled with fine
sand, a silent crowd waited outside in the gathering dusk
of his antechamber. Lackeys with soft-soled shoes, tall,
spare hidalgos with goatees, commissioners of the *Santa
Hermandad*, conquistadors on holiday, legates, and peti-
tioners—all spoke in hushed tones. Now and then an opaque
light played on pale foreheads, white collars, and military
insignia, and an aroma of leather, faded velvet, and medi-
cinal unguents pervaded the room. Everyone was waiting
for the king. Bold captains just returned from Peru, their
rapiers concealed under their armpits, trembled in anticipation of the monarch's verdict (his splutterings sounded like
the buzz of an insect) and at the thought of his stony presence. His frown, his reptilian stare, were a thousand times
more frightening than the wild beasts of the jungle!

Was he a Demon of the Noon Hour, or merely the Prudent
King? Probably neither. Philip II's virtues—his dogged
work habits, his austerity and punctiliousness—were doubtless inherited from his German ancestors; Charles V had
been a Burgundian, but Philip was all Habsburg—a genius
of the North. It was his religious intolerance that led him to

commit political errors from which Spain was never to recover. A profile of the king's character could never be more
than an approximation, so full of contradictions was this
strange prince. Humble toward God, he was proud in his
dealings with men, merciless yet scrupulous, fanatical but
shrewd, several times married yet chaste; he was a creature
whom nobody loved, except perhaps his daughter, the
Infanta Clara-Eugenia.

Two tragedies wrought havoc in his personal life. His
son, Don Carlos, an unfortunate degenerate, had conspired
with Philip's enemies. The plot was discovered and Don
Carlos died in despair. Antonio Pérez, the king's trusted
secretary, had betrayed his royal master and fled to France.
Abandoned by the people he counted on, widowed four
times, his life endangered by one of his own sons, Philip had
neither friends nor even collaborators, only employees. He
ruled just as he faced his God—alone.

With the exception of the Netherlands, he had managed
to safeguard most of his possessions. Indeed, at the price of a
short war waged by the Duke of Alva, he had conquered
Portugal. Against the Netherlands, France, and England,
neither arms nor diplomacy proved effective. He had served
his God with all his might, yet the Protestant and the
Mohammedan had not been conquered. What a bitter end
for this Christian prince whose every battle was fought in
the name of Catholicism! Perhaps he had been too ambitious.
Stubborn in his determination to expand the Christian domain, and to crush all enemies of the faith, he had turned
away from his own people. Antonio Pérez commented: "I
very much fear that if men do not become more moderate,
if they continue to behave like God on earth, God will grow
weary of monarchies." Grandiose plans which took too long
to mature blinded Philip to the fact that he was ruining
Spain. Wanting too much power for his country, he only succeeded in impoverishing it.

Philip II was now seventy. For a long time he had not
set foot outside the Escorial. He no longer greeted the people from the high balcony which led from his private apart-

ments to the chapel. Rarely did the Grandees of Spain catch a glimpse of him—perhaps once or twice a year. The candle that burned late at night in the window of his study was the only sign that the king was not dead. For a few more months the bald, white-bearded man, dressed in black velvet, could be seen walking up and down the Hall of the Ambassadors, stopping to glance at a map of the world which stood on a silver pedestal, or softly caressing an illuminated prayer book. A young girl guided him by the arm. Then he was bedridden, and the Infanta Clara-Eugenia attended him, cooling his brow. His body, lacerated by ulcers and covered with sores, was rotting away. His last words were: "Never weary of listening to the laments of the poor." Like his ancestor Ferdinand the Saint, he mustered his last bit of strength to grasp a candle that had been blessed. He died holding Charles V's crucifix.

Beneath the emblazoned granite of the Pantheon of Kings, two corpses lay side by side—the hermit of Yuste and the penitent of the Escorial. Both men had just missed being truly great figures, and both died in an unusual fashion. With macabre pleasure, each had prepared for his own death well in advance. But a terrible surprise awaited Philip II, as if God had elected to recompense his blind servant with a terrible death—fifty days of frightful martyrdom! Like St. Lawrence on the rack, on which he had patterned the Escorial, the Prince of God suffered torture by fire.

One more year and the sixteenth century would be over. The death knell of Philip II heralded the decadence of the Habsburgs and the decline of Spanish power. As his coffin was lowered into the crypt, the Golden Century drew to a close.

❦ PART · IV ☙

THE AGE OF
Goya

"Goya is doubtless one of those artists who, as early as the eighteenth century, foreshadowed the accomplishments of the [Spanish] Revolution, although with a bit of democratic rancor, somewhat akin to a Beaumarchais, but a sycophantic Beaumarchais, a child of the people who rubbed shoulders with the social elite of the period."　　　—EUGÉNIO D'ORS,
The Art of Goya

I

The Days
of the Enlightenment

To his successors, Philip II bequeathed intact, or almost intact, the legacy he had inherited from Charles V. To be sure, the Protestant Netherlands were lost, but Naples, Sicily, Milan, Franche-Comté, Artois, Flanders, and, recently, Portugal, to say nothing of the "Empire of India," still belonged to the King of Spain. True to its lot, which always fluctuated, Spain fell from the dizzy heights to which the Habsburgs had raised it. Its task was no longer to conquer, but rather to preserve what it still possessed, or at least to safeguard the major part of it.

Philip III, Philip IV, Charles II . . . we might better say Lerma, Olivarez, Nithard, for from now on favorites, or *validos*, were to govern. To complete the triptych, three French names—Richelieu, Mazarin, Louis XIV—must be added. The first half of the seventeenth century was marked by France's efforts to wrest from Spain the hegemony it retained for a time in Europe; but Spain's political decadence, which conformed to the inexorable law of falling bodies, proceeded at a uniformly accelerated tempo and gradually isolated it from the family of great nations. First it lost Portugal, then Catalonia, which the monarchy barely managed to recover. The Austrian alliance did not have the desired effect; the Treaty of Westphalia recognized the independence of the United Provinces of the Netherlands and deprived Spain of Artois; the Treaty of Utrecht gave Austria the so-called Catholic Netherlands, that is to say, German Flanders, Hainaut, southern Brabant, Limburg, Luxembourg, Namur, Antwerp, and Malines. Then proud Spain saw Franche-Comté, the Italian possessions, Minorca, and Gibraltar break away. Within the space of a century it had ceased to be a great power.

Between the death of Philip III and the advent of Philip V the "Great Century" of France supplanted the Golden Century of Spain, and the management of European affairs slipped from the hands of the weak Habsburgs; nevertheless, they did not give up their secular struggle against the enemies of the faith. The frontiers of Spain were under constant attack, and endless wars had impoverished and bled the country, yet it refused to surrender what it considered to be its spiritual sovereignty. There was something rather touching, quixotic, about its pale, lymphatic, weary kings who defied the pressure of *camarillas* and favorites and resumed the fight their fathers had waged against the Moors and Protestants. Philip III, the Pious, triumphed over the German Protestants in the famous Battle of the White Mountain. Victorious over the Huguenots, he launched an attack on the last Moriscos. Scattered throughout Spain and strictly supervised ever since the Alpujarras revolt and Philip II's edict, the Moriscos persisted in their stubborn resistance. They plotted with the sultan and conspired with the French. Philip III, deciding to implement his father's plans, took drastic action. The last of the Moriscos, some 100,000 in all, were banished.

Philip IV was sixteen when he mounted the throne. He named his chamberlain, Don Gaspar de Guzmán, Count Olivarez, first minister of the realm. Olivarez ruled Spain for twenty years. Tremendously ambitious, he did not await the death of Philip III to declare: "Everything is mine." And, indeed, everything was his, but he made very poor use of it. Only after he had suffered many bitter defeats did

Philip IV decide to rid himself of his evil genius. The third Habsburg was gloomy—he reportedly laughed only three times in his whole life. Although he liked diversion and women, he took his pleasures grimly. However, he had a great appreciation for art; his sole distinction, perhaps, was the discovery of Velázquez, the only friend he had. The story is told that when "Las Meninas" was finished, the king seized Velázquez's brush and drew the cross of Santiago, which he later awarded him, on the artist's doublet. Thanks to Olivarez's mistakes and Richelieu's genius, a series of disasters punctuated Philip IV's reign. Richelieu followed the traditional French policy of trying to weaken the House of Austria and acquiring territory that was geographically part of France—Artois, Flanders, Franche-Comté, Alsace, and Roussillon. Olivarez had no policy whatsoever, save that of following the whim of the moment. At first the Franco-Spanish conflict seemed to go well for the armies of Philip IV, which got as far as Compiègne and threatened Paris. But Richelieu's energetic intervention halted them not far from the capital.

The Catalonian revolution soon demanded the full attention of the Spanish monarchy. The ancient principality of Catalonia had never renounced its independence. The blunders of the Castilian administration aroused the people's ire against the government of Madrid and precipitated the revolution of the *segadors*—the harvesters—who fought to the tune of the "Harvest Song," the Catalonians' "Marseillaise": *"Grans cops de falç, Defensors de la Terra, Grans cops de falç."* French muskets went to the aid of Catalonian scythes, and a chaotic war ensued between Frenchmen, Catalonians, and Castilians, with Roussillon as the prize. It had a dramatic epilogue: after several months of fierce battle, Flores, the marquis of Ávila, surrendered Perpignan to the French. Before leaving the city he dismounted, bowed in front of the sculptured escutcheon above the gates, and with his right hand traced in the air a large cross. He thus bade farewell to Perpignan.

The year of Olivarez's disgrace and dismissal also witnessed Spain's most disastrous defeat. Encouraged by Richelieu's death and the grave illness of Louis XIII, the governor of the Netherlands, Don Francisco de Melo, invaded northern France. Fiercely determined, he was also powerfully armed; but he encountered "the Great Condé." The battle of Rocroi which followed has been vividly described by Bossuet in his *Funeral Orations:* "The enemy army was composed of that old combination of Walloons, Italians, and Spaniards which until now we had not been able to disperse." Although the Spanish army was by far the more powerful, the French were commanded by "a young prince of royal blood who had about him an air of victory." He was to be seen galloping from one end of the battlefield to the other, "his blazing eyes dumfounding those who had escaped his blows." There was a mass attack by "the Spanish infantry, whose large serried ranks, resembling the kind of towers whose every breach could be mended, remained immovable in the midst of the confusion, firing in all directions." Meanwhile Louis XIII died and Condé won the battle.

The Catalonian rebellion had been only temporarily suppressed. Portugal shook off the Spanish yoke and chose its own king, the Duke of Braganza, who was proclaimed João IV. France made peace with Austria. Weary of fighting uselessly, Spain had no choice but to sign a peace with France at Bidassoa. It ceded Cerdagne, Roussillon, a part of Artois, and a few Flemish cities. At St.-Jean-de-Luz, the young French king, Louis XIV, married the Spanish Infanta, Maria Theresa. As for Philip IV, whom Olivarez impudently, or ironically, called "Philip the Great," he ended his days devoutly under the aegis of a pious nun, María de Agreda.

With the advent of Charles II the pathological decadence of the Habsburgs reached its height. The son of Philip IV was an unfortunate, sickly man with a long, moon-shaped face. This frail prince, whose life hung by a thread, was surrounded by drama. Foreign influences, palace conspiracies, dagger thrusts, mysterious poisonings, transformed the

Spanish court into a setting for tragedy in the grand manner. *Validos*, ministers, confessors, vied for the favor of the Queen-Mother, Mariana of Austria, and for that of the gloomy monarch. Nithard, a German Jesuit, Valenzuela, a poet, Juan José of Austria, the illegitimate son of Philip IV and the Calderona, the Duke of Medinaceli—each, in turn, enjoyed the royal favor and each exerted an influence that occasionally worked for the good of the country but more often proved disastrous. The sickly Charles II was but the shadow of a king, yet he was not without some majesty. The lower part of his sallow face bore traces of the Habsburg heavy lower lip and stubborn jaw. Yet his bearing was noble, for, while fully aware of his physical defects, he was nonetheless conscious of the importance of his role and of the grandeur that was Spain's. He loved and was loved by his subjects. Plots and intrigues were rife during his reign and continued even as he lay dying; he had no direct descendant and there were several pretenders. All Europe waited for him to breathe his last, eager to know whom he had named as his successor. Agents of the great powers besieged him. It was even said that he was possessed by evil spirits, and people called him "the Bewitched," whereas actually he was merely subject to epileptic seizures. The poor man occasionally indulged in extravagant acts which caused some to doubt his sanity. From his ancestor Philip II, he had inherited a macabre nature and spent a good deal of time in the Pantheon of Kings at the Escorial, where he insisted that the coffins of members of his family be opened. Moved by the sight of the decaying remains of his first wife, Marie Louise of Orléans, he had to be restrained from embracing them.

Finally, after changing his mind a hundred times, Charles II named as his successor his grand-nephew, Philip of Bourbon, duke of Anjou. Actually it was his entourage who suggested the Duke of Anjou, feeling that only Louis XIV was strong enough to uphold the integrity of the Spanish monarchy. When his last will was read to him, Charles II burst into tears. "Only God grants empires and takes them away," he sighed. He was heard to murmur from

time to time: "We no longer amount to anything." No one
mourned his death. Two centuries earlier Charles V had
been born at Ghent. 1500–1700 . . . The five Habsburgs
that represented the Golden Century were gone, disappearing down the somber lane of history.

"The Pyrenees Are No More"

When Louis XIV presented his grandson, the young Duke of
Anjou, at the court of Versailles, he said to him: "Your first
obligation is to be a good Spaniard. But remember you were
born a Frenchman and be sure to maintain the unity of the
two countries." Philip V, the first Bourbon of Spain, never
forgot his grandfather's advice. However, for a number of
reasons, some of which cannot be related, he was always
more French than Spanish.

Likable and high-spirited, Philip V was full of good intentions, but he had no capacity whatsoever for making decisions. The women of the crown assumed control. For a long
time Spain was subject to the influence of the Princess des
Ursins, maid of honor to the queen, Marie Louise, Philip's
first wife. From the moment of her arrival at the austere
Escorial palace she shocked the old noblemen of the court by
her initiative, which the king accepted only too readily. She
insisted on doing away with rigid etiquette and cold, formal
ceremonies. The royal couple were soon dancing, and Mo-
lière's comedies replaced the endless, tiresome Spanish
tragedies. The pizzicato of gay Italian music offended the
ears of the duennas, accustomed to hymns and sacred music.
And, to the great scandal of Philip's courtiers, the monarch
approved the removal of the train (the *tontillo*) from the
gowns which ladies wore so that their ankles would not be
exposed when they mounted their carriages. But the Princess des Ursins did not confine her activities to such trivial
matters. With the help of the French ambassador, Amelot,
and that of the French financier Orry, she was able to renew
the flow of Spanish currency and to improve the public fi-

nances, which had suffered during the preceding century, when Spain had been bled by its many wars. Nor did she hesitate to grapple with the Inquisition, whose excesses she sought to moderate. Philip gave the industrious lady, whom he called "my heart," a free hand.

If Philip seemed indifferent to Spanish affairs, it was because he had another, bolder ambition: to become King of France upon the death of the young Louis XV, who was said to be extremely ill. Despite the fact that in 1713, by the Peace of Utrecht, he had solemnly renounced the throne of France, Philip not only intrigued for the French crown but encouraged his ambasssador in Paris, Cellamara, to foment intrigues against the Regent. The plot failed and Cellamara's accomplices, including Cardinal Polignac and the Marquis de Pompadour, were sent to the Bastille. Thereupon France, Holland, England, and Austria formed an alliance and demanded that Philip officially renounce his claim to the French and Austrian thrones. When his daughter, Marie Anne Victoire, was three, he planned to marry her to Louis XV, who was only eleven! From the Austrian emperor he obtained an option on the Italian duchies. Finally, convinced that his interests coincided with those of France, Philip concluded the first Family Compact with the Bourbon princes. As a consequence, France dragged Spain into the Wars of the Polish and Austrian Successions. In return, the duchies of Parma and Tuscany were restored to Spain. On the other hand, Gibraltar, which the Anglo-Dutch fleet had seized in July 1704, was retained by the English. Thereafter Spain continuously demanded the return of this national *peñon*, "the thorn in the heart of the country."

Philip V will be remembered as the most unfaithful of kings. Weak and charming, he was influenced by a succession of favorites whose conflicting interests proved mutually destructive. After placing the fate of the Spanish kingdom in the hands of the Princess des Ursins, he eventually had her arrested and ignominiously banished. This he did on the advice of the new favorite, Alberoni, a simple gardener who had won the heart of the Duke of Vendôme because of the special way in which he prepared macaroni. Dispatched to the court of Madrid as councilor, Alberoni became the favorite of Philip V, who named him cardinal and chief minister. Blamed for subsequent Spanish reverses, Alberoni was banished in turn. Philip now came under the influence of his second wife, Elizabeth Farnese, who turned his attention to Italy, where she hoped to find thrones for her sons. The Italian policy of the queen, and her encouraging attitude toward José Patiño, the Spanish Colbert, resulted in the creation of a powerful navy and placed Spain once again in the forefront of the great Mediterranean powers.

One day, for reasons unknown—in imitation, perhaps, of Charles V?—Philip decided to abdicate in favor of his son. Accompanied by Elizabeth Farnese, he retired to the palace of San Ildefonso, which he had built in the heart of the Guadarrama. Luis I's career was brief and scandal-ridden. After reigning for several months he died of smallpox and Philip V resumed power. Elizabeth Farnese persisted in her Italian plans and was partially successful. But the sudden death of Philip V interrupted her intrigues for a time. The reign of this unstable prince can be summed up in a few words: King of Spain for over forty-six years, he was neither a king nor a Spaniard; others governed in his place and, although distrustful of France, he never ceased to covet the French crown. Never were the Pyrenees more formidable than during this period when Louis XIV declared that they no longer existed.

In view of his tendency to let others rule in his place, a distinction must be made between Philip V of Spain and the Spain of Philip V. Although it is rather easy to see through his personality, the complications of successions and alliances which constitute the pattern of Spanish politics from the death of Charles II on November 1, 1700, to that of Philip V on July 9, 1747, are less readily comprehensible. Spain's policy can perhaps best be likened to a mountain landscape bathed in fog whose crest is barely discernible. Philip V, grandson of Louis XIV, became King of Spain not only because he was so designated by his grandfather. Like

Louis XIV, the German emperor, Leopold I, was a son-in-law of Philip IV. He renounced his right to the Spanish throne in order to promote the candidature of his second son, the Austrian Archduke Charles. Supported by a powerful coalition consisting of England, Holland, Denmark, Germany, Portugal, and Savoy, Archduke Charles laid claim to his Spanish legacy; it was imperative to prevent a fusion of the French and Spanish monarchies. On the other hand, Louis XIV could not permit a German to reign at Madrid, for this would constitute a first step toward the encirclement of France which the determined policies of Richelieu and Mazarin had succeeded in preventing. Thus began the War of the Spanish Succession. Victorious at Friedlingen and Höchstädt, defeated at Oudenaarde, Lille, and Malplaquet, saved just in time from a frightful disaster at Denain by the sudden victory of Marshal de Villars, France signed a peace treaty with England, Holland, Portugal, Savoy, and Prussia at Utrecht, with Austria at Rastatt, and with the Italian and German princes at Baden. Supplementary pacts attached to the treaties settled the Spanish question. Philip V retained his throne but ceded Naples, Milan, Sardinia, and the Spanish Netherlands to Austria, Sicily to Savoy, Gibraltar and Minorca to England. Furthermore, the English obtained important privileges in the Spanish colonies which they exploited in such a way as to supplant Spain gradually in the New World. What mattered most to Philip V was the retention of his crown, which he owed in large part to the French. What would have become of him had the Duke of Vendôme failed to break up the Anglo-Austrian offensive at Villaviciosa? And, indeed, Archduke Charles, who had been proclaimed King of Spain and acclaimed in Catalonia and had staged a victorious entry into Madrid, very nearly replaced his French rival. Greatly indebted to France, Spain plainly followed its lead, siding with it in the Wars of the Polish and Austrian Successions. As a result, it acquired Naples for Prince Charles, and the duchies of Parma, Piacenza, and Tuscany for Prince Philip.

Such were the contours of the mountain peak during the

reign of Philip V. The landscape was majestic but night was falling. Although still a mighty European power, enriched by its American possessions, Spain was on the verge of decline. England, its enemy in the colonies and on the seas, soon would prevail. We must now bid the Spain of Philip V farewell; to do so we must go to San Ildefonso, where this grandson of Louis XIV, who hated Madrid even more than the Escorial, had built a palace that was reminiscent of the Versailles of his youth. La Granja. . . . Pink marble and gray stone, spouting fountains, French gardens, vast green parks adorned with statues and urns—it was here, in the shade of poplar trees, that Philip V liked to relax. In the *sala del Panteón*, on a mausoleum of red marble, Rigaud has painted the young Duke of Anjou bowing at the court of Versailles.

Philip V's successor, Ferdinand VII, was the second son of his first wife. A rather insignificant figure, the new king vacillated between England and France, unable to take a firm stand. His half brother and successor, Charles III, King of Naples and son of Elizabeth Farnese, definitely chose to ally himself with France. The Family Compact was renewed and strengthened; Louis XV ceded Minorca and Louisiana to Spain. The common enemy was England. Both Frenchmen and Spaniards dealt it hard blows on the high seas as well as along the borders of its colonial empire.

The eighteenth century, although an era of decline, was nonetheless one of the most brilliant periods in Spain's history. From the moment that French princes mounted the throne, a fresh and salubrious wind blew over the country. Intolerance was not completely dead, but it was disappearing. Religion still commanded respect, but it was now possible to smile at the extremely devout. Gone were sectarian persecutions and expulsions! Within the space of one century the population almost doubled, increasing from six to eleven million! The New World had become profitable. Powerful companies were set up which systematically exploited the commercial potentialities of Spanish America. For example, the Real Compañía Guipúzcoana de Caracas, which had a monopoly of the cocoa trade, handled more than 100,000 quintals of cocoa a year. Great viceroys like Amat and O'Higgins lent their talents to the achievement of prosperity in the colonies. In every domain Spain adopted modern methods. New fields of endeavor were explored, new villages established, new industries created and old ones improved. Under the dynamic leadership of such men as Jovellanos and Campomanes, Spain began to build public works worthy of the Romans. Within fifty years, more than 600 miles of roads were constructed, and at least 300 bridges. The postal service functioned expertly; a letter mailed in Madrid and destined for Cadiz could be answered in two weeks—very rapid service in view of the distance covered and the difficulty of the route.

Spain was no longer the great political power it had been under Charles V and Philip II, but it began to be a great commercial, economic and colonial power.

While agriculture was being modernized and technical improvements were being made, and while the population increased, a great storm raged. Doggedly impervious until then to external intellectual influences, the Spain of Charles III reacted violently to French philosophy. Encyclopedist ideas erupted suddenly in a spiritual atmosphere that had not altogether broken with the Middle Ages. Two centuries after Luther, a second revolution was to trouble the minds of some men and delight others: the shadow of Voltaire had joined that of Erasmus.

Moreover, Charles III bore a slight resemblance to Voltaire—long, pointed nose, piercing eyes, prominent cheekbones. Discriminating, a man of taste, patron of arts and letters, he prided himself on being an "enlightened prince," and indeed he was. A persistent builder, an excellent administrator, he adopted measures that were bold yet wise. He built the Museum of the Prado, personally planned the layout of new roads, and saw to the organization of the army and navy. He selected competent ministers like Count Aranda and the Marquis of Floridablanca. Some of his biographers claimed that the third Spanish Bourbon was as "stubborn as a mule and as weak as a woman," but these were probably the same men who criticized him for his love of France.

The Jesuits and Freemasonry

Charles III apparently did show some weakness in regard to the expulsion of the Jesuits. Actually, it was Aranda, the chief minister and captain-general of Castile, who first gave him the idea. A strong-minded man and a "philosopher," according to the disciples of French thought, this Aragonese had been maligning the Jesuits for a long time. When the minister Esquilache was disgraced for having forced Madrileños to wear three-cornered cocked hats in place of the large sombreros, he finally convinced the monarch that the Jesuits were plotting against him and accused them of having fomented the "revolt of the capes." Aranda revived old grievances: the Jesuits persecuted the Indians and the Chinese, they wanted a universal monarchy, they spread religious terror. But as Charles III seemed not altogether persuaded, his councilors adduced some telling evidence they had been holding in reserve. They showed him a letter supposedly written by Father Lorenzi Ricci, a Jesuit General. It claimed that Charles was the son not of Philip V but of Cardinal Alberoni and Elizabeth Farnese. This spurious document convinced the king. Without further ado, he had all the Jesuits of the kingdom arrested. Twenty-four hours later they were taken under guard to Spanish ports. Almost 5,000 Jesuits landed on the Italian coast. In spite of Pope Clement XIII's sharp protests, the King of Spain was adamant and urged his son, the King of Naples, to follow his example. Six years later, upon the insistence of the Spanish ambassador, Moñino y Redondo, Clement XIV published the encyclical *Dominus ac Redemptor Noster*, abolishing the Society of Jesus throughout all of Christendom. As a reward for this diplomatic victory, Charles III conferred the title of Count Floridablanca upon Moñino.

For forty years—until Pope Pius VII re-established it—
the Society of Jesus suffered. Banished from France, Portugal, and Russia, the Jesuits continued to protest the treatment to which they were being subjected. But what hurt
them the most was their eviction from Spain; that such measures should be taken by the most Catholic nation in the world
was totally unexpected. Certain Jesuits must have behaved
most undiplomatically to awaken so much hatefulness among
the Spanish ministers, one of whom, the Minister of Justice,
wrote to Choiseul: "We have killed the son, now all we have
to do is kill the mother, our Holy Roman Church."

The introduction into Spain of Encyclopedist philosophy
as well as Voltaire's writings, the close contact between the
ministers of the French Regency and those of Charles III, the
emergence of a new ideology based upon liberty—all these
helped to engender the brutal reaction against the Jesuits.
But the Spanish Church was soon to pit its strength against
another formidable if slippery foe—Freemasonry.

Of very ancient origin, perhaps going all the way back to
the Eleusinian mysteries, Freemasonry had already played
an important role in England by the time it reached France
via the Jacobites during the first years of Louis XV's reign.
From France it spread to Spain. The first lodge was founded
in 1726 at Gibraltar, which by then was English. More
lodges were established at Madrid, Cadiz, Barcelona, and
Valladolid. Since Freemasonry was hostile to the Catholic
Church, although not to theism, the Church countered by
taking every possible measure to protect itself. In his bull
In Eminenti of April 28, 1738, Pope Clement XII excommunicated the Freemasons. In 1740, Philip V promulgated a
severe edict against them, and eleven years later, Pope Benedict XIV, in his bull *Romanorum Pontificum*, renewed the
excommunication.

Until the advent of Charles III, Spanish Freemasonry,
controlled by the English lodges, played in insignificant
role. The appointment of Aranda, a friend of the philosophers, as chief minister lent fresh impetus to the secret
society. He was given the task of reorganizing Spanish Free-

masonry along the lines of its French model. Upon his appointment as Grand Commander of the Order, Aranda put his mind to giving the Masonic institution a Spanish character. Freeing it from English control, he brought it closer to the Grand Lodge of France, among whose initiates were prominent contributors to the *Encyclopédie*. There is no evidence that Charles III sympathized with Freemasonry, but he was well aware of his chief minister's Masonic activities. In any event, the Catholic sovereign could not openly oppose the wishes of Popes Clement XII and Benedict XIV, which had been clearly expressed not once but twice. He merely closed his eyes to the Freemasons' ever-increasing activities at the court. They zealously assisted the philosophers. And if they were especially hostile to the Church, this was because the Church had a monopoly of education and therefore held the keys to culture. The "Friends of Enlightenment" were less resentful of the temporal privileges of the Church than of the control it had wielded over the minds of the people ever since the Middle Ages.

In Paraguay, which was pre-eminently the domain of the Jesuits, a handful of Guarani, siding with the missionaries, took up arms against the royal decree, but their resistance was short-lived. Meanwhile, to prevent the clergy from attempting to substitute its authority for that of the viceroys in the New World territories, Charles III appointed special intendants with extensive powers. They gradually limited the clergy's field of action and at the same time disseminated French philosophical thought in Latin America. These were the first currents of the revolution to reach the peoples of America, who, until then, had been accustomed to associate government with religion. So adroit was the propaganda of Charles III's ministers that the new governor of Buenos Aires wrote Aranda quite sincerely: "I am going to try to conquer the Mission villages and free the Indians from the slavery and ignorance in which they live." The clever and persistent campaign initiated at the court of Madrid had borne fruit. The *Encyclopédie* was disseminated throughout the vast overseas empire and thus the foundations of future universities were laid. At the same time, Freemasonry gained a foothold and established lodges in the principal cities of Spanish America. "New ideas" were making rapid headway.

It was inevitable that a conflict should arise between the Frenchified disciples of the *Encyclopédie* and the descendants of Loyola. Jesuit education at the beginning of the eighteenth century showed serious gaps. The imperatives of religion called for such rigid control over Catholic teachers that subjects considered dangerous had to be eliminated from their curricula. Instruction in mathematics and the natural sciences was very elementary. The Jesuits certainly were not lacking in erudition, but their teaching methods, at best dogmatic, were frequently childish, leaving much to be desired. The most Catholic of Spanish historians, Menéndez y Pelayo, admitted: "In my opinion it was most unfortunate that the Renaissance fell into the hands of the Jesuits, where it degenerated into college rhetoric." Indeed, Ignatius Loyola's successors seemed to look upon their pupils, even those about to don the scholar's cap, as perennial children.

French ideas were quite naturally popular in Spain in view of the new light they shed on science, economics, law, and sociology. Literary societies multiplied. Spain prided itself on becoming as "enlightened" as pre-revolutionary France, and this perhaps revealed vanity rather than a desire to imitate. During this period the Royal Library, the Academy of Languages, and the Academy of History were founded. Not content to be a mere Francophile, Charles III wanted to be another "enlightened despot," and he turned to France for inspiration in the domains of government and thought. With great difficulty he imitated the French monarchy, centralizing the royal authority, limiting local privileges, abolishing viceroyalties, and replacing favorites of the old regime with responsible ministers. To be sure, the spirit of the century affected only a small segment of society. Actually, only the leading classes—ministers, noblemen, courtiers, high officials, a few men of letters and jurists—were fired with enthusiasm for *The Social Contract* or *The Spirit of the*

Laws. Fashion played an important part in their infatuation with the intellectual "sensitivity" of Jean Jacques Rousseau; many claimed they were inspired by Montesquieu's philosophy when, in fact, they had not read a single line of his work! For one Cabarrús, who hoped to "obliterate in twenty years the mistakes of twenty centuries," there were a number of scholars—Fernando de Cebellos y Pier, Diego de Cádiz, Juan Pablo Forner—who remained true to traditional philosophy. Furthermore, the peasants, the lower clergy, provincial hidalgos—all stubborn *cristianos viejos*—would have nothing to do with these writers whose very fame seemed highly suspect. Frenchification brought about a confrontation between two attitudes: one liberal and revolutionary, the other fiercely Catholic and nationalistic—in other words, between progressivism and conservatism. The entire history of contemporary Spain is marked by the conflict of these two tendencies.

The most representative figure of the eighteenth century was Gaspar Melchor de Jovellanos. Born in Gijón and slated at first for a career in the Church, Jovellanos soon displayed great aptitude for administration. He quickly acquired a reputation as an economist and jurist. His competence and honesty were so esteemed that Charles IV turned to him in the very serious situation that had arisen in foreign affairs and entrusted him with the portfolio of Foreign Affairs and Justice. But he was disliked by Godoy, the favorite, and this proved fatal to his political career. During the last ten years of his life, he was sent from prison to prison, accused of imaginary intrigues by enemies jealous of his powerful personality. He died at the port of Vega as he was fleeing from the French.

"A liberal in the English sense, an innovator yet mindful of tradition, a guardian of human dignity and true intellectual emancipation within the confines of faith and adherence to Church dogmas"—thus one of his biographers has described him. Jovellanos combined all that was best in Christian tradition with the message of the Revolution. He bluntly criticized the Church when he spoke of "eras of superstition and ignorance." Nor did he spare the Revolution. "In our day a ferocious and somber sect has sought to reduce mankind to its original barbaric state, to break our ties with society, claiming them to be unnatural, and to envelop all the principles of civil, natural, and religious morality in a chaos of absurdities and blasphemy." In his treatise on theoretical and practical methods of education, he countered the Declaration of the Rights of Man by claiming that "inequality is not only necessary but essential in civil society." Finally, in a work dealing with the Cortes, he plainly qualified as "political heresy" the principle of national sovereignty. Thus, while acknowledging the importance of the "new ideas" and the benefit Spain might derive from them, Jovellanos was not totally indifferent to Christian tradition. He was pious, attended Mass, received Communion, and spoke of the author of the *Imitation* as his "old friend." But when church was out he went to his lodge, for this good Catholic was a Freemason.

Jovellanos took a middle position between the past and the future. Honest and sincere, he was unable to choose between a fixed and rigid Spain and one that was Frenchified. This indecisiveness was with him to the end; he died loving France yet unwilling to borrow from Frenchmen, imbued with a deep love of his own country, which was not without merit in view of his imprisonment and exile. Jovellanos's uncertainty was characteristic of the latter part of the eighteenth century. "New ideas" or tradition? Spain itself could not make up its mind. The University of Salamanca remained true to traditional methods of education while the Universities of Valencia, Granada, and Alcalá readily accepted the new doctrines. Theism and rationalism tried to be good bedfellows. Age-old "truths" were put to new tests. Thanks to Newton and to advances in mathematics, technology and mechanics were competing with philosophy. The old scholastics bewailed this state of affairs, complaining that theirs was a terrible period in which to live. Revision of chronological data and objective examination of the archives opened new historical perspectives. Idols were being smashed. Economics stepped on the toes of theology, and hygiene vied with ethics.

What was the effect of the French enlightenment on Spanish politics? It was still too soon to speak of a Left or a Right, but it was early enough to perceive among the Hispano-Catholic majority a liberal and free-thinking minority. Already the enemies had taken sides; they were still peaceful, but their positions paved the way for the harsh conflicts of the nineteenth century and foreshadowed, from this great distance, the tragic bloodshed of 1936. Does this mean that Spain was in danger? Doubtless Robespierre, and subsequently Napoleon, believed it was. Only a few more years were to elapse, however, before both men were to be confronted with the unity of the Spanish people which they themselves had forged. Faced with invasion by the French, Spaniards of every political affiliation formed a united front. As soon as the emperor's small hat and the plumed cocked hats of his marshals appeared on the horizon of Saragossa, Catalonians, Basques, Andalusians, and Castilians, divided until then, rose up as one man. This was the same people that Voltaire described in his *Essay on the Manners of Nations:* "Everyone played the guitar, yet sadness was no less widespread throughout Spain." But the strummers of *malagueñas* were equally adept at intoning the song of the *segadors.*

2

The Fall of an Emperor

HARLES IV succeeded
Charles III. The new sovereign bore a curious resemblance
to his ill-fated cousin, Louis XVI, both physically and
morally. One has but to examine Goya's extraordinary painting "Charles IV and His Family." What a king and what a
family! In the foreground is Charles IV, massive and thick-
set, one foot forward as if he were about to step out of the
picture. The build of a day laborer, the Bourbon nose, fleshy
chin, and flabby lip were quite reminiscent of the corpulent
and rustic majesty of Louis XVI. Similar, too, were their
personalities—indecisiveness, weakness, and guilelessness.
Charles's passions were hunting and clockmaking; he desired
only good food. Women did not interest him, which perhaps
explains why he was the only one at court who was blissfully
unaware of the situation in his own household. When he
naïvely praised his wife's virtues to anyone who cared to
listen, his old father could be heard to murmur: "How stupid
you are, my poor child!" The queen was Marie Louise of
Parma. . . . For a true portrait of her one must again turn
to Goya: gimlet eyes, the head of a bird of prey perched on a
long neck, beautiful arms, patrician hands—her only marks of
beauty—for otherwise she was poorly endowed as a woman.
In one corner of the canvas, blurred by the gathering dusk,
Goya smiles. Did he guess that the royal couple, who thought

they were being immortalized by the greatest painter of the day, would soon know the fury of the mob, as well as exile and death on foreign soil? The contemporary judgment of Charles IV and his wife confirmed Goya's impression. The First Consul's two ambassadors in Madrid expressed their opinion quite frankly. One, Lucien Bonaparte, had this to say about Charles IV: "He is the flower of ancient Castilian honesty, religious, generous, trusting—too much so—because he judges others according to his own lights." The other ambassador, Alquier, in referring to the queen, exclaimed: "No woman ever lied with such effrontery, nor is there a creature as completely treacherous as she! At the age of fifty she has the conceit and coquetry one would scarcely pardon in a young and pretty woman. She is fit only to rule over valets. She has no love for anything, not even her lovers, and has been beaten and insulted by Godoy and by others as well." Yet Spain was never so great as during the time of these bad shepherds.

The court of Madrid observed France anxiously, for events there were approaching a climax. Louis XVI convoked the Estates-General; the Tennis Court Oath, the storming of the Bastille, the Declaration of the Rights of Man, and the Constitution of 1791 followed. Apprehended at Varennes, Louis XVI was imprisoned in the Temple. Invoking the Family Compact, Spanish diplomacy attempted to come to his rescue. In a letter addressed to the Minister of Foreign Affairs, the Spanish ambassador in Paris, speaking in the name of Charles IV, expressed indignation at the way Louis was being treated. Alone among the sovereigns of Europe, Charles openly sided with his "relative and ancient ally." But the Convention was unmoved. Louis was judged, condemned, and beheaded.

While relations between the two governments grew increasingly bitter, revolutionary propaganda continued to spread throughout Spain. The rumbling voice of Mirabeau could be heard as far away as Madrid. The Declaration of the Rights of Man and Necker's writings, concealed beneath coats, inside beaver hats, and in mother-of-pearl boxes, were surreptitiously handed around. Nevertheless, the execution of Louis XVI and the religious persecution unleashed by the Mountain provoked great anger among Spanish monarchists and Catholics. Emigré French officers and refractory priests crossed the border: the reign of the Terror had begun. Meanwhile, in Madrid a palace revolution occurred. The foreign policy of Spain had been controlled first by Floridablanca, then by Aranda; but the latter was soon replaced by the queen's favorite, Manuel Godoy. This handsome man, who was an excellent dancer, had been a mere Estremaduran guardsman. Suddenly, within the space of a few months and thanks to Marie Louise, he rose to become Commander of Santiago, Duke of Alcudia, Grandee of Spain, and Knight of the Golden Fleece. Barely twenty-five, he now was the chief minister. The Convention offered him a choice between alliance and war. Godoy chose war.

The first Franco-Spanish conflict of the nineteenth century lasted two years, with military operations localized in Catalonia and in the Netherlands. Realizing the uselessness of fighting, Spaniards offered Jacobin France a renewal of the Bourbon alliance. Peace terms were concluded at Basel and the Bourbon Family Compact was renewed at San Ildefonso. Godoy, who had become the "Prince of Peace," once again turned to France, now under the Directory. His aim was no longer to wage war but rather to conclude an alliance.

Thereupon the 18th of Brumaire burst upon the French horizon. Returning in haste from Egypt, Bonaparte overthrew the Directory and had himself proclaimed First Consul. Three years later he became permanent Consul, and shortly afterward was crowned French Emperor by Pius VII. On the steps of the great central altar in Notre-Dame, among the ranking diplomats, stood the proud figure of the Spanish ambassador. Did this signalize the re-establishment of good relations between the old Catholic monarchy and the new revolutionary empire?

Bailén Heralds Waterloo

When Napoleon made his triumphal entry into Madrid, he went to the Royal Palace, and he is reported to have exclaimed after gazing at length at Philip II's portrait: "I possess it at last, this Spain so ardently desired"—a phrase that has the ring of literary invention, although perhaps he actually did utter the words, as grandiloquent expressions were characteristic of the emperor. He seemed to know that his pronouncements would become "historic" and worked over phrases in advance, or revised them after the fact. Napoleon posed for eternity. Whether authentic or not, this utterance was like so many others which doubtless were manufactured out of whole cloth but which summed up, in their eloquent conciseness, a dramatic event, a situation, or a personality. It is quite true that Napoleon passionately coveted Spain, but it is equally true that he never achieved possession of it. Why?

What a trump card Spain would have been in the great contest between France and England! Naturally each side tried to bring Spain into its camp. Godoy's preferences, as well as his interests, inclined him toward the emperor. He had blind faith in Napoleon's ultimate triumph, and his faith persisted even after Nelson's fleet sank the Franco-Spanish squadron at Trafalgar, thus destroying forever Napoleon's cherished hope of effecting a landing in England. Lending their support to the heir presumptive, the future Ferdinand VII, Godoy's enemies were closing in on him from all sides, like hunters stalking a deer. They, too, were inclined to collaborate with France, but their devotion to the emperor was not as sincere as they proclaimed it to be. Confusion reigned at the court of Spain, and reached its height when, taking advantage of a domestic intrigue, Ferdinand attempted to seize his father's throne by force. But Charles IV's police had discovered the plot, and they arrested the prince and his friends. The people sided with

Ferdinand, but the nobility and the army rebelled. A bloody uprising broke out at Aranjuez. Completely disheartened, Charles IV abdicated in favor of his son. Godoy was removed from office. Napoleon chose this moment, which seemed propitious, to make his appearance on the scene. Taking advantage of the dynastic crisis, he ordered his troops to occupy a certain number of strategic positions. The time had come, he believed, to implement his plan to capture Spain and use it as a bastion against England; he further hoped to utilize his key position in the Mediterranean, as well as his overseas empire, to destroy English commerce. He knew the full value of the reliable Spanish infantrymen, who were as fearless as his own veterans. His only task was to settle the dynastic problem.

Headed by Murat, the emperor's brother-in-law, the imperial army entered Madrid. The regimental staff was impressive, but not the troops, who were exhausted and in tatters. Then, on the following day, Ferdinand VII made his entrance. He was greeted by enthusiastic crowds waving hats, handkerchiefs, and fans. The French, however, were looked upon with suspicion. No sooner had he set foot in Madrid than Ferdinand received an "invitation" from Napoleon—the kind of summons one can hardly decline—to meet him at Bayonne. Ferdinand complied, but a few days later he found to his surprise and embarrassment that his father, Charles IV, the queen, and Godoy, the favorite, were in Bayonne too, having stopped there after fleeing Madrid. There were explanations, harsh words, and a general settling of accounts under the jeering eye of the Corsican. To have drawn the three nominal heads of Spain into his trap—what a stroke of genius! Convinced that he was the master here, Napoleon proceeded to dictate his wishes: Charles IV was to abdicate in his favor and Ferdinand was to renounce his claim to the throne. Both would find refuge in France. As for the crown, Joseph Bonaparte, the emperor's brother, would find it quite suitable. Napoleon had turned the trick! Gone were the Spanish princes, and he was certain that he had won.

It was easy for this astute chess player to place upon the Spanish chessboard crowned heads who only looked like kings. But one important chessman, destined to checkmate him, was missing—the Spanish people. He had scarcely given them a thought, believing them to be backward and ignorant. The only thing he valued in Spain was its army, whose fame still graced the annals of world history. On the other hand, he had utter contempt for the court, which he had come to know all too well, and for the clergy. "Spain? A country of parish priests and monks"—thus he described the prey he had just devoured. Perhaps, too, the son of the Revolution was sincere when he spoke of "liberating" the Spanish people, but the liberation proved different from the one he had intended.

While the crown of Spain was the subject of negotiation at Bayonne, tempers were rising in Madrid. Abandoned by their kings and held captive by a foreign army, the people suddenly realized that they had been tricked. A spontaneous uprising against the French broke out on May 2, 1808—the famous *Dos de Mayo*. It began at the Puerta del Sol. The day before, the handsome Murat, commander of the French expeditionary forces, had been booed by Madrileños yelling: "Cabbage head!"—a reference to his green-and-white uniform. The situation had not yet got out of control; but the next day, May 2, the same angry mob, assembled at the Puerta del Sol, clashed with Murat's Mamelukes and dragoons. Pérez Galdós wrote: "All Spain descended into the streets." In frightful confusion, the insurgents, armed with picks, daggers, and iron bars, attacked the imperial soldiers. "Death to the *gavachos!*" Mamelukes in broad red pantaloons and white turbans desperately twirled their scimitars while the rebels, slipping under the horses, stuck daggers into their bellies. A hail of stones fell on the cuirassiers' helmets. In panic, the French fired their cannons. When evening fell, Murat decided to put an end to sedition. A manhunt was organized. Any Spaniard caught with arms in his possession was shot on the spot. Goya immortalized the episode. He lived at 9 Place de la Puerta del Sol—he was then over sixty—and this page of history he knew at first hand. It is impossible to forget the Spaniard in a resplendent white shirt, standing on an ocher-colored hillock, his arms crossed. In the background was Madrid, its sky translucent, and crowded around a yellowish lantern light were the men waiting their turn, their eyes covered to avoid watching the fate that awaited them—and the streams of black blood!

The insurrection was put down in Madrid. But, like a poorly extinguished fire, it continued to smolder, cropping up here and there, first of all in Asturias. Juntas, or local committees, governed and directed operations. Very soon, Old Castile and New Castile, Andalusia, Valencia, Aragon, Catalonia, the Balearic Islands, Navarre, and the Basque region joined the resistance movement. Before Joseph Bonaparte arrived in Spain, seventeen juntas had been organized and the War of Independence had begun. And still Napoleon did not take Spanish resistance seriously. One of his generals declared: "The conquest of Spain will be the French army's lunch"—a lunch of poisoned hemlock or, like some Roman banquets, one that ended in massacre.

The fact that Spanish forces were scattered compelled the French army to disperse, a very poor strategy for an offensive but excellent for purposes of defense. The French were thus at a disadvantage. Lefebvre was held in check before Saragossa by Palafox. In Catalonia, General Schwarz lost the battle of El Bruch. Duhesme was not able to conquer Gerona, and Moncey struggled in vain before the gates of Valencia. At Cadiz, the junta seized the English flotilla. Murat, stricken suddenly with illness, which the Spaniards regarded as the work of Providence, had to give up his command and return to France.

The imperial armies met with better fortune in the north, where they captured Santander, Bilbao, and Valladolid, but they suffered their worst defeat in Andalusia, at Bailén, a small town not far from Las Navas de Tolosa, which, six hundred years before, had witnessed the victory of the kings of Castile, Aragon, and Navarre over the Moors. More than 20,000 Frenchmen, commanded by General Dupont, an old soldier of the Revolution, surrendered their arms, while their conqueror, Castaños, with a typically Spanish gesture, placed on the tomb of Ferdinand the Catholic a crown of laurels made by the Sevillians.

When Napoleon learned of the defeat at Bailén he flew into one of his towering rages, threw Dupont into prison, and took matters in hand himself. "I will put the machine back together again," he informed the members of his entourage, who trembled with fear. He assembled an army of 200,000 men and swooped down on Madrid. At his side were his most illustrious marshals, Ney and Masséna. In a few days they reached the Spanish capital. The junta was ordered to surrender the city. "Long live Ferdinand VII! To hell with the tyrant-emperor!" was the prompt response. However, faced with total destruction, Madrid capitulated. For the moment it looked as if the French had gained the upper hand.

But what about Joseph? His actions have been alternately censured and defended. But he "merited neither excessive honor nor indignity." He was certainly a very fine man, full of good intentions that came to nought. Fortune turned against him. His awesome brother had pried him loose from the gentle kingdom of Naples and insisted, without consulting him, that he wear the crown of Spain. After temporizing as long as possible, Joseph decided to leave Bayonne for Madrid, arriving two days after Bailén, at the very moment when the population was seething with the excitement of victory. Soldiers were lined three deep to protect Joseph from the mob's enthusiasm; but there was no mob. An atmosphere of mourning prevailed, a deathlike silence punctuated now and then by the cry: "Long live Ferdinand!" Then all was still. It was enough to freeze the heart of the poor sovereign—who had no sovereignty. To his brother he wrote: "The spirit here is everywhere bad"—so bad, indeed, that Joseph felt it prudent not to remain in Madrid. He returned to Bayonne and waited six months before making a second entry into the capital, this time with the emperor himself leading the way. The capital received him just as it had the first time: the streets were deserted, the people silent. This obvious indifference concealed a burning hatred for the foreign monarch whom the Spaniards called Pepe Botellas— a reference to his love of the bottle, which, however, has been greatly exaggerated. In public prayers, "Father of Our Savior" was replaced by the name of Joseph. Was he a pathetic figure? Possibly not. In any event, he made a genuine effort to win popular favor. Every morning he was the first to attend Mass, and instead of riding at the head of processions, he went on foot. He even forced himself to eat Spanish food, which many thought delicious but which Joseph really disliked. A half century later, Maximilian did likewise in Mexico, to please the people whom Napoleon III had chosen to rule. In public proclamations as well as in letters to his brother, Joseph displayed noble sentiments. Nor was he devoid of a certain political sense and of a kind of good-natured, easy humanity. What, then, did he lack? He was not a Spaniard, that was all. Moreover, he was overwhelmed by the shadow of his brother, but not completely, for on occasion he did venture to rebel. At such times his appeals were heart-rending. He wrote to the emperor: "Your interests, sir, and I might even say your glory, make it impossible to prolong the ignominious agony of your brother on the Spanish throne." And, to his credit, he went on to say: "I am King of Spain only because of the strength of your army. I could become King of Spain because the Spaniards have come to love me, but in order to achieve this, I would have to govern in my own way."

To govern in his own way? He certainly tried, but he lacked the skill. It was not very clever of him to do away with the Spanish Grandees and the military orders. He should not have attempted, by a single stroke of the pen, to rid Spain of all its convents, seeking thereby to outdo Napoleon, who had already closed two thirds of them. Furthermore, he was surrounded by mediocre men, the *afrancesados* and the *josefinos*, who had rallied to his side in the hope of personal gain. A few, mostly "intellectuals," looked upon Joseph's rule as a first step toward progress. Actually, he had no true partisans, only a scattered following whom the rest of the country repudiated. Two governments headed Spain: that of Joseph Bonaparte, with headquarters in Madrid, and the Central Junta at Seville, later at Cadiz, an offshoot of the earlier juntas, which favored the legitimate king, Ferdinand VII; two rival factions, one factitious, the other elusive, moving from city to city according to the fortunes of war.

Thus, with Napoleon in Madrid, Joseph was installed on the throne once occupied by the Catholic Kings. The capital watched the old soldiers of the Guard as they paraded on the Calle de Alcalá; their aides-de-camp wore white dolmans with gold braid, crimson shakos adorned with glittering aigrettes, and wide black-and-gold belts. The horses, covered with garnet-braided panther skins, their heads held high, walked at parade pace. The whole spectacle was intended to serve as a demonstration of strength. One might have gained the impression that Spain, occupied almost everywhere by a tough and disciplined foe, would give up the struggle. Nothing of the kind was true. The war, or rather guerrilla warfare, lasted four years. Pitched battles between Spanish troops and the imperial army were rare. But hardly a day passed without guerrilla fighting, which was ferocious, unrelenting, and ruthless.

This type of combat had begun in Spain. During the Roman era, the Iberians had assembled their forces and hidden in the mountains, where regular army units could not attack them. Viriathus, the first hero of Spanish independence, who defied the legions of Vetilius in the Sierra Morena, had also been the first *guerrillero;* next had come King Pelayo, victor over the Moslem army at Covadonga. Guerrilla fighting was distinctively Spanish, encouraged somewhat by the lay of the land, especially in the north. Even in modern warfare a natural obstacle can not only slow and in the end completely halt an army on the march, but may also serve as an excellent base for offensive operations; to understand this fully one would have to lose one's way among certain mountains in Aragon, or wander about in that inextricable tangle of hilly ramparts called the Maestrazgo. Later on, guerrilla techniques improved, reaching their highest level of perfection during the Civil War. This kind of fighting served as a model for other countries and was used successfully during World War II in Greece, the Balkans, and France, where *guerrilleros* were called *maquis*.

Like the forays of the medieval raiding parties, the warfare against Napoleon was spontaneous and unpremeditated, but the juntas tried very hard to control it. It was precisely this diffuse, elusive aspect of Spanish resistance that proved most demoralizing to the imperial soldiers, who had been trained to fight pitched battles. Of what use to them was the famous "square formation"? The enemy was everywhere and nowhere; routed in one place, it reappeared elsewhere. Napoleon's veterans longed for their billets in Germany and Poland, for the battlefields of Austerlitz, Jena, and Friedland. There, at least, the enemy fought according to the rules; that was the real thing, a thousand times preferable to guerrilla warfare.

Who were these *guerrilleros?* They were an extremely varied group of men—unemployed officers, students, monks, some deserters and smugglers. It was a difficult task, requiring not so much virtue as courage. What was expected of them? "To spread terror and confusion among the armies of the tyrant." What were the rewards? "The means of acquiring wealth honorably from booty captured from the enemy"—according to the Central Junta. The *guerrilleros* were organized into groups called *partidas*, or *cuadrillas*, led by men whose authority commanded respect. There were many *guerrilleros*, and each had a history of his own. Goya has immortalized them in almost photographic fashion. The guerrilla fighter can be recognized by tanned skin, dark eyes, heavy eyebrows, and bared forehead, by hair brushed back and tied in a bright-colored kerchief, and by a felt hat with a rooster feather. He wears a silk belt, black velvet trousers, and leather strips laced tight around the calves of his legs. Occasionally he trades his hat for the busby of a French drum major.

Who were the most famous *guerrilleros?* Juan Palarea, nicknamed El Médico—he actually was a doctor—who displayed such courage against Joseph's troops that Wellington himself awarded him the saber of honor; Juan Díaz Porlier, El Marquesito—captain-general of Asturias; a Franciscan, Father Nebot, called El Frayle, who declared: "Napoleon, the commander of the square of Valencia, and myself—we are three devils, but I am the worst"; Francisco Espoz y Mina, whose exploits in Navarre have become legendary; the Basque Jaureguy, El Pastor; Merino, the priest who wrought havoc in the countryside of Burgos and wore the insignia of a colonel under his cassock. But the most famous of all was Juan Martín Díaz, called El Empecinado—"the pitch-black"—because his native village, Castrillo, was traversed by a river of viscous waters the color of pitch. He was a fearsome, lusty man with a face covered with black hair and a long lock that fell over his forehead. He abandoned the plowshare for the first time when he was eighteen, to fight against France under the Convention. Fifteen years later, he joined the fighting forces again, this time clandestinely, becoming the leader of a group of men whose numbers soon reached the proportions of a small army. Soldier, prophet, and justiciar, he called his soldiers "freedom seekers." They were a fine-looking outfit. Their uniform was brown, with red lapels for the infantry and green for the cavalry. El Empecinado was also a popular leader. He knew that if men were to give their lives to a cause their chief would have to be eloquent. Everywhere along the banks of the Tagus his rough voice could be heard: "From all over Numantia we have flown with the wings of patriotism to the fields of Saguntum." His soldiers worshipped him and risked their lives for him happily. The junta of Cadiz made him a general. But he clashed with another general, who held him constantly in check, General Count Sigisbert Hugo.

Victor Hugo's father was indeed his most formidable adversary. Severely defeated by him at Cifuentes, near Sigüenza, El Empecinado was forced to flee to the province of Cuenca, where he tried several times to re-establish his position, but in vain. His career was over. General Hugo had brought him bad luck, just as he had brought bad luck to others: in the course of the Napoleonic Wars, which lasted almost a quarter of a century, Hugo captured three of the principal partisan leaders. A lieutenant in the Vendée, he was a member of the company that seized Charette, and as head of his battalion in Catalonia, he had collared Fra Diavolo, who was serving the Bourbon cause; El Empecinado surrendered to him at Cifuentes, where Hugo at long last was made a general. No, he certainly did not bring good luck to his victims; Charette was shot, Fra Diavolo hanged, and El Empecinado beaten to death.

While General Hugo was battling it out with El Empecinado, the young Hugo, who was nine at the time, his two brothers, and his mother were slowly making their way to Madrid. The keen memory Victor Hugo retained of this hazardous journey may well explain his penchant for things Spanish. Of course the Hugo family traveled in a shell-proof stagecoach safe from bullets, and they were escorted by the "royal treasure," an armed convoy that accompanied the twelve million in gold which constituted King Joseph's quarterly stipend. What a trip it was! The crossing of the Bidassoa, Irún and "its wooden roofs," Burgos, Valladolid, Segovia, the Escorial—"From a distance I took the Escorial for a tomb"—Madrid. Later, Victor Hugo was to write: "Spain displayed its convents, its Bastille to me—Burgos, its ribbed Gothic cathedrals—Irún, its wooden roofs—Vitoria, its towers—and thou, Valladolid, thy family palaces, proud of the rusting chains in the courtyards." Thus he remembered this journey of his childhood. As soon as he arrived in Madrid, Victor was sent to board at the Seminary of Nobles, in the Calle San Isidro, where two Jesuits were entrusted with his education: the thin, severe Don Basilio and the smiling, plump Don Manuel. They were all cold and hungry, and Don Manuel said to Victor Hugo: "Draw a cross on your belly, it will nourish you."

The harder Napoleon fought, the stiffer grew the resistance. Ferocity increased on both sides. Why was there such

an outbreak of hatred between two peoples who only yesterday were allies? Herein lies the true significance of the
drama that was being enacted. The war waged by the Spaniards against Napoleonic France was both nationalistic and
religious. Catholic, monarchist Spain looked upon the emperor, heir of the French Revolution, as something of an
Antichrist. Moreover, he relied heavily on Freemasonry,
which, although not yet as anti-religious as it was to become
later, was nonetheless profoundly anti-clerical. Encouraged
by King Joseph, its lodges multiplied. Murat created the
Grand Orient of Spain, establishing it in Madrid in former
buildings of the now defunct Inquisition. Actually, these
lodges were primarily social centers, *tertulias*, where imperial officers would meet to kill time when not on duty instead of gathering in cafés or theaters. Very few Spaniards
frequented the lodges—perhaps a few *josefinos* who entered
on tiptoe. And so the war assumed the character of an ideological struggle between Freemasonry and Catholicism. The
Freemasons, however, were not in agreement themselves.
The *afrancesados* supported Napoleon; the rest sided with
the insurgents. A minority, who sincerely believed in the
"new ideas," were faced with a tragic dilemma. The invader,
to be sure, had brought with him a political and social
program that was in harmony with the objectives of "enlightened" Spaniards, so that, inevitably, they had to choose
between two alternatives: to yield to their intellectual aspirations and side with Napoleon, thus betraying Spain, or to put
patriotism first and oppose the national enemy, thus promot-
ing reaction and doing violence to their convictions. However, a majority of Spaniards—whether traditionalists or
progressivists—wanted only to be rid of the occupiers and
to restore Ferdinand VII to the throne. Political and religious problems could be settled later among themselves;
resistance must come first.

That the relentless war the Spanish people were waging
against the imperial army was as much ideological as nationalistic was demonstrated not only by the events themselves but also by the testimony of contemporaries. One in

particular is noteworthy for his sincerity: Rocca, one of Madame de Staël's husbands, who, after the Peace of Tilsit, was ordered to leave Prussia and go to Spain with his regiment. His memoirs read like an exciting novel. He excelled in the portrayal of personalities. He saw the emperor only twice, but each time described him so vividly that he seemed to come to life. Here is the first description: "He was on horseback. The simplicity of his green uniform set him apart from the lavishly uniformed generals who surrounded him. With a wave of his hand he greeted each officer individually as if to say: 'I am counting on you.' Frenchmen and Spaniards gathered in great crowds to watch him go by. The French felt he alone epitomized the fate of the entire army, while the Spaniards tried to decipher from his expression and bearing what was in store for their unhappy country." In the second description, Rocca wrote: "He was accompanied by five or six of his aides-de-camp, who could barely keep pace with him so swiftly did he ride. All the trumpets were blowing. The emperor rode a hundred paces from the center of our regiment and asked the colonel for a list of officers, noncommissioned officers, and soldiers who had earned military distinction. The regimental colonel called off the names. The emperor spoke informally to the simple soldiers presented to him, then addressing the general who commanded our brigade, he quickly asked a few brief questions. The general began to give a rather long-winded answer, whereupon the emperor wheeled about without waiting for him to finish. His departure was as unexpected and sudden as his arrival." The scene emerges as plainly as if a master like Goya had painted it. One can also imagine the expression of bewilderment on the face of the stammering colonel.

During his stay in Madrid, Rocca was billeted with an elderly and illustrious man, whose name he has withheld. He says of his host: "He went to Mass regularly twice a day and once a day to the Puerta del Sol to gather news. On his return he sat in his living room, where he spent the entire time doing nothing. Occasionally he lit a cigar to dispel his boredom and distract his mind. He spoke only rarely. I never heard him laugh. Every half hour he exclaimed: 'Ay! Jesus!' His daughter answered him in similar vein and then both fell silent." This noble Castilian, frozen in an attitude of negation, resembles the work of some Spanish master painter, so lifelike does he seem. Are we not reminded of Vercors's *Silence of the Sea* by this country gentleman and his daughter, who also were immured in silence?

Even more interesting are Rocca's remarks on the Spanish mentality: "The Spaniards were a religious and warlike people, but not militaristic. They actually despised and scorned anything that had to do with line troops. As a consequence, they had neither good officers, noncommissioned men, nor any other of the elements that make for a well-ordered army. They looked upon war as a religious crusade for king and country." Rocca adds: "The Spanish character bears no resemblance whatsoever to that of other European nations. Their patriotism is religious in nature, as it was among the ancients, when despite reverses people never gave themselves up to despair or admitted defeat so long as the altars of the protective gods remained intact. . . . Only political or religious patriotism makes a people indomitable. . . . These events demonstrate as forcibly as does the protracted resistance of the Spanish people that the struggle between governments is determined less by the size and strength of armies than by religious, political, or patriotic sentiments powerful enough to attract to a public cause all the individuals of a nation, as if it were their very own." And Rocca concludes with the kind of honesty that does him credit: "Europe must not forget that for more than five years Spain bore up alone under the weight of Emperor Napoleon's immense power. . . . The French had won ten consecutive battles and seized almost all the fortresses, yet they were unable to achieve the permanent subjugation of a single province. . . . It was the *soul* of each and every man that had to be attacked, a stronghold impervious to cannon and bayonets." The soul of Spain—Rocca had hit the nail on the head. The phrase shows remarkable insight, coming as it did from this freethinker, this atheist who ordinarily did not accept the notion of the soul's existence.

The mystical nature of Spain's resistance to the emperor asserted itself at Saragossa. For a month the French artillery pounded the ramparts of the city. First Moncey, then Junot, and finally Marshal Lannes directed the imperial army. For the second time Palafox organized the defense of Saragossa. While the emperor's grenadiers besieged the ancient Iberian city, *guerrilleros*, astride the walls and holding crucifixes in their hands, sang the hymn of freedom: "The Virgin of the Pillar says she does not want to be French." Finally Napoleon's soldiers pierced the defenses, but at what a price! Every house was a small fortress that had to be demolished. Inside the cathedral, gathered around hundreds of piled-up coffins, the few survivors, mainly women and children, sang the *Dies Irae*. On the very spot where St. James, eighteen centuries earlier, had allegedly placed the Virgin of the Pillar, Frenchmen discovered an image of the Virgin, but it was stripped of its jeweled dalmatic and seemed as dead as its defenders. Surrounding the Madonna, close to this small figure atop its marble pillar, Spanish soldiers fought primarily for their faith rather than for king and country—or, to be more precise, country, king, and religion became one. At all events, the encomium *Zaragoza siempre heroica* had been well earned. Even Lannes, the conqueror of Saragossa, later admitted: "It is a grave error to attack men's convictions."

The war was to last another four years, and during this time there were many ups and downs. But the intervention of the English, particularly Wellington, the Iron Duke, clearly weighed heavily in favor of the Spanish armies. French divisions were pushed back to Burgos; at the end of April 1813, they had to recross the Bidassoa. For the second and last time Joseph returned to France. Napoleon signed a peace treaty with Ferdinand VII. Defeated in Russia, at Leipzig, and in Spain, the emperor's star was dwindling. In a few months he was to withdraw to Elba. One of his most bitter memories would certainly be the Spanish campaign, in which he lost not only prestige but a tremendous amount of matériel and 500,000 men.

The failure of the Napoleonic adventure must be attributed primarily to psychological causes. The emperor had misjudged the Spanish people's capacity to resist. Was he overconfident or inadequately informed? The various opinions he himself expressed about the situation are contradictory. To his brother Louis, king of Holland, he wrote: "The Spanish people summon me to help them." Yet at the time such things as these were being said from Cadiz to La Coruña: "What are Napoleon's origins? He was born of sin. Who are the French? Former Christians who have become heretics. Is it a crime to be born a Frenchman? No, a Frenchman is damned only after he has reached the age of seven. Is it a sin to kill the French? No, it is a worthy deed that frees the country from its oppressors." Imperturbable, Napoleon wrote Fouché a few days after May 2: "A lot of nonsense about Spanish affairs has been spread in Paris. In actuality, not a single drop of blood was shed either in Toledo or in Burgos. Blood flowed only in Madrid. The Spaniards that were killed were all insurgents and rabblerousers. Not a single peaceful individual [whom did he call peaceful?] was killed." However, this fine optimism vanished a few months later as his temper gradually got the better of him. At that time he wrote Joseph: "We must hang some twenty rascals, and if we don't get rid of a hundred firebrands and bandits we shall have accomplished nothing." And he added: "I never had any peace of mind in France until I arrested two hundred firebrands, killers, and bandits and sent them to the colonies. After that, the atmosphere in the capital changed as if a whistle had been blown." In a letter to Talleyrand he expressed sympathy for Godoy: "The Prince of Peace arrives tonight. The poor man is pitiful. For a month his life has been threatened and he has been on the brink of death. Can you imagine that during this time he never changed his shirt and his beard grew seven inches? The Spanish nation has demonstrated an unexampled inhumanity." On the other hand, in another letter, also addressed to Talleyrand, he alluded harshly to the Prince of Asturias, the future Ferdinand VII: "He is very stupid, very mean, and a great enemy of France." How sincere was Napoleon in expressing such opinions? Did he write in this manner merely to further his cause or did he really believe what he said?

For a long time Napoleon remained doggedly optimistic. He refused to admit that his Grand Army could be defeated by guerrillas and went so far as to declare: "It is laziness not heroism that makes the Spanish peasant prefer the dangers of smuggling to the wear and tear of cultivating the land. There is nothing patriotic about this"—an unjust and false accusation that demonstrates anew how completely he misunderstood the Spanish mentality. At Bailén he began to worry and took it out on his generals: "My lieutenants have always made foolish mistakes, and whenever I am not on the spot my armies are defeated." Napoleon called Murat "an idiot" even though he was a favorite to whom he had given his sister in marriage, the kingdom of Naples, and a marshal's baton. However, the emperor promptly contradicted himself by adding that Murat "is a hero." Why did he give his generals political responsibility if he thought they were lacking in astuteness?

Only after he had experienced the sting of defeat did Napoleon finally acknowledge the valor displayed by his adversary. "On the whole the Spaniards behave like men of honor. I have nothing to say about them save that they have been victorious," he commented. Much later, from his rock at St. Helena, he admitted: "That unfortunate war was my undoing." And it is quite true that the imperial eagle was first wounded at Bailén; it received its second wound at Moscow and its third and fatal one at Waterloo.

The Cortes of Cadiz and the Constitution of 1812

At the height of the struggle the Cortes met at Cadiz. Composed for the most part of judicious men holding a wide range of opinions, the Assembly's first task was to define the political regime of the future. Acting on a proposal made by Don Diego Muñoz Torrero, former rector of the University of Salamanca and deputy from Estremadura, the Cortes assumed the powers of national sovereignty and recognized Ferdinand VII as the only legitimate king. But the Assembly's primary task was to create a new constitution. The Asturian Agustín Arguelles, called "the Divine" because of his great personal charm and eloquence, drafted the constitution which, several years later, was to divide Spain. Placed under the protection of "Almighty God, the Father, the Son, and the Holy Ghost, creator and supreme legislator of society," the Constitution of 1812, while recognizing the hereditary monarchy, proclaimed the sovereignty of the nation, guaranteed civil liberties and private property, and decreed indirect universal suffrage. Providing for freedom of the press and the irremovability of judges, the Constitution of Cadiz was one of the most "progressive" in Europe, although the influence of its French model was apparent. Nonetheless, one article stated categorically: "The religion of the Spanish nation is and will always be the Catholic, apostolic, and Roman faith, the only true one. The nation will protect it by wise and just laws and prohibit the practice of any other religion." This clause is quite surprising, particularly in view of the fact that almost all the guiding lights of the Cortes of Cadiz had been greatly influenced by the Encyclopedists. Many were Freemasons. The lodge of the Sons of Oedipus played an important role in the work of the Assembly. In short, the Constitution of Cadiz represented the revolutionary and Masonic tendencies of the late eighteenth century. More clever than Napoleon's advisers, however, the legislators of Cadiz knew very well that any charter that threatened the primacy of the Catholic religion would prove inapplicable in Spain. "Religious tolerance" was therefore not to be countenanced. Three years before, the junta of Seville had unanimously refused to include in any draft constitution the following clause suggested by the economist Álvaro Flores Estrada: "No citizen will be persecuted because of his religion, *no matter what it happens to be.*" Venturesome and "enlightened" though they were, the writers of the Constitution of 1812 did not dare to include freedom of worship in their bill of rights. It was still too early to suggest that Catholicism was not Spain's only religion. Would such a time ever come? What legislative clause, what parliamentary assembly, would ratify a rupture of the alliance between Spain and Catholicism, engraved in blood on the ancient Iberian soil? In spite of their desire to prove themselves even more liberal than the French, the jurists of Cadiz hesitated to launch a direct attack on the Church. Besides, it was politic at this juncture to spare the clergy; large groups of *frailunos* were fighting before Cadiz, offering heroic resistance to Napoleon's army. The only anti-clerical measure adopted was the abolition of the Tribunal of the Inquisition and the confiscation of all its property by the Treasury, but it was enough to precipitate a rupture of diplomatic relations between the Holy See and the Spanish government.

Thus, the nineteenth century began with a basic inconsistency. The people, the riffraff or *canaille*—a word coined by Joseph Bonaparte which Alfonso XIII appropriated—patriotic, monarchist, and loyal to the Christian tradition, fought furiously against Napoleon, the symbol of impiety. Fiery and impetuous, they cared not at all that Ferdinand VII was a man of insignificant stature—he was their king! The mediocrity of the exiled prince dissolved, from a distance, into the noble features of a legendary figure, somewhat akin to the Virgin of the Pillar. He stood for the magnificence of the early Habsburgs, for a return to the *fueros*, to absolute authority and closer union between politics and religion. In similar fashion, an intellectual elite, which continued to resist, met at Cadiz. The city was under heavy crossfire. While the *guerrilleros*, bedecked with holy images and pious mementos, were dying for God and king, the Cortes, assembled in the chapel of San Felipe de Neri, drafted and proclaimed a constitution inspired by the French Revolution. One can almost visualize these liberals of recent standing deliberating in their Andalusian retreat.

What a tragic irony it was that "enlightened" men should fight the French with relentless obstinacy while building simultaneously a political system borrowed from the Convention! They would pore avidly over *The Social Contract* and *The Spirit of the Laws* and keep issuing orders to fire on the enemy. Like an iron band, the Spanish people—peasants, monks, regular soldiers—surrounded and protected Cadiz, the capital of the insurrectionary junta. What conclusions are to be drawn from this?

Napoleon had inspired this sacred union of Spaniards, whether traditionalists or liberals, just as, from the very outset, he became the unwitting fomenter of revolutionary ideas. In the wake of the emperor's receding cocked hat there arose those bastions of Left and Right between which the Spanish people were to vacillate endlessly.

3

Aspects of Liberty

ERDINAND VII's triumphant return to Madrid on March 22, 1814, marked the complete failure of the Napoleonic adventure and served to restore internal peace. Scarcely had Spaniards recovered from their heady victories when they found themselves confronted with a new problem—that of self-government; they learned that it is easier to expel the enemy than to choose new masters. "Long live our chains!" the people cried when Ferdinand VII —"the Desired"—rode by, little knowing how wisely they spoke.

Intent on following the policies of Ferdinand and Isabella, Ferdinand VII hastened to reinstate the Inquisition. Refusing to support the Constitution of Cadiz, he resumed diplomatic relations with the Holy See, abrogated Charles III's edict against the Jesuits, and restored the privileges of the clergy. The minutes of the Cortes were to be destroyed in a public bonfire. A state of war existed between "absolutists" and "constitutionalists," or liberals. While Ferdinand and his *camarilla* attempted to govern, compounding brutality with blunders, the liberals were secretly organizing. Freemasonry played an important part in the resistance to absolutism. Officially suppressed and tracked down by the royal police, these secret societies had never been more active. They insinuated themselves into a variety of areas, and they counted among their adherents ministers, deputies, and high-ranking bureaucrats. In the Basque region, in Navarre and Catalonia, the army, roused to action by the lodges, rebelled, but it was quickly put down. In the end, however, the liberals triumphed. The hero of the War of Independence and a commanding officer, Rafael Riego, proclaimed the reestablishment of the Constitution of 1812. The action occurred at Las Cabezas de San Juan, near Cadiz. At the head of an Asturian battalion, Riego marched on Madrid. Sensing the danger, Ferdinand did not await his arrival, but quickly convoked the Cortes and announced his intention of adopting the constitution. As the Asturians entered Madrid, singing "The Hymn of Riego"—the liberals' "Marseillaise"— the Cortes met in great haste. *Moderados* and *exaltados* were at each other's throats, although both were constitutionalists. The king swore to uphold the constitution and even went so far as to abolish the Inquisition. Released from jail, the constitutionalists of Cadiz became ministers. But, although the liberals were victorious in Madrid thanks to the activities of the Masonic lodges as well as to military intervention, the absolutists were holding their own in the provinces. Heading the struggle against the liberals, monks and priests bestirred themselves, just as they had done during the recent Napoleonic invasion. At Seo de Urgel a junta was organized. It called upon Spaniards to take up arms to "free" the king, a prisoner in his own palace, and to defend the Catholic religion. Navarre and the Basque country rallied to the cause of God and king. Priests and *frailes* left their parishes and monasteries to join guerrilla bands. The leader of the absolutist insurrectionaries in Catalonia was a Trappist monk, "tough, enthusiastic, fanatical, who combined the exaltation of the cloisters with the battle fever of the camp." The Viscount of Martignac saw him in Madrid and penned the following description: "There was nothing unusual about the figure he cut, but he looked serious, lively, and self-assured. Garbed in his monk's robe, a crucifix on his breast, a sword and pistols in his belt, and a whip in his right hand, he rode alone amidst crowds that knelt as he passed by. Glancing coldly right and left, he distributed his blessings with a kind of disdain, even indifference." A cross driven into the ground in the middle of a field served as a rallying point. Entire populations, led by their priests, would flock to the Trappist's banner shouting: "Long live religion! Long live the absolute king!"

Once again—still black with powder, the walls of Saragossa attest to this—Spain fought for an idea rather than for a king. In the eyes of the absolutists, who called themselves "apostolic," the constitutionalists were atheists and revolutionaries. United only yesterday, Spain was again torn and divided. Forgotten was Napoleon—what mattered now was a settling of accounts. But the Holy Alliance was worried that the Spanish revolutionary movement might cross the Pyrenees and, by a curious reversal of circumstances, contaminate the very country that had inspired it—the French monarchy and all Europe as well. The imposing voice of Chateaubriand was heard at the Congress of Verona. Ferdinand's crown was being threatened, France must hasten to the rescue! In a speech from the throne, Louis XVIII solemnly declared: "One hundred thousand Frenchmen are ready to march in the name of St. Louis in order to save the Spanish throne for a descendant of Henry IV."

Ten years after the emperor's division had left the Franco-Spanish frontier for good, the army of the Restoration was to cross it again. The leader of the expedition, the Duke of Angoulême, was welcomed as a liberator by the very same peasants, monks, and priests who had embodied the spirit of the resistance to Napoleon. On both sides the enemy had changed. Now it was the spiritual heirs of the French Revolution, the *afrancesados* of yesterday, who had become the "liberals," that Louis XVIII's soldiers were pushing back to Andalusia.

The liberal government sought refuge in Seville, then in Cadiz, taking the king with them as hostage. The two constitutionalist armies fought halfheartedly, aware that the country was not really in sympathy with them. French troops, advancing rapidly, entered Madrid, pushed on to Cadiz, and took possession of the Trocadero fortress with relative ease.

The legal government resigned, the Cortes capitulated, and Ferdinand was "freed." Now, perhaps, he would prove himself to be a true king. But unfortunately he once again was more intent on revenge than on devising a worthy solution. Victorious throughout the land, thanks in large part to the army of the King of France, he might have shown clemency, but he was not merciful by nature. The purge—*la purificación*—was terrible. Riego, who personified the revolution, was transported to the gallows in a wicker basket drawn by a donkey; he was hanged and his body dismembered. El Empecinado, the hero of the War of Independence, suffered an even worse fate. For fourteen months he was kept in a dungeon; on market days he was taken out and placed in a cage to be exposed to public scorn. On the way to the gallows one of his torturers jabbed him with his own sword, a sword which had once covered him with glory. Mad with rage, El Empecinado tore at his chains until they broke and rushed at his tormentor. He stumbled, fell, and was beaten to death. The constitutionalists were hunted down and persecuted; the Freemasons, declared "enemies of the throne and the altar," were threatened with the death penalty. The so-called White Terror became the order of the day. Its heroic martyr was Mariana de Pineda, condemned to be strangled for having embroidered the forbidden words "Law, Liberty, and Equality" on the standard of Castile.

Blood dries quickly in Spain. The last years of Ferdinand's reign were peaceful. Remembering his grandfather, Charles III, the king tended to become an "enlightened despot" toward the end of his life. He created the Museum of the Prado, the Pharmaceutical School, and the Conservatory of Arts. The country's financial situation was improving. The establishment of corporations and the introduction of a commercial code turned people's thoughts away from politics for a while. But there prevailed in the hearts of men a sadness, an abiding bitterness. Moreover, the news from America was discouraging. One by one, almost simultaneously, the colonies of the New World shook off the Spanish yoke and became republics—Mexico, Venezuela, Colombia,

Peru, and Chile. Fifteen years earlier, a half-breed priest, Miguel Hidalgo, of Dolores, in Mexico, had brandished the banner of the Virgin of Guadalupe and roused the Mexicans to rebel against their viceroy. So profoundly did his appeal —*el grito de Dolores*—penetrate the empire that within a few years it split up and collapsed. Meanwhile, during the first half of the nineteenth century, Spain was like an immense tree bent by storm. Its colonies were nought but scraps of bark torn loose by the winds of revolution; its sap, the blood shed needlessly in fratricidal wars. The battle of Ayacucho, which Peruvians fought and won against Spaniards, sounded the death knell of the empire. What wine could quench Spain's terrible thirst for absolutism?

In Favor of Don Carlos

While Ferdinand VII was belatedly attempting to draw closer to the liberals, the absolutists split into two groups: the Moderates, who stood for a policy of compromise, and the Apostolics, or Ultras, who favored the re-establishment of a monarchy worthy of Spain's past, for they no longer harbored any illusions about Ferdinand. He had demonstrated the full measure of his weakness and instability. Even before he died, the Ultras rallied to the cause of his brother, Don Carlos, who was in line to succeed Ferdinand, as the king's three marriages had produced no heirs. The Federation of Pure Royalists was organized in Catalonia, and it soon recruited additional members in the Basque region, in Navarre, and in Aragon. Thus "Carlism" was born. Ferdinand chose this moment to marry a fourth time, much to the disappointment of the Apostolics, whose hopes were dashed by the event. María Cristina of Naples was beautiful and lively. She brought to the dull Spanish court something that had been missing since the time of the Princess des Ursins—gaiety. Laughing and dancing, she gave her husband, who was nearing his end, a renewed sense of life. She also brought him joy of a kind he no longer dared to hope for—that of fatherhood. María Cristina presented him with a daughter, Isabella. To insure the throne for his newborn child, the king hastened to re-establish the Pragmatic Sanction which abolished the so-called Salic law. Three years later he died.

Ferdinand was buried with the usual pomp. As the coffin was being lowered into the Escorial crypt and before the lid was nailed down, the captain of the guard called out three times: "My Lord! My Lord! My Lord!" After a moment of silence he gravely proclaimed: "Since His Majesty does not answer, the king is truly dead." Then he broke his baton and tossed the pieces at the foot of the coffin. Who would now reign? Ferdinand's widow, María Cristina, was to serve as regent until her daughter, Isabella, should come of age. But Don Carlos had other ideas. Disregarding the last wishes of his brother, he claimed the crown of Spain for himself. Thus began a struggle between Carlists and partisans of María Cristina that was to last until the end of the century.

Like its predecessors, this new civil war soon developed into a conflict between ideologies as well as parties. María Cristina favored liberalism and "enlightened despotism," while Don Carlos represented the traditional monarchy and religion. At the head of his army was the Virgin of Sorrows. The Cristina-Carlos war lasted seven years, during which time both extraordinary courage and dreadful cruelty were displayed by both sides. Don Carlos entrusted the command of his army to Tomás Zumalacárregui, a Basque soldier with inexhaustible energy to whom flight and defeat were unthinkable. Any man who flinched or retreated in the face of enemy fire was shot on the spot. But Zumalacárregui was wounded at the siege of Bilbao, and his career was brought to an abrupt end. Other Carlists known for their fierce devotion to the prince were Orbe y Elio, marquis of Valdespina, Ignacio of Uranga, Simón de la Torre, and, above all, the priest Merino. At first a simple shepherd, then priest of his native village of Villabiao, Merino was never without his ecclesiastical garb or his heavy cavalry sword and huge powder-filled blunderbuss. He did not smoke, drank only water, and reportedly never slept. At night he would go on long, solitary walks in the mountains. Then there was Cabrera. His mother, it was said, had been killed in reprisal for Carlist atrocities, and he had responded to the news by exclaiming: "I will make a pyramid of corpses higher than any the world has ever seen." He kept his word. These men fought without mercy under extraordinarily difficult circumstances, stranded among rocks, lost in endless forests, holed up in deep ravines. Such was guerrilla warfare.

On María Cristina's side the leaders were equally brave— Rodil, Mina, Valdes, and, last but not least, Espartero. Military operations were complicated, limited as they were to a small area. Zumalacárregui besieged Bilbao, but the attack was short-lived because of his wounds. A second attempt to capture Bilbao failed. Undaunted, Don Carlos marched on Madrid, but as he was about to enter it he was seized with fear and gave orders to retreat. His troops were tired and probably disappointed. Moreover, treason was rife among the general staff. Don Carlos surrendered. The Carlist army, facing Cristina's troops on the plain of Vergara, saluted them. "Embrace each other, my children," Espartero cried.

Perhaps the Carlists would have won had the pretender been more inspired and had his military command been less makeshift. In any event, his troops had waged war according to traditional guerrilla tactics, hiding behind rocks and praying to the Virgin as they fired. Carlists had embroidered a sacred heart along with the following inscription on their coarse woolen robes: "*¡Detente, bala, que Sagrado Corazón está conmigo!*"—"Stop, bullet, for the sacred heart of Jesus is with me!" A fierce piety, hatred of political innovation, devotion to the *fueros*, and desire for a close union between throne and altar—in other words, fanatical intolerance—all these characterized Carlos's partisans. In the same spirit other soldiers had fought the Moors, joined King Pelayo, or waged war under King Sancho. In certain Basque and Catalonian villages one can still see the stone walls on which Carlists sharpened their bayonets. These marks on the granite symbolize the spirit of Carlism, which did not dis-

appear with the compromise of Vergara. Carlist hearths
burned brightly in the Basque and Navarrese mountains
long after defeat. Just when they were thought to be extinguished, sudden sparks could be seen. Carlism—the expression of blind absolutism and uncompromising Catholicism—
survived Don Carlos himself. Poorly served by a mediocre
prince, it was to be revived by another soldier a century later,
almost to the day.

Matanza de Frailes

While traditional Catholic trends crystallized in the mountains of the north, María Cristina was attempting to govern.
The liberals were split into "Moderates" and "Progressivists." The former were eager to maintain the royal authority
and the Church's privileges; the latter boldly championed
democracy and anti-clericalism. Although sincerely anxious
to keep an even balance between the two, the regent was soon
overpowered by the Progressivists. While the Cortes continued to revise an inapplicable constitution, and ministers succeeded one another—Martínez de la Rosa, Mendizabal,
Toreno—a wave of anti-clericalism spread over María
Cristina's Spain. When a cholera epidemic broke out in Madrid, the monks were immediately accused of poisoning the
fountains. One warm day in July, eighty priests were massacred—this was the *matanza de frailes*. At Puerta del Sol,
a blind guitarist was heard to intone: "Death to Christ!
Long live Lucifer! Death to Don Carlos! Long live Isabella!" Monasteries were burned; the police, confronted with
a raging mob, did nothing. The government was in full sympathy with the popular sentiment and took strong measures
against the Church. Once again the Society of Jesus was
abolished, and, with the exception of about ten, monasteries
were either suppressed or converted into barracks. Since
Pope Gregory XVI's intervention proved ineffectual, diplomatic relations between Rome and Madrid were severed.

Blood spattered the sidewalks of Alcalá and the Rambla

at Barcelona. At the Café Nuevo the severed fingers of an unfortunate general were used to ladle out the punch. From her palace, María Cristina could hear the sinister crackling of the firing squad. If only she could temper the ferocious zeal of the Progressivists! Espartero dissuaded her from trying, advising her to abdicate. She had lost the confidence and respect of her subjects. Madrid could not forgive her her love affair with an obscure officer, the son of an official in the Revenue Department. Easily convinced, the regent abdicated and took refuge in France. Espartero, called the Duke of Victory since the Vergara Convention, was appointed regent by the Cortes.

The brief reign of Espartero was marked by a stiffening of official anti-clericalism. Pope Gregory XVI reminded Espartero that, although he had broken all ties with the government of Madrid, the Church of Spain remained under his jurisdiction, and it was therefore up to him to appoint the bishops. Too preoccupied with other matters, Espartero not only ignored the Pope's claim; he banished the head of the nuncio's office and closed the nunciature, thus definitively severing relations between Rome and Madrid. Gregory completed the rupture by solemnly condemning Spanish policies since the death of Ferdinand VII. Copies of the pontifical statement were seized to prevent the people from reading it. Soon Spaniards began to regret the abdication of María Cristina, so brutal was Espartero's rule. Generals of the opposition were shot, the Cortes was dissolved, and Espartero personally supervised Barcelona's firing squads, which executed anyone guilty of "republicanism." Finally, making way for Moderates returning from exile, Espartero fled to London. Once the most popular figure in Spain, he was now condemned to "public contempt" by a special decree. His final gesture before leaving Spain was to bombard Seville. But he was destined to return.

Narváez, leader of the Moderates, succeeded Espartero. The Church was to know better days, for the Progressivists were evicted from governmental posts. A new constitution stipulated that "the religion of the Spanish nation is the

Catholic, apostolic, and Roman faith," and that the "State is committed to uphold the Church and its ministers." While Madrid was negotiating for peace with the Holy See, Pope Gregory XVI died and was succeeded by Pius IX. At the same time, the news from Paris was grave. Louis Philippe had been overthrown and the Second French Republic proclaimed. Standing in front of the Hôtel de Ville, Lamartine brought cheers for the tricolor. The revolutionary fever that swept through Italy, Austria, and Germany also affected Spain. In the working-class districts of Barcelona and Madrid, people were heard to exclaim: "Long live the Republic!" Narváez suppressed the movement with severity and it had no further repercussions. However, Pius IX, forced to flee the pontifical states, sought refuge in Gaeta. Promised protection by the Spanish ambassador, he planned to go to the peninsula. But, with the help of Narváez, a French expeditionary force marched on Rome and re-established Pius IX in St. Peter's. The Concordat of 1851 was signed; it reconciled Spain with the Holy See.

Although she was only thirteen, Isabella was declared of age by the Cortes; a little later her marriage to Francisco de Asís was arranged. Called Francisquet or Paquita, he was a grandchild of Charles IV, as was the young queen; thus they were cousins. When Isabella went to bed with him for the first time she was both surprised and disappointed—surprised because under his clothing he wore petticoats and frills, disappointed because the mass of lace covered absolutely nothing. From then on, the court of Spain became a stage for Renaissance comedy. Upon it appeared the minions of the king, the lovers of the queen—her nature grew ever more ardent—the favorites of her mother, María Cristina, whom the Moderates had recalled from exile, and a certain nun, Sister María de los Dolores y Patrocinio, who claimed to be a visionary and said that she suffered the stigmata; apparently her role lent an air of respectability to this royal bedroom farce.

The people of Madrid either tittered or raged at the goings on in the palace. Everyone knew about the intrigues spun by the favorites; they knew that the financier Salamanca had grown rich through fraud, that the minister Sartorius was guilty of extortion. Narváez's personnel were either mediocre or corrupt—sometimes both. The Progressivists sniffed this foul air and sneered, waiting until the moment was ripe for action. A military rebellion gave them their chance. Espartero returned to Madrid and a new star appeared on the political horizon—General O'Donnell. The religious question cropped up again, just when it had supposedly been solved. One article of the draft constitution stated: "No Spaniard or foreigner will be persecuted because of his opinions or faith, provided he commits no public act detrimental to religion." The Holy See considered this leaning toward tolerance an offense against the Concordat. Once again the Pope broke off diplomatic relations with the Spanish government. As María Cristina, fearing for her safety, went into exile a second time, an almost adolescent orator, Emilio Castelar, uttered at the Royal Theater the famous phrase: "I salute thee, young democracy."

But the dawn of democracy, so ardently desired by some, so greatly feared by others, was not yet to come. Progressivist reaction was short-lived. Three years after Espartero and O'Donnell had seized power, they were forced to yield to Narváez. The fickle Isabella announced to the Cortes: "The Concordat has been re-established in all the fullness of its strength and vigor. . . . Further measures have been taken to give the Church the liberty with which its holy founder endowed it." These measures provided for the return of Church property and the restoration of bishoprics suppressed by the previous regime. Thus the ups and downs of Spain's relationship with the Holy See reflected the vicissitudes of Spanish politics during the middle of the nineteenth century. Was the nuncio in Madrid? If so, the conservatives were in power. The closing of the nunciature indicated that the Progressivists were in the saddle. But a more serious and significant fact lay behind these swings of the pendulum. By dint of its efforts to "integrate," and because of its stubborn refusal to break with the past, Spanish Catholicism became far less a tool of the state than the weapon of a party determined to acquire power by force. Because of the obstinacy of the conservatives, the gulf between Catholic tradition and the democratic ideal grew constantly wider. Hundreds of thousands of dead Spaniards were to topple into this abyss.

While Narváez's Moderates and O'Donnell's "Liberal Union"—the Left-Center—took turns governing, democratic parties were being organized. Among these were the "Republicans" of Castelmar and Salmerón and the "Federalists" of Pi y Margal. Generals also attempted to gain power. Prim ventured seven pronunciamentos within the space of four years. Everyone hated the queen, who had behaved very badly. To the tune of "Down with the Bourbons!" the troops of the triumvirate, Prim, Serrano, and Topete, fought Isabella's soldiers, commanded by the blundering González Bravo; simultaneously a revolutionary junta in Madrid proclaimed "the basic freedoms" and universal suffrage. The queen fled to France. Had the hour of the Republic struck?

The Two Spains

The Republic was not yet an accomplished fact, but clearly there were now two Spains. The Right represented the absolutist trend—the divine right of kings, a concept more Gallic than Catholic; and traditionalism, a confusion of reason of state with religion, nostalgia for the *imperium*. The Left stood for a revolutionary trend which, by successive stages, resulted in republicanism. Both camps harbored extremists—Carlists and Socialists. On the Right were the nobility, the clergy, the court, the local leaders; the Left comprised the "new men," powerfully supported by Freemasonry and the "intellectuals." From time to time there rose up, on both sides, the generals of the pronunciamento. Their methods were the classical ones. Secret societies, exiles, or interested foreign agents would work out plans to land the chosen person on Spanish soil. Troops previously subjected to clandestine propaganda were summoned to agitate for the new leader. People were threatened, arrested, or shot. The rest was up to the current government. If it was weak, the pronunciamento succeeded, if strong, there would be a brief purge followed by the restoration of order. But often a movement took on the form of a spontaneous uprising or an urban revolt. The leaders became lost in the crowd. Where were they to be found? Certainly not at the Royal Palace, in any event. Isabella formed and dissolved ministries at will and according to her whims. "My beautiful general!" she said to Serrano, her first lover, and subsequently her prime minister. She liked handsome men and rewarded them politically for their prowess as lovers. Monarchists as well as Republicans had nought but contempt for this caricature of Catherine the Great, who at least had not confused her love affairs with matters of state.

Thus, the royal power deteriorated because there was no monarch worthy of exercising it; generals of the pronunciamento appeared and disappeared like comic-opera tyrants, the boulevards grumbled, the country whispered, the hidalgos sighed. A Left and a Right existed, but where were they and who represented them? In any case, Isabella's flight marked a new era in Spain, one in which the Right and the Left were to confront each other. Here was the first hint of a "black" and a "red" Spain. The very year that the last Spanish queen crossed the French border, an Italian deputy, Giuseppe Fanelli, disciple and friend of Bakunin, came to Madrid from Barcelona. He founded the Workers' International as well as cells of the Bakunin Alliance. Within a few months, 100,000 Spaniards became Bakuninists, and Spain, like *communarde* France, served as a laboratory for world revolution. From his Swiss chalet, Karl Marx watched with keen interest the evolution of the Spanish movement. It was still quite precarious and limited to a few centers in Catalonia and Andalusia. Twenty years were to elapse before a real workers' party came into existence. Nonetheless, there were great changes since the death of Ferdinand VII— from enlightened despotism to Bakuninism—although only a tiny minority, tracked by the authorities, were disciples of the International. At least the infiltration of the Russian ideology into Spain, or rather the injection of infinitesimal doses of a new dogma, was surely a far more important phenomenon than Isabella's insipid love affairs with the lymphatic Puig Molto.

The fifty-year period from Ferdinand VII's return to Madrid to Isabella II's abdication witnessed the disappearance of three dynasties. It also saw four pronunciamentos, five constitutions, and several dozen ministries. Gone was Spanish America. There was fighting at the border and within the country. Just as during the days of the *taifas*, entire provinces were free from control by the central government. The monarchy trembled. It repressed revolts ferociously or came to terms with them. Who governed Spain? The endless political crises were also crises of growth for the Spanish people. Trampled by some, betrayed by others, the will of the people was trying to express itself. Would it be heard? Faces convulsed with hatred or exuding hope, glimpsed in the flickering light of revolutions, express the uncertainty of a people too often deceived. The Right offers order and eternal hope; the Left promises freedom and a better way of life. Which would the people choose?

PART · V

THE AGE OF
José Antonio
AND
García Lorca

"The flag thou art sewing will flap in the streets amid the clamor of the people of Granada and thanks to thee, Liberty, so ardently desired, will trample the hard earth with its large silver feet."
—FEDERICO GARCÍA LORCA,
Mariana Pineda

I

Guerrilla Warfare
for Bread

EW Spaniards missed Isabella II. On several public squares portraits of the queen were burned; customs officials at the border at Irún presented arms to the discredited queen with ill grace and indifference. On the other hand, Prim, Serrano, and Topete were welcomed with open arms in Madrid. A few days after they had assumed power, they set up a provisional government and issued a manifesto. Quite explicit in regard to principles—the evils of the Bourbon rule, universal suffrage, freedom of worship, education, and the press—the manifesto was much less precise about the constitutional form of the new regime. Sternly cautioned against revolutionary action, the people were told very plainly that a republican system, similar to that of the United States, "is possible only for a young people; it is not suitable for a country with ancient, indestructible traditions." The provisional government seemed primarily concerned with calming the populace. Actually, public opinion was aroused, and numerous riots broke out. At Jerez and Málaga, the *jornaleros* occupied the haciendas; at Valladolid, Republicans and Monarchists fought in the streets. The governor of Badajoz broke up a disturbance with his sword. At Cadiz, the peasants pillaged the ammunition depot and fired on the troops. The electoral colleges were convoked and a political campaign of unwonted violence was unleashed. Although many big landowners supported the new parties because they sensed the way the wind was blowing, Cabrera, the traditionalist, won a triumphant victory, and the Carlists, reopening the civil war, used gunfire as propaganda. Finally, the constituent Cortes plumped for the monarchy. Serrano was named regent, and Prim became President of the Council. Both men sought a suitable king. Prince Leopold of Hohenzollern was their first choice, but France did not take kindly to the idea and he withdrew his candidature. Then they considered the son of the King of Italy, Amadeus, duke of Aosta. News of his consent arrived during those dark days when French and German armies clashed at Sedan. Amadeus left Florence for Cartagena, where Prim was to welcome him. Prim quit the palace of the Cortes in great haste to go home and prepare for the trip. It was difficult for his carriage to force its way through the unusually large gathering. A berlin stationed in the road prevented the carriage from moving. From a tavern on the Street of the Turks several men came running. One, short and bearded, rushed to the door of the carriage and fired five shots at the president. The carriage took off. In spite of his wounds, Prim stoically climbed the stairs of the War Ministry but collapsed on the landing. He died three days later. A gloomy, snowy afternoon two days after Prim's demise, Amadeus arrived in Madrid. Facing the stricken Cortes, he took the oath of office. Then he visited the chapel where the corpse of the man who had made him king reposed. This was the first act of his brief reign.

The year 1868 was not to pave the way for a republic, although perhaps the circumstances were conducive. The triumvirate had resisted the clamor of the people. But neither the failure of the 1869 elections nor the monarchical plans hatched by the combined efforts of Progressivists and Moderates could obscure the essential importance of that year— the emergence in Spain of a new social category: "the working class"—also described by an ancient word the Romans used in referring to the poor: the proletariat.

A peasant proletariat, to begin with. By as late as the end of the nineteenth century, the agrarian system had scarcely changed since the Middle Ages. In the south, the *latifundia*, or contracts for collective labor, and in the north, the *foros*, a seigniorial survival, made heavy demands on the tenant farmers and benefited the landowners. Vast tracts of land had been inherited by men whose privileges were very similar to those of feudal lords. These landowners, former captains and conquistadors, had become politicians. They used the votes of their workers to send deputies of their choice to the Cortes. It is scarcely surprising that in time the peasant proletariat should have become angered by the knowledge that the protection of throne, altar, and property was closely linked to the political ambitions of their local suzerains. Under liberal and progressivist governments, the sale of Church property had aroused hopes among the peasantry, but these were soon dashed. The men who acquired Church property were merchants whose main concern was to make money by reselling quickly and profitably. Indifferent to agrarian betterment, they did nothing but speculate. This was a far cry from sharing the land. Moreover, the big landowners did not attempt to increase the yield of their property. Of the 40,000 acres owned by the powerful Medinaceli family, only 2,500 were used for farming, the rest being set aside for hunting. Furthermore, it cost no more to work the land with outmoded methods, using cheap labor, than to cultivate it with the aid of modern equipment. Doubtless such an attitude was shortsighted, but the men concerned had always been hoarders, from father to son; they had never learned the virtues of investment or that their selfishness might prove their undoing. It was easier to move mountains than to persuade them. The situation, however, was becoming very clear to the agricultural proletariat. Confined to small towns of ten to fifteen thousand inhabitants, working seasonally for scandalously low wages, the Andalusian day laborers were among the poorest in the country. They had the reputation of being passive and resigned. But one day they were seized with rage. Peasants were observed marching on the city, led by the anarchist Fermín Salvoche. An agrarian organization, the Federale, incited the farmers to revolt. Brave groups of men even went so far as to occupy uncultivated land and to abolish the *latifundia*. But the incident was an isolated and fruitless one.

The urban proletariat . . . a class recently created as a result of the developing industry. Mines tripled their output and railroad networks expanded. In Catalonia industries abounded—2,000,000 cotton spindles and 50,000 cotton weavers; hosiery mills, leather tanneries, and pelt refineries, to say nothing of paper and light-machinery factories. The population of Barcelona increased fivefold. But only a few profited from this rapid growth. Industry had given birth to the proletariat but made no effort to care for it. So long as workers labored in small or average-sized enterprises associated with the guilds, they were able to ply their own trades. But under the impact of "new ideas," the guilds, or *gremios*, were abolished. Far from improving the condition of industrial workers, this merely emphasized their isolation and widened the gulf between them and their employers. Economic liberalism certainly promoted the prosperity of Spain, but it in no way benefited its artisans, who, with utmost difficulty, organized in order to protect their interests. Thus, for example, the Catalonian worker Muntz founded an association of weavers that later became known as the Unión de Clases.

The proletariat was testing its strength and trying to gain recognition for its legitimate claims, while employers stubbornly resisted. Very unwisely, they occasionally resorted to public agencies to stamp out popular movements. The authorities secretly supported the employers, or, at any rate, remained obligingly neutral. If help from the state was not forthcoming, employers had recourse to the services of the "Cudgel Party," whose self-imposed mission was to foil plots against the government. In earlier times, Ferdinand VII had done likewise, making use of a secret society called "The Exterminating Angel." Strikes, uprisings, arson, sabotage, the destruction of railway ties, and the felling of telegraph poles

—all these attested to the deep-seated resentment of workers against their employers and marked the beginning of prolonged periods of social unrest. Following on the heels of national and religious wars, another civil war—disguised, variable, muffled—threatened Spain's economic progress. Apparently the issue was not so much ideas and principles as needs and realities. The proletariat was struggling to obtain better living conditions, but very quickly a mystique arose to overshadow the social issues. In typically Spanish fashion, the guerrilla war for bread became a battle of ideas.

The new guerrillas required a dogma and a faith, both of which Fanelli supplied, for he was the prophet of the new religion. The first Socialist newspapers, Fernando Garrigo's *La Atracción* and Terrades's *La Fraternidad*, disseminated the collectivist doctrine. At a meeting in the Madrid stock exchange of the innocuous "Association for the Reform of Registration and Custom Laws," one of the founders of the Workers' International suddenly spoke up. "Tariffs concern only the bourgeoisie. The workers need an entirely different kind of reform!" A manifesto was issued which urged the emancipation of the laboring class by means of a union for all working-class people. Shortly thereafter, a new weekly, *La Solidaridad*, appeared. One of its editors, Anselmo Lorenzo, who was imbued with Marxism but inclined to interpret it in his own fashion, became the founder of Spanish Anarchism. Another newspaper, *La Federación*, appeared in Barcelona, just as the first Workers' Congress met. One hundred Castilian, Andalusian, Valencian, Catalonian, and Aragonese delegates were present. Important decisions were reached, but a basic disagreement arose between the Marxists and the Bakuninists. The former advocated statism, whereas the latter opposed any kind of authority. From then on the working class was divided into two factions: a right and a left wing—authoritarian and anti-authoritarian, Socialist and Anarchist. But most important, hereafter governments would have to contend with a social class.

At the Madrid School of Architecture, or in certain secular churches of Catalonia, on Sunday mornings when people were going to Mass a new kind of sermon was being preached. Socialists and Anarchists would take turns mounting the rostrum to advocate the class struggle and denounce capitalism. Occasionally, liberal intellectuals, eager to move with the times, participated in discussions and contributed their arguments. One of the outstanding figures of Spanish Socialism was the Galician Pablo Iglesias, publisher of *El Socialista* in Madrid and a contributor to *Emancipación*. Dogged, selfless, a spokesman for Socialist authoritarianism, Iglesias was in favor of pooling industrial profits but insisted it had to be done under the strict direction and control of the state—in other words, he favored nationalization. The Anarchists, whose organ, *Tierra y Liberdad*, was published in Madrid, opposed the notion of authority. Rather, they glorified individual action and rejected coercion, especially that of religion. These two Socialist movements, one with headquarters in Castile, the other in Catalonia and Andalusia, were represented a little later by two powerful organizations: the General Union of Workers and the National Confederation of Labor. The latter, also called the Anarcho-Syndicalist Central, counted among its affiliated organs the Iberian Anarchist Federation. It preached "direct action" and did not hesitate on occasion to resort to terrorist methods.

How did Amadeus's government react to this revolutionary movement? After first underestimating its importance, it became alarmed only when the Paris Commune led to bloodshed in the streets of the French capital. The Minister of the Interior, Sagasta, forbade the International to hold meetings and the police were ordered to hunt down left-wing leaders. There was disagreement in the Cortes; Pi y Margal, Carrigo, and Salmerón defended the workers, while Castelar, although a Republican, violently opposed Socialism. "Wherever Socialism appeared, it pressed its secular claims with an eye, first of all, to violating freedom, regarding itself as a superior form of democracy." In the end the Cortes reached no decision whatsoever, merely condemning the Workers' International, whereas the rightist deputies referred to it as "the philosophical utopia of crime." While the deputies were hurling insults at one another in the Cortes, while Socialists and Anarchists were extolling their respective systems in public meetings, a third contender mysteriously made his appearance in Madrid. Unnoticed, Paul Lafargue, Karl Marx's son-in-law, had just arrived, bringing with him the *Communist Manifesto*.

The First Spanish Republic

During the course of his two-year reign, Amadeus never ceased to ask himself what on earth he was doing on the Spanish throne. The two parties that had brought him to power—the Progressivists and the Moderates—were worn out and had fewer and fewer followers, while the extremists —the Carlists and the Republicans—enjoyed equal popularity. Amadeus announced that he had every intention of ruling as a "constitutional" king—he would be an arbitrator. "Not to intrude"—this was the motto of the ready-made monarch, of whom Pi y Margal said: "He made a virtue of not being or wanting to be ambitious." In actuality, the Spanish monarchy had never been so poorly represented. Receptions at the palace were few and devoid of any pomp. The Italian gave the impression of being a petty bourgeois who economized on candles, scraped, and pinched. Punctilious about etiquette, the aristocracy despised him, and the masses made fun of him; yet he was really neither contemptible nor ridiculous. He had merely realized, from the moment of his arrival in Madrid, that he was not the man to resolve the grave problems confronting Spain. Well aware of the rising temper of the people, and realizing that the situation called for more radical steps than those taken by the government —secularization of the cemeteries, confiscation of religious art objects—he was liberal and open-minded, but not prepared to initiate revolutionary measures; rather he was a king of the transition, and this role satisfied him—he had no further ambitions. Congratulating the palace architect for some changes he had made, Amadeus said quite simply and sincerely: "You must do more next year, if I am still here."

Since Amadeus was ineffectual, his ministers—Sagasta, Ruiz Rorillero, and Serrano—attempted to govern in his place, but it was an uphill affair. First they had to stamp out a Carlist flare-up. Serrano took care of this by forcing Don Carlos's troops, which had reached Navarre, back across the frontier. This was the only success of Amadeus's government. Subsequently, Sagasta, who was mixed up in a scandal involving political corruption, was forced to resign. An attempt was made to assassinate the king; the army rebelled. In vain did the Cortes try to legislate; factionalism triumphed over the national interest. Meanwhile, on Christmas Day 1872, forty-eight delegates of the Spanish Workers' Federation met at the Moratín Theater in Cordova. A workers' organization, Syndicalist in character, was established. Its members grouped according to profession or trade rather than on the basis of political or religious tendency. Thus, a few months before the Hague Conference, the charter of Syndicalism was formulated. After the Hague Conference, political problems were discussed at a public meeting at which the Workers' International proclaimed its faith in collectivism and Anarchism. Thus, from the very outset and throughout the ensuing years, Spanish Syndicalism and Anarchism were closely linked. The fate of the working classes was no longer in the hands of the Socialists; instead, the Anarchists had taken over.

A seemingly trivial incident brought about the end of the regime. A new Minister of War had just been named. The artillery officers, who disliked him, resigned en masse. The government immediately replaced them, but apparently many of the newly promoted officers had Republican leanings and might have infected the rest of the army. "Who would then protect the family, order, property, and religion?" wondered those generals who favored a *coup d'état.* The moment was indeed propitious for the king to arbitrate, but he chose "to take leave of noble and unfortunate Spain" —in short, he abdicated. Apprised of the king's resignation, the Cortes proclaimed the Republic by a vote of 258 to 32. Amadeus left Madrid amid dancing and the noise of exploding firecrackers. With exuberant lightheartedness, the people celebrated the change of regime. Amadeus sighed with relief. He was finally back in Italy! As for the deputies of the Cortes, they stared at one another in amazement. They were overcome by the lopsided vote, little realizing how Republican they had become! Actually, they got more than they had bargained for.

"When will you have a republic?" Gambetta had jokingly asked the Catalonian Estanislao Figueras at the end of his visit, early in 1873. The answer was clear: "In February." The following day Gambetta wrote his friend Castelar asking if Figueras was mad. But Figueras knew whereof he spoke; in February he was made President of the First Spanish Republic. A clever and cultivated man, Figueras did not have the makings of a statesman, or at least not the kind of statesman required by the circumstances. Scarcely had this Republic, which nobody had expected, come into being when it was ringed by enemies. Castelar admitted: "The monarchy is dead, but only Providence can take credit for this." Against the new regime stood the Monarchists who backed Alfonso, Isabella's son, Republicans who disapproved of federalism, as well as Anarchists and Carlists who had never relinquished their arms. Now, when a leader with an iron fist was needed, or a figure so dazzling as to silence partisanship by the mere mention of his name, the Republic proposed only intellectuals, well-intentioned men but unskilled in government. Pi y Margal, a brilliant theoretician and translator of Proudhon's writings, succeeded Figueras. Considered too soft by the Cortes, he was replaced by Nicolas Salmerón, a philosopher and jurist. Salmerón came a cropper over the question of agrarian reform, refused to sign a decree re-establishing the death penalty, and himself suggested that Emilio Castelar govern in his place. A close friend of Gambetta's, Castelar resembled him in one respect: his stormy and occasionally bombastic eloquence concealed a complete lack of vitality. Like all weak men, he resorted to strong measures, and there were many who did not like his methods. While he was earnestly trying to govern, a pronunciamento, inspired by General Pavía, was being prepared. One evening in January 1874, Castelar waged his last battle before the Cortes. He lost it. A vote of confidence went against him, 120 to 100. At six o'clock the following morning, a messenger from Pavía announced that the assembly must vacate the room. Soldiers filled the corridors. Concealed in the garden, Pavía awaited his hour; it was not long in coming. In a burst of indignation, the deputies swore they would die for the Republic, then wormed their way to the exits. Their faces concealed under capes, they departed in the icy mist of the early-winter morning. The benches were empty. Pavía entered.

Now, between a Republic that had just breathed its last, after 327 days of precarious existence, and a monarchy in the offing, a transitional government ruled. Who would be chosen? Alfonso, the son of Isabella II, had a very good chance provided an effective campaign prepared public opinion. While Serrano was dealing a final blow to Don Carlos's troops, Martínez de Campos was urging the army to rally to Alfonso's side. As the young prince was leaving the Hotel de Castille in Paris to go to the theater, a note was handed to him. "Sire, Your Majesty was proclaimed King yesterday by the Spanish army. Long live the King!" A few days later Alfonso left for Barcelona from Marseille. "I am the king of no political party," he told the *Times* correspondent. Actually, it was not possible to belong to a political party; until the advent in 1931 of the Second Republic, which comprised many parties, no truly representative political group existed in Spain. One could scarcely call the conservatives and liberals, whose leaders were, respectively, Cánovas and Sagasta, sincere democrats. By tacit agreement they managed to take turns governing in order to oppose the Republican and Carlist factions. As for the elements of the extreme Left, the Socialists and Anarchists, they continued to organize semi-clandestinely. Their efforts bore fruit much later; for the present, they had no intention of becoming involved in important public issues or in political life generally. The monarchy of Alfonso, known as the regime of the Restoration, followed an essentially middle-class policy, while conservatives and liberals shared both power and prebends. The *cesante*, or temporarily unemployed official, could be seen strolling about the Puerta del Sol, waiting for his friends to return to office and restore his sinecure, always at the disposal of the party in power. This was known as the *turno político*, or, as the people put it, "lamb-chop politics," with each side taking a turn at being broiled by the fire. In the provinces, the government representative was called the cacique, a term derived from the name of Indian chiefs who, during the era of conquest, placed their authority at the disposal of the Spanish administrators. Similarly, in rural nineteenth-century Spain, bureaucrats, moneylenders, all those acquainted with people in office, influenced their clients to vote for the candidate selected by the party in power. Would anyone indebted to the cacique refuse his vote? Usually he was either employed by him or owed him money. To insure his election and avoid accusation of fraud at the polls, the candidate had to have all the caciques in the palm of his hand. Cheating during an election was a common practice; among the devices used were trick ballot boxes, the registration of deceased persons or minors, prearranged ballot lists. This was the way conservatives and liberals of the capitalist bloc handled universal suffrage.

One could hardly accuse Alfonso's ministers of ill will. The Constitution of 1876 proved the opposite. Freedom of speech, religion, and assembly, recognition of the legality of civil marriage—all this seemed liberal enough. One clause, however, stipulated that the government could suppress constitutional rights and that, in such an eventuality, the military command of a given region would enjoy full powers. During Alfonso's reign this clause was never invoked and Spain knew a period of peace and order, despite certain disturbing external events. The Holy See sulked over Spain's constitution, which it considered too tolerant. It was further irritated by the street demonstrations occasioned by the

death of Pius IX. Grave incidents precipitated a quarrel between Arab rebels and Spanish colonials in Algeria, and this
prompted the government of Madrid to protest sharply to
France. Two years later, the combined blunders of King Alfonso and President Grévy once again troubled Franco-
Spanish relations. Before his announced official visit to
Paris, Alfonso went to Germany. Accompanied by Emperor
Wilhelm and Moltke, the latter decked out in the light-blue
uniform of a Bavarian colonel, he witnessed the military ma-
neuvers. French national feeling ran high at the time and did
not take kindly to the King of Spain being entertained by a
colonel of the Uhlans who had covered himself with glory
in the Franco-Prussian War. Alfonso was greeted in Paris by
catcalls and cries of "Down with the Uhlan King!" Grévy
made his excuses, but they were obviously mere formalities.
Returning to Madrid, the monarch was greeted enthusiasti-
cally by cries of "Long live the Uhlan King!" It has often
been noted that the masses have amazing insight. Could the
French, and subsequently the Spanish, have guessed that
during his visit with Emperor Wilhelm, Alfonso had promised to ally Spain with Germany in the event of war?

Alfonso married his cousin Mercedes of Orléans, the
daughter of the Duke de Montpensier; after her death he
took as his second wife an Austrian archduchess, María
Cristina of Habsburg and Lorraine. When he died of tu-
berculosis at the age of twenty-eight, his wife was pregnant
with the future Alfonso XIII. Entrusted with the regency,
she ruled for fifteen years—a period marked by the Cuban
affair. The loss of this island in the Antilles sounded the
death knell of what had once been Spain's vast empire. For a
long time Cuba had resented Spanish control and on various
occasions had taken up arms against the local authorities.
But for once, and with the aid of great cruelty, the government won out. The United States chose this moment to
threaten intervention. In a show of strength, the American
battleship *Maine* dropped anchor in Havana Bay. A few
days later it exploded and sank. The Americans accused the
Spaniards of having planted a bomb aboard; the Spaniards

fiercely denied the charge. The incident, however, gave the Americans a perfect pretext for declaring war on Spain. The government of Madrid received McKinley's ultimatum with less enthusiasm than courage. The Spanish fleet, commanded by Admiral Cervera, headed for Cuba, while the people, grossly misinformed, awaited news of Spanish victory. How could these "sausage eaters" defend themselves against the bravest fighters in the world? "One, two, three, and the jig is up with McKinley," Madrileños sang. But the battle ended as the experts had predicted. The Spanish fleet was surrounded in the port of Santiago and, one after the other, its ships were sunk by American artillery fire; in the Philippines, Admiral Montojo's squadron suffered a similar fate.

The unfortunate admiral reportedly said: "Spain prefers honor without ships to ships without honor"—a noble statement that glossed over a terrible defeat. A few months later, in accordance with the terms of the peace treaty, Spain relinquished Cuba and ceded to the United States Puerto Rico, Guam in the Mariana Islands, and the Philippines. The Balearic and Canary Islands, a narrow strip of Guinea, and the three Moroccan enclaves of Ceuta, Melilla, and Ifni were all that remained of its overseas possessions. The sun had indeed set on the defunct empire.

"Oh, Sad and Noble Land!"

So sighed the poet of Soria, Antonio Machado, as he contemplated the countryside around Old Castile and bitterly branded Spaniards as having "empty stomachs and empty heads." There were a few who, like him, delighted in expressing contempt compounded of strange inconsistencies: a rejection of tradition yet a feverish search for original sources, a yearning for regeneration coupled with respect for national originality. The failure of the monarchy, the collapse of the colonial empire, the illiteracy of the masses which no government sincerely tried to remedy, the unbelievable poverty of certain regions, the scandalous corruption

of the caciques, the mediocrity of the king and his entourage—all this bred profound pessimism. Spain was rotting.
Like a drifting ship, it moved farther away from Europe.
New life had to be breathed into it; it had to be restored
to the European family of nations—such were the imperatives of the generation of 1898, who still hoped to see Spain
become a great power once again. But the past would have
to be forgotten. A lawyer, Joaquín Costa, said: "We must
now make our schools a political instrument and put a double lock on the sepulcher of the Cid to prevent him from
coming back and prancing about on his horse." Some there
were who maintained that the grandeur of Spain lay dead
and buried. And, indeed, it was difficult to believe in its
grandeur when field workers lived on acorns in winter and
the windows in certain villages of the province of Teruel
were without panes; when inhabitants of the Jurdes lived in
caves and hundreds of thousands of Galicians and Basques
emigrated to America, where, not so long ago, their grandparents had ruled as masters.

For a time the generation of 1898 took an active interest
in social problems. Costa was the guiding light of this group,
which, on the whole, was more inclined to speculate than to
act. He tried to apply practical solutions to the ills of the
agrarian proletariat, but discovered there was no real pana-
cea—the entire system had to be changed. Long before
Pierre Poujade had the idea, Joaquín Costa made a desperate effort to abolish the income tax. He incited the Aragonese
peasants to revolt, and openly exhorted people to use illegal
means since legal action had proved ineffectual. To those
who came to complain about the landowners, Costa roughly
replied: "What about your pitchforks? Don't you know how
to use them?" But the intellectuals of 1898 soon wearied of
the endless struggle. Their every tendency, their middle-
class origins, their religious training, plus an obvious lack of
enthusiasm that was evident to the masses, made them unfit
for collective action. Despite their sincere and rather touching efforts, they were incapable of ridding themselves of a
certain academic stiffness of manner and the peremptory

tone of the professional philosopher. Nonetheless, the ideas they implanted influenced the Syndicalist leaders and the members of workers' parties. They adapted these ideas to the level of their comrades and transposed them into dynamic slogans. The working class would be saved by the workers themselves.

Although the men of 1898 failed in their earnest efforts to change the living conditions of the proletariat, they did achieve great success in the purely intellectual domain. The fact that they represented neither a school of thought nor a current of opinion, that each individual made his own special contribution, only added to their luster. Among them were essayists—Ganivet, Azaña, Azorín, and, later, Ortega y Gasset; sociologists such as Hurtado and Azcarate, and a historian, Altamira; two poets, Ramón Jiménez and Antonio Machado, and the musicians Falla, Granados, Albéniz; a novelist, Baroja. Finally, one of the greatest geniuses of Spain, Miguel de Unamuno, reacting to the disenchantment of the philosophers of 1898, suggested that Europe regard Spain as its ideal and Don Quixote as a model.

To the intellectual movement of 1898 a curious educational doctrine must be added, one that permeated university circles during the second half of the nineteenth century and persisted until the outbreak of World War I— "Krausism." A fiery young Castilian, Julián Sanz del Río, introduced the doctrine in Spain, having brought it in from Germany. At first the preserve of a small group, the new theory had become very popular by the end of the century, due in large part to the personality of its guiding light, Francisco Giner de los Ríos. Eventually it exerted a considerable influence on Spanish culture and education. The "Krausists" professed faith in science and modern pedagogy and a respect for strict moral values. They founded the Institución Libre de Enseñanza, which, after overcoming many initial difficulties, finally won official recognition and became a veritable lay seminary. All the academicians and intellectuals who later paved the way for the coming of the Second Spanish Republic were trained in the Institución.

But "Krausism" was limited to an avant-garde elite which later became an intellectual aristocracy. It shocked Catholic and traditionalist circles because of its somewhat crude approach to sexual problems, its emphasis on biological rather than religious studies, its encouragement of outdoor life, with girls and boys mingling freely instead of engaging in pious diversions. Deliberately denied higher education, the masses were not affected by "Krausism." In the end, the cold spirituality that stemmed from the hazy German systems of thought, the pretense of religious neutrality which concealed a basic pantheism, did not take root in ancient Spain. To be sure, "Krausism" made an important contribution to the Spanish universities by giving impetus to scientific research. It added something to the talents of a Menéndez Pidal or a Marañón; but it did not transcend the framework of a fascinating but narrowly circumscribed pedagogical experiment. Although they were both generous and clever, these "lay apostles" failed utterly in their plan to extend to Spain Bismarck's *Kulturkampf*. But was this actually their purpose?

How can we evaluate the men of 1898? Their writings, works, and influence made nineteenth-century Spain a "Silver Century" of sorts, the century of a philosophical Counter Reformation. In this respect, their appearance on the stormy horizon during this period of decline was salutary. The grandeur that was Spain's had crumbled, but its spiritual values, which perhaps had never before shone with such radiance, were safeguarded. On the other hand, they had failed utterly to solve the social problem. Presumably Spain was not yet ready for a republic headed by professors; furthermore, despite their almost naïve benevolence, they had no political backing whatsoever. It was quite natural that traditionalists should spurn them, since they, in turn, spurned tradition; and it was also natural that the proletariat should eye them with suspicion, since they belonged in the enemy camp. What did workers and peasants have in common with these bourgeois disguised as apostles? Brains—but not brawn. Having incautiously become "involved," the intellectuals of 1898 felt it wise to withdraw to their ivory towers. Finally—

and this is perhaps the main reason why their mission failed —these talented men who specialized in synthesis were not able to reconcile tradition with modern thought. Not until fifty years later were the ancient Hispanic themes realized in the aesthetic domain by García Lorca and by the Pablo Picasso of the early period.

Alfonso XIII—A King Who Was Too Hesitant
Primo de Rivera—A General Who Was Too Determined

As soon as he came of age, Alfonso XIII was proclaimed King of Spain. During the first twenty years of his reign the atmosphere was stormy. Scarcely had the country recovered from the American fiasco when it experienced another defeat in Morocco. Although relations between the Triple Alliance and the Entente were strained, the young king, whose pleasing personality made him popular with everyone, visited Edward VII, Loubet, and Wilhelm II in turn. In this way the monarch plainly showed how important he felt it was to remain neutral in a conflict that was generally regarded as inevitable. His marriage to Princess Victoria Eugenia of Battenberg, Queen Victoria's niece, who unfortunately transmitted to his heirs the terrible disease of hemophilia, was proof of his desire to please all concerned. Actually, he satisfied nobody; none of his allies was fooled by his attempts to play one country off against another, giving the nod now to France, now to Germany, and then to England. Spain's internal situation was fraught with unrest. Separatist movements were gaining ground while Syndicalism, moving toward anarchy, prepared for direct action. Catalonia rebelled. In Barcelona, the "Tragic Week" ended in bloodshed. Alejandro Lerroux's exhortations incited the people to murder. "Burn all records of landownership. Kill. Lift up the skirts of novitiates and raise them to the status of mothers." By far the gravest incident was the execution of Francisco Ferrer, a militant Anarchist who directed the École Moderne. In spite of a world-wide campaign to save him, he was hanged. Strong feelings were aroused both inside and outside Spain. The Socialists portrayed Ferrer as a victim of intolerance and tyranny, and the Left deified him. 1914 . . . Sarajevo. The world fixed its gaze on the Rhine. World War I began. Spain remained neutral, although it was said that the king secretly sympathized with Germany. But he also liked France, and the French had taken him to their hearts ever since the day when, saved by a hairbreadth from an attempt to assassinate him, he stood up in his carriage on the Paris boulevard and called out pluckily: "Long live France!" Nor did Frenchmen forget a remark he made in 1914: "Only the rabble and I love France." Officially, Alfonso XIII adopted a "humanitarian" policy, organizing a service in his palace designed to serve prisoners and wounded men as well as to act as a clearinghouse for letters and packages. He hoped to make himself popular in both camps. To the heads of states he suggested a daily period of truce to bring in the wounded. Meanwhile, the Spanish army, and especially its very partisan navy, seized every opportunity to help the Germans. German submarines sought shelter and fresh supplies along the Spanish coast, and Madrid became a center of espionage. On the other hand, a group of Catalonian volunteers, who considered themselves compatriots of Joffre (a native of Rivesaltes in the eastern Pyrenees), headed for the French front, delighted that the French general had halted the German invasion at the Marne. As for the Spanish bourgeoisie, they grew rich on the war. Orders poured in to tanneries and clothing and canned-goods factories. Wages increased 50 per cent and profits 500 per cent. Many hoped the war would last a long time.

Meanwhile, domestic affairs reached an acute phase. The economic boom that resulted from foreign orders, the smell of powder wafted from beyond the Pyrenees, the pretense of neutrality which concealed partisanship—all this inflamed the revolutionary spirit. And the ensuing political agitation affected the army, which established juntas more powerful than the government. Catalonia aspired to provincial autonomy and established a *Mancommunitat*. For the first time, Republicans, Catalonians, Socialists, and intellectuals made common cause. There were strikes, workers remained idle, trains stopped running. Strikers were fired on. The Russian Revolution erupted like a thunderbolt. "Long live Lenin!" the Spanish peasants shouted, demanding that land be divided and shared. The rout of the Spaniards in Morocco came as a shock. An armchair strategist, the king ordered General Sylvestre, the governor of Melilla, to cross the Rif, where Abd-el-Krim was stirring his people to revolt, and proceed to Alhucemas Bay. "I will arrive at the bay on St. James's day," Sylvestre telegraphed Alfonso. On his way he clashed with the Moors, who inflicted a resounding defeat on the Spanish army: 12,000 killed, including General Sylvestre, and 1,500 taken prisoner. When the king was told that the Arab leader demanded a ransom of five million pesetas for the prisoners, he exclaimed: "Damn! The price of poultry is exorbitant!"

The Moroccan fiasco did not upset Alfonso too much. In search of a big name to attract customers, the head of the Deauville Casino invited the king to Deauville, with all expenses paid. "Why not?" said the king, and off he went while Spain was still brooding over its misfortunes. Each day his popularity declined a little more. This spoiled child, who had the manners of a nobleman and was the soul of frivolity, no longer appealed to the masses. Blasco-Ibáñez did his bit to expose him. Moreover, the internal situation was tense. Two powerful groups confronted each other— the army and the proletariat. As for Parliament, it was helpless, caught between the political activity of cliques and the slow, muffled erosion of anarchy. After hesitating a long time, the king decided that the army might bring about law and order. He asked General Primo de Rivera to take over. Well-meaning, an excellent orator, a lover of literature, Primo de Rivera was courageous but lacking in political acumen. He dissolved Parliament and substituted a military directorate for constitutional government. First he dealt with the Moroccan affair. At the head of his troops, he landed at Alhucemas Bay and, with the help of the French, crushed the Rif rebellion, forcing Abd-el-Krim to sue for peace. The Moroccan leader's surrender, together with the restoration of peace, not only enhanced Rivera's personal prestige but also served to cement Franco-Spanish relations. Indeed, Spain signed a treaty permitting French African troops safe passage to Spain in the event of a Franco-German war.

Primo de Rivera did not fare nearly as well in his internal policy. His slogan can be summed up in three words: nation, religion, monarchy. His social program was more than generous; it was utopian. But he must have known that it could not be realized. He advocated an end to the class struggle and the establishment of parity commissions to arbitrate conflicts between workers and capitalists, an improvement in working conditions, and agrarian reform. In short, his intentions were excellent. He studied the possibility of an ambitious plan for technological expansion which, to be feasible, should have been accompanied by an economic plan. But was it reasonable to expect increased production in a politically divided country? "The twenty-five million educated, understanding, industrious, tolerant inhabitants, inspired by the sacred flame of love and by Christian doctrine," referred to by Primo de Rivera, existed solely in his imagination. In reality, the people were implacably bitter. Like Mussolini, whose example he denied following, Primo organized a single party, the Patriotic Union, composed in large part of his own supporters and local caciques; but he refrained from suppressing the Socialist party and the General Union of Workers, both of which were merely vegetating. The Anarchists had been eliminated. Most Republicans had emigrated, and they confined themselves to journalistic attacks. The most celebrated figure among them was Blasco-Ibáñez, who sought refuge in France. His many pamphlets, dropped on Spanish soil from airplanes, fanned the flames of revolution. The dissolution of the *Mancommunitat* and the banning of the Catalonian language and flag only served to excite the separatist movement there. Colonel Francisco Macía, head of the *Estat Catala*, and likewise an exile in France, made a gallant attempt to do his bit. Gathering a group of friends near the Franco-Spanish border, at Prats-de-Mollo, he tried to slip into Spain in order to mobilize the enemies of the dictatorship. But before Macía could cross the border, his plot was discovered. At the same moment, Unamuno was deported to the little island of Fuenteventura because of an article he wrote which displeased the dictator. Commenting on the incident, Primo de Rivera said: "I do not believe that a little Hellenic learning gives a man the right to mix into everything." Shortly thereafter, Unamuno too sought refuge in France.

Primo de Rivera remained in power for seven years, and during this time he tried in all good faith—his Andalusian shrewdness was not devoid of a certain guilelessness—to solve by military methods economic and social problems whose extreme complexity was beyond his understanding. Discouraged, and perhaps sensing the approach of revolution, whose first victim he would certainly be, Primo resigned. A few weeks later he died in Paris.

After the withdrawal of the dictator, the regime seemed doomed. In spite of its dramatic beginnings, the praetorian experiment had not fulfilled its promise. Once again the king hestitated between restoration of constitutional liberties and continuation of the dictatorship. Alfonso XIII had changed a great deal since his gay accession to the throne, when the masses adored him—or perhaps it was they who had changed. They no longer remembered the dark, slender, handsome young man who drove racing cars at breakneck speed or, with slow tread, headed the Good Friday procession at Seville. Whether he played polo or reviewed his troops, officiated at the opening of a bull fight or ran his horses at the tracks, the masses had loved their *enfant terrible*. They had admired his plumed military cap and his numerous uniforms—he wore everything with such an air of elegance! Disappointed now, the people muttered: "To the frontier with the King!" But the moment had not yet come. Alfonso XIII's last political act was to hand over authority to General Berenguer, an old soldier who had distinguished himself both in Cuba and in Morocco. Sincerely desiring to do his best, the general appealed to all the political parties, but their only response was sarcasm. Two grave incidents occurred. Fermín Galán, the head of a company at Jaca, in

Aragon, had had his fill of the regime. He was an exceptional young man. After studying at the military academy of Toledo, which he had entered as a top-ranking pupil, he was made a captain at the age of twenty-five, and received the Red Cross of María Cristina for bravery. A disciple of Saint-Just, Galán was eager for action but did not know where to begin. He and his friend Ángel García Hernández joined forces and started off down the road with their troops a little earlier than the day fixed by the civilian conspirators. Their triumphant march ended with a court-martial at Huesca. The two rebels were condemned to death. "Don't lower your heads. Take a good look at your captain," Galán called to the firing squad.

Three days later, on a beautiful, clear morning, two planes took off from the Madrid airport and headed for the capital. A shower of pamphlets fell on the streets and barracks of Madrid. "Soldiers . . . last night throughout Spain the long-awaited Republican movement, so eagerly desired by all those who want justice, came into being. . . . If your barracks do not surrender, you will be bombarded within the half hour. . . . Soldiers, long live Spain and long live the Republic!" The planes then described a circle and disappeared. Those in the know claimed the two fliers were none other than Commander Franco and General Queipo de Llano. No further information was forthcoming, since the government immediately established complete censorship and decreed martial law. By evening, one hundred Republicans had been arrested. Friends of Ortega y Gasset and of Alcalá Zamora were worried about their whereabouts.

Although Berenguer displayed great calm, he was discouraged. His final attempt to rally the various parties to his side had failed. Military experience having taught him that a general staff cannot fight without troops, he resigned. The cabinet that replaced him decided that municipal elections were in order. Socialists and Republicans joined forces against the Monarchists and were victorious at the polls in most of the large cities—Madrid, Barcelona, Valencia, and Seville. Although considerably more Monarchists than Republicans were elected—22,150 as against 5,775—the popular vote was decisively anti-royalist. Thereupon, Admiral Aznar, the last of the crown's leaders, published a manifesto signed by the king. Alfonso explained that, although he was not abdicating, he would withdraw in order to avoid bloodshed. "In the spring we will see the lilacs triumphant," a lady friend of Alfonso's quipped, alluding to one of the colors of the Republican flag. And, indeed, one lovely spring day, April 14, 1931, the Spanish Bourbon walked out of the palace gates, bowing courteously to the crowd, and climbed into his car. A boat awaited him at Cartagena to take him to France. Spain had lost its amiable king. Already—in fact, the day before—the Socialists' red flag flew from the People's House in Madrid. The Republic's colors—lilac, yellow, and red—were hung from every window. In the streets crowds were singing the "Marseillaise."

The Second Spanish Republic

The first concern of a Socialist government must be to satisfy at least to some extent the masses that brought it to power. The advent of the Republic awakened great hope among the workers and peasants, and it was imperative not to disappoint people who had been so slow to unite. All this was very much in the minds of the leaders of the new regime. Who were they? Alcalá Zamora was named head of the state and President of the Council. The principal cabinet members were Alejandro Lerroux, Miguel Maura, Manuel Azaña, Indalecio Prieto, and Largo Caballero. The chief theorists of Republicanism did not participate in the government, but remained in their studies to advise and meditate. These included Dr. Marañón, whom the people called the "Republic's midwife," and Ortega y Gasset, author of *Invertebrate Spain*. Harping on themes so dear to the generation of 1898, Ortega insisted that it was essential to give the people the education which the monarchy had denied them and to Europeanize the nation.

The government first tackled its most urgent problem, that of agrarian reform. It proved a serious stumbling block because Communists, Socialists, and liberals disagreed on basic principles. Who should own the land? Those who farmed it? The state? The family? Special commissions studied the problem and offered suggestions. But reform was postponed and the peasants began to grumble. Finally, a statement was issued in a clause of the Republican constitution: "The wealth of the country, regardless of ownership, is to be subordinated to the interests of the national economy. It will be nationalized if necessary." In accordance with this article, the basic law of agrarian reform called for the expropriation of land (many property owners had left the country when the monarchy fell) and its division among 50,000 peasants per year. Moreover, farmers were given loans and authorized to organize collectives or syndicates. The reform applied only to the *latifundia* in Andalusia, Estremadura, La Mancha, and the regions of Salamanca and Toledo—a dozen provinces in all—and expropriation was limited to a maximum of 25 acres of fertile land or 1,700 acres of poor land. Property owners were indemnified according to tax rates and land-survey figures. Within two years, fewer than 9,000 families were settled and only 225,-000 acres expropriated. To increase the disappointment, agricultural wages rose, thus resulting in greater unemployment. In the end, land ownership was assigned to the state, and the farmers merely changed masters. A planned economy replaced "caciquism." Improvement in working conditions proceeded in similar fashion. The state controlled production, and the rise in the cost of living, which was caused by the world-wide economic crisis, nullified any benefits the proletariat might have derived from higher wages. Trade unions and government agencies were at each other's throats, and strikes became more frequent. Dissatisfied and disappointed, workers and farmers were increasingly attracted to Anarcho-Syndicalism and more receptive to Bolshevik propaganda. In Seville and Barcelona the *ley de fuga* was proclaimed, and Andalusian peasants hummed the well-known refrain: *¿Cuando querrá dios del cielo Que la justicia se*

vuelva? ¿Y los pobres coman pan Y los ricos coman hierba?
"When will God in Heaven wish justice to return, so that the
poor will eat bread, and the rich, grass?"

The problem of local autonomy solved itself. In Barcelona, Colonel Macía proclaimed the Catalonian Republic just
as the government of Madrid established its own republic.
This was going far in the direction of separatism. A deal was
made between the central government and Macia's ministers
which brought the Catalonian Republic back into the general
framework of the nation. A statute conferring independence
on Catalonia received the unanimous support of the people
and was ratified by the Cortes. The Basque country, Navarre, Galicia, and Aragon, stimulated by this example, feverishly prepared their own statutes of independence. The
danger of this separatist contagion, which threatened the
still somewhat fragile unity of Spain, did not escape the
attention of the central government.

What attitude would the Republic assume toward the
Church? The municipal elections of 1931 were directed not
only against the monarchy but against the Church as well.
Most significant was the first statement the President of the
Council made to the Cortes: "Spain is no longer Catholic."
The anti-clerical deputies—the *jabalíes*—responded with resounding applause. Appropriations were voted for the immediate establishment of 6,000 schools and several thousand
scholarships. The illiteracy of more than 65 per cent of the
population was a sore that the Republic resolved to heal by
means of lay therapy. Freedom of worship was likewise proclaimed and cemeteries secularized. Naturally, the Spanish
Church had no intention of allowing itself to be stripped,
without a fight, of the spiritual monopoly it had enjoyed for
twenty centuries. High Church officials protested the measures. Cardinal Segura, archbishop of Toledo and Primate of
Spain, openly expressed his hostility to the new regime,
whereupon the Governor of Guadalajara, following orders
from the government, had the cardinal escorted to Irún
under guard. After heated debate, the Cortes enacted several measures against the Church and Christian morality:
the establishment of divorce and civil marriage, the abolition

of schools connected with religious congregations, the dissolution once again of the Society of Jesus and the seizure of its property, the withdrawal of state subsidies for religious purposes. At the time the Church possessed about 12,000 rural properties, 8,000 city properties, 4,000 tracts of land, 3,000 convents, and 800 monasteries. The religious personnel, all of whom were appointed by the state, included 36,-000 nuns, 8,000 monks, and more than 35,000 secular priests. How were they to live?

The authors of the Constitution of 1931 committed a grave error when they decreed that Spain no longer had an official religion and brutally announced their anti-clericalism. They alienated liberal Catholics and a sizable minority of the clergy who, disillusioned by the monarchy, had voted for the Republic. The Second Spanish Republic had been proclaimed at Eibar, not far from Guernica, the Basques' holy city. The federal banner flew from the top of the Montserrat monastery, the sanctuary of Catalonia. Did the Republicans imagine that legislative clauses, press campaigns, intellectual professions of faith—even when expressed with unquestionable generosity and in the noblest terms—would suffice to destroy at one stroke the deep-seated religious sentiments to which the Spanish people, often unconsciously, had nonetheless remained faithful?

Soon all the elements hostile to Marxism joined forces in an attempt to safeguard religion: the nobility, the upper classes, and the landowners. Of course, the motives of many of these people were questionable. Some, who had ostentatiously proclaimed their Republican leanings, still favored the monarchy. Others, publicly associating their cause with that of Christ, were merely hoping to retain their privileges. Once again, and not for the last time, capitalism leaned heavily on religion to protect its position and its property. For example, the banking monopoly did its share to sabotage agrarian reform by refusing credits to businessmen and landowners while claiming to be in favor of both Republicanism and Catholicism. From the moment it came to power, the Republic had to protect itself from both the Right and the Left, and even from the Center.

As the months went by, the new regime's inability to govern became increasingly evident, and this was understandable, so heterogeneous was the National Assembly. On the Right were the Navarrese traditionalists, the Catholic Popular Action party, and the Agrarians, those defenders of property rights, nation, and religion; the Center consisted of Progressivists, headed by Zamora and Maura, Radicals who backed Lerroux, a few Radical Socialists and "Federalists"; on the Left were the Socialists led by Largo Caballero. The Catalonians belonged to none of these factions but were themselves split into two groups: The Liga Regionalista and the Esquerra de Catalunya. The slogan of the Catalonian middle-class minority was simply: *"la caseta y l'hortet"*—"a little house and garden." But Azaña's cabinet, which succeeded Alcalá Zamora's, had more ambitious plans. Influenced by Largo Caballero, the secretary-general of the General Union of Labor, the Spanish C.G.T., it tended more and more toward the Left, but its policies were less effective than those of the General Confederation of Labor, an organization plainly tinged with Communism. The Left was definitely outbidding the other parties, a situation which inevitably led to a Rightist reaction.

There had been no pronunciamento in Spain for a long time, but a pronunciamento against the Republic, which had been in the making for quite a while, exploded like a bombshell in Seville on August 10, 1932. General Sanjurjo was its author. As he paraded on the Calle de las Sierpes, garrisons were revolting in northern and central Spain. The government reacted vigorously and the rebellion was swiftly put down. Sanjurjo fled, was captured on his way to Portugal, and was brought back to Madrid, where he was tried, condemned to death, and subsequently pardoned. A little later, after elections held in several parts of the country had gone against the cabinet, Azaña resigned. Lerroux succeeded him, and was followed by Martínez Barrio, who was firmly resolved to win a majority in the forthcoming national elections. To everyone's surprise, the popular vote was a triumph for the Right, represented by one party, the Confederación Española de Derechas Autónomas, known as the C.E.D.A ,

and inspired by Gil Robles, a pupil of the Jesuits and a Salamancan lawyer. During the campaign, José Antonio Primo
de Rivera, son of the dictator, surrounded by *pistoleros*,
made a spectacular speech in Madrid's Comic Theater. "The
only dialectics are fists and guns!" he exclaimed. Would
Gil Robles be able to stem the rising tide of the Right?

Was a rightist Republic possible or feasible? More surprised than anyone by the victory of the C.E.D.A. (it won
115 seats out of a possible 473), Gil Robles apparently was
doubtful, since he refused to assume power; rather, he tried
for several months to steer the government toward ministries
made up of members of various parties in the hope of achiev-
ing some unity. But neither the Right nor the Left tended
toward conciliation. The unhoped-for opportunity of check-
ing the Spanish crisis by legal and sensible means was seriously impaired, first by Robles's indecisiveness and then by
the stubborn attitude of big business, which hoped to ham-
per the application of the C.E.D.A.'s social program.

Bewildered at first by the rightist victory, the parties of
the Left quickly recovered and began to reorganize. Exploiting the Right's failure to keep its promises, the opposition had no difficulty in winning back an important segment
of the proletariat. Under the red banner of the *Frente popular*, the Left was victorious once again in the February 1936
legislative elections. For the first time it presented a united
front, which embraced the Republican Left (Azaña), the Republican Union (Martínez Barrio), the Catalonian *Esquerra*
(Companys), the Socialists (Caballero and Prieto), the
Communists (Díaz), the P.O.U.M. (the Worker-Peasant
and Left Communist bloc), and a few isolated Catalonian
groups. Neither the Anarchists nor the C.G.T. signed the
pact of alliance, but both supported candidates of the Popular Front. The leftist coalition obtained 4,500,000 votes
against 4,300,000 for the Center and the Right. Three
months later, a Popular Front was victorious in France.

It did not take long for the opposition to react. For some
time the Falange, founded by José Antonio, had been
watchful. Primo de Rivera's son had sworn he would fulfill his father's dream—to revive the Golden Century in

Spain, in imitation of Mussolini, who, at that very moment, was trying to imprint upon modern Italy the stamp of the *Impero romano*. But the hour of Spanish Fascism had not yet struck; it was the Monarchists, led by Calvo Sotelo, who brought to a head the opposition to the regime. Gil Robles, the rightist Republican, was completely overwhelmed and swept aside by the anti-Republican tide. At Cadiz, General Varela, seated on a dais, harangued the people in the streets. No Falangists were present, but their spirit hovered over the forum. From now on there were no more moderates left in Spain: people were either for or against the Republic. The crisis was reduced to its simplest form—either a clenched fist or an outstretched arm. At Yeste, in the province of Murcia, the civil guard fired on the crowd. Churches were converted into arsenals. Two generals, Goded and Franco, whom the government eyed with suspicion, were traveling in Berlin, and José Antonio was attending a Fascist congress at Chamonix. While the Socialists' left wing was increasingly infiltrated by Anarchist elements, the Falange tried, at first without success, to rally to its side old Monarchist groups such as the Spanish Action and the Spanish Renovation. For the moment it merely existed as an ideological movement with very few members—eleven in all, *los once!* It took the Falangists quite a while to rally their forces when Queipo de Llano called them to arms in Seville. He found only two or three members.

Thus ideological positions were dangerously divided and taut. No further compromise was possible; the country's very foundations were shaken. A record for the period from February 16 to June 15, 1936, showed: 161 churches burned, 269 dead, 1,287 wounded, 213 attempted assassinations, 113 general strikes, 228 limited strikes, 146 bomb explosions. Half the population of Spain was affected by the Comintern's propaganda; the other half feverishly eyed Mussolini's Fascism and Hitler's National Socialism. This panicky oscillation between two political extremes marked the beginning of the kind of unrest that was to end in bloodshed. The Cortes declared "a state of emergency." The government, its anxious gaze fixed on the army, expected the worst.

2

Under the Shadow
of Swords

HERE IS NOTHING more effective than the assassination of a political figure to precipitate a major catastrophe. The murder of Archduke Francis Ferdinand and his wife at Sarajevo served the cause of those who desired war in 1914. The die had been cast a long time before. The same was true of the Spanish Civil War. During the night of July 12, 1936, storm troops, presumably eager to avenge the death of their comrade Lieutenant Castillo, who had been killed in the streets, went to the home of the Monarchist leader Calvo Sotelo, deputy from Toledo and "silver-tongued" orator. At dawn his body was found beneath the walls of the Eastern Cemetery. There had been a good many killings prior to this, but now the victim was one whose death could not be ignored. A few days earlier, during a passionate debate in the Cortes, Calvo Sotelo had reminded his listeners of the army's impatience and threatened the Republic. Hardly had he finished his speech when, amid the general hubbub, the dry voice of La Pasionaria could be heard: "That man is speaking for the last time." Calvo Sotelo paid for his recklessness. His funeral provoked such violent demonstrations that the police had to fire on the cortege, killing two people. Three days later, on July 17, legionaries took over post offices, barracks, and airfields in the Moroccan protectorate. The same day, General Franco, Captain-General of the Canary Islands, boarded a plane at Tenerife and landed at Tetuán. Beforehand he had issued a manifesto: "The army has decided to re-establish order in Spain. . . . General Franco has been asked to head the movement and he appeals to the Republican sentiment of all Spaniards who want to work for Spain's recovery." Now he declared war on the Republican government. The authorities at Madrid demanded Franco's surrender, but since he did not deign to answer, they bombarded his headquarters during the night of July 18. On Sunday morning, the nineteenth, a troop transport ship, accompanied by a cruiser, crossed the Strait of Gibraltar, dropped anchor at Algeciras, and fired at the fort, which surrendered. Most of the troops were Moors. They landed and took possession of the city. Twelve centuries earlier Tarik's Berbers had landed along the same shores.

Vae Victis!

Two years before, José Antonio had sent a long letter to Franco in which he detailed his political aspirations and misgivings. In conclusion he alluded to the "inevitable." Now the inevitable occurred. The terrible war which many Spaniards foresaw had begun and there was no reason to believe that it would be brief.

From the very beginning it was possible to foresee the alignment of the various political groups. The Republic could count on four middle-class parties: the Republican Left (Azaña), the Republican Union (Martínez Barrio), the Catalonian Left (Companys), and the Basque Nationalists. In addition, it had on its side the workers' parties: the Socialists (Caballero and Prieto), the Communists (Díaz), the Unified Socialists of Catalonia, the Trotzkyite Communists—the P.O.U.M.—and the Anarchist Federación Anarquista Ibérica, plus the two big trade-union organizations: the U.G.T. (Union General del Trabajo) and the C.N.T. (Confederación Nacional del Trabajo), the former Socialist, the latter Anarchist. Behind Franco were the C.E.D.A. (Gil Robles), or the *Acción Popular* (a Catholic movement), the

Agrarians (Martínez de Velasco), the Spanish Renovation (Calvo Sotelo), the Falange (José Antonio), and the Carlists. The Radical (Lerroux), Conservative (Maura), and Liberal Democratic (Álvarez) parties did not participate in the conflict.

Actually, the position of the various political parties or groups was not as clear-cut as it seemed. There were many nuances. For example, within the Republican camp, the extreme left wing did not make a distinction between war and revolution, while the *Esquerra* and the Basque Nationalists generally assumed that there would be no reform of the government until the war had been won. The Communists denied that in fighting Franco they were pursuing their own political ends. "It is entirely untrue that the purpose of the present movement is to establish a proletarian dictatorship once the war is over. We cannot be accused of having a political motive in intervening in this war. Our sole objective is to defend the democratic Republic." The same discord existed in the rebel camp. Among the generals, one was purely and simply in favor of a dictatorship while the others, the most important men—Sanjurjo, Mola, Varela—favored a return of the monarchy. But who was to be king? Alfonso XIII or Alfonso Carlos? The monarchy, represented by Alfonso XIII, approved of Franco's action; Alfonso's son, Don Juan, joined the navy. The Church was divided, although the bishops on the whole sided with the rebels. The Basque clergy made no attempt to conceal its disapproval—in fact, it acted accordingly. A statement made by Ortega y Gasset fifteen years earlier might well have applied to the rebels: "The colonels and generals of the nineteenth century believed that when they raised their voices in the barracks all Spain would hear them. Their purpose in rebelling was not to fight but to seize power." The Falange was on the alert because it now knew what it wanted and had developed a doctrine. Its ranks grew daily, attracting those who had been undecided, opportunists, and Republicans hostile to the monarchy. Moreover, Fascism was fashionable, but it required a leader. José Antonio, imprisoned by the Loyalists at

Alicante, was shot in November; Calvo Sotelo was no more; General Sanjurjo died on August 2 in an airplane accident as he was flying from Lisbon to Burgos. The way was clear for Franco, who had just entered Burgos. The Junta "of National Defense" proclaimed him "supreme head of the Spanish state," thus solving the problem of leadership. For the first time in the history of Spain, the word "Franquista" was used.

While the Falange—like the Italian Blackshirts and the Nazi Storm Troopers—became the guiding force in the *Movimiento*, the rebellion's principal instrument was the army. Although he lacked numerical superiority, Franco had one important advantage over his adversaries: almost all the military cadres rallied to his side—the cream of the army, the Moroccan regiments, or *regulares*, the Civil Guard, and, above all, the *Tercio*, the Foreign Legion—all well-trained and thoroughly disciplined soldiers. This was all he needed to get the rebellion off to a good, if somewhat slow start with many initial setbacks.

But the navy and most of the air force were on the side of the Loyalists. The Republican army, brave and enthusiastic, was the very antithesis of Franco's. Its generals—Hernández, Sarabia, Asensio, Miaja, Riquelme—were pressed into service in impromptu fashion; they were full of courage, but their subalterns were few and inexperienced. Pointing from the window of his study to barracks recaptured from the Franquistas, Azaña remarked to a foreign visitor: "We seized them with four artillery officers." Franco's army was composed primarily of mercenaries, experienced in the technique of war. Later, they were joined by volunteers and conscripts. The entire northern front was held by *Requetes*, peasants who, like their forebears during the Carlist wars, came from the Navarrese mountains. They were preceded by priests, crosses, blunderbusses, and banners bearing the motto: "For God and for King." The Loyalist army was mainly composed of militiamen. Why? Out of respect for its principles and the Anarchist credo, the government was not willing to order a general mobilization. Many who served as militiamen would have balked at being conscripted. Giral, the new President of the Council, finally called up twelve classes, but they were too small to be of help. However, workers' organizations, despite their distaste for discipline, soon realized that their freedom was at stake. They formed isolated columns of partisans. Armed and trained in great haste, these guerrillas managed to forge an army, for everyone realized the urgent need to fight. In fact, both sides were well aware that this was not a struggle over a mere pronunciamento, nor even a military conflict between the army and the people. Besides, ever since the days of Primo de Rivera, the people had changed and so had their slogans. The Republican army was now a people's army—sailors and petty officers—who had rid themselves of officers and taken their places. The people were no longer a sentimental entity, but a human one, taught to think politically by the trade unions and the parties. The battle was no laughing matter, no musical comedy or farce, but a real civil war. To be sure, there were moments of respite, and entire areas remained free of strife. Certain parts of the country were never bombarded or bombed and there were times when the war seemed less like a battle than the kind of guerrilla warfare Spain had waged against Napoleon. The front was not a continuous line; large segments were not manned. Between Toledo and Seville during the campaigns of 1938, little more than one thousand men guarded the front on either side. Nor was there a lack of colorful incidents, such as the seizure of Seville by General Queipo de Llano, a Republican who joined Franco at the last minute. Thanks to his jovial nature and his knowledge of the Andalusian dialect, he took over the radio station with the help of his ordnance officer and two Civil Guards. A half dozen *Moros* who had just landed from Morocco paraded up and down the Calle de las Sierpes, brandishing their guns and screaming, to give the impression that they were the vanguard of a powerful column. Queipo held Seville by this trick until the arrival of Moroccan reinforcements, who were dropped along the Andalusian coast in groups of twelve. But

such incidents were rare. The Spanish Civil War was neither "phony" nor amusing.

From the very outset, Franco was faced with major strategic problems arising from the nature of the battle area.
Besides Morocco and the Spanish-owned islands, he held
within the peninsula the mountains of Aragon, Navarre, and
Galicia, a part of Old Castile, and the Andalusian coastline
from Algeciras to Huelva. These zones were connected by
Portugal. Consequently, it was necessary to close as quickly
as possible the gap between the north, where General Mola
was in command, and the south, which was in the hands of
Queipo de Llano. Furthermore, Franco had to bring Moroccan reinforcements to Spain, since in the beginning his contingents were weak numerically: five divisions in Saragossa,
Burgos, Seville, Valladolid, and Galicia, and 34,000 men in
Morocco, of whom 9,000 were natives. The first imperative
of any land operation was control of the Strait of Gibraltar.
But the navy, almost all of which had remained faithful to
the government, guarded the coastline vigilantly, and
Franco's air force was not strong enough to transport troops
by air. He bought planes from England, probably with the
help of Juan March, the tobacco king, a friend and very
probably a financial backer of the Falange. An Italian
squadron, commanded by Rossi, patrolled Majorca, and the
authorities at Tangier ordered the Republican squadron to
withdraw from the Strait. Thus, Franco was able to establish
an air bridge between Morocco and Algeciras that was protected by Italian bombers. At Gibraltar, the English closed
their eyes. All this made it possible for Franco to win control
of the Strait.

Free passage through the Strait of Gibraltar for the troops
of the *Caudillo*—the Spanish equivalent of *Duce*, or "leader"
—was of major importance because it enabled him to keep
pouring his Moroccan shock battalions into the struggle.
While no junction was effected between the north and the
south, the south could come to the rescue of the north.
General Yagüe's Moroccan column descended on Seville,

which Queipo de Llano was holding firmly, and entered Estremadura. Frightened, confused, and pursued by both Republicans and Franquistas, part of the population fled to adjacent Portugal, only to be pushed back into Spain. Franquista troops halted before Badajoz; the city fought furiously but was finally forced to yield. Republican losses were heavy; the Franquistas used every and any means to capture the city. Alleging that the inhabitants of Badajoz fought "without wearing uniforms," the Franquistas pursued them into fields and machine-gunned them. No prisoners! Woe betide the losers! Two to three thousand people, men, women, and children, were said to have been slaughtered in this fashion. A neutral Catholic newspaper lashed out in disapproval: "We protest against murder, the burning of churches, and the extermination of religion's servants. But we also protest violently against the atrocities at Badajoz. Murders have been committed there in the name of Jesus Christ and the Holy Virgin." In the name of freedom, as well. While Yagüe was cleaning up Badajoz, Queipo de Llano, with all the zeal of a recent convert, was sustaining the morale of his soldiers by nightly broadcasts. His oratorical style was colorful in its brutality: "Our valiant legionaries and our *regulares* have taught the Reds what it means to be a man. The Reds' women have also learned that our soldiers are real males and not castrated militiamen. Howling and kicking won't save them." Of the Catalonian president, he said: "Companys deserves to be bled like a pig." His verbal violence was not devoid of humor. "I have given orders to shoot three members of the family of every coast-guard sailor who bombarded La Línea. In conclusion, I want to assure my daughter that we are in excellent health and that we hope to hear from her soon." Republican reprisals were also horrible. Unfortunately, violence begets violence!

While the south-north junction was being effected, General Mola seized Irún and San Sebastián, thus isolating the Basque-Asturian region. Meanwhile, Yagüe was marching on Madrid. He seized Oropesa and hurried on to Toledo. Republicans held all of this legendary city except the Alcazar, where Colonel Moscardo's cadets were entrenched. After repeated but futile infantry and artillery attacks on the garrison, the desperate Republicans resorted to blackmail. Luis Moscardo, son of the colonel, was a prisoner. It was arranged for father and son to speak over a telephone. The following dialogue ensued between them:

"Father."

"What's the matter, son?"

"Nothing. They say they're going to shoot me if the Alcazar doesn't surrender, but don't worry."

"If they do so, commend your soul to God; say: 'Long live Spain!' and you will become a hero who died for his country. Farewell, son. All my love."

"Farewell, father. All my love."

To the head of the militiamen who was listening in and who had announced a ten-minute time limit for the surrender of the Alcazar, the colonel said: "The time limit has expired. The Alcazar will not surrender!" A few days later his son Luis was shot. When Moscardo was freed by the Franquista general, he saluted and merely said: "*Sin novedad en el Alcázar, mi general*"—"Nothing new at the Alcazar, General."

The Farce of Non-Intervention

The seizure of Toledo opened the road to Madrid. With lightning speed the Franquistas marched toward the capital. By the end of October it was encircled. On November 6, the government left, loading its archives onto trucks and transferring full powers to the Junta of Defense, over which General Miaja presided. On the following day, legionaries took possession of Carabanchel, on the outskirts of the city. To the astonishment of the Madrileños, Moors, black with dust from the roads and from gunpowder, were seen running after a streetcar at University City. The Franquista command had already made preparations for a triumphal entry into Madrid. Every officer carried instructions in his pocket detailing the manner in which he was to conduct himself. The general staff figured that they would enter in a few hours. Three attacks were launched simultaneously. One, from the west, was stopped at University City, where Miaja was entrenched just as Moscardo had been at the Alcazar. The second attack came from the Jarama Valley and was also halted. Finally, the third, from the direction of Guadalajara, an attack that was motorized and heavily supported by the Italians, was broken up by a furious counterattack. Madrid remained in the hands of the Republicans. What was the reason for the Franquistas' failure? What happened?

First of all, the Republican army, organized by the Communists, no longer fought in small groups each under its own party or Syndicalist flag; it had accepted the idea of training and discipline. Military schools were established, and they turned out officers of various ranks. It was still too early to talk of a unified command, but large-scale co-ordinated operations were now feasible. Moreover, droves of foreign volunteers had arrived to swell the Republican ranks. International Brigades were formed. According to the Republic's statistics, in June 1937 there were 25,000 Frenchmen, 5,000 Poles, 5,000 Americans and Britons, 3,000 Belgians, 1,000 South Americans, 2,000 from the Balkans, and 5,000 Italian and German émigrés. Their leaders were for the most part Communists—Lukas, Tito, Kléber, Beimber—or Socialists —Deutsch, Gallo, and Nenni. One of the most celebrated was a Frenchman, André Marty, vividly described by Ernest Hemingway in *For Whom the Bell Tolls:* "A large man, old and heavy, in an oversized khaki beret, such as *chasseurs à pied* wear in the French Army . . . He recognized his bushy eyebrows, his watery gray eyes, his chin and double chin under it, and he knew him for one of France's great modern revolutionary figures who had led the mutiny of the French Navy in the Black Sea. . . . He did not know what this man had become with time, disappointment, bitterness both domestic and political, and thwarted ambition . . . His face looked as though it were modelled from the waste material you find under the claws of a very old lion."

Besides manpower and leaders, money and arms were needed. Funds were collected in the United States, France, Sweden, Australia, China, and the U.S.S.R. The greatest problem was the lack of arms. Pierre Cot, the French Minister of Aviation, authorized the transfer of one hundred planes—a small enough number—to Republican Spain, while Soviet Russia provided war equipment that was of good quality but somewhat antiquated. Subsequently the U.S.S.R. sent the Spanish Republic pursuit planes and bombers—Moscas, Chatos, and Katiuskas—which were very difficult to ship because the Mediterranean was heavily patrolled by Italian submarines. This was the counterpart of the much more ample help received by Franco from both Germany and Italy. Indeed, Hitler and Mussolini sent him considerable support. Germany contributed technicians and an air force which, while it was not very large, was of superior quality—the Condor Legion. Teams of German fliers took turns practicing dive-bombing on real objectives. Junker planes, considered very much up to date at the time, easily outclassed the Republic's ancient Bréquets. On the seas the *Deutschland* engaged the *Libertad* in battle at Ibiza to insure safe passage for the German ship *Kamerun*, which was loaded with war matériel for the Franquistas. This naval engagement was followed by the bombardment of Almería by the *Graf Spee*. The reason for the presence of German specialists in the Catalonian campaign became clear a few months later: it was marvelous preparation for their *Blitzkrieg* in Poland and France! Italy's intervention was both more extensive and less disguised. Active in the Balearic Islands, at Guadalajara and Tortosa, the Italian contingents also patrolled the approaches to the Strait, bombarded Barcelona, and machine-gunned Santander. Reinforced by Spaniards, they were spread over almost the entire theater of operations. Although statistics published by both Republicans and Franquistas on the number of foreigners fighting on Franco's side must be taken with a grain of salt, it is well to cite them: several thousand Germans, composed largely of teams of pilots who spelled one another every month; a few

thousand Italians, who received half their pay from Franco
and the other half from Mussolini, and whose divisions, the
Littorio, the Black Arrow and the Blue Arrow, were commanded by Generals Gambara and Bergonzoli; one thousand Irishmen; and one Portuguese *Legião*, primarily of
symbolic value. According to reasonable estimates, the foreigners did not exceed 50,000. However, the Italian government also provided considerable military equipment: 2,000
cannons, 10,000 automatic weapons, 200,000 guns, in addition to a far from negligible number of tractors and various
types of other vehicles.

"The Spanish Civil War was a blood-stained bull fight:
the arena was the peninsula, but a good many of the toreadors were foreigners." This statement by Martín Blasquez is
a clear summation of the situation. Spain had become a training ground on which European armies were limbering up for
the impending conflict. Rarely in military history had bel-
ligerents had an opportunity to engage in such an ideal dress
rehearsal. But the powers that intervened soon realized the
game was growing dangerous. Italo-German and Franco-
Russian confrontation on foreign soil might develop into an
international war. It was not yet time. For the moment it was
preferable to maintain the European status quo. At the instigation of the French, a Non-Intervention Committee was set
up in London. It comprised the French, of course, the
U.S.S.R., Germany, Italy, and a few secondary powers. At
this point the United States declared an embargo on arms
for Spain. However, Rome and Berlin, having officially recognized Franco's government, noisily withdrew from the
Committee after the *Libertad* attacked the *Deutschland*.
While legal minds gravely discussed non-intervention proce-
dures in London and Geneva—for the League of Nations
was also drawn into it—foreign volunteers and equipment
continued to pour into Spain. And while Count Grandi
haughtily announced that his country would not withdraw a
single volunteer from Spain, while Germany loudly demanded reparations for the damage done to the *Deutschland*,
while the U.S.S.R. called for the withdrawal of all foreign

elements—including the Moroccans!—"control ships" symbolically cruised the Mediterranean. The flag they flew—white with two black balls—typified the farce of nonintervention.

Actually, the powers involved in the Spanish Civil War were not merely seeking to perfect their war machines or to learn strategic lessons that would be of value for the future; the conflict in Spain was also a struggle of ideologies. Some of these powers were divided internally on the Spanish question. While it is true that the German and Italian peoples were almost unanimous in their desire to see Franco win, and the U.S.S.R. ardently hoped for Republican victory, the French government, although officially neutral, had not convinced public opinion. The right wing was for Franco. Jacques Maritain and François Mauriac were for the Republic and said so openly. These differences, or rather these divergent principles, were reflected in political circles. Thus, Édouard Herriot urged Léon Blum not to authorize the dispatch of planes, armaments, and oil to the Spanish Republicans. The Socialist premier allowed himself to be persuaded, but, wringing his hands, he exclaimed: "My soul is torn in two!"

Despite the triple attacks of the Franquistas, Madrid did not fall. Franco withdrew from the capital for the time being and bore down on the Basque-Asturian area. A little earlier, important changes had been made in both the Republican and Franquista governments. Largo Caballero succeeded Giral and became supreme chief of the army; Franco established a "single party," composed of Carlists, Monarchists, *Requetes*, Spanish Traditionalist Falangists (the F.E.T., founded by José Antonio), and the Juntas of Syndicalist Nationalist Defense (J.O.N.S.). The *Movimiento* had become unified. Its symbol was the Catholic Kings' coat-of-arms—St. John's eagle, the yoke, and the bundle of arrows. A few months later, named head of the state, Franco established his headquarters in Salamanca, but the government junta remained in Burgos.

Ever since the battles at Irún and San Sebastián, quiet

had reigned in the Basque country. Would it be spared civil war? Alas! On April 16, 1937, a market day, Guernica was black with people. The crowd was lighthearted, for in the evening there would be dancing around the sacred oak tree which for centuries had sheltered the deliberations of representatives of the ancient Euskarians. Six months earlier, the Basque Republic had been proclaimed beneath this legendary tree. It was 4:40 P.M. Suddenly the sky grew dark and a tremendous explosion shook the houses, shattering window panes. Flying in tight formation, planes swooped down on the town, fired machine-gun blasts, then dropped explosives and incendiary bombs. Fires broke out and gradually engulfed the entire city. One could glimpse, through the veil of flames and smoke, women clutching their children to their breasts and praying. People tried to flee to the mountains or to the woods, but they were pursued by planes. The bombing lasted until 7:45—about three hours.

Two months later it was the turn of Bilbao, besieged by General Mola's army, to fall into the hands of Franquista troops. The indomitable city, which thrice during the preceding century had resisted the Carlist troops, succumbed in spite of its reputedly indestructible fortifications. The men who had built these ramparts went over to the Franquista camp with the plans in their pockets. Mola, the hero of the north, did not witness the fall of Bilbao, for he had been killed in an airplane accident prior to the siege. The Italian Black Arrows were among the first troops to enter the city. Bread was distributed to the starving population. Meanwhile, the Republican troops retreated to Santander, which they were also forced to abandon. Diversions were attempted in order to delay the Franquista advance. At Brunete, on the outskirts of Madrid, they were able to pierce the front after three days of fierce fighting, but they could not advance any further. In Aragon they seized Belchete, near Saragossa, but were unable to gain access to the city itself. Despite the furious resistance of the miners, Asturias was conquered by Franquista troops. Republican Spain now controlled only fifteen provinces out of fifty, and eleven million inhabitants out of twenty-five. Besides his fighting forces, Franco had at his disposal an unused army of 70,000 men, which he held in reserve for a massive attack on Barcelona. Hopelessly beaten in the north, the Republicans would not admit defeat. Nor were they defeated.

At the end of 1937 they recovered. The government moved to Barcelona in order to push war production in Catalonia and to gain control of the workers, who were leaning toward anarchism. Prieto was now Minister of War. He wanted very much to win an important engagement, no matter what the cost, in order to raise the soldiers' morale and restore an approximate balance of military strength, which might lead, if not to a compromise peace, at least to an armistice.

On December 14, the Republican army attacked Teruel in a supreme effort to pierce the important southeastern flank of the Franquista line. For two weeks Franco's soldiers resisted repeated assaults, only to surrender in the end. This coincided with the failure of Franco's big offensive to isolate Catalonia and cut off Madrid from the sea. Encouraged by their success, the Republicans swept on toward Saragossa, their final objective. Unfortunately their ammunition was running low and they had been tramping about in the snow in espadrilles, completely exhausted. A furious counterattack led by General Aranda proved decisive. Once again the Franquistas took the offensive; their leaders were General Varela, who had served in Morocco, and General Vigón, former tutor of Alfonso XIII's son, who, until the outbreak of the war, had been living in retirement in Argentina. After seventy days of continuous fighting against a rejuvenated enemy, the Republicans had to abandon Teruel. Very little was left of the city. The Loyalists had placed dynamite in the grottoes that lay under the city, and when Teruel exploded, thousands of innocent people were buried under the ruins—a tragedy not unlike Guernica. From now on the Franquistas could look toward the sea. In April 1938, Catalonia was cut off from Valencia at the delta of the Ebro, and Republican-held territory was split in two. Franco's troops marched on Valencia, passing through Castellón de la Plana. At the gates of Valencia they encountered a fortified line, powerfully defended by Loyalists under the command of Generals Sarabia and Meléndez. Would fortune smile on the Republicans? Risking their all, the Loyalists executed a bold plan conceived by General Rojo, chief of the general staff. On July 24, Republican troops crossed the Ebro and took the Franquistas by surprise. They advanced to Gandesa but could go no further. The battle of the Ebro, one of the most fearful of the war, lasted four months. Military historians have likened it to the engagements of World War I. Although certain military operations of the Spanish Civil War foreshadowed the fighting that was to occur two years later, the battle of the Ebro, on the contrary, was reminiscent of the Marne and Verdun. Huddled in trenches, soldiers would leap out to engage in fierce hand-to-hand combat. Artillery and air support was virtually nonexistent. Both sides lacked equipment, fought in the mud, and displayed superhuman courage, but bad news affected the morale of the Loyalists. Negrín, who succeeded Largo Caballero, had told the League of Nations he would agree to the withdrawal of the International Brigade. Furthermore, exactly one week later, the Nazis won a diplomatic victory—the Munich agreement—an indication that democracy was not strong enough to withstand the Hitler-Mussolini combination. A great gust of fear blew over Europe, its bitter breath contaminating the Valencian *huerta*. Inch by inch, the Republicans were pushed back to the Ebro. On November 15 they retreated across the river, leaving 10,000 dead behind. The way through Catalonia was now clear.

On Christmas Eve the Franquistas attacked first in the mountains near the Segre, and then along the Ebro. Employing new tactics—assaults with motorized units and the encirclement of "pockets"—they reached the last defense of Barcelona within ten days. The Republicans had to fight off simultaneous attacks, one from the north by the troops of Moscardo (he was now a general), the other from the south by General Yagüe's soldiers. They fell back after a supreme but futile effort to hold the line at Igualada and Vendrell. On January 26, the Franquistas and their allies entered Barcelona. While Negrín conferred with a rump Cortes at Figueras, Azaña and Companys crossed the frontier at La Junquera. Republican troops, followed by refugees, crossed the Pyrenees. On the opposite side the French police kept the pitiful procession moving—almost 400,000 soldiers and civilians. Negrín and his government managed to reach Valencia, where fighting still raged. On February 27, by a vote of 323 to 261, the French Chamber of Deputies decided to recognize Franco. England and most of the other countries followed suit. Only Soviet Russia and Mexico refused. Yet many Spanish exiles found a warm, fraternal welcome in France while they waited to become naturalized citizens, a step their children were never to regret. These sons of Spain, born on the banks of the Garonne or in some village near the Ariège, became excellent Frenchmen—possibly because of the dynastic marriages of an earlier day—while retaining their native traits.

What was happening in Madrid? Azaña resigned and went to France. A Junta of National Defense, headed by Colonel Casado, who was prepared to negotiate with Franco and surrender to the symbol of anti-Communism, replaced Negrín, considered an extremist. Determined to resist to the very end, Negrín rallied all the remaining Communists and Anarchists for a last stand at Valencia. While "Negrínists" and partisans of the Junta fought each other in the streets of Valencia, Madrid, and Cartagena, negotiations began and failed. By dawn on March 30, all of Spain except Alicante was in Franco's hands. During the evening of this last day of battle, an Italian division, the Littorio, landed at Alicante under a gentle drizzle. With the exception of a few hide-outs in the Pyrenees, Asturias, and Andalusia, Spain had been "recaptured" by the army of the *Movimiento*. On April 1, 1939, after 986 days of relentless warfare, the victorious general issued his last communiqúe: "Today the Red Army has been captured and disarmed. The National troops have accomplished their final objectives. The war is over—

Burgos, April 1, 1939, the year of Victory—Generalissimo Franco."

The war was over, but at what a price! One million two hundred thousand dead—almost as many as the French losses of World War I. Four hundred and fifty thousand of these were soldiers—150,000 Franquistas and twice as many Republicans; 750,000 were civilians. On both sides cruelty reigned. How many crimes were committed in the name of religion, how many assassinations perpetrated for the Republican cause! Here are a few examples: at Ávila, Civil Guards who had sought refuge in the *Ayuntamiento* were forced to emerge one by one. The Republicans clubbed them, then pushed them over the edge of the plateau into the valley below. Those who did not move fast enough were beaten to death. In November 1936 several thousand Madrileños were assassinated at Paracuellos del Jarama. At Saragossa, Franco's firing squad crackled lugubriously. To recall these horrors, to compare the Red Terror with the White, to attempt to exonerate some or point an accusing finger at others, to assess the amount of blood shed or the number of bullets fired—such is not the task of a historian. Rather, distressed by the spectacle of Spain's martyrdom, noting the names of its heroes, whether of the Left or the Right, he can but hope that one day the cadets of the Alcazar and the defenders of University City will be posthumously reconciled because of their equal love for their country. Macabre incidents neither add nor detract from the individual worth of each soldier, nor do they help to clarify the "Goyaesque" features of the Spanish Civil War.

Over and above the fray, two raging archangels stand out: José Antonio, shot in the prison of Alicante on November 20, 1936, whose body, "as handsome and harmonious as the Spain he loved," lies buried in the Escorial beside the remains of Charles V and Philip II; and Federico García Lorca, assassinated on August 19, 1936, at Viznar, near the Alhambra. If ever two Spaniards epitomized two ideologies, they were these—one the son of Primo de Rivera, the other the poet of Andalusia. Harking back to ancestral themes,

José Antonio wanted a traditionalist, unitary, imperial Spain. With the help of the Church and the army, he hoped to see his country recover the position it had lost. The sword and the cross. . . . His ideal was both militant and mystical. García Lorca belonged to no political party; not a militia-man, he wore no uniform. He, too, hoped for a revival of Spanish grandeur, but he did not differentiate between his country and the masses. It was the peasant, the worker, not the hidalgo, and even less the banker, who was to forge the future of Spain. Lacking a precise political program, García Lorca contributed two profound sentiments to the Revolu-tion: love for the Spanish people—whom he knew well—and love for his own small region of Granada, which was fused in his heart with all of Spain. "Oh, city of gypsies! Who has not seen thee and cherished thee? Let people seek thee on my brow—tricks of moonlight, play of sand."

The Solitary Man of the Pardo

In the annals of nations as well as in men's memories, the dead are soon forgotten. While José Antonio and García Lorca gradually became legendary, each in his special way, a very real figure emerges from the cold light of reality— that of Generalissimo Franco, head of the Spanish state. He was born on the shores of the Atlantic, at Ferrol, in Galicia. His father was a naval officer and all his ancestors had mari-time careers. He himself was about to enter the Naval Acad-emy when he learned that competitive examinations had been abolished. And so he went to the Alcazar in Toledo. Upon graduation from the military academy he was sent to Mo-rocco. There he organized the Spanish Foreign Legion, the *Tercio*, and won his stripes. Promoted to Brigadier-General at the age of thirty-four—for a long time he was known as "the youngest general in the world"—he brought to his study of North African problems exceptional intelligence as well as endless diligence. Moreover, as a soldier he dis-played exemplary courage, and his exploits against Abd-el-

Krim won him fame. He owed his rapid promotion solely to his accomplishments and his brilliance as a leader of troops. Not a single political recommendation blemishes his military record. When the monarchy fell in 1931, he quite properly supported the Republic, but without enthusiasm. Like so many career officers, who have a rigid concept of duty and pride themselves on their readiness to serve whatever government happens to be in power, Franco did not become involved in politics. However, when Gil Robles appointed him Chief of the General Staff, he began to think about the future of Spain. He followed developments closely until the Popular Front, which viewed him with distrust, exiled him to the Canary Islands.

Franco is short, stocky, slightly potbellied, always well groomed. His round head set firmly on a thick neck is bald, except for a fringe of black hair. He has an aquiline nose, long, almond-shaped eyes whose expression is very dark and soft, almost sad, and a pepper-and-salt mustache. A smile appears fleetingly, rarely. He is in excellent health, leads a well-ordered, sedentary life, eats little, neither smokes nor drinks. What little leisure he has he spends walking, hunting, fishing on the high seas, and at his favorite pastime—painting. In short, as a personality, he is healthy and well balanced.

As a politician he is more complex. A fervent Catholic, he is quite certain that one of his missions is to make Spain a great Christian country. His chaplain never leaves his side. During moments of crisis, Franco spends much time praying in his private chapel. He thinks of himself as a man of destiny, and perhaps he is right, for he survived those who could have claimed power: José Antonio, Sanjurjo, Mola. He feels closely identified with a Spain steeped in blood and tears. This is hardly surprising: he himself fashioned it according to his own concepts; for better or worse, he is its leader. In any event, of all the heads of state in the mid-twentieth century, he is at once one of the most hated, discussed, and admired. He is also a figure who can be assessed only when enough time has elapsed to give us a proper perspective. It is still too early to form a definite judgment of his rule. However, it is only fair to credit him with having spared his country the ordeal of World War II. Such a trial, coming in the wake of the Civil War, could have meant the end of Spain. But the debits are considerable. Therefore, although the man himself is morally irreproachable, it is uncertain how the future will judge him as a military leader and statesman. ¿Quién sabe? Perhaps history, which is the final arbiter, will rectify the harsh opinion of certain comtemporaries. Cloistered in his Pardo Palace, Franco seems as indifferent to praise as he is to criticism. He has chosen silence and solitude. He emerges from isolation only to make shattering proclamations; some are so courageous they command respect—for example, those in which, like David confronting Goliath, he defies the Soviet colossus. Is it true that he is "as popular as a bull fighter" or that many secretly wish he were dead? This, too, probably leaves him indifferent. He demands obedience, not affection. He distrusts people, even his own ministers, whom on occasion he dismisses suddenly, when they least expect it. In a few minutes they are through. One evening in February 1957, Martín Artajo, who had served as Foreign Minister for eleven years, was informed by telephone of his dismissal. Serrano Suñer, his brother-in-law, was relieved of an important post within the space of a single day. What is this calm, vigorous man like who, in spite of everything, continues to be responsible for the fate of Spain? A militant monk or a Machiavelli? Perhaps merely a Galician, with all the characteristics of his native land—energy, sobriety, and dogged persistence. Viewing his country with the nostalgic spleen of an exile, he also looks upon it as a family fishing establishment which he operates with the shrewdness of a Ferrolese sailor.

"Not a Dictatorship, But a Hierarchy"

On May 20, 1939, the victorious army paraded in the streets of Madrid; by October 18, Franco's government was installed in the capital. How, according to what precepts, did the generalissimo intend to rule? As soon as he seized power, Franco made plain his plan to pattern his regime on the Fascist model. At the same time he proposed to adapt the principles of Hitler and Mussolini to the special needs of Spain. Interviewed in July 1937 by a United Press correspondent, Franco declared: "Spain will utilize corporate formulas and shun liberal institutions, which have corrupted the people. It will respect the law, develop a respect for the state, promote social justice, and protect the bourgeoisie and the working class. In short, it will draw its inspiration from the German-Italian experience, but will adapt it to our national characteristics." Twenty years later, in response to questions on the same subject from a reporter for *Le Figaro*, Franco stated: "Our present regime is founded exclusively on Spanish history, traditions, institutions—on the Spanish soul. These had been ignored or polluted by liberalism. Neglect of Spain's spiritual needs throughout the nineteenth century and well into our own cost us our empire and led to a disastrous decline. While other world powers were able to marshal their strength, we sank into a hundred-year sleep." The interval between these two interviews was used to create a political structure for the new Spanish state. Franco has thus described the Constitution of July 18, 1942: "Spain is not a dictatorship, but a hierarchy." The hierarchy is embodied in the Cortes, a consultative body composed of *procuradores* named by the government or elected by the various cultural and economic corporations. Franco claims that national decisions originate not at the top of the pyramid, but at its base, since the people's wishes are expressed through families, municipalities, trade unions, and professional associations. At various times Franco has insisted that his government is not a dictatorship, for under the Spanish constitution he has fewer prerogatives than does the President of the United States. But his attitude toward democratic institutions has never changed; no words are harsh enough to characterize political systems based on parliamentary assemblies or the interplay of political parties. "Petrified democracies," he contemptuously calls them. Thus he rejects anything remotely resembling a liberal republic. From the very outset, he has leaned heavily on three powerful organisms—the Falange, the Church, and the army.

The Falange sets the tone for the new regime. It is the originator and disseminator of the slogans: "For the Empire which looks to God!" "No home without bread, no Spaniard without light." "One must speak not of rights but of duties." The Falangist hymn, "Cara al Sol," the "Oriamendi," a song of the *Requetes*, and the Royal March are national anthems of the new Spain. Numerous Falangist subsidiary organizations reach every social category: the Flechas y Pelayas for children, the Youth Front for young people, the Feminine Section for women, the Social Mutual Aid for the charitably inclined, the Spanish University Syndicate for students, the Section for Education and Relaxation for the leisure classes, Workers' Fraternities for peasants, and Vertical Syndicates, called the Central National Syndicate when combined, for employers and employees. The Falangist doctrine can be summed up in the three words that appear on the new Spanish coat-of-arms: "United, Great, Free." The word "united" signifies condemnation of localism. With the Catalonians and Basques primarily in mind, the Falange has stated: "Separatism is a crime we will not condone." "Great" means fidelity to historical tradition, while "Free," of course, refers to liberty within the framework of the new order. But the Falange's arrogance has softened with the passage of time. Its imperatives have been reduced to mere propaganda themes. Although it trumpets the same old slogans, the Falange has gradually assumed a "leftist" tinge, thus foreshadowing a less intransigent attitude. Not the least of Franco's concerns has been to curb this turbulent, at times troublesome, band which raised him to his present eminence.

Since the Nationalist army won the war, it is naturally a great favorite of the regime. All important posts—in the national administration, with the police force, in local government—have been held by the military or by service-connected individuals among the Falangists. Most of the young people served in the army during World War II, when the Spanish frontiers were in a constant state of alert. The army comprised not only regular troops and conscripts but also innumerable auxiliary organizations. The majority of the population, including ministers, were in uniform from the end of the Civil War to the end of World War II. Many young men, bewildered, without jobs, or orphaned, were naturally drawn to a military career that offered both prestige and security. Peasants left their plowshares and workers their factories to join the army. Moreover, never before has the army been so submissive or so unified. It no longer needs to fear a pronunciamento, and there is no safety anywhere except with Franco.

A privileged institution, closely linked to authority—the cardinal-bishop has a seat on the council of the kingdom— the Church occupied a pre-eminent position in the Spanish state. Thanks to a clever concordat, it was sure of preferential treatment by the pontiff; and it also controlled education and morals. At no time since the Golden Century has the Church, so often victimized by revolution, encountered a more congenial political system. A return to Hispano-Christian traditions, to a heroic regime and a mystical ideal —this represented unbelievably good luck after two centuries of trials and vicissitudes. Franco's promise—"Spain will be the empire that looks to God"—was an explicit assurance that the Church would resume all its authority. What a temptation for an institution that had once sat on the king's right! For its own sake we can but hope that in accepting the generalissimo's embrace, it will not forget the persecutions suffered by the clergy and the Basques for espousing the Republican cause. The bombing of Guernica —the Basques' holy city—should give it pause. In the light of such an experience, it would do well to keep its vision clear. Exclusive reliance on Franco's regime could prove imprudent. Can it hope to retain the privileges it enjoys today? Should it fail to deserve them, fortune might turn against it. The spiritual strength which the Spanish Church has represented throughout the centuries must be its sole pillar. It must depend only on its own virtues and values, for the cause of Christ is irretrievably lost whenever social injustice dons the mantle of the clergy.

"An Edifice of Crosses and Swords"

In the course of his rule, Franco has attempted little by little to improve his system, to make it less rigid in certain respects. On July 14, 1945, the Cortes approved a "Charter for Spaniards," which defined the rights and duties of the nation. On October 27, a law was promulgated providing for a referendum in the event of a national emergency. Three days later, the press was ordered to cease referring to Franco as the *Caudillo*. Hereafter he was to be called "Chief of State." Gradually the Falangists were deprived of some of their functions. In the very same year, facing up to the dynastic problem for the first time, Franco announced that he favored the restoration of the monarchy, the only regime likely to succeed his own. However, he did not say when this was to occur. Finally, on March 31, 1947, he issued a manifesto which declared Spain a Catholic and unified country and described it as a kingdom, over which he presided. As Chief of State he was to be assisted by a council of the kingdom composed mainly of the president of the Cortes, the cardinal-bishop of Spain, and the head of the general staff. Should the Chief of State die or become incapacitated, the council of the kingdom and the government were together to summon the most qualified individual of royal blood to head the regime. This would have to be approved by two thirds of the Cortes. Should no such individual be available, the choice was to fall on whoever was most suitable from the standpoint of prestige and ability. However, he too would eventually have to receive the nation's endorsement. The manifesto was submitted to a popular referendum. On July 6, 1947, it was approved by 87 per cent of the voters.

"A Catholic state." There was nothing equivocal about this. Franco intended to show the world that his system was essentially Catholic. Accordingly, under the sign of the cross, the *Movimiento* was broadened and transformed. It is necessary to see this in order to understand the Franco's ideology. Catholicism not only was made the official religion of the state; it permeated the nation's modes of expression. Christian Spain was neither a myth nor a legendary kingdom, but a living and present reality. In their religious sentiments, many present-day Spaniards still maintain a close relationship with the spirit of the Crusades. They are quite convinced that they have been chosen by God to safeguard *the* truth, or at least that form of truth which alone seems valid. Convinced that no moral or material progress can be achieved without religion, they vehemently deplore today's emphasis on the individual. They also denounce those organizations in modern society that tend to reduce the human being to purely mechanical functions, to degrade the "human person," as the Society of Jesus used the phrase.

An article in the Spanish periodical *Ecclesia* indignantly related incidents that precipitated a quarrel between Catholic and non-Catholic students at the University of Mexico. The director of the university settled the argument by saying: "Here we teach the phenomena of life and nature strictly in the light of Science." The author of the article added: "In other words, without God." The very opposite occurs in Spain. In all educational centers, "whether or not they are operated by the state, and regardless of their nature or intellectual level," religious instruction is obligatory, save for non-Catholics, who constitute an infinitesimal minority. The professors are carefully supervised by the ecclesiastical authorities. The Church also censors public performances, publications, and radio and television broadcasts, and "appropriate time is reserved for the exposition and defense of religious truth." Public opinion is entirely permeated with Catholicism.

In one of a series of speeches he gave at Santiago de Compostela, Franco warmly urged Spanish families to devote time to religious practices: prayer, acts of grace, good works which might lead to a priestly vocation. Moreover,

immediately after the Civil War, Franco showed a special
concern for the plight of the clergy, which had been decimated by the conflict. He had a twofold objective: to increase
the number of priests and to raise their intellectual level.
Modern seminaries were built which combined the functional
with the pleasurable, thus satisfying the requirements of
religion amid comfortable living quarters—individual
rooms, gardens, parks. There are two categories of seminaries, one for younger students aiming at the bachelor's
degree, the other for graduate students seeking an advanced
degree. In addition to subsidies for these schools, the state
pays a large part of the professors' salaries. The government's efforts to recruit candidates for the priesthood have
proved successful. The number of priests increased 160 per
cent—from 7,000 in 1934 to 18,000 in 1952. Yet there are
still not enough. The population has increased; so have the
needs of the flourishing Spanish missions in Latin America.

The mistress of culture, Catholicism has also dominated
the concept of war. The word "crusade" appears frequently
in Franco's speeches, and if he shows a special attachment to
St. James of Compostela, it is because of gratitude for his
protection during the Civil War. Was it not St. James who
turned away a ship carrying arms to the "Reds"? The God
of Thought, the God of Battles, the God of the Spanish
State, was he not also the God of the People? It is important
to emphasize in this connection the social work the Spanish
Church has accomplished, often on the basis of personal initiative. Making the most of every available means—the Social Weeks, the Confederation of Catholic Propagandists,
and, above all, the powerful Catholic Action—the Church
has attempted to reach the people. To this end, it founded a
"Social Sacerdotal School" in Málaga whose purpose it is to
train peasants for the priesthood. The curriculum of these
future rural clerics includes modern languages, sociology,
and political economy as well as religion. Every social doctrine is explored and discussed, mainly Marxism and Communism. Spain also has its working-class priests, who are
under the aegis of the *Hermandad del Cristo Trabajador*.

Franco's religious policies were amply rewarded. The concordat signed on August 27, 1953, between Spain and the Holy See constituted not a mere resumption of diplomatic relations, but rather a "juridical systematization of an almost ideal relationship of Church and State, both considered perfect societies." The concordat recapitulated, clarified, and perfected all the measures favorable to the Church which Franco had enacted and which gave the clergy a dominant position in traditionally Catholic Spain. It regulated the relations of Church and State in regard to such matters as education, law, and finance; it transformed Catholic Action into an apostolic organization for laymen and gave the Church full responsibility for the preservation of Spain's artistic heritage. Furthermore, it established Catholicism as the official religion of the state and entitled the Church to generous monetary aid from the government. In fact, the state acknowledged the right of the Church to acquire, retain, and enhance its properties, most of which were not subject to taxation. Moreover, the concordat stipulated that the state would "subsidize all dioceses that it might establish in the future" and would share the expense of building or restoring churches, episcopal palaces, ecclesiastical offices, and diocesan seminaries. The concordat fixed the status of matrimony in Spain and restored the country's privileges in regard to Santa María Mayor. Finally, it designated Spanish as one of the three languages acceptable to the Holy Congregation of Rites for purposes of beatification and canonization.

Thus, Spain has become officially and avowedly Catholic. What is her attitude toward non-Catholics and toward the so-called "free world," a phrase signifying either democratic or Communist regimes? Non-Catholics constitute a small minority: 20,000 Protestants, half of whom are foreigners, 7,500 Sephardic Jews, and a handful of Moslems. In spite of its ideological affinities with Fascist states which were doctrinally anti-Semitic, Spain has never showed hostility toward the Jews. Quite the contrary. During the years of persecution the Jews were helped and protected by Franco's

government and by its representatives both in and outside
the country wherever Sephardic colonies of very ancient
Spanish stock existed. Spain's attitude toward them was
more than tolerant; it was charitable. When Israel's delegate
to the United Nations voted against admitting Spain, arguing that the country was the last representative of a regime
responsible for pogroms, the Spanish government countered
with a report stressing how often it had interceded with the
Nazi authorities in order to save thousands of Spanish Jews
from extinction. At all events, Jews were entirely free to
worship in their own synagogues, and the Center for Hebraic
Studies received special assistance from the government.

Acceptance of Protestants by the Spanish state has been
very gradual. For a long time they were looked upon as "false
brothers." In 1947, as a consequence of propaganda spread
by certain Protestant elements against worship of the Virgin, three Protestant churches, in Madrid, Barcelona, and
Granollers, were sacked and burned by groups of Catholic
youths. Since then the Protestants have lived in peace and
attended services without fear. There are 210 Protestant
churches in all of Spain, half of which belong to the Church
of England. Of the 117 ministers, one third are foreigners.
However, proselytizing is forbidden. Franco has made this
crystal clear: "Tolerance in regard to beliefs and various
forms of worship does not mean freedom to propagandize,
which would only engender religious discord. . . . We will
give dissidents an opportunity to practice their faith, but we
will not allow them to proselytize, which would outrage
everyone."

Thus, intolerance within the framework of tolerance is a
specific characteristic of the Franco regime. The "free
world" was taken by surprise, finding itself in the position of
being reproached by Franco for the very thing it accused
him of—suppression of freedom. If, in examining the Marx-
ist ideology, one compares it with "Francoism," one arrives
at an identical definition for both: in each, total freedom
exists only insofar as it is exercised within the authoritarian
structure. Paradox? Ingenuity? Political humbug? Can any-

one except Spaniards read Article VI of the *Fuero de los Españoles* without smiling? "Nobody will be persecuted for his religious beliefs or for worshipping according to his faith. No ceremonies or other external manifestations will be permitted save those of the Catholic religion." In philosophical parlance, such a statement would be called a contradictory proposition.

An Evolutionary Policy

In remarks collected by Martin Bormann, Adolf Hitler had this to say about Spain: "I have sometimes wondered if we did not make a mistake in 1940 when we failed to drag Spain into the war. It would have taken very little to get her in, for she was really anxious, after the entry of the Italians, to join the winning side. Evidently Franco thought his intervention was worth a high price. Nevertheless, I believe that in spite of all the systematic sabotage by his Jesuitical brother-in-law, he would have agreed to go along with us on reasonable terms: the promise of a small strip of France to satisfy his pride and a substantial bit of Algeria for its material advantages. But since Spain could not contribute anything tangible to us, I felt that her direct intervention in the conflict was not desirable. To be sure, it would have enabled us to occupy Gibraltar. On the other hand, we would then have had to defend miles and miles of the Atlantic coast, from San Sebastián to Cadiz; and we would have risked the additional danger of reviving the Civil War, which the English would have encouraged. Thus we would have been tied for better or worse to a regime that I like less and less, a regime of capitalist profiteers, maneuvered by priests. I cannot forgive Franco for failing, once the Civil War was over, to make peace among his countrymen, for shoving aside the Falangists, whom Spain can thank for the help we gave her, and for treating former enemies, not all of whom were Reds —far from it—as thieves. . . . In short, Spain did us the greatest possible favor during the war by behaving in such a way that the Iberian Peninsula remained out of it."

Franco's observations on the same subject strike quite a different note. According to him, in his interview with Hitler at Hendaye on October 23, 1940, he declined the Führer's invitation to join the war, pointing out, among other things, that England had not yet lost, that it had the advantage of enormous support from America, and that, in any event, Spain wanted peace more than anything else. "He greeted me warmly, but his farewell was frigid," the Spanish Chief of State later reported. Four months after that, on February 12, 1941, Franco met Mussolini at Bordighera. Their conversation was apparently far more frank and cordial owing to the much closer affinity between the two men. Toward the end of their talk, Franco asked: "If you could get out of this war, would you do so?" And Mussolini reportedly answered, throwing his arms in the air: *"Claro que si, hombre, claro que si!"* On his way back from Bordighera, Franco stopped at Montpellier to see Marshal Pétain. Amenities were exchanged, but nothing more.

What Franco, Hitler, Mussolini, and Pétain said to one another in private, man-to-man talks without witnesses is of purely anecdotal interest, as are all *a posteriori* confessions. Actually, Franco's policy toward the Great Powers was, according to his own definition, "evolutionary." Caught between sympathy for Italy and Germany—the Berlin-Rome Axis—and a desire to save his country from foreign occupation or war, the Spanish Chief of State shaped his attitude according to the fortunes of the war; Spaniards could scarcely blame him for this, but what about others?

On September 3, 1939, France and England declared war on Germany. Marshal Pétain, whom Franco had known in Morocco in 1925, was the French ambassador in Madrid. Spain announced its strict neutrality. On June 10, 1940, Italy intervened on Germany's side and France was defeated. Pétain, who had become Chief of State, requested and obtained an armistice. His intermediaries in the negotiations

with Germany and Italy were Lequérica, the Spanish ambassador to France, and the nuncio. In spite of repeated appeals from Berlin and Rome, with whom he maintained
friendly relations, Franco managed to remain neutral. To be
sure, he applauded the victories of the Axis, told Mussolini
he would move from "vigilant neutrality" to "active non-
belligerency," and closed his eyes to the ceaseless anti-
British propaganda of the Falange. But he did resist mounting pressure from the Italians and the Germans. Although he
occupied the international zone of Tangier, incorporating it
into Spanish Morocco, he postponed from day to day military
operations against Gibraltar, which Hitler was urging. German troops were ordered into the Iberian Peninsula on January 10, 1941, but Franco persuaded the Führer to defer
the "Spanish operation." However, shortly after Soviet Russia entered the war against Germany in June 1941, Franco
felt it wise to make a token gesture to the Axis. He sent the
Azul Division, commanded by General Muñoz Grande, to
fight the "Bolsheviks," and at the same time affixed his signature to the anti-Comintern pact. From Germany, the volunteers of the Azul Division were dispatched to the Russian
front under the German flag and equipped with weapons.
They fought courageously at Lake Ilmen, Novgorod, and
Leningrad. In 1944 the division returned from the Russian
theater of operations, leaving behind more than 40,000
dead.

Meanwhile, Franco had not fulfilled the expectations of
the Axis. The "million bayonets" which, in a speech at Seville, the Spanish Chief of State had boasted he would use
against Bolshevism were still sheathed. Foreign Minister
Serrano Suñer, who was known for his pro-Axis leanings,
was dismissed and replaced by Count Jordana, a man of less
definite views. On November 8, 1942, the Americans landed
in North Africa, and Franco received President Roosevelt's
personal guarantee that Spain had nothing to fear from the
Allies. He then retreated from "active non-belligerency" to
"vigilant neutrality." But his attitude differed perceptibly
from that of three years before. One has but to look at the

Spanish press of that period, which had been instructed to report military events "objectively"—in other words, to report them in a way less favorable to the Axis. Was Franco already planning to go over to the enemy? In any event, his shilly-shallying, whether deliberate or not, served the Allied cause, as the Allies were to acknowledge later. Churchill told the House of Commons in 1944: "There is no doubt that our burden would have been much heavier had Spain yielded to German flattery and pressure at this critical moment. . . . Certainly Spain's resolve to remain outside of the conflict was most important." And Cordell Hull, the American Secretary of State, admitted in turn that the "invasion of Africa would have been impossible had it not been for Spain's neutrality."

The year 1943 marked the turning point of the war. On February 2, the Red Army won the battle of Stalingrad. At the same time, in the Mediterranean, in Tunisia, and at Cape Bon, the Axis was defeated. The African campaign ended. On July 10, Anglo-American forces landed in Sicily. The fall of Mussolini and the Italian armistice followed. Berlin and the principal German industrial and railroad centers were bombed mercilessly. At this juncture, Franco went over openly to the Allied side. He offered to serve as mediator in ending the war and wrote to Churchill with this in mind; he also went to see Sir Samuel Hoare, the British ambassador. It took him a long time to win their good graces.

Filled with anguish, Germany regarded Spain with distrust and mounting anger. If only it had invaded Spain while there was still time—a country that had been friendly but was now renegading! Early in 1944 Franco was harshly reprimanded by the German government for giving safe passage through his territory to Frenchmen answering General de Gaulle's appeal of June 18, 1940, to join the Free French in North Africa. The *National Zeitung*, which appeared in Madrid, raged at the sight of so many young Frenchmen strolling about the Puerta del Sol. "Where once only Italian or German was heard one now hears nothing but French. A rough estimate of these future soldiers would run to about 50,000. And all this time Spain offered us only the

help of its Azul Division on the eastern front!" The Frenchmen who strolled the Gran Via in Madrid or the Rambla in
Barcelona were not idling; they were waiting for the British
consul to direct them to Algiers. And if they engaged in
animated conversation, it was because they were eager to
compare notes on their journeys from the French border to
the Spanish capital. Many had left from Perpignan and, accompanied by a guide, had boarded a train to Osséja. From
there they walked to Puigcerdá, expecting to go directly to
Barcelona. But unluckily they fell into the hands of customs
officers, who took them to the *Jefatura* of Barcelona. There
they spent twenty days in prison, in the *Carcel Modelo*,
under observation. Hunger, the lack of tobacco, religious
services in the *Cobla* penitentiary to the accompaniment of
the strains of a tango—such was their lot. When the twentieth day was up they were transferred to the Miranda del
Ebro camp for internment. They found themselves with
Republican prisoners—*los Rojos*—and black-market profiteers—*los straperlos*. Again there was hunger despite the
distribution of Red Cross packages. "More bread and fewer
scapulars!" was their cry. The chaplain's sermons, the
Falangists' political harangues, news of the war, whether
true or false, whispered from ear to ear—all this helped to
kill the time. Finally liberated, the French arrived in Madrid,
changed into fresh uniforms (many of them were still wearing the garb of the Todt Organization, which marked the
date of their escape), and sped toward Gibraltar! Memories
of their stay in Spain were not pleasant, but at any rate
Franco had allowed them to pass through the country.

On June 6, 1944, General Eisenhower landed on the
beaches of Normandy. On August 25, Paris, which had
staged an insurrection six days before, welcomed General
Leclerc's Second Armored Division as well as the Allied
troops. On the twenty-sixth General de Gaulle paraded down
the Champs-Élysées to the Arc de Triomphe. At Madrid,
Franco was beginning to fret. He knew that French Resistance forces included many Spaniards. In some border zones,
the *maquis* were commanded by Spanish Republican of-

ficers. Might they not cross the Pyrenees and attempt a leftist pronunciamento? Frontier outposts were firmly secured and garrisons reinforced. But nothing of the kind occurred. So Franco concentrated on "normalizing" his relations with the United States and agreed to all the guarantees Hayes, the new American ambassador at Madrid, demanded. The year 1945 began with a massive and victorious Russian offensive in the east, supported by Allied campaigns in the west. On April 26 the French, British, and Americans established contact with the Red Army at Torgau on the Elbe. Berlin fell on May 2. Hitler committed suicide. Mussolini was shot by partisans; his corpse was strung up on a butcher's hook and exposed to the public. On May 4 the German Army surrendered to Marshal Montgomery, and on May 7 an armistice was signed in Reims. The terms were unconditional surrender. World War II was over.

Germany and Italy had lost the war and their leaders were dead. The Fascist ideology was completely discredited. Franco could no longer make use of it. Now, more than ever, if he was to continue in office, his policy would have to "evolve." And indeed, the Allied military victory resulted in greatly increased opposition to his regime. The General Union of Workers and the General Confederation of Labor, for a long time quiescent, now joined forces under the name of National Alliance of Democratic Forces. At the end of 1945, and for the first time since Franco had seized power, strikes broke out in Manresa, in Catalonia, and even in Madrid and Valencia. In the mountains of Castile, hastily formed bands of guerrillas attacked the Civil Guard. But Franco had the army well in hand: 150,000 soldiers guarded the Pyrenees and 350,000 protected the peninsula. Order was restored within Spain, but hostility from outside the country increased. The rough and ardent voice of La Pasionaria—Dolores Ibarruri—was heard on radio broadcasts from Moscow. The separatist Basque government and the *Generalitat* of Catalonia, led by José Antonio Aguirre and Irla respectively, had headquarters in Paris. Moreover, about a hundred deputies of the Cortes, exiled in Mexico, proclaimed Martínez Barrio President of the Spanish Republic, to succeed Azaña, who had died in Montauban. Barrio accepted Negrín's resignation in August 1945 and established a provisional government under the premiership of José Giral. In 1947 it was replaced by the Llopis cabinet. But Prieto disapproved. Relations between Republicans of various shades became bitter when a quarrel over money complicated ideological differences. The Republican leaders who left Spain in 1939 had taken with them large sums in currency and coin that belonged to the Treasury or to political organizations; they had been anxious to prevent the money from falling into the hands of the Franquistas. Who was accountable to the Spanish people for this sacred trust?

While Prieto quarreled with Negrín, while the Anarcho-Syndicalists, meeting in Toulouse, challenged the Llopis government, and former members of the *maquis* agitated in organized groups in the Haute Garonne or in Hérault, Spanish émigrés toted up their forces. Of the 400,000 men and women who had crossed the French border in 1939, half had returned to Spain almost immediately. Of the rest, a good many had likewise gone back a few years later, after the promulgation of an amnesty decree (Rojo, the famous Republican general, was among these), while others had settled in the United States (a few hundred), Russia, England, the South American republics (about 30,000), Belgium, France, and North Africa. Those who went to North Africa proved excellent recruits for the Free French forces; some of them fell at Bir Hakeim under the French flag.

The game that Franco was now about to play had as its setting chancelleries and powerful international organizations. Early in 1946, the Republican government was officially established in Paris. It was recognized by Mexico, Guatemala, Panama, Poland, Yugoslavia, Rumania, Hungary, Bulgaria, and Czechoslovakia. The French government did not take a stand. It merely sent a diplomatic note to London and Washington suggesting the adoption of a common policy toward Franco's regime. At the same time, the question was brought before the United Nations; on February 9, 1946, by a vote of 45 to 2, the United Nations decided to exclude Spain. Having received no definite answer from the American and British governments, and anxious to elicit one, France decided to express its own moral judgment by concrete action. On February 26 it closed the Franco-Spanish frontier. But the Allies were very slow to follow France's example. While, in effect, they agreed to sign a joint declaration denouncing the Franco regime, they completely evaded the question of breaking off diplomatic relations, stating that it "must be decided in the light of future events; account must be taken of the efforts of the Spanish people to free themselves." Theirs was a neutral stand that satisfied nobody, France least of all, since it alone bore the consequences of its principles, which were not only courageous but also costly to its economy. Undaunted by the excessive caution of its partners, France urged that the issue be presented before the Security Council of the United Nations. It also demanded a rupture of diplomatic and economic ties with Franco's Spain. The Americans and British demurred, but a little later the Polish member of the Security Council took up France's demand. A committee was appointed to look into the matter. Although the conclusions it drew stressed the threat the Spanish situation presented to world peace and security, the question was not debated until the General Assembly of the United Nations met in October 1946. On December 12 a recommendation that the powers recall their diplomats from Madrid and that Spain be excluded from all United Nations organizations was adopted by a vote of 34 to 6, with 13 abstaining. Henceforth there would be no further crossing of swords on this burning issue in the United Nations. Platonically condemned, Franco's regime survived.

Its survival was due in large measure to the United States. Perhaps it would be an exaggeration to describe the attitude of the State Department toward Franco as not wanting "to cause any trouble, even the slightest," but actually it never departed from the policy that Roosevelt laid down on March 10, 1945, in a letter to the American ambassador in

Madrid: "It is not our custom to intervene in the internal affairs of other countries unless international peace is in jeop-
ardy. The form of Spain's government and the policy it pur-
sues are the exclusive concern of the Spanish people." To be
sure, Washington had loyally backed its Allies in supporting
diplomatic action against Franco. Both at Potsdam and at
San Francisco, the three great powers unanimously condemned the Franco regime. In July 1945, Norman Armour
invited Franco to rid himself of the Falange. In December
of the same year, Dean Acheson warmly welcomed Negrín,
the representative of the Spanish Republic. On February 21,
Washington gave France the idea of creating a provisional
Spanish government and, in the United Nations, the United
States voted against Franco's regime. Nonetheless, as early
as the spring of 1945, the United States opposed the plan of
the Latin-American republics to sever diplomatic relations
with Franco. A few weeks later, Byrnes announced that
America would put no pressure on Franco and would con-
tinue to buy textiles from Spain. In March 1946 the United
States plainly refused to co-operate with France in bringing
the Spanish question before the Security Council. While the
United States could not prevent discussion of the issue at
Lake Success, it managed to turn it into a harmless debate
on procedure which culminated in the following resolution:
"Franco's regime is not a threat to peace; however, it might
lead to a situation that could endanger international peace."
What could be vaguer than this? And what conclusions are
to be drawn from America's inconsistencies? The United
States was apparently torn between sincere aversion for to-
talitarian systems, whose leaders it had recently defeated,
and awareness of the need to adopt a new diplomatic policy.
And indeed, the day after the end of the war it felt obliged
to alter its objectives. Hardly had the common enemy been
vanquished and effusions of comradeship ceased, when yesterday's allies began to take each other's measure. Whiskey,
vodka, and champagne continued to flow freely, but the initial enthusiasm vanished. The threat of Soviet imperialism
had been overlooked in the fever of battle. Would Russia be

the future enemy? Overcome with joy at being once again at peace, the British and French did not think so. But the Americans, reacting to the crushing burden of their responsibilities, prepared to face the worst. In planning a system of defense for the protection of Western Europe against a hypothetical Soviet invasion, how could they exclude Spain? Its excellent strategic position, its natural military bases, its large, well-equipped army, its leader, who happened to be the last champion of anti-Bolshevism—all this influenced the practical Americans, who looked upon Spain as their trump. In 1947, Washington began negotiations with Madrid for the possible use of Spanish airports in case of need. The same year, General Marshall urged the large banks of the United States to make loans to Spain. Although the country was not yet an ally, it was already a customer.

Three years after the end of World War II, Franco did not count himself among the losers, even though he was morally condemned by the United Nations, censored by a large section of world opinion, and hated by Republican Spain. He knew that the United States needed Spain because it could contribute to both America and Europe precious military help as well as raw materials, to say nothing of its traditional values. Spain is acutely aware that Americans need an anti-Communist Spanish government which has full control over its own people. It is merely waiting for passions to subside before suggesting to the world that it serve as a bridgehead for Europe. There is no hurry. Franco's friends would certainly agree with his worst enemies in giving him credit for one virtue—patience.

3

That Stranger,
the Spaniard of the
Mid-Twentieth Century

$\mathbb{L}$OGICALLY, a book that purports to cover the history of the Spaniard from the time of the caveman of Altamira should end with a description of the mid-twentieth-century man. But this is difficult, for the documents a historian ordinarily uses are lacking. It is too early and we are too close to the subject to have a proper perspective. The real nature of the contemporary Spaniard, who is still in the midst of writing his history, is as yet barely perceptible. However, by proceeding cautiously, step by step, we may perhaps disclose the true features of this stranger.

From Hundreds of Millions of St. James's Pilgrims to a Hundred Thousand Knights of St. Louis

As early as the ninth century, the Codex of St. James of Compostela gave pilgrims not only practical information but also a few hints about the Spanish mentality. Thus, the author states, one must beware of the "crude and barbaric"

Navarrese, enemy of the Gallic race; they are very unlike the Galicians, who are "hot-tempered and quarrelsome." Much later, during the reign of Henry IV, Barthélémy Joly, who accompanied the Abbé of Cîteaux on his mission to Spain, described Spaniards as follows: "They are short, with dark, rough, dry skin, black hair, and very short beard. . . . Melancholy, taciturn, wise, sparing with advice, serious, stern, religious, choleric, they are good warriors and patient workers." This opinion, which on the whole is both flattering and accurate, lacks a touch of humor, so we add: "They eat each other up, the Old Castilians claiming and believing themselves to be the best in the world." Already!

Fifty years later, a certain Van Aerssen and his brother, accompanied by their tutor, undertook a trip to Spain in order "to become acquainted with this haughty and prudent nation in its own land, a nation that hardly ever leaves the country save to issue orders to others." The interesting thing about their remarks is the parallel they draw between Frenchmen and Spaniards, who were then in a state of "diplomatic tension." The hostility existing between the two peoples seemed artificial to the travelers, created out of whole cloth by their respective governments. Actually, they were made to get along well together, for each complemented the other. The authors' criticism of Spaniards is not devoid of an unconscious humor at their own expense: "Reserved and speculative, slow and backward, patient, circumspect, admirably steadfast, persevering and energetic in good fortune, discreet and secretive in their negotiations, Spaniards are the exact opposite of Frenchmen." The Van Aerssen brothers made their trip to Spain the year of Philip IV's death. His weakness proved fatal to both his lineage and his country. His death occurred a few months before the lightning campaigns of Turenne and Condé in the Netherlands and Franche-Comté. Thus, just when the Habsburg dynasty was evidencing symptoms of the languid disease that was to carry it off, when French diplomacy was at its most successful, and the famous Spanish infantry came under the fire of the "Sun King's" guns, these honest men were praising the Spaniards. In their opinion, politics had nothing whatsoever to do with the fine qualities of the Spanish people, who, despite a declining monarchy and major military reverses, retained the virtues that were peculiar to them.

Now, we might ask, what do women travelers thing of Spaniards? One woman of distinction, Marie Catherine d'Aulnoy, went to Spain about 1680 and stayed there for a long time. Her account, written in the form of letters, which were then very fashionable among literary women, was not flawless, but the lady was shrewd and a good observer. "They are born with more wit than most people. . . . They speak and express themselves well, have keen memories, write with clarity and conciseness, and possess a ready understanding. They learn easily whatever interests them; they have a perfect grasp of politics, are sober and industrious when necessary." And Madame d'Aulnoy concludes that Spaniards have all the qualities of "perfect gentlemen."

While the seventeenth century was generally sympathetic to Spaniards, the same cannot be said of the eighteenth, which was influenced by Voltaire's false and categorical judgments. Spain, he claimed, could boast only a few second-rate painters. "Everybody played the guitar." Abbé Delaporte compared the Spaniards to the early Egyptians. Brave soldiers, slow and patient, good diplomats, loyal subjects, sober, frugal, faithful, slaves to honor, they were, nonetheless, or so he maintained, boastful and lazy. The Abbé thought them well built, but cold and phlegmatic. François de Bourgoing, a French minister in Madrid, tried to be impartial, though he was a *philosophe* and a disciple of the Encyclopedists. "In speaking of a nation . . . one must beware of two pitfalls—sounding either too eulogistic or too satirical." He objected to the charges of laziness and coldness leveled against Spaniards; he found them to be both industrious and enthusiastic. A contemporary of his, the Chevalier de Fonvielle, though shocked to see "little ladies" smoking cigars, said that "nowhere else does one find friends more trustworthy or sincere." Gradually, as the eighteenth century was nearing its end, the influence of the *philosophes* waned and views about Spain changed accordingly. To explain his surprise at discovering that no other people were comparable to Spaniards, the Marquis de Marcillac said: "Far from boasting that he is the ape of Europe, he takes pride in being forever himself"—a description already tinged with romanticism. Soon the purple dawn of the nineteenth century appeared. Cautious objectivity, or what passed for it, gave way to passionate hyperbole. And the sire of the Romantics, Chateaubriand, long before the publication of his *Adventures of the Last of the Abencerages*, quoted in *The Genius of Christianity* an émigré's opinion of the Spaniards: "I have great respect for these people who respect themselves, who do not go off to serve other nations and have preserved truly original characteristics. . . . What fine people they are!" Chateaubriand himself heartily subscribed to this judgment. He visited Andalusia and Old Castile a year before the *Dos de Mayo*. Just as Spaniards were about to become the darlings of Europe, Murat entered Madrid.

Under Fire from the "Orientals"

A century ago, in 1862, Gustave Doré, who had been wildly successful with his illustrations of Perrault's *Fairy Tales*, was contemplating a trip to Spain. Davillier, his friend and inseparable traveling companion, addressed him in this vein: "You will give us a splendid *Don Quixote* upon your return. . . . You will have tramped the dusty roads of La Mancha, which the valiant *manchego* and his faithful squire followed; like them, you will sleep on the hard ground, visit the little inn of Cárdenas, for it still exists, and the wild Sierra Morena, so conducive to repentance in knights-errant. . . . But banish all memories of Bacchanalian feasts, for Spain is not a country of fine foods. And when you come back you will remember with pleasure the deprivations you endured." A few days later, the two old cronies took a train from the Gare de Lyon to Perpignan and from there a stagecoach through the Perthus Pass to Barcelona. Thus, even at such a relatively recent date, a trip to Spain seemed a formidable expedition, and Spain itself a country where the least one might suffer was starvation.

The fact is that twenty years earlier the Romantics had done their share to create what was perhaps not a legend, but the next thing to it. At that time Théophile Gautier grimly stated: "A journey to Spain is a romantic and perilous undertaking. It demands great personal endurance, courage, patience, and strength." He stressed the "infernal heat," the "sun that gives one a splitting headache," and the need to go armed with a gun because of thieves, brigands, and innkeepers. However, the dangers he encountered at every moment did not affect his high spirits or enthusiasm—or so he says! Upon leaving the Burgos cathedral, he exclaimed: "We came out dazzled, overwhelmed, intoxicated by the masterpieces." But of major interest are his comments on the Spaniards themselves. One might have supposed that the Romantic image of Spain with which he was imbued even before he crossed the border would have enveloped the people he saw in a mirage tinged with Oriental mystery. Nothing of the sort was true. He noticed that the women of Madrid were gowned in the French manner, save for their headdress. "One sees very few women's hats at the Prado. With the exception of a few sulfur-yellow pancake-shaped coifs which must have once adorned learned fools, they wear only mantillas." He also observed that what was known in France as "the Spanish type" was but another Romantic invention. The señorita with the pale, elongated face and flesh-colored lips was to be found only in Andalusia; there were many ardent *malagueñas* and cigarette girls as dark as prunes. Yet blue-eyed blondes were legion. The Spanish bolero, the guitar —these were there too, but Gautier realized that Spaniards did not like to hear them mentioned. He frankly admitted: "One cannot achieve deep insight into a people within the space of six weeks." One day, from a distance, he saw a bandit surrounded by constables, but never did he meet one on the road or in the Sierras. This led him to write: "The Spanish bandit is a purely mythical being." The houses were clean, the people industrious, and everyone knew how to read and write. The rhythm of life was slower than in France, but one lived better. As for the Spaniards' excessive pride, he found no trace of it. On the contrary, they were "extremely simple and natural." He came across no slatterns, no vermin in the beds, few castanets, not many beggars, lots of oil in the *puchero*—but Gautier loved food cooked in oil.

Stendhal, who had preceded Gautier by three years along the roads of Spain, was also most favorably impressed. His mind had been made up before his departure. In his book *De l'Amour*, he gravely asserted: "I look upon the Spanish people as the living representatives of the Middle Ages." He added: "I like the privacy of Spanish life. I respect the *Spanish silence.*" His first contact with the country confirmed his opinion: "I like the Spaniard because he is an individual, not a copy of someone else. He is the last individual left in Europe." These are profound observations. While it is true that silence is characteristic of the country and the people, it is also unquestionably true that, contrary to the general opinion, Spanish individualism is destined to enjoy enduring eternity.

Altogether different was the reaction of George Sand, who settled the following year in Chartreuse de Valdemosa, on the island of Majorca. With her were her children and the unhappy Chopin, who was already very ill. Of the Spaniards, with whom she had but little contact, she wrote: "They have wounded my heart in its most vulnerable spot; before my very eyes they have stuck needles into a suffering human being. Never will I forgive them, and if I ever write about them it will be with rancor." She kept her word and expressed great bitterness in a book, *Un hiver à Majorque*, published in Parma—which proves that Majorcans bear no grudge.

Edgar Quinet was the next great traveler after Gautier to go to Spain. Even more than Stendhal he had preconceived notions about the country. The Spain he was prepared to visit was that of the Cid. Having decided this in advance, he did not change his mind. The bandits whom Gautier never saw, Quinet sought out at every street corner, his heart beating wildly; sometimes he even convinced himself that he had encountered a few. Such a mood could not fail to influence the judgment of this Sorbonne professor. After watching a bull fight he hit upon an apt formula: "Who can say that the finest attributes of the Spanish people are not sustained by the example of the toreadors—their *sang-froid*, tenacity, heroism, and contempt for death? According to Nordic legends, Siegfried bathes in the blood of the monster in order to become invincible."

Alexandre Dumas's *Impressions de voyage* contains some admirable descriptions—the mountains of Guipúzcoa likened to "the coats of poor people, full of large yellow, red, and green patches," or the Giralda, "vanishing in the dying night like a golden bee." But Dumas sees the Spaniards through the halo of his imagination. He is more fascinated by his own reactions than by his surroundings, and he blandly asserts, with the kind of naïve conceit that caused his friends to smile and irritated his enemies: "I am better known in Madrid than in France . . . Spaniards believe there is something of the Castilian about me, which tickles their fancy." In any event, Dumas's Romantic attitude toward the Spaniards showed a human sympathy which was absent from the haughty comments of Maurice Barrès, for example. To him Spain was nothing more than a pretext for intellectual vituperation and brilliant aesthetic sallies.

Castanets and the Chinese Quarter

We now come to the early years of the twentieth century. Romanticism has been dead a long time, but apparently not in Spain; or rather it lived again. In the style of Victor Hugo, the Countess de Noailles recalled imaginary wanderings: "Beneath a sky without pallor, without shade, without birds, In the yellowed and parched vales of the Toboso . . ." But the Spain of the poetess, "violent, streaked with ocher, pitch, and lime, ravaged by light—pimento of the world," is even more unreal than the Spain of the *Orientales*. In the admirable pages of *Éblouissements* and *Forces éternelles* one looks in vain for even the semblance of a judgment. It is of course true that the fervent countess's knowledge of Spain was limited to Fontarabie.

René Bazin gives us precise information about the Spanish temperament. It abounds, he says, in civility, pride, and a sense of honor. While Claude Farrère, visiting the Alhambra, is nostalgic for the grandeur of the Saracens, Louis Bertrand, on the contrary, sings the praises of Catholic Spain. Jacques de Lacretelle cautions the traveler against excessive illusions, while Montherlant, author of *Bestiaires* and *Service inutile*, claims that the Spanish character rests, paradoxically enough, on a mixture of mysticism and sensuality. As for Francis Carco, he writes in his *Printemps d'Espagne:* "Whether we talk about bulls, museums, women, or churches, our friends and neighbors are never satisfied." Of course not! Such topics are precisely the ones which should be approached with the utmost circumspection. He goes on to speak of the Chinese quarter with the same lack of tact. Meanwhile, French travelers who flocked to Spain between the end of World War I and the beginning of World War II have studiously and with varying skill harped on Spanish themes. They are usually benign, although at times somewhat heavy-handed. The points of view vary. In contrast to the Romantics, Albert Dauzat criticizes the Spanish people, their food, their railroads, whereas Maurice Legendre confesses: "I like Spain. I believe I know the country, not perfectly, of course, but well enough to like it, while those that speak ill of it do not know it at all and therefore have no right to criticize." All his writings amount to one long cry of friendship and admiration. Enchanted by eternal Spain, he does not judge it; he merely loves it.

"How Can One Be a Spaniard?"

One might suppose that improved facilities and better traveling conditions for tourists, which have prevailed since

1950, would have modified the attitude of Frenchmen to
Spain. Every year during the summer holidays, hundreds of
thousands of travelers rush to the Spanish border. In 1955,
during August alone, more than 10,000 cars, half of them
French, drove over the Roman aqueduct at Tarragona. One
cannot say, therefore, that Spain is not open to foreigners.
Accessible to the world along the five sides of its pentagon,
in ten years it has welcomed the equivalent of its total population. Explored, examined in all its parts, photographed,
filmed, interviewed, interpreted on the stage, on the screen,
in concert halls, exposed to cameras, flash bulbs, paint
brushes, microphones, literally dissected by professionals
and amateurs alike, Spain, one would assume, should hold
no further mystery. Yet there are still foreigners whose
stupefied countenance seems to say, in imitation of Montesquieu's quip: "How can one be a Spaniard?"

In the face of their astonishment one must admit that although Spain is no longer a kingdom of mystery, it nonetheless remains full of surprises. In spite of his ingrained
urbanity, how can a Chicago businessman fail to be somewhat
disconcerted when he enters a Madrid restaurant at eight
o'clock in the evening—a late hour for dining in the United
States—only to find the *muchachas* busy sweeping the
place? Should he go to the Ritz Gardens for a breath of fresh
air, the hat-check girl will hand him a tie, because no man
is admitted without one. For a whole fortnight he has been
bombarding some minister with letters in an effort to wind
up his affairs, but has received no reply. Should he happen
to meet this minister at a social gathering, the matter is settled in a few minutes. At the end of the day he strolls along
the banks of the Castellana, which is lined with stately
homes. Here beribboned nurses walk with their starched and
already haughty little charges. One would think this was
Eton. After a few hundred yards, our American finds himself in the narrow streets of the suburb of Vallescas, where
other children—unaccompanied by maids!—are playing on
the doorsteps of small, poorly built workshops. Our Babbitt
wonders: Are Spaniards rich or poor? He has no way of

knowing, for, when he goes to a café with a Spaniard and reaches in his pocket to pay for his drink, he discovers that the bill is already taken care of: *"Permítame, España para los españoles."* He is also struck by their air of accepting dollars as if it were their due! Money, then, is not everything? To make his bewilderment complete, he is refused an interview with a Spanish duke. *"Es un indio . . . ¿Qué más?"* the great-great-great-grandson of the Conquistadors whistles between his teeth. He, an Indian, this steel magnate? One can reign supreme in Chicago and yet have no ancestors. And so he returns to the Middle West with his contracts signed, to be sure, but also feeling a vague respect for this people wrapped in its legendary cape.

"Special and Noble"

That Spain, a victim of its own colorful legend, has always been misunderstood by Europe, that absurd judgments distort its true features, is not the whole story. A basic question remains to be answered: What is the Spaniard?

First of all, which Spaniard? For everyone realizes that a Sevillian and an Aragonese differ as much as a Marseillais and a man from Roubais, a Rhinelander and a Pomeranian. The characteristics of each province are well known. The Galician is sober and nimble and willingly emigrates. The Asturian's obstinacy is mistaken for stupidity, which his glorious history belies. The Basque, a descendant of the Euskarian race, claims to be the first Spaniard; he worships his language, which he says was spoken by Adam and Eve in the Garden of Eden. Fiercely attached to his traditions, the Navarrese still sings the hymn of the red berets: *"Por Dios, por la Patria, por el Rey!"* The Aragonese, so stubborn that he is said to be capable of "hammering a nail with his head," is nonetheless henpecked by his wife, *la dueña de la casa.* The Catalonian dances the *sardana* and is a hard worker. The Valencian and the Murcian, despite their bad reputation —"in Murcia the sky and ground, good; the first floor, bad"

—are close to the earth but prefer sailing about in their tar-
tan coasting vessels to working in the mines. As for the Castilian, his arrogance and pride are legendary. A yearning for
power, the desire to dominate—as strong today as it was
during the time of the Cid—a sense of his historic superiority over other Spaniards, make him the last representative of
the "Grandees of Spain." Should one conclude from this that
there are several Spains? Perhaps, but the Spanish individual is still distinctive. Like trees of various species nourished
by the same soil, all Spaniards stem from the same leaven,
and their invisible roots are intertwined. Rather than differences in traits or complexion, it is important to stress the sub-
terranean oneness that makes Spaniards, despite ephemeral
dissimilarities, all sons of the national *hombre*.

Stripped of the tinsel of folklore, with the paint of his
province removed from his face, what is the Spaniard's true
countenance? Montherlant has written: "Spain, like Italy, is
one of the most hated nations of Europe because it is both
special and *noble*, two characteristics which would be for-
given if it had power—and it has none." A rather harsh statement, but true, provided one substitutes "misunderstood"
for "hated." Unamuno finds a happier phrase: "The Spaniard is conscious of his manhood, his total masculinity."
Whether he be a Galician or a Catalonian, the Spaniard then
is special, the descendant of a noble race. One senses this
from the start, if only by the familiar way he looks at others,
asks them whence they come and who they are. And that
word *hombre*, which crops up endlessly in his conversation,
expressing a warm welcome, an affirmation, illustrating the
importance he attaches to what only a paraphrase of the word
can convey—the humanity of man. The Spaniard is an indi-
vidualist; he feels his manhood keenly. Consequently, no
government, regardless of its nature, is likely to make him a
citizen in the British or French sense of the word. Although
respectful of order, he does not accept hierarchy readily. He
resists integration into groups. He is perhaps accepting of the
army and the Church, although both evoke criticism and, on
occasion, rebellion. The only group to which the Spaniard

unreservedly adheres is the family, or rather *his* family, therefore himself; his only love is for his country—*la tierra*, his soil, the land he treads. Himself, his own people, the field he cultivates—this is Spain for the Spaniard.

Observers have tended to attribute a certain political indifference to the Spaniard. At heart he does not acknowledge authority; he submits to it because he is a fatalist but even more because he is not interested in the political policies of his government. However, his apparent submission to established authority does not last. Although patient, he is hot-tempered. Salvador de Madariaga has defined Spain's political evolution as "a series of horizontal lines of tranquillity intersected by bouts of activity." This activity is somewhat similar to that of volcanoes, which erupt without warning.

This fundamental, individualistic tendency is apparent in the way Spanish revolutions have been conducted. In France they are fought in the name of principles. The men of 1789 wanted to introduce Encyclopedist ideas into the government of the nation. In Spain principles are strikingly personified in individuals who are able to impose their ideas through their prestige and physical prowess. And this explains why Spanish revolutions are shocking and frightening in their violence. Unlike England, where revolutions are almost a sporting event, a kind of rugby match, and unlike France, where they represent a conflict of ideas, Spain experiences sudden moments of drama upon which a leader—a *caudillo*, usually unanticipated—imposes his own imprint, his iron fist.

Fiercely individualistic, the Spaniard is no less fiercely patriotic, for his country is but a kind of passionate extension of himself. Just as love of family and love of the soil, his *tierra*, are cherished as one and the same thing, so religion and country are fused in his heart. This leads one to say that the Spaniard regards religious observance as a patriotic duty and patriotism as a religious rite, even when he combats religion. Every Spanish revolution, every war, whether foreign or civil, revolves around religion and the Church. What could be more natural in a people whose roots are embedded in metaphysics? Until the beginning of the nineteenth century, the history of Spain was a religious epic. The liberal movements of the nineteenth and twentieth centuries, some of which were savagely anti-clerical, were based primarily on doctrines of religion. Catholic fanaticism or Masonic atheism—each aroused an equal amount of love or hatred. Like those ancient scepters with ivory faces that confront each other, the Church of Spain is destined to see before it now the profile of El Greco, now that of Goya—monk or rebel. "All the people of Spain run behind the Church, half of them with a candle, the other half with a stick," an old saying has it. Alternately praised and beaten, the Spanish Church is still in good health even though it has been assassinated several times.

This is a rough sketch of the Spaniard in his "Hispanicism"—the only possible translation of the word *castizo*, unless one uses many words to define it: a way of being, of acting, and of thinking that is common to all men of Spanish blood and rests essentially on love and concern for *la tierra*. The Spaniard's nation is something he savors greedily, as well as a metaphysical concern that fills him with anxiety. *Comer* and *estar* are verbs the Spaniard utters a hundred times a day.

— Himself, first of all, then *his* family, *his* language, *his* country, *his* religion—one might say *his* God—the world if he can have it, and once he did. The Spaniard is possessive, and more than possessive, a conqueror. He leaves the self to conquer others, by successive leaps and bounds, like a dancer.

And indeed, there is nothing that gives a better idea of this psychological process—the gradual and passionate extension of the Spaniard's personal universe—than the dance, a solo of course. Listen to the long hoarse cry of the *cante jondo*, a cry that comes from deep inside—prelude and conclusion. Then the *flamenco* dancer leaps onto the stage, his waist so tightly sheathed in his broad black belt that he resembles a fragile insect in a watered-silk corselet. Look at him, alone on the stage like a farmer on his land—a man laid bare, *hombre a secas*. And the "profound song" that heralds him is called "solitude," *soledad*. Alone and motionless, he stands, eyes half closed, chin high, a look of suffering on his face. His hips are still, finger tips touching, the wrists turned outward. He scarcely moves. Now he moves, slowly, very slowly. Leaning backward from the waist, head to one side, he revolves, seeming to point with outstretched finger to the edge of the wide circle where he is master. But now the dancer slips away from the enchanted circle, as if, at one stroke, the magic wand were broken. Pirouetting just once, he disappears through an invisible wall. Contriving to work loose from himself, he walks away from the exacting earth. He approaches the two guitarists and the singer, who beat time for the long glide of this feline within reach of his prey. With something akin to anguish one awaits the moment when the Andalusian finally breaks the chains that still bind him to himself, to his land, to his friends. The music of the guitars swells—they speak rather than play, says Antonio Machado—the castanets make a storm of noise; from the depths of her entrails the woman calls the *ay-ahi*—which was once the *Magnificat* of the Moors of Granada. Little by little, the dancer enlarges his circle. He runs from set to set, profiled at last in shadow pantomime against the final backdrop. Revolving, he flies from one end of the stage to the other, present everywhere at once, stretching his realm to infinity, like those sons of hidalgos who, never having left their ancestral manor, one day went off to Seville, sailed from Cadiz, and found themselves at some Indian outpost along the shores of the Amazon. Finally, with a prodigious effort, the dancer leaps wide and is carried off to the wings, his arms curved in the shape of an amphora, one leg flexed, the other outstretched. He comes down with one knee on the ground, crosses his arms over his chest, and, in a sudden gesture, lowers his head, readying himself to receive the baptism of death. A last, heart-rending sound from the guitars; the castanets clap once, twice, like the shrill rattling of bones. Wildly stomped by the clicking heels, the floor still vibrates. The man who thought he could possess the world returns to his solitude. Bending his knee, his hands joined behind his

back, he bows his head and falls, alone, on the verge of ultimate conquest—the Kingdom of God—but before he has at-
tained it.

Feet on the Ground

This typical dancer who, leaping, lands on the ground, symbolizes the Spaniard's return to reality. His head is still
seething with Don Quixote chimeras—crossed swords, prizes
laid at the feet of ladies, displays of physical prowess—but
his feet are on the ground. The mid-twentieth-century Spaniard is well balanced and clear-headed. He can no longer be
fooled. Many years have elapsed since the Security Council
of the United Nations refused, in June 1948, to present the
Spanish problem to the Assembly, thus implicitly accepting
Franco's right to continue in office. What has transpired
since then? Franco is still in power, Spain has opened its
doors wide to foreigners, but the Spaniard, although now
better informed about the world as well as his own country,
nevertheless is still preoccupied with the same traditional
problems that have always beset him: bread, religion, freedom, the leader. How has he evolved since the end of World
War II?
  Bread . . .
  Spain is poor. Franco can do nothing about this; it is the
fault of the soil. One third of the land is fertile, while the
other two thirds have to be furiously broken up and turned
over to keep them from being covered with dust. Yet 70 per
cent of the population is employed in agriculture or related
activities. In spite of the government's attempts to initiate
agrarian reforms, the system of large estates still prevails
and the old adage remains true: soil without men, men without soil. Consequently, the national income is one of the low-
est in Western Europe: about $220 per capita annually com-
pared with $515 for France and $1,000 for Switzerland.
True, it increased 8 per cent between 1956 and 1957. But
Spaniards consume three times less meat than do Frenchmen

and half as much sugar. They have more natural elegance, but are not as well dressed, for they use less material or goods of inferior quality. One out of every 110 Spaniards owns a car; in France the figure is one out of seven. Spain's primary agricultural problem is irrigation; the annual rainfall is 14 inches, whereas an average harvest requires a minimum of 20 inches. The ten-year plan begun in 1939 to double the area under irrigation failed to fulfill expectations although it did improve the situation considerably. Aridity still remains the peasant's unconquerable enemy. There is too much sun and not enough water. This likewise retards the development of electrical power, although in this field Spain has achieved spectacular progress, increasing its consumption fivefold between 1936 and 1956. The country is poor, yet its industry prospers. It leads the world in the production of mercury and is second only to the United States in the mining of lead. In Europe it is first in the production of olive oil. Its output of cereals is third highest. It has copper and iron as well as wolfram, from which tungsten, so essential to hard steels, is made. Between 1945 and 1950 its industrial production increased 60 per cent. While agriculture leaves much to be desired, the same is not true of cattle breeding—1,200,000 horses, 20,000 lambs, and 65,000 bulls for bull fights.

In the autumn of 1957 Franco opened the first blast furnace for a giant sheet-metal factory at Avilés. One hundred thousand houses were built in five years, and the railroad network, the RENFE, which early in the century had been the target of tourists' gibes will soon be entirely electrified. Such progress is most gratifying, but who, one wonders, is financing it? Spaniards pay a small part of the cost. In 1957 investments did not exceed one sixth of the amount expended in France for the same purposes. Most of the big companies in Spain are supported by foreign capital, in spite of a certain number of official restrictions on foreign credit. The industrial prosperity of Spain therefore depends in large measure on foreign investments and American help. In carrying out the important projects of the National Industrial Institute—

THE AGE OF JOSÉ ANTONIO

a nuclear-science center, a uranium plant, more than 9,000 miles of new highways—Spain runs the risk of eating up its capital and increasing its debts. Therefore it is trying very hard to stimulate its export trade. In 1958, Spain took in more than $6,000,000 from exports, mainly oranges. Its books are balanced so far as the banks are concerned, but it is sadly deficient in dollars. In short, Spain lacks the money to import the goods and equipment so essential to her economy. Recently she joined the International Monetary Fund and the International Bank for Reconstruction and Development, which can and should help her. This could be essential, for without ample financing and a stable currency continuous industrial expansion is quite impossible. When expenditures cease to exceed the limitations of the national budget, when Spain relies more on its own resources and less on borrowed American money, when abnormally low wages are offset by a decrease in the cost of living (from January 1953 to December 1957 the index soared from 100 to 132), then the country's general situation would improve and Spaniards would not be as poor as they are now.

The Church . . .

Almost all Spaniards, even those who are not pious, attend services. But what do they think of the Church, or rather how does the Church regard the Spanish people? Has it finally achieved that synthesis between Christianity and democratic ideals which the Catalonian Jaime Balmes dreamed about more than a hundred years ago, when the "breath of the century" blew over Christian Spain? "The two Spains drew apart from each other instead of uniting. They fought instead of helping one another. . . . As a consequence, revolutions replaced reforms. . . . It is not politics that must save religion, but religion that must save politics. . . . Political power belongs to the people." Thus spoke the young priest of Vich, a distant precursor of the *Sillon* and of the French Mouvement Républicain Populaire. Later, inspired by Leo XIII, the "Workers' Pope," fervent and courageous priests founded Christian trade unions in opposition to the employers, who confined themselves to organ-

izing an association of their own. These priests distributed
rosaries and scapulars. Carrying candles, they led workers'
demonstrations and felt they had done their duty.

In the middle of the twentieth century the Spanish Church
cannot continue to ignore social conditions. It has come to
realize that the proletariat, goaded by poverty, will not be
satisfied with a free pass to the hereafter, that the workers
demand more immediate rewards and will turn against official Catholicism whenever, consciously or unconsciously, the
Church connives at social injustice. If the Church fails to address itself to the people, the people will desert it. However,
not all churchmen realize the urgent need of a different attitude. Some bishops, concerned solely with politics, are eager
to conform to the dictates of the existing regime. Others,
immersed in their mysticism, intend to keep the faithful
within the confines of a rigid Catholic orthodoxy. Their arguments have not changed since the Middle Ages. The thundering voice of Cardinal Segura in the cathedral of Seville,
threatening the Lenten congregation with hell fire for the
slightest infraction of the Church's commandments, struck
terror in the hearts of some penitents. Listening to these
pious but shortsighted prelates, one would think that all
Protestants are doomed to damnation, that Ortega y Gasset
is the devil incarnate. On the other hand, there are some for-
ward-looking bishops who do not hesitate to remind the ruling classes that religion cannot serve as an alibi. Ángel Her-
rera, archbishop of Málaga, is unrelentingly active in his
efforts to promote Christian democracy. The most recent
evidence of the concern of a fraction of the Spanish episco-
pacy is the pastoral letter which Archbishop Morcillo of
Saragossa addressed to his diocese in 1958. After describing
"the spiritual tragedy of the working class," the prelate set
forth the principles of the Young Catholic Workers (the
J.O.A.C.), whose dynamic action he deliberately stressed.
This was followed by remarks that it takes a great deal of
courage to make in a country where the state church is reluctant to part company with the moneyed interests. "The
worker has the right to expect everything from the Church.

The glorious mission of freeing the workers from proletari-
anization is the task of Christ's priests." In conclusion, the
Archbishop of Saragossa urged the clergy and the entire
Spanish community to "respond to the clamor of the working-class youth who wants a place in the life of the nation,
not in order to destroy it, but rather to improve it." We might
add that periodicals like *Esprit* and *Témoignage Chrétien*
are read in the seminaries, that young priests are protesting
from the pulpit against the inadequate living conditions of
industrial employees, that priests have taken up collections
for strikers—all of which would seem to indicate that the
Spanish Church is attaining a new conception of its duties toward those formerly referred to, and not without condescen-
sion, as "the poor." As Archbishop Morcillo said: "Today in
Europe the poor are the workers."

Freedom . . .

Between 1926 and 1958 the population of Spain rose from
twenty-four to thirty-two million. Preoccupied primarily with
practical, material matters, the majority of the people are not
interested in politics. *Primum vivere.* . . . An opposition
party as such is virtually nonexistent, or if it does exist, it
has no effective means of action. Although Franco has re-
laxed his repressive methods appreciably, any pressure
group, however slightly politically tinged, is quickly suppressed. The streetcar strike in Madrid, the student uprising
that was put down in a few days, resulted in a few gains for
those involved. Is the Spaniard free? In his personal life, yes.
No police regulation prevents him from choosing a profession or from leaving it for something else, from going to
Mass or not going, from marrying and raising a family as he
sees fit, from moving about at will within Spain, even from
grumbling about the regime on the terrace of some café. On
the other hand, he does not have the right to give public expression to his opinion of the regime. If he disapproves of it,
he must remain silent. Is it true that Spaniards who want to
work in another country are subjected to a thousand formalities and regulations? An American newspaperman cited the
case of a young woman, who, in order to obtain a visa to

leave Spain, was obliged to do a six-month stint of social-service work and to learn by heart the 176 pages of the Falangist manual! Of course, she was not the wife of a diplomat. . . . But the real question is not whether Spaniards are free, or half-free, as individuals, but rather how much influence they can exert on the government. In this respect, they enjoy no freedom whatsoever. The average Spaniard does not belong to any powerful organization and consequently has virtually no way of expressing himself politically. Through the syndicates and corporations which are represented in the Cortes, he can advance a technical or professional opinion, but he has no right to say what he thinks about the existing regime. One might say that the Spaniard is absent from the forum. Who, besides Franco and the Cortes, can wield any influence? The Church, represented by the bishops; the Falange, although it no longer plays much of a role save as a kind of "Club of Good Fellows"; the army, the regime's praetorian guard; the old nobility and the moneyed interests, whose members are often related. Then there is the Opus Dei. Calling itself the "Canonical Institute" and boasting the approval of the Holy See, it constitutes a Third Order of sorts. It represents Catholics of every kind (with the exception of the Christian Democrats) and its purpose is to train good Christians, but also to inculcate the proper political attitudes. Viewed from the heights of this shining fortress, built of steel, gold, and subtle shades of blue, the producer, the worker, looks very tiny.

The leader . . .

At the closing session of the Cortes on July 15, 1957, Luis Carrero Blanco, ministerial secretary to the President and Franco's right-hand man, declared: "We must not close our minds to the establishment of a traditional, Catholic, monarchical state while the *Caudillo* is in power." And to make his meaning clearer, he added: "When he [Franco] should no longer be with us, a monarchy neither absolute nor liberal, but traditional, like that of Ferdinand and Isabella, will preside over the destiny of Spain. The person who symbolizes such a monarchy must loyally serve the principles of the national movement. . . . This future monarchy would not be invested with the powers enjoyed by the *Caudillo*, since he is an exceptional being who won the war and reconquered the nation." This speech was important because it was the first time since the July manifesto of 1947 that Franco referred openly to the question of the succession. What is the dynastic situation? Alfonso had four sons: Alfonso, duke of Covadonga, Jaime, duke of Segovia, Juan, prince of Asturias and count of Barcelona, and Gonzalo. Alfonso and Gonzalo, the first and fourth sons, both victims of hemophilia, died as a result of an automobile accident. The second son, Jaime, a deaf-mute from birth, renounced his own rights to the throne as well as those of his sons, Alfonso and Gonzalo. The presumptive heir to the Spanish crown is therefore Don Juan, count of Barcelona. He is a very tall, healthy, athletic-looking man with cold blue eyes. He lives in Portugal, near Lisbon, in a villa called La Giralda, which looks out over the Estoril. "My suitcase is packed to leave for Madrid at any moment," he recently announced. The Count of Barcelona married María de las Mercedes de Borbon y Orléans, daughter of Louise of France, and fourth child of Louis Philippe Albert, count of Paris. They have had four children: Margarita, blind since birth, Alfonso, accidentally killed at the age of fourteen, Pilar, and Juan Carlos. Will Juan Carlos, born in Rome on January 5, 1938, and baptized by Pope Pius XII, wear the crown of Spain in place of his father? We have no reason to be sure of this, although with the consent of both Don Juan and Franco (the two men met to discuss the matter in the summer of 1954 on board the *Azor*), Juan Carlos is being groomed for the succession. "I will never renounce my prerogatives in favor of my son!" the Count of Barcelona has declared, and Juan Carlos himself stated plainly: "My father is the only legitimate king . . . and for the time being, politics is not my concern." True, the grandson of Alfonso XIII is a cadet in the Spanish army. He is studying at the naval school as well as at the center of the army air force. But there is always a considerable difference between official pronouncements and secret understandings.

Everyone in Franco's entourage knows who his favorite is. One cannot help liking this prince in his early twenties, so slim and elegant, who tears over the roads at the wheel of his jeep, his hair ruffled by the wind; like his grandfather, at once tender and willful, he is the idol of the girls.

Will the pretender be the heir of Alfonso XIII or Franco's successor? If Carrero Blanco is to be believed, the future King of Spain will have to accept the guidance of a military directorate and follow the path already outlined by the *Movimiento* and its leader. Thus, by tacit agreement, the monarchy would be a continuation of the Franco regime, and the sovereign would obediently follow in the footsteps of its Falangist survivors. Naturally, it would be better if the transition from one regime to another took place with a minimum of disturbance, but it is doubtful whether a Spanish prince, no matter how constitutional, would accept a *capitis diminutio* once he had ascended the throne. *Ya veremos!*

While awaiting resurrection in monarchical form, voluntary withdrawal, or, possibly, destruction in a bloody uprising—which nobody can envisage with indifference—the Franco regime is trying to revamp its foreign policy. To begin with, it seems to have renounced the role of mediator between Europe and the Arab world. The idea of trying to achieve Charles V's dream in the middle of the twentieth century by building a bridge between Christianity and Islam, with the traditional West, personified by Franco, bestowing the kiss of peace upon the Moslem Orient, personified by Nasser, was indeed a seductive one. But Morocco's independence shattered this naïve and grandiose scheme. While loudly proclaiming its secular rights to its "presidios" and justifying them on both historical and legal grounds, Spain cannot possibly preserve its "positions of prestige," whether in Ceuta, Melilla, and the Chafarinas Islands off the Mediterranean coast or in the Saharan enclave of Ifni. On the other hand, the Spanish government is resolutely turning to its immediate neighbors, thus showing a sincere desire to join the European community. Fortunately, the relations between France and Spain have changed as a result of this realistic policy. A Franco-Spanish legalistic quarrel has existed for a long time. French ministers—Mendès-France, Pinay, Pineau, and Maurice Faure—wisely took the initiative in attempting to remove the main stumbling blocks that created the impasse. The arrival in Paris, in April 1958, of Castiella, the new Spanish Minister of Foreign Affairs, in connection with the tenth anniversary of the Organization for European Economic Cooperation (O.E.E.C.); the many contacts between the Municipality of Paris and the *Ayuntamientos* of Madrid and Barcelona; commercial contracts between French and Spanish firms as well as increasingly meaningful cultural exchanges—all these attested to a desire on the part of both countries to put an end to the antagonism they have felt for each other and which has lasted too long. One of the first visitors General de Gaulle received after the events of May 13, 1958, was Count de Casa Rojas, the Spanish ambassador to France. This was an excellent prelude to the celebration of a tercentenary of which both Frenchmen and Spaniards were especially aware: for indeed, on June 6, 1660, in the modest church of St.-Jean-de-Luz, Louis XIV was wed to the Infanta Maria Theresa, daughter of Philip IV of Spain.

1959 . . . Three hundred years have elapsed since the Treaty of the Pyrenees was signed at the Isle of Pheasants on the Bidassoa; twenty years since Franco's triumphant announcement at Burgos ended the Civil War. Spaniards born in 1939 today are in their twenties. They have been nurtured not on legends but on tales of battle. When Guernica or Teruel is mentioned, their faces grow sad. Yet this story is merely history to them. Time has done its work, the future dominates the past, and one cannot build on memories. *"Nuestra guerra,"* the veterans say, with melancholy pride. But the young people are looking ahead. They listen to those who promise them a better tomorrow. To the 10,000 monarchists assembled at Lourdes in October 1958, Don Juan declared: "Political power that serves only one class is no longer conceivable, and if the scale of justice tips at all, it will always tip in favor of the weakest." Friends of Spain willingly accept the pretender's statement. The regime that follows Franco's, whether it be Junta, Monarchy, or Republic, will have to take into account the needs and aspirations of the Spanish people. Similarly, the Spain of tomorrow, if it is to survive, must become an integral part of Europe. It already belongs to the O.E.E.C.; its persistent efforts to forge an economy worthy of the name indicates its intention of joining, at least for a time, the Common Market, Euratom, and the Free Trade Zone. Speaking in October 1958 on the occasion of the opening of the largest electrical plant in Spain, and just after the U.S.S.R. had launched its first satellite, Franco had this to say: "It is impossible to minimize the political importance of any nation that has successfully launched the first artificial satellite. . . . Such an event would not have been possible in ancient Russia, but it is inevitable in the new Russia. To accomplish any great undertaking, political unity and discipline are indispensable. Whether we like it or not, the fact remains that this could never have happened in a politically divided or chaotic nation." Remarks such as these would have been unthinkable ten years ago.

Spain and Euratom . . . This is something for the poet to dream about as he roams the open fields of Old Castile. As yet nothing has changed in this legendary country which seems to extend all the way to the sea—vast stretches bathed in a medieval light, dotted with foreign ruins, with battlefields, and here and there with sanctuaries. Not a sound, not a soul, is present—only an occasional city that seems to be slumbering beneath the heavy blue sky. A city that is also a name. Ávila? Theresa? Madrigal de las Altas Torres? Isabella? Bivar? The Cid? It is heartbreaking to know that deafening bulldozers will split open this fiery desert down whose paths raced the heroes of both the Reconquest and the Conquest. Is it possible that the hissing furnaces of atomic factories will appear in this noble, solitary land where the noon sun hovers and trembles, and where once the Empire of Mankind and the Kingdom of God were conceived?

Oh, to breathe one last time the almost Mongol air! . . . But the nostalgia of poets has never altered the course of history.

Puerto de Alcudia (Majorca), July 1957
Paris, January 1959

*Chronological Summary
of Major Events*

Genealogical Charts

Index

Chronological Summary
of Major Events

Origins

The emergence of the first religions: Celts, Iberians, Celtiberians, Phoenicians, Greeks, and Carthaginians
221 B.C.:   The death of Hamilcar Barca at Helica (Elche)
200–150 B.C.:   The Lady of Elche

Roman Spain

218–201 B.C.:   Second Punic War (the Siege of Saguntum)
149–146 B.C.:   Third Punic War
139 B.C.:   The death of Viriathus
133 B.C.:   The capture of Numantia
26 B.C.:   Cantabrian wars
39:   The Virgin appears before the apostle St. James at Iria Flavia(?)
58:   St. Paul's mission in Spain(?)
66:   The death of Seneca, the precursor of Christianity(?)
320:   The emergence of Arianism

Visigothic Spain

567:   Toledo becomes the capital of Visigothic Spain
568–586:   Leovigild
586–601:   Reccared

560–636:   St. Isidore writes his *Etymologies;* he founds a school at Seville; the persecution of Christians
633:   Fourth Council of Toledo, presided over by St. Isidore
636–638:   Fifth and Sixth Councils of Toledo
653:   Eighth Council of Toledo; the law of the *Fuero Juzgo* applies to both Goths and Hispano-Romans alike
702:   Seventeenth Council of Toledo
709:   The advent of Roderic

Moslem Spain

710:   The battle between Rodrigo and Achila(?)
711:   The battle of the Guadalete; the downfall of the Visigothic monarchy
718:   Pelayo; the battle of Covadonga
724:   Constitution of the state of Sobrarbe
732:   The battle of Poitiers
740:   The Berbers recapture Tangier
756:   Abd-er-Rahman, the caliph of Damascus, seizes Cordova
778:   Charlemagne's campaign(?); the death of Roland at Roncesvalles
791:   Oviedo, the capital of Asturias
912–961:   The reign of Abd-er-Rahman III
932–970:   The founding of Castile
997:   The sack of Compostela by the Infidels

The Reconquest

1033:   The French Cluniac Movement appears in Spain
1063:   Ferdinand I conquers Seville
1085:   Alfonso VI seizes Toledo
1086:   Alfonso VI is defeated at Zalacca by the Almoravides
1091:   The Almoravides settle in Cordova
1095:   The Cid conquers Valencia
1109:   The death of Alfonso VI
1118:   Alfonso I, the Battler, founder of the kingdom of Aragon, takes Saragossa
1156:   The founding of the Order of Alcántara
1158:   The founding of the Order of Calatrava
1161:   The founding of the Order of Santiago
1170:   The founding of Teruel; the birth of St. Dominic
1195:   The Almohades replace the Almoravides and defeat Alfonso VIII at the battle of Alarcos
1198:   The death of Averroës
1204:   The death of Maimonides
1209:   New offensive against the Moors; the Pope encourages the Crusade

1212:   The battle of Las Navas de Tolosa; the Almohades army is dispersed
1213:   The Albigenses are defeated at Muret
1215:   St. Dominic founds his first community
1217:   Ferdinand the Saint becomes King of Castile
1221:   The death of St. Dominic; the founding of the cathedral of Burgos
1227:   The founding of the cathedral of Toledo
1232:   James I of Aragon conquers the Balearic Islands
1236:   Ferdinand the Saint captures Cordova
1248:   Ferdinand the Saint captures Seville
1252:   The death of Ferdinand the Saint; the birth of Alfonso X, the Learned
1256–1265:   The drafting of the *Partidas*
1276:   The death of James I of Aragon
1284:   The death of Alfonso X, the Learned
1314:   The death of Raymond Lully
1369:   Henry of Trastamara kills Pedro I, the Cruel, with the help of Du Guesclin
1394:   Benedict XIII, the anti-pope
1411:   The founding of the University of Valencia
1453:   The Turks capture Constantinople
1464:   The founding of the University of Saragossa
1469:   Marriage of Ferdinand and Isabella
1474:   Isabella becomes Queen of Castile
1478:   The bull of Pope Sixtus IV establishing the Inquisition
1479:   Ferdinand becomes King of Navarre
1480:   The Inquisition is established at Seville
1491:   The birth of Ignatius Loyola
1492:   The Catholic Kings capture Granada; the Jews are expelled from Spain; Christopher Columbus discovers America
1497:   Rojas writes *La Celestina;* Amerigo Vespucci discovers the Gulf of Mexico, Yucatán, and Honduras
1500:   The birth of Charles V
1503:   Gonzalo de Córdoba defeats the troops of Louis XII at the battle of Cerignola
1504:   The death of Isabella the Catholic
1506:   The death of Christopher Columbus; Cisneros becomes regent of Castile; the birth of Francis Xavier
1509:   The founding of the University of Alcalá by Cisneros
1513:   Vasco Núñez de Balboa discovers the Pacific
1515:   The battle of Marignano; the birth of Theresa of Ávila; Solís discovers the Río de la Plata
1516:   The death of Ferdinand the Catholic; the death of Cisneros

Spain of the Golden Century

1516: The death of Ferdinand the Catholic; the death of Cisneros
1517: Charles V takes possession of the kingdom of Spain; Martin Luther draws up his theses at Wittenberg
1519: Charles V is elected emperor
1520: The Pope condemns Luther; Magellan rounds South America and reaches the Pacific Ocean
1521: Hernando Cortes seizes Mexico; the Diet of Worms; Ignatius Loyola is wounded at Pamplona
1525: The battle of Pavia
1526: Ignatius is tried by the Inquisition
1527: Erasmianism is condemned at Valladolid, an imperial letter guarantees its orthodoxy; the Sack of Rome; the birth of Philip II
1532: Francisco Pizarro sails for Peru
1533: The conquest of Colombia
1534: Ignatius Loyola takes his vows at Montmartre
1535: The first book is printed in America
1536: The death of Erasmus; St. Theresa becomes a nun at the Convent of the Incarnation at Ávila; the death of Garcilaso de la Vega
1540: The Society of Jesus is founded; the conquest of Venezuela and Chile; Miguel Serveto discovers the circulation of the blood
1541: Francis Xavier departs for India
1542: The birth of John of the Cross; law to protect the American Indians (Las Casas)
1545: First meeting of the Council of Trent
1546: The death of Luther; Morales paints "The Virgin and Child"
1547: The birth of Cervantes; the battle of Mühlberg, the Protestants are defeated
1548: The Interim of Augsburg; the birth of Suárez
1552: The death of Francis Xavier on the Chinese coast; the Treaty of Passau
1555: The Peace of Augsburg; the death of Juana the Mad; Charles V abdicates
1556: Philip II becomes King of Spain; the death of Ignatius Loyola
1557: Charles V retreats to Yuste; the battle of St.-Quentin
1558: The death of Charles V at Yuste
1559: The Treaty of Cateau-Cambrésis between France and Spain; auto-da-fé at Valladolid; Philip II lands at Laredo
1562: First Reform Carmelite Convent founded by Theresa of Ávila; the birth of Lope de Vega
1562–1563: Termination of the Council of Trent
1563: John of the Cross dons the garb of the Carmelite Order
1564: The death of Calvin
1566: The Pragmatic Sanction against the Moriscos

1567: John of the Cross meets Theresa of Ávila
1571: The Battle of Lepanto
1572: The Massacre of St. Bartholomew
1573: El Greco arrives in Spain
1575: Theresa of Ávila is humiliated
1577: John of the Cross is imprisoned at Toledo
1578: John of the Cross writes *Spiritual Canticle, Climbing to Carmel, Dark Night*
1582: El Greco paints the "Burial of Count Orgaz"; the death of Theresa of Ávila
1588: The "Invincible Armada" is defeated; the death of Luis de Granada
1591: The humiliation and death of John of the Cross
1598: The death of Philip II

The Twilight Epoch

1598: The advent of Philip III; the Peace of Vervins
1599: The birth of Velázquez
1605: The publication of *Don Quixote;* Pedro Fernández de Quiroga again discovers Australia
1609: The last Moriscos are banished
1616: The death of Cervantes and Shakespeare
1620: Spain participates in the Thirty Years' War; the Battle of the White Mountain
1621: The death of Philip III; the advent of Philip IV
1626: The siege of Breda
1630: Tirso de Molina's *The Sevillian Deceiver* appears
1633: The Infante-Cardinal is named Governor of Flanders
1636: The siege of Corbie
1642: The death of Richelieu
1643: The battle of Rocroi
1648: The Treaty of Westphalia; the Treaty of Münster
1659: The Treaty of the Pyrenees
1660: Louis XIV's marriage to the Infanta Maria Theresa; the death of Velázquez
1665: The death of Philip IV and the advent of Charles II
1668: The Peace of Aix-la-Chapelle
1678: The Treaty of Nijmegen
1681: The death of Calderón
1700: The death of Charles II
1700: The advent of Philip V
1713: The Treaty of Utrecht
1715: The death of Louis XIV in France
1720: The Peace of Cambrai
1726: The first Spanish Masonic lodge is established at Gibraltar

1744:   The birth of Jovellanos at Gijón
1746:   The death of Philip V; the advent of Ferdinand VI

The Age of Goya

1748:   The birth of Goya
1751:   Ferdinand VI's decree against Freemasonry and Benedict XIV's bull, *Romanorum Pontificum*
1759:   The advent of Charles III
1761:   The Family Compact is signed
1762–63:   War between Spain and England
1766:   The Revolt of the Capes
1767:   The Jesuits are banished from Spain
1779:   The siege of Gibraltar
1781:   The Spaniards land on the Isle of Minorca
1783:   The signing of the peace
1788:   The death of Charles III; the advent of Charles IV
1789:   The French Revolution; the Declaration of the Rights of Man
1791:   The French Constitution; Louis XVI is arrested at Varennes
1793:   Louis XVI is executed; Spain declares war on the Convention
1795:   The Treaty of Basel and the end of the Franco-Spanish War
1796:   The Treaty of San Idelfonso; Spain declares war on England
1797:   Jovellanos, Minister of Foreign Affairs and Justice; the siege of Cadiz
1799:   18th of Brumaire
1802:   The Peace of Amiens
1804:   Napoleon is crowned Emperor
1805:   The naval battle at Trafalgar
1807:   The Treaty of Fontainebleau between France and Spain
1808:   French troops enter Madrid; May 2, 1808
1809:   The birth of Donoso-Cortés; the French attack Saragossa
1812:   The Cortes of Cadiz and the Constitution
1813:   The Treaty of Valençay; Napoleon acknowledges Ferdinand VII as King of Spain; the end of the Franco-Spanish War; the abolition of the Inquisition; St. Theresa made patron saint of Spain

Restoration and Revolution

1814:   Napoleon goes to Elba; the return of Ferdinand VII; the decree of Valencia suppressing the Constitution of 1812; the Inquisition is reinstated; the Jesuits return to Spain; Freemasonry is suppressed in Spain
1820:   Riego's pronunciamento; Ferdinand swears allegiance to the Constitution of 1812; civil war between absolutists and liberals
1821:   Venezuela becomes independent

1822: Colombia becomes independent
1823: The French army attacks; Ferdinand VII resumes power; the White Terror
1824: Peru and Mexico become independent
1833: The death of Ferdinand VII; the regency of María Cristina
1835: The Carlists besiege Bilbao; the death of Zumalacárregui
1839: The Convention of Vergara ending the first Carlist war
1840: Abdication of María Cristina; Espartero's dictatorship
1843: Espartero is overthrown and Isabella comes of age
1844: Narváez, leader of the Moderates, assumes power
1847: The Carlist war begins again
1848: The downfall of Louis Philippe; the Second French Republic
1854: *Coup d'état;* Espartero returns; the Progressivists return to power with O'Donnell
1855: The first general strike in Spain; the birth of the future Alfonso XII
1866: Prim's first pronunciamento
1868: Prim's second pronunciamento; the triumvirate of Prim, Serrano, and Topete defeat the queen's troops; a revolutionary junta is established at Madrid
1869: The convocation of the Cortes
1870: Isabella II abdicates in favor of her son, Alfonso XII

The Road to the Republic

1870: The Cortes selects Amadeus of Savoy, son of the King of Italy, as King of Spain; the assassination of Prim; Amadeus lands in Spain
1872: The first Anarchist Congress of Cordova
1873: Amadeus abdicates and the First Republic is proclaimed; the Federal Constitution is promulgated; Salmerón succeeds Pi y Margal to the presidency; Castelar succeeds Salmerón
1874: General Pavía's *coup d'état;* Alfonso XII ascends the throne
1875: The Carlist war resumes
1876: The Constitution of the Kingdom is promulgated
1879: The Workers' Socialist party is founded
1885: The death of Alfonso XII; María Cristina becomes Queen-Regent
1886: The birth of Alfonso XIII
1888: Pablo Iglesias founds the newspaper *El Socialista;* the General Union of Workers is established
1889: Slavery is abolished in Cuba
1890: Universal suffrage is established
1891: Leo XIII publishes his encyclical *Rerum Novarum*
1892: Peasant uprising at Jerez

1895:   Cuba's Proclamation of Independence
1898:   The Spanish-American War; the Treaty of Paris; Spain loses Cuba, Puerto Rico, and the Philippines
1902:   Alfonso XIII ascends the throne
1903:   General strike in Barcelona
1904:   Franco-Spanish agreement relating to the zones of influence in Morocco
1905:   Attempted assassination of Alfonso XIII and President Loubet in Paris
1906:   Spain participates at the Algeciras conference
1909:   The "Tragic Weeks of Barcelona"
1909:   The execution of Francisco Ferrer
1914:   The assassination at Sarajevo; the beginning of World War I
1917:   Social and political crisis; general strikes throughout the country; the war in the Rif
1921:   The Abd-el-Krim rebellion; the disaster at Melilla
1923:   Alfonso XIII hands the government over to Primo de Rivera; Constitution of the military directorate
1925:   Spanish troops land at Alhucemas in Morocco
1926:   Abd-el-Krim's surrender to the French; attempted invasion by Colonel Macía at Prats-de-Mollo and his failure
1927:   The Constitution of the National Assembly
1930:   Primo de Rivera withdraws and is succeeded by Berenguer; the execution of Galán and García Hernández; Commander Franco and General Queipo de Llano seize the Quatre-Vents Airport and shower Madrid with tracts

The Republic and the Civil War

1931:   The collapse of the Berenguer government; the Republic is proclaimed; the departure of Alfonso XIII; separation of Church and State; the Spanish episcopate's letter forbidding recourse to violence
1932:   Abolition of the Society of Jesus; General Sanjurjo's uprising in Seville; approval of a law for agrarian reform; General Macía is elected President of the Catalonian *Generalitat*
1933:   Legislative elections and success of the C.E.D.A.; José Antonio founds the Falange
1935:   General Franco is named Chief of State
1936:   Elections to the Cortes; the Cortes removes Alcalá Zamora from the presidency of the Republic; Azaña is elected President of the Republic; Lieutenant Castillo is assassinated; Calvo Sotelo is murdered; General Franco makes his appeal in Morocco; General Franco lands at Algeciras; General Sanjurjo is killed in an accident; October: the beginning of the battle for Madrid; José Antonio is assassinated

1937:   March: the end of the first battle for Madrid; Guernica; May: naval engagement between the *Deutschland* and the *Libertad;* the Republicans capture Teruel

1938:   The birth of Juan Carlos, son of the Count of Barcelona

1938:   July: the battle of the Ebro

1939:   The fall of Barcelona; the French government recognizes Franco; the capture of Toledo; Madrid surrenders; the end of the war

The Spanish State

1939:   France and England declare war on Germany; the beginning of Franco's regime

1940:   Italy enters the war; Hitler and Franco meet at Hendaye

1941:   Franco and Mussolini meet at Bordighera; June: the Azul Division is formed; the death of Alfonso XIII

1942:   The Constitution of the Spanish state; the Americans land in North Africa

1943:   Russian victory of Stalingrad; the Allies land in Sicily

1944:   Allied landings on the Normandy beaches; Leclerc's division enters Paris

1945:   Berlin falls; the end of World War II; the Cortes ratifies the "Charter for Spaniards"; law on the referendum

1946:   The United Nations votes to exclude Spain

1947:   Franco creates the Council of the Kingdom; referendum

1953:   Concordat with the Holy See

1957:   Statement by Luis Carrero Blanco to the Cortes inaugurating a traditional, Catholic, monarchist state

1958:   April: the Spanish Minister of Foreign Affairs calls on General de Gaulle; October: Don Juan's declaration to the Spanish monarchists at Lourdes

The Kings of Castile

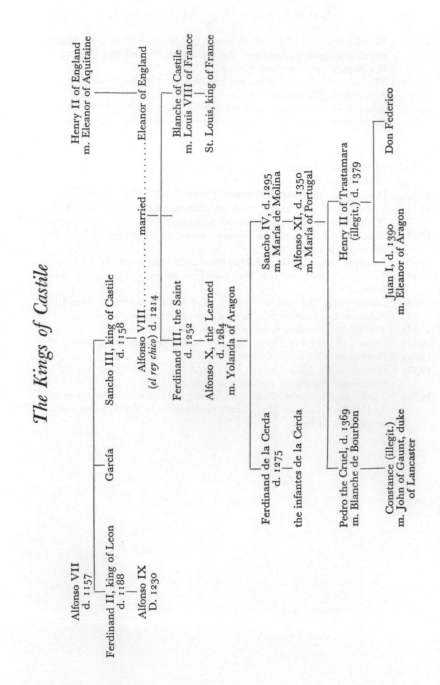

Alfonso VII
d. 1157

├─ Ferdinand II, king of Leon
│   d. 1188
│   └─ Alfonso IX
│   D. 1230
│
├─ García
│
└─ Sancho III, king of Castile
    d. 1158
    └─ Alfonso VIII
        (el rey chico) d. 1214

Henry II of England
m. Eleanor of Aquitaine
└─ Eleanor of England

Alfonso VIII .... married .... Eleanor of England

├─ Ferdinand III, the Saint
│   d. 1252
│   └─ Alfonso X, the Learned
│   d. 1284
│   m. Yolanda of Aragon
│
│   ├─ Ferdinand de la Cerda
│   │   d. 1275
│   │   └─ the infantes de la Cerda
│   │
│   └─ Sancho IV, d. 1295
│   m. María de Molina
│   └─ Alfonso XI, d. 1350
│   m. María of Portugal
│   ├─ Pedro the Cruel, d. 1369
│   │   m. Blanche de Bourbon
│   │   └─ Constance (illegit.)
│   │   m. John of Gaunt, duke
│   │   of Lancaster
│   │
│   └─ Henry II of Trastamara
│   (illegit.) d. 1379
│   ├─ Juan I, d. 1390
│   │   m. Eleanor of Aragon
│   │
│   └─ Don Federico
│
└─ Blanche of Castile
    m. Louis VIII of France
    └─ St. Louis, king of France

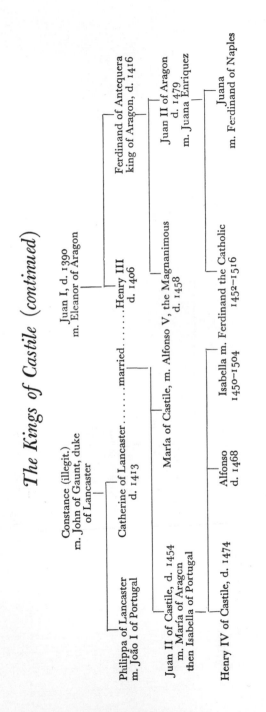

Constance (illegit.)
m. John of Gaunt, duke of Lancaster

Juan I, d. 1390
m. Eleanor of Aragon

Catherine of Lancaster.......married.......Henry III
d. 1413   d. 1406

Ferdinand of Antequera
king of Aragon, d. 1416

Philippa of Lancaster
m. João I of Portugal

María of Castile, m. Alfonso V, the Magnanimous
d. 1458

Juan II of Aragon
d. 1479
m. Juana Enriquez

Juan II of Castile, d. 1454
m. María of Aragon
then Isabella of Portugal

Isabella m. Ferdinand the Catholic
1450-1504   1452-1516

Alfonso
d. 1468

Henry IV of Castile, d. 1474

Juana
m. Ferdinand of Naples

The Ancestry of Charles V

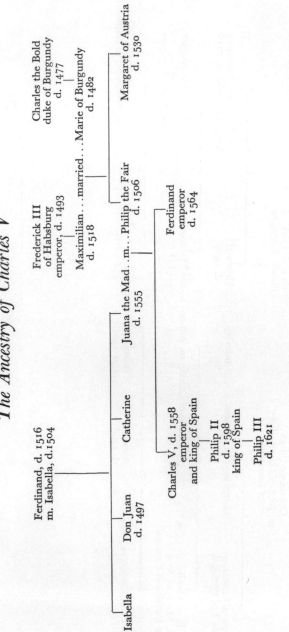

Ferdinand, d. 1516
m. Isabella, d.1504

Frederick III
of Habsburg
emperor, d. 1493

Charles the Bold
duke of Burgundy
d. 1477

Maximilian...married...Marie of Burgundy
d. 1518   d. 1482

Margaret of Austria
d. 1530

Isabella

Don Juan
d. 1497

Catherine

Juana the Mad. .m. . .Philip the Fair
d. 1555   d. 1506

Ferdinand
emperor
d. 1564

Charles V, d. 1558
emperor
and king of Spain

Philip II
d. 1598
king of Spain

Philip III
d. 1621

m. Marie de Médicis

Louis XIII married Anne of Austria

Louis XIV d. 1715
m. Marie Thérèse

Philip
duke of Orléans
m. Henrietta of England,
then Charlotte Elizabeth
Princess Palatine

Marie Louise of Orléans
queen of Spain

Louis the Grand Dauphin
m.
Marie Christine of Bavaria

Louis d. 1712
duke of Burgundy
m. Marie Adélaïde
of Savoy

Philip V
king of Spain
duke of Anjou
d. 1746
m. Maria Louisa of Savoy then........Elizabeth Farnese

Charles
duke of Berry

Louis XV d. 1774
m. Maria Leszczyńska

Louis I
d. 1774
m. Louise of Orléans

Ferdinand VI
d. 1759

Charles III
m. Marie Amélie
of Saxony

Philip
duke of Parma
m. Louise of France

Louis dauphin
d. 1765
m. Marie Josèphe of
Saxony

Charles IV
d. 1819
m. Maria Louisa
of Parma

Ferdinand IV
king of the Two Sicilies
d. 1825
m. Maria Carolina
of Austria

Marie Amélie....married...Louis Philippe

Louis XVIII d. 1824
Charles X d. 1836

Louis XVI
d. 1793
m.
Marie Antoinette
of Austria
d.1793

Ferdinand VII
d. 1833
m. Marie Christine
de Bourbon

Don Carlos
d. 1855
m.
Francisco
of Portugal

Don Francisco
of Paule

Don Francisco
of Assisi

Marie Thérèse
duchess of Angoulême

Louis XVII
d. 1795

Don Carlos
count of Montemolin

Don Juan d. 1887
m. Maria Beatrice
d'Este

The Habsburgs and the Bourbons (*continued*)

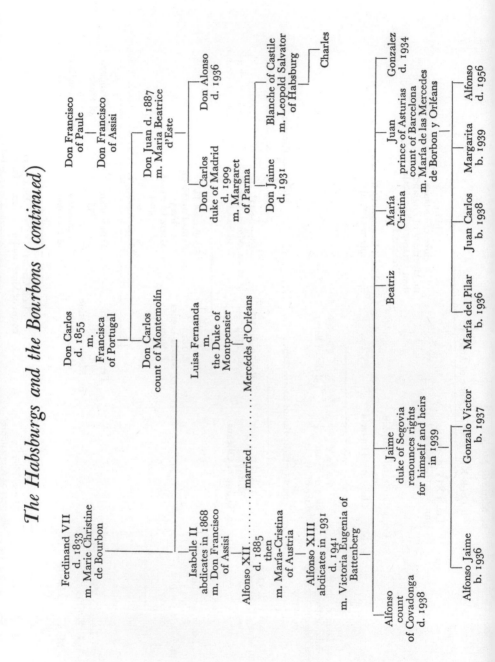

The Habsburgs and the Bourbons (continued)

Philip III d. 1621, m. Margaret of Austria

- Philip IV d. 1665 m. Isabelle of Bourbon, then.... Mariana of Austria d. 1664 / d. 1696
- Ferdinand the Cardinal-Infante
- Maria of Hungary

- Anne of Austria m. Louis XIII
- Charles II m. Marie Louise of Orléans then Anne of Bavaria-Neuburg
- Margaret Theresa

- Charlotte Elizabeth Princess Palatine m. Philip duke of Orléans
- Philip regent of France
- Louis d. 1752
- Louis d. 1785
- Louis Philippe Joseph "Philippe Égalité" d. 1793 m. Louise of Bourbon-Penthièvre
- Louis Philippe, king of the French m. Marie Amélie of the Two Sicilies
- Antoine Marie Louis Philippe duke of Montpensier d. 1890 m. the infanta Luisa Fernanda

The Habsburgs and the Bourbons (continued)

Maria of Hungary, m.
Ferdinand III, emperor
d. 1657

Mariana of Austria
d. 1696
queen of Spain
m. Philip IV

Margaret Theresa
married..........

Leopold I,
emperor, d. 1705

Joseph I
emperor, d. 1711

Charles VI
archduke, then emperor
d. 1740
m. Elisabeth Christina
of Brunswick-
Wolfenbüttel
d. 1750

Marie Antoinette
m. Joseph Leopold of
Wittelsbach
Elector of Bavaria

Maria Theresa
empress
d. 1780
m. François of Lorraine
d. 1765

Joseph II
emperor
d. 1790

Leopold II
emperor
d. 1792

Marie Antoinette
m. Louis XVI
d.1793

Marie Caroline
d. 1814
m. Ferdinand IV
king of the Two Sicilies

Francis II
emperor of Austria
in 1804
d. 1835

Ferdinand
d. 1875
abdicated in 1848 in
favor of his nephew

Francis Charles
d. 1878

Francis Joseph
d. 1916

Index

A Note about the Author

JEAN DESCOLA was born in Paris in 1909, and educated there at the Lycée Buffon and at the Institut des Etudes Hispaniques of the Sorbonne. His work as a Hispanic scholar has won him wide respect and recognition as well as a number of honors and awards, including the Grand Prix d'Histoire, the Prix Thiers of the French Academy, and the orders of Chevalier de la Légion d'Honneur and Commandeur d'Isabelle la Catholique. Among his many books on Spain and Latin America are a work on the Conquistadors, *A History of Christian Spain*, and a translation of the *Spiritual Canticle* of St. John of the Cross. M. Descola now lives with his wife and two children in Paris, where he is a lecturer at the Institut Catholique and a director of the Centre d'Etudes et de Recherches Ibéro-Américaines.

January 1963

A Note on the Type

THE TEXT of this book is set in MONTICELLO, a Linotype revival of the original Binny & Ronaldson Roman No. 1, cut by Archibald Binny and cast in 1796 by that Philadelphia type foundry. The face was named Monticello in honor of its use in the monumental fifty-volume *Papers of Thomas Jefferson*, published by Princeton University Press. Monticello is a transitional type design, embodying certain features of Bulmer and Baskerville, but it is a distinguished face in its own right.

Composed, printed, and bound by
Kingsport Press, Inc., Kingsport, Tennessee.
Typography and binding design
based on originals by
W. A. DWIGGINS

ST. MARY'S COLLEGE OF MARYLAND LIBRARY
ST. MARY'S CITY, MARYLAND

31417

E DUE

OCT 16 '71	
DEC 19 1980	
JAN 17 1983	
DE 10 '84	
AP 25 '88	
	PRINTED IN U.S.A.